DEMOCRATIC BRAZIL DIVIDED

PITT LATIN AMERICAN SERIES
John Charles Chasteen and Catherine M. Conaghan, Editors

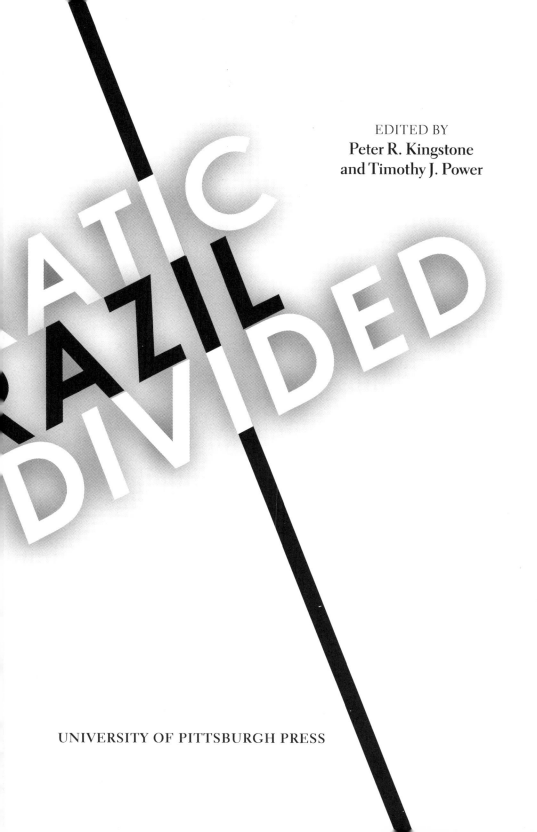

EDITED BY
Peter R. Kingstone
and Timothy J. Power

UNIVERSITY OF PITTSBURGH PRESS

Published by the University of Pittsburgh Press, Pittsburgh, Pa., 15260
Copyright © 2017, University of Pittsburgh Press
All rights reserved
Manufactured in the United States of America
Printed on acid-free paper
10 9 8 7 6 5 4 3 2 1

Cataloging-in-Publication data is available from the Library of Congress

ISBN 13: 978-0-8229-6491-9
ISBN 10: 0-8229-6491-0

Cover art: "Manifestação" by Geraldo Magela/Agência Senado is licensed under CC BY 2.0;
"#ForaTemerOlimpico" by Flickr user IdeasGraves is licensed under CC BY 2.0.
Cover design: Joel W. Coggins

CONTENTS

ACKNOWLEDGMENTS

SOME POLITICAL EVENTS happen so suddenly and unexpectedly they shake up much of what we believed to be true. The collapse of the Soviet Union and the Arab Spring both revealed the profound weakness of regimes believed to be much more durable and overturned years or even decades of social science "wisdom." Brazil's rapid rise from "feckless" democracy to BRIC and back again is perhaps not as surprising or as disruptive of social science and public wisdom. But it is in the neighborhood.

The simplest way to illustrate the speed of change for us is to chart how our effort to organize, frame, and name this volume changed over the course of the project. When in 2013 we first assembled the contributors to comment on the state of democracy in Brazil, the proposed title of the future volume was *Democratic Brazil Ascendant*—a testament to Brazil's stability and global leadership and example for developing countries everywhere, including the coining of the term the "Brasília Consensus" as a contrast to the much criticized Washington Consensus. The "Vinegar Revolution" protests of June 2013 had not yet broken out in São Paulo, but then again, nobody predicted this massive wave of demonstrations either. With mounting evidence of economic malaise, social unrest, and corruption, we spent much of 2013 and 2014 wondering whether we were witnessing the exhaustion of a virtuous cycle. Would the ruling Workers' Party (PT), which presided over an impressive period of social inclusion after 2003, be able to hold on to power? Was this the end of an era? Dilma Rousseff's reelection in October 2014 should have provided an answer, but in reality it provided only a fleeting veneer of stability, which proved illusory just months later. In 2015 charges of budgetary crimes and the impeachment process brought the PT's dominance of politics to an end and revealed a high level of polarization and anger as Brazilians divided against themselves. Thus, the final name of the volume, *Democratic Brazil Divided*. We moved from a framing device of ascendance to one of division in only two years.

For our Brazilian colleagues and friends, this period has been painful and has divided friendships, institutions, and even professional associations. For those *brasilianistas* like ourselves, Brazil's sharpening polarization evokes an unwelcome sense of déjà vu. The first *Democratic Brazil* involved a group of young United States–based political scientists who had all begun their doctoral research work shortly after the restoration of democracy. We saw ourselves as a distinctive cohort who had no experience of authoritarian Brazil and believed that this lent the volume a cohesive viewpoint. The Brazil we came to know in our research was indeed volatile—politically and economically. Our more senior colleagues, Brazilian and non-Brazilian, coined a wide variety of phrases to capture the apparent chaos of the late 1980s and early 1990s (including the term above, "feckless democracy"). Public opinion polls and many scholarly analyses suggested that Brazil was the Latin American laggard in consolidation of democracy.

The twenty-first century, then, brought great satisfaction. Brazil was still a moving target, but we were now charting the important ways in which democracy was indisputably deepening. Both of our earlier volumes capture this sense of progress even amidst great challenges. Indeed, a very important strand of political science literature, driven by leading Brazilian scholars, argued that the political system had always been more governable than critics imagined. This Brazil rested on a functional and even effective form of "coalitional presidentialism" that brought economic stability and then prosperity, generated and diffused world-leading social policy innovations, and became a regional leader and an emergent global power on the basis of these achievements.

The return of crisis—economic and political—has terrible human consequences, and the circular sense of returning to our starting point as observers of Brazil is disheartening. Yet, beneath the tensions of the moment, we retain the awareness of great strides and of people dedicated to making the country a more democratic, prosperous, and just society. The current volume in the Democratic Brazil series refers to a nation divided, but with the hope that the next iteration returns to celebrating a forward trajectory.

As with the first two volumes of this series, the project began as a series of panels and public presentations. Earlier collaborations took advantage of the annual conferences of the Latin American Studies Association. This iteration benefited instead from the fortuitous fact of Peter Kingstone's decision to follow Timothy Power to the United Kingdom in the summer of 2012. Tim had moved to Oxford in 2006, and for the first time in our careers, we found ourselves within a short distance of each other. The result was a two-day conference involving all the contributors, the first day at King's College London (KCL) and the next day at Oxford. The resulting volume benefited as a result from the lively comments and questions from the knowledgeable and diverse London and Oxford based audiences, including academics, policy makers, diplomats, journalists, and businesspeople. We were also very fortunate to have comments from outstanding discussants drawn from our colleagues and visitors at the two institutions. Leslie Bethell, Olivier Dabène, Mahrukh Doctor, Anthony Hall, Leigh Payne, Miriam Saraiva, Matias

Spektor, and Laurence Whitehead all served as chairs and discussants and greatly contributed to the quality of the papers.

We are grateful to King's College London, the University of Oxford, and Santander Universities UK for financial and logistic support for the conference. But the challenging task of managing a conference over two days in two cities at two universities depended on the flawless coordination of David Robinson of the Latin American Centre (LAC) at Oxford, Jacqueline Armit of King's Brazil Institute, and Flo Austin of King's Department of International Development. We are indebted to Alison Walsh, a graduate student at Oxford's Latin American Centre, who prepared the final manuscript for publication. Finally, we are grateful to Peter Kracht and Josh Shanholtzer for their enthusiastic support for the ongoing Democratic Brazil enterprise and their patience as this volume made repeated changes to respond to the rapidly changing landscape of Brazilian democracy.

Peter Kingstone would like to thank KCL's Department of International Development for its support. Tim Power is grateful to the Latin American Centre and to its parent department at Oxford, the School of Interdisciplinary Area Studies.

Finally, as in all our endeavors, we would like to thank our families, Lisa, Ben, and Lara Kingstone and Valéria Carvalho Power, for their unflagging love and support.

ACRONYMS

ABCP	Brazilian Political Science Association
ABI	Brazilian Press Association
ALACIP	Latin American Political Science Association (Asociación Latinoamericana de Ciencia Política)
APSA	American Political Science Association
BASIC countries	Brazil, South Africa, India, China
BNDES	National Development Bank (Banco Nacional de Desenvolvimento Econômico e Social) / National Bank for Economic and Social Development]
BNDESPar	BNDES Participações
BPC	Continuous Cash Benefit (Benefício de Prestação Continuada)
BRASA	Brazilian Studies Association
Brasil Sem Miséria	Brazil Without Extreme Poverty
BRIC	Brazil, Russia, India, China
CAP	Retirement and Pension Fund (Caixa de Aposentadoria e Pensão)
CCT	conditional cash transfer
CEBRAP	Brazilian Centre of Analysis and Planning (Centro Brasileiro de Análise e Planejamento)
CELAC	Community of Latin American and Caribbean Nations
CEPAL	Economic Commission on Latin America (Comisión Económica para América Latina y el Caribe)
CESOP	Center for Studies on Public Opinion
CGU	Comptroller General's Office (Controladoria-Geral da União)
CIRI	Cingranelli and Richards (CIRI) physical integrity scale
CNBB	National Confederation of Brazilian Bishops
CNJ	National Judicial Council (Conselho Nacional de Justiça)
CONADEP	National Commission on the Disappearance of Persons [Argentina] (Comisión Nacional sobre la Desaparición de Personas)
CPF	a federally issued taxpayer identification card (Cadastro de Pessoas Físicas)
CPI	Congressional Investigatory Committee (Comissão Parlamentar de Inquérito)
CRAS	Social Assistance Reference Center (Centro de Referência de Assistência Social)
CSES	Comparative Study of Electoral Systems Project
DEM	Democrats (Democratas)
EIA	Environmental Impact Assessment
EMBRAPA	Brazilian Agricultural Research Corporation (Empresa Brasileira de Pesquisa Agropecuária)

ENCCLA	National Strategy to Combat Corruption and Money Laundering (Estratégia Nacional de Combate à Corrupção e Lavagem de Dinheiro)
ENEM	National High School Exam (Exame Nacional do Ensino Médio)
FAO	Federal Accounting Office
FARC	Revolutionary Armed Forces of Colombia (Fuerzas Armadas Revolucionarias de Colombia)
FAT	Workers' Support Fund (Fundo de Amparo ao Trabalhador)
FCPA	Foreign Corrupt Practices Act
FDI	Foreign Direct Investment
FECAMP	Campinas Foundation for Economics (Fundação Economia de Campinas)
FIFA	International Federation of Football (Fédération Internationale de Football) Association (World Cup)
FIOCRUZ	Oswaldo Cruz Foundation (Fundação Oswaldo Cruz)
FOI law	Freedom of Information Law
FPA	Perseu Abramo Foundation (Fundação Perseu Abramo)
FPM	Municipal Transfer Fund (Fundo de Participação dos Municípios)
FPS	Federal Prosecution Service
FRL law	Fiscal Responsibility Law
FTAA	Free Trade Area of the Americas
FUNAG	Alexandre de Gusmão Foundation (Fundação Alexandre de Gusmão)
Funai	National Indian Foundation (Fundação Nacional do Índio)
FUNDEB	Fund for the Improvement of Basic Education and Valorization of Education Professionals (Fundo de Manutenção e Desenvolvimento da Educação Básica e de Valorização dos Profissionais da Educação)
FUNDEF	Fund for the Improvement of Basic Education (Fundo de Manutenção e Desenvolvimento do Ensino Fundamental)
FUNRURAL	Fund for Assistance to Rural Workers (Fundo de Assistência ao Trabalhador Rural)
GHG	greenhouse gases (carbon dioxide, methane, and nitrous oxide)
GNI	Gross National Income
IADB	Inter-American Development Bank
IBAMA	Brazilian Institute of Environment and Renewable Natural Resources (Instituto Brasileiro do Meio Ambiente e dos Recursos Naturais)
IBASE	Brazilian Institute of Social and Economic Analysis (Instituto Brasileiro de Análises Sociais e Econômicos)
IBGE	Brazilian Institute of Geography and Statistics (Instituto Brasileiro de Geografia e Estatística)
IBOPE	Brazilian Institute of Public Opinion and Statistics (Instituto Brasileiro de Opinião Pública e Estatística)
IBSA	India-Brazil-South Africa Dialogue Forum

ICONE	Institute for International Trade Negotiations (Instituto de Estudos do Comércio e Negociações Internacionais)
IESP	Institute for Social and Political Studies, State University of Rio de Janeiro (Instituto de Estudos Sociais e Políticos)
IFPRI	International Food Policy Research Institute
IIRSA	Initiative for the Integration of the Regional Infrastructure of South America
ILO	International Labor Organization
IMF	International Monetary Fund
INAMPS	National Health Care Institute (Instituto Nacional de Assistência Médica de Previdência Social)
INDC	Intended Nationally Determined Contribution (under the UN Framework Convention on Climate Change)
INEP	National Institute for Education Research (Instituto Nacional de Estudos e Pesquisas Educacionais)
Infraero	national airport authority of Brazil (Empresa Brasileira de Infraestrutura Aeroportuária)
IPEA	Institute for Applied Economic Research (Instituto de Pesquisa Econômica Aplicada)
ISI	import-substituting industrialization
LAC	Latin American and Caribbean region
LACEA	Latin American and Caribbean Economic Association (Asociación de Economía de América Latina y el Caribe)
LASA	Latin American Studies Association
LDB	National Education Guidelines and Framework Law (Lei de Diretrizes e Bases da Educação)
MDS	Ministry of Social Development and the Fight against Hunger (Ministério do Desenvolvimento Social e Combate à Fome)
MERCOSUL (Portuguese) / MERCOSUR (Spanish)	South American Common Market (Mercado Comum do Sul/ Común del Sur)
MP	Prosecutorial Service (Ministério Público)
MPL	Free Fare Movement (Movimento Passe Livre)
MSBs	Micro and small businesses
MST	Landless Peasants' Movement (Movimento dos Trabalhadores Rurais Sem Terra)
NC	National Congress
ND	new developmentalism
NECI/USP	Comparative and International Studies Research Center, University of São Paulo (Núcleo de Estudos Comparados e Internacionais)
NM	National Meeting
NTC	Brazilian National Truth Commission
OAB	Brazilian Bar Association (Ordem de Advogados do Brasil)
OAS	Organization of American States
OECD	Organization of Economic Cooperation and Development

OGP	Open Government Partnership
PAC	Program for the Acceleration of Growth (Programa de Aceleração do Crescimento)
PCB	Brazilian Communist Party (Partido Comunista Brasileiro)
PCdoB	Communist Party of Brazil (Partido Comunista do Brasil)
PDT	Democratic Labor Party (Partido Democrático Trabalhista)
PED	Process of Direct Elections (Processo de Eleições Diretas)
PISA	Programme for International Student Assessment
PL	Liberal Party (Partido Liberal)
PMDB	Brazilian Democratic Movement Party (Partido do Movimento Democrático Brasileiro)
PMN	National Mobilization Party (Partido da Mobilização Nacional)
PNUD	UN Development Programme (Programa das Nações Unidas para o Desenvolvimento)
PP	Popular Party (Partido Popular)
PPP	Purchasing Power Parity
PPS	Popular Socialist Party (Partido Popular Socialista)
PROUNI	Brazilian scholarship program for higher education, aimed particularly at low income students (Programa Universidade para Todos)
PSB	Brazilian Socialist Party (Partido Socialista Brasileiro)
PSDB	Party of Brazilian Social Democracy (Partido da Social Democracia Brasileira).
PSI	Sustainable Investment Program
PSL	Social Liberal Party (Partido Social Liberal)
PSOL	Party of Socialism and Liberty (Partido Socialismo e Liberdade)
PT	Workers' Party (Partido dos Trabalhadores)
PTB	Brazilian Labor Party (Partido Trabalhista Brasileiro)
PTS	Political Terror Scale
PV	Green Party (Partido Verde)
REDD+	(Reducing Emissions from Deforestation and Forest Degradation)
RG	National Identification Card Number (Registro Geral); RG
RS	Rio Grande do Sul
SAE	Brazilian Office of Strategic Affairs (Secretaria de Assuntos Estratégicos)
SAEB	System for the Evaluation of Basic Education (Sistema de Avaliação de Ensino Básico)
SEBRAE	Brazilian Micro and Small Business Support Service (Serviço Brasileiro de Apoio ás Micro e Pequenas Empresas)
SELIC	Brazil's basic overnight interest rate, Special System for Settlement and Custody (Sistema Especial de Liquidação e de Custódia)
SOE	state-owned enterprises
STF	Supreme Federal Tribunal (Supremo Tribunal Federal)
SUAS	Unified System of Social Assistance (Sistema Único de Assistência Social)

TCU	Federal Accounting Court (Tribunal de Contas da União)
TSE	Supreme Electoral Court (Tribunal Superior Eleitoral)
Título de Eleitor	voter registration card
TJLP	long-term interest rate, the rate at which BNDES borrows (Taxa de Juros de Longo Prazo)
UERJ	State University of Rio de Janeiro (Universidade Estadual do Rio de Janeiro)
UN/DESA	UN Department of Economic and Social Affairs Unasul
UNASUL (Spanish)/ UNASUR (Portuguese)	Union of South American Nations
UNCAC	UN Convention Against Corruption
UNCTAD	UN Conference on Trade and Development
UNDP	UN Development Programme
UNE	National Union of Students (União Nacional dos Estudantes)
UNFCCC	UN Framework Convention on Climate Change
Unicamp	State University of Campinas
USD	US dollars
USP	University of São Paulo
VAT	Value Added Tax
WAPOR	World Association of Public Opinion Research
WHO	World Health Organization
WTO	World Trade Organization

DEMOCRATIC BRAZIL DIVIDED

INTRODUCTION

Peter R. Kingstone and Timothy J. Power

A Fourth Decade of Brazilian Democracy

Achievements, Challenges, and Polarization

IN 2009 THE *Economist* magazine celebrated Brazil's meteoric rise as an emerging power with a cover featuring Rio de Janeiro's mountaintop icon, "Christ the Redeemer," taking off into the stratosphere. Four years later, with the economy in decline and protestors marching in the streets, the magazine again featured the *Cristo*, this time in a horrific nosedive, asking "Has Brazil blown it?" Brazil's situation had deteriorated but still remained hopeful enough to allow the incumbent Workers' Party (Partido dos Trabalhadores; PT) president Dilma Rousseff to win reelection in October 2014. Within months of her victory, however, the country was plunged even deeper into recession and was caught up in the sharpest and most polarizing political crisis in the young democracy's history. In a short period, Brazil had moved from triumphant emerging power to a nation divided against itself.

At the heart of the political crisis was the impeachment of Dilma, a process that began barely a year into her second term. Dilma's reelection campaign had withstood declining economic performance and a rapidly widening corruption investigation—the Lava Jato (car wash) scandal that ensnared dozens of leading business people and politicians, including many key PT figures, though not Dilma herself. In October 2015, the Federal Accounting Court (Tribunal de Contas da União; TCU) rejected Dilma's budget accounts, having identified a series of practices that violated federal budget and fiscal laws—actions that could be construed as impeachable offenses ("crimes of responsibility") under the 1988 Constitution. The next several months witnessed a sordid process that featured accusations, counteraccusations, and clear evidence of accounting irregularities as well as of conspiracy presented by opposition lawmakers to bring down the president, leaks of recorded conversations by both politicians and judicial officials, and the realization that in fact a broad swath of the political class was implicated in large-scale graft.

Tainted by corruption and economic crisis, the increasingly unpopular president lost nearly all her political allies outside the PT. In December 2015 the speaker of Brazil's lower house, Eduardo Cunha of the Brazilian Democratic Movement Party (Partido do Movimento Democrático Brasileiro; PMDB), a PT ally for more than a decade, decided to retaliate against the PT for failing to defend him on the Ethics Committee against charges of misconduct. Cunha, who as speaker had unilateral authority to decide the admissibility of impeachment requests, announced that the Chamber of Deputies would investigate Dilma's accounting practices as a potential crime of responsibility. Cunha's decision unleashed a series of dramatic events. In April 2016 the Chamber approved the articles of impeachment against Dilma with a vote of 367 to 137. This vote had the effect of immediately suspending her from office for 180 days and setting in place an interim government led by Vice-President Michel Temer (like Cunha, a member of the PMDB). His was the first cabinet without the PT—or indeed any party of the left—since 2002. Ironically, Temer, like Cunha, was under investigation for corruption as well.

The impeachment process then moved to a trial in the Federal Senate. After Dilma defended herself for over twelve hours of questioning on the floor of the Senate (more of an exit interview than a meaningful cross-examination), on the morning of August 31, 2016, the upper house by a vote of 61 to 20 voted to convict the president. This definitively ended her presidency, and Michel Temer took the oath of office the same afternoon. Only two weeks after Dilma's final conviction the man who triggered the impeachment process, former speaker Eduardo Cunha, was expelled from Congress for lying under oath about secret bank accounts in Switzerland. By mid-September 2016, Cunha had been stripped of his political rights for eight years, Dilma was a private citizen living in Porto Alegre, and Temer was the only one left standing—now as the thirty-seventh president of Brazil.

In the midst of this political soap opera, millions of Brazilians took to the streets in competing demonstrations, protesting both for and against impeachment. For Dilma and PT supporters, the impeachment was a coup (*golpe*) led by conservative forces eager to remove a progressive government that had improved the lives of millions of poor people. Leaked audio recordings made clear that at the very least it was an effort by some members of the political class to remove Dilma in a bid to stop further corruption investigations. For critics of the PT, however, the impeachment was a constitutional process to remove a government that had become arrogant and abused its power. While political elites and academics argued over whether the impeachment was a golpe or not, polls showed that a majority of ordinary Brazilians held both Dilma and Temer in low regard and supported impeaching both of them. How did the country arrive at this point?

Never Trust a Regime over Thirty?

None of this would have been expected when Brazilian democracy entered the twenty-first century. The historic 2002 presidential victory of the PT's founder, Luiz Inácio Lula da Silva, augured the arrival of a new Brazil that featured stable democratic politics, economic growth with equity, and innovative social policies that were lauded and copied all around the world. Under two PT presidents, first Lula and then his chosen successor Dilma, Brazil had gone from a "feckless" democracy to a BRIC country—an emerging power, recognized globally in myriad ways, not least by winning the right to host the 2014 World Cup and the 2016 Olympics. When Dilma celebrated the inauguration of her second term as president of Brazil on January 1, 2015, it marked a stretch of political domination by the PT dating back to 2003. For a country once described as "ungovernable" or "drunk," this stability and continuity of political rule should have been an opportunity to reflect on the great successes of the party and the country. Only ten weeks after being sworn in for her second term, Dilma was slated to preside over what should have been a momentous occasion for celebration: the thirtieth anniversary celebrations for Brazilian democracy, commemorating the military's return to the barracks on March 15, 1985.

Instead, 2015 opened with crises and scandals that evoked memories of the uncertainties and volatility of the early 1990s—the period that produced the large collection of unflattering labels such as "drunk," "ungovernable," or "feckless democracy." Perhaps the most dramatic element was the explosion of protest around allegations of large-scale corruption involving politicians, major private firms, and at the center of it all, Petrobras, the jewel in the crown of state-owned firms. In March and then again in April 2015, roughly a million Brazilians took to the streets—the third year in a row of mass protests—clamoring against corruption and calling for Dilma's impeachment. Drowned out by the loud banging of pots and pans, the thirtieth birthday of democracy was barely noticed.

The investigation into improper kickbacks began in early 2014, well before the presidential elections. Initially, it focused on money laundering and foreign exchange manipulation centered around car wash services offered at Petrobras service stations. As the investigation expanded, however, it stumbled onto a much larger bribe and kickback scheme with audits showing over 8 billion dollars' worth of suspect payments. Federal police had dozens of individuals under investigation, indicted, or arrested and a dozen private firms under scrutiny. While President Rousseff avoided direct implications, the scandal tarnished her image and that of the PT. Key allies fell victim to the investigations, including Dilma's close personal friend Maria das Graças Foster, the CEO of Petrobras (forced to resign), and João Vaccari Neto, the PT party treasurer (arrested by the federal police on suspicion of receiving bribes). By April 2015 Dilma's electoral triumph had changed to a new record: the worst presidential approval rating in Brazilian history. Polls in mid-April showed only 13 percent public support, with 62 percent disapproving and 63 percent believing she should face impeachment hearings.

But corruption and new worries about governability were hardly the only challenges for Dilma's ill-fated second term. Perhaps even more threatening was the precarious state of the economy. The euphoria over Brazil's rise to global prominence as a BRIC country was already over before the 2014 election. The enthusiasm had always been exaggerated—it arose partly in sharp contrast with the chaotic 1980s and early 1990s, partly by the active promotion of enthusiastic foreign observers, and partly through the PT's own public relations efforts to promote the "Brasília Consensus" around the world. But, aside from 2010 (a year in which the economy rebounded strongly from the 2009 global economic/financial shock), Brazilian growth had not been extraordinary. There had been real achievements, especially regarding poverty and inequality. But the good news concealed the underlying weaknesses present throughout the BRIC years and worsening throughout Dilma's first term in office. These included inadequate investment in infrastructure, weak health and education performance, considerable weaknesses in microeconomic competitiveness, low investment in research and development, inadequate supply and quality of skilled labor, and a steady worsening of macroeconomic conditions.

By 2014 many Brazilians, especially those in the rising new "middle classes," were feeling the pressures of falling growth, stagnant real wages, a growing tax burden and increasing cost of living, resurgent inflation, and rising unemployment. The weak economic performance of 2014 soon deteriorated to a full-blown recession, with 3.8 percent contraction of Gross Domestic Product (GDP) in 2015 and another 3.6 percent decline in 2016. Inflation was running at 8–10 percent per year (well over the government's maximum target of 6.5 percent) and the loss of the country's hard-won investment grade credit rating. During the BRIC years, Brazil had moved from a country racked by macroeconomic crisis propelled by political deficiencies—a scenario that Bolivar Lamounier (1996) had called "the hyperactive paralysis syndrome"—to a model of fiscal prudence and macroeconomic strength. Yet in Dilma's second term, Brazil's global image fell quickly from being an "economic superpower" to being a leading example of the inherent risks of placing too much stock in the "emerging economies."

By 2015 the twin challenges of corruption and macroeconomic deterioration clearly exposed the limitations of both Dilma as a political leader and the Brazilian political system as a set of institutions that shape governability. The BRIC years under PT domination led to a new way of understanding Brazil's "governability"—a coalitional form of presidentialism that involved trade-offs and concessions to other parties and leading politicians but led to a stable, functional, and at times very effective form of governance. Yet, the crisis revealed that the stability and effectiveness of the system depended on a leader who could manage the complex bargains inherent in such a fragmented system. Further, it also highlighted the dependence on a healthy macroeconomic environment and a growing economy to provide the resources to cement those bargains. But the rapid deterioration of the economy forced hard budgetary choices that increased Dilma's unpopularity while removing from her the most important patronage and clientelistic resources for coalition management.

Dilma's political fortunes declined notably when the TCU rejected her government accounts in October 2015 and pointed to evidence of *pedaladas* ("pedaling," or delaying obligatory government payments) in an effort to appear to be in line with laws governing fiscal responsibility and government accountability. Added to this, the Dilma administration illegally extended new lines of credit for government social programs. The implication was that both sets of accounting manipulations were designed to allow the Dilma administration to put off spending cuts that could affect the 2014 presidential election. With Dilma directly implicated in a criminal offense, not only the opposition but also "allied" politicians—acting opportunistically when the government began to crumble—seized on the chance to bring Dilma and the PT down.

With Dilma impeached, the weak Temer government already discredited by ongoing discoveries of corruption, and the country divided bitterly, it is reasonable to ask "what happened?" Years of impressive accomplishments and political stability had altered the way scholars and other observers discussed Brazil. A large number of new works emerged to explain how and why Brazil was indeed governable or to explain Brazil's newfound economic and political strengths. How did Brazil's situation shift so dramatically over the course of the PT in government? What are the origins of the sudden-onset malaise that tarnished democracy's thirtieth birthday and clouded the prospects for the future? What conclusions should we draw about the state of democracy and development?

In this volume, the third in a series of studies on the state of Brazilian democracy, we address a range of vital aspects of Brazil's ever-changing polity. If there is one overarching thesis of the book, it is that the story of Brazilian democracy is not as bad as the worst-case scenario suggests, nor was it ever as good as the excessively optimistic versions made it appear. In that sense, this collection of essays and its two earlier companion volumes continue to resist simple classification and overreaction to the events of the moment. Democratic Brazil in 2017 is much as it has been for these past three decades: a work in progress in which the patterns of direction of change are mixed, complex, and never linear. After the discouraging performance in the early years of democracy (1985–1993), an interregnum of stabilization and reform (1994–2002), and a decade of growth with social inclusion (2003 to roughly 2012), Brazilian democracy and its economy are once again recalibrating.

The essays in this book address a moving target: the challenging period from 2013 forward is one for which Brazilians are struggling to develop a consensual narrative. For a start, Brazilians need to find a way forward that reconciles divergent understandings of the impeachment process and of the PT's more than thirteen years in power. While many ordinary citizens simply want to move beyond the conjunctural crisis, large numbers of mobilized citizens and opinion makers hold beliefs about the Dilma endgame that point to profound distrust, anger, and betrayal, that is, the potential for lingering divisions. But the impeachment process of 2015–2016 highlights another crucial legacy: institutions of accountability grew undeniably stronger in the PT years. As a result, so did the ability of the Brazilian state and media to monitor, identify, investigate, and ultimately prosecute individuals on corruption charges. Brazilian society has grown notably less tolerant of graft and malfeasance, yet the political system has not adapted to this new reality. The path that Brazilian democracy takes going forward will depend on how these two seemingly irreconcilable tensions are resolved.

Challenges and Changes since the Previous Volume in Assessing Brazil

Observers of Brazil have long tended to paint the country in extremes, moving between the euphoria of "greatness" (*grandeza*) and the sense that some sort of collapse is just around the corner, and this current period is simply the most recent example. There is, however, a lot of analytical space between "emerging power" and "regional laggard." Brazilian reality is always complex, with important elements of continuity and change intertwining in marble-cake fashion across the dimensions of politics, economics, and society. In *Democratic Brazil: Actors, Institutions, and Processes* (2000) and *Democratic Brazil Revisited* (2008), the authors problematized different aspects of Brazil's political economy and asked to what extent things had changed and whether they had improved, remained the same, or worsened. While all three volumes in this series (2000, 2008, and the present collection of essays) yield complex portraits, the country had shifted in important ways from the first to the second volume. In 2000 our collaborators were still concerned with the extent to which democracy had taken root and what that actually meant. The temporal focus of *Democratic Brazil* was on the governments of José Sarney (1985–1990), Fernando Collor (1990–1992), Itamar Franco (1992–1994), and the first term of Fernando Henrique Cardoso (1995–1998), while the substantive focus was on the key actors, institutions, and processes critical for preserving and deepening democratic rule in Brazil. By the time of the second volume, *Democratic Brazil Revisited*, which covered the historic transition from Cardoso to Lula and the PT, there was much less concern about a return to authoritarianism. Instead, the question was on whether democratic *quality* was deepening in any meaningful way. The emphasis, however, remained on dynamic rather than static features of the post-1985 regime.

Despite the concerns facing Brazil in 2017, our focus has shifted again. None of the contributors to this volume questions whether Brazil is an established democracy. Even with the twin crises of economic contraction and impeachment, they see this as a moot question. Brazil's democracy as of 2017 may be overshadowed by a cloud of crisis, but the country is still marked by a record of considerable policy innovation and policy achievements (Melo and Pereira 2013). Citizens are participating in a denser network of civil society associations that organize interests in ways that influence policy and protect interests much more effectively (Abers and von Bülow 2011; Pogrebinschi 2012; Wampler 2015). New accountability institutions have emerged stronger than ever and together with the media and judiciary are pushing toward higher levels of transparency and challenging long-standing traditions of impunity. Despite the divisions over Dilma Rousseff's ouster, both politicians and the public have followed democratic rules and procedures and demonstrated restraint despite the anger. In brief, Brazilian democracy faces many challenges, but it is not clear these are markedly different from, say, the slightly older democracies that comprise the European Union's southern fringe (Greece, Spain, and Portugal). Brazil shows many of the qualities of a mature democracy, even as it confronts problems of corruption, protest, and economic backsliding.

The Political Context

As depicted by our collaborators in *Democratic Brazil*, the current democratic regime had a rocky start in the late 1980s and early 1990s. This was a period in which Brazil suffered inflation rates upward of 2000 percent yearly, poverty rates soared, and the first popularly elected president (Fernando Collor) was impeached and removed from office. But in the two decades after 1994, the year of the Plano Real economic stabilization plan, the country began a long cycle of reformist social democracy that led to widely praised advances. The government of Fernando Henrique Cardoso (1995–2002) ended hyperinflation, improved government finances, renegotiated the federal pact, and implemented reforms that increased state capacity. Cardoso was followed by Luiz Inácio Lula da Silva (2003–2010), who had been defeated on his first three attempts to win the presidency (twice by Cardoso). Lula maintained a responsible macroeconomic policy while dramatically expanding the social safety net, lifting 30 million Brazilians out of poverty and reducing income inequality to its lowest level in fifty years. Lula's chosen successor, Dilma Rouseff, attempted to maintain both Cardoso's legacy of economic stability and Lula's legacy of social inclusion — a tall order by any standard. Her election in 2010 was indisputably owed to strong public approval of the eight years of Lula's government, and in her first two years in office Dilma herself was a very popular president (Power 2014; Campello and Zucco 2015). While her second term in office was controversially interrupted, there is no question that Dilma herself — especially as Lula's presidential chief of staff from 2005 to 2010 — played a major role in Brazilian democracy's successful third decade.

As the regime enters the fourth decade of its life, observers generally concur that it has proved its sustainability through thick and thin. Brazil had only three finance ministers in the twenty years between 1994 and 2014, the lowest number among major economies. And with Dilma's second victory in October 2014, Brazil became the first Latin American country to have three consecutive reelected presidents. Beginning with Fernando Henrique Cardoso, who sought and won a constitutional amendment allowing consecutive reelection for executives, presidential competition stabilized around two poles: the Workers' Party (PT) and the Party of Brazilian Social Democracy (Partido da Social Democracia Brasileira; PSDB). In the six presidential elections between 1994 and 2014, these two parties jointly won 70–90 percent of the first-round vote (Table I.1). This persistent duopoly was surprising in what is probably the most fragmented party system in the modern democratic world: over the past two decades, the largest party in Congress has controlled less than 20 percent of the lower-house seats. Yet in a system that currently has thirty-five registered political parties, with twenty-eight of them represented in

Table I.1. The PT-PSDB Duopoly in Presidential Elections, 1994–2014		
Election Year	*PT + PSDB Joint Vote for the Chamber of Deputies (%)*	*PT + PSDB Joint Vote for the Presidency (%)*
1994	27	81
1998	31	85
2002	33	70
2006	38	90
2010	35	80
2014	26	75

Note: Presidential vote shares refer to the first round of competition in each election year.
Source: Tribunal Superior Eleitoral.

Congress, the PT and PSDB notably occupied privileged positions in these years—not only as the two main sources of competitive presidential candidates but also as the suppliers of most of the main ideas that have dominated national policy debates since the 1990s.

The PT emerged as a key player in Brazilian macropolitics after Lula's impressive presidential bid in 1989, in which he vaulted over nineteen other candidates in the first round only to lose to a neoliberal populist, Fernando Collor, in the runoff. After Collor's impeachment on corruption charges in 1992, Lula was the heir apparent to the presidency, yet his head start was not enough to stave off Cardoso (PSDB), the finance minister who laid the groundwork for the successful Plano Real in 1994. Politics in the second half of the 1990s revolved around the struggle between Cardoso's liberalizing reforms and the PT's efforts to preserve a statist model. As analyzed in *Democratic Brazil Revisited*, Cardoso departed office during the financial turbulence of 2001–2002, allowing the PT to capture the presidency at last. The PT's winning strategy involved a dilution of socialist discourse, new alliances with center-right parties, and explicit promises to maintain the macroeconomic policies of the second Cardoso term. Beginning in 2002, the PT reeled off four consecutive presidential victories, two by Lula and two by Dilma—one of the most impressive electoral records of any governing party in a Third Wave democracy. In each of those elections, the PSDB candidate—propelled by the party "brand" and by strong subnational bases in São Paulo and Minas Gerais, the two most populous states—forced the PT candidate into a runoff election, losing all four of them but also displaying a resilient national organization even twenty years after the Plano Real.

We acknowledge that a focus on the two "presidential parties" can obscure the political diversity that exists in Congress, in state governments, and in municipal-level politics in Brazil, and there is certainly no guarantee that the PT-PSDB duopoly will survive in 2018 and beyond. Public support for the PT fell dramatically during the second Dilma government, and Lula's ambition to return to the presidency may be thwarted by continued corruption investigations. Similarly, the PSDB is plagued by an aging leadership and a lack of policy innovation; despite taking three seats in Temer's cabinet in 2016, the party did not benefit in any direct or unconditional way from the PT's fall from grace. Yet there is no doubt that these two actors strongly flavored Brazilian democracy in the period from 1994 (the Plano Real) to 2014 (Dilma's reelection), and their respective legacies will impact the regime for many years to come.

The two parties differ from other Brazilian parties in three main ways. First, the PT and the PSDB are *modernizing* parties that inject an important element of programmatic politics into a system long dominated by personalism and clientelism. The PT modernized the Brazilian left by divorcing it from union bossism and by establishing authentic new connections to civil society; the PSDB, although sometimes described as a "right-wing" organization in the Brazilian context, is probably better described as a party of the modernizing center. The party brought actual programmatic proposals (economic stabilization and state reform) to the center space, traditionally an ideological wasteland occupied by opportunists willing to support any government. Second, the PSDB and PT have clear *party brands* (Lupu 2016) based largely on their time in the national presidency. Simplifying broadly, the PSDB is associated with inflation control and state reform, while the PT is associated with pro-poor policies and social inclusion. Third, the PT and PSDB are *formateur* parties—that is, for the past twenty years they have been the only two parties capable of forming the multiparty alliances that are necessary to win office and govern in Brazil's system of coalitional presidentialism (Power 2010). In these ways and more, the PT and PSDB have helped to anchor not only Brazil's notoriously fluid party system but also the democratic regime itself.

Brazil's most recent presidential election in 2014 revealed how much the post-1994 duopoly has shaped national politics. A casual observer of the presidential debates could have been forgiven for believing that, in such a relentlessly backward-looking campaign, Cardoso and Lula themselves were on the ballot. Dilma Rousseff positioned herself clearly as the heiress to Lula's legacy of poverty reduction and rising personal incomes for the poor, stressing not only the Bolsa Família but other popular social programs in the areas of housing, health care, electrification, and university access. Given mounting inflationary pressures, the PSDB candidate, Aécio Neves, attempted to remind voters of his party's successes in stabilizing the economy in the 1990s. The runoff between Aécio and Dilma was the closest election in modern Brazilian history, with Dilma winning by only 3.28 percent. The closeness of this margin and the fact that Aécio demanded (and failed to obtain) a recount of the votes cast a polarizing shadow over the eventual impeachment process in 2015–2016.

The election also confirmed new patterns of presidential voting that had first been observed in Lula's reelection in 2006. After several years of pro-poor policies including conditional cash transfers and strong increases in the real minimum wage, voters in Brazil's poorest regions—especially the Northeast —voted massively for PT presidential candidates (Hunter and Power 2007; Zucco 2008). The so-called new middle class had strong reasons to support the Lula and Dilma governments. Social indicators also suggested that more prosperous voters in the South and Southeast, where the "traditional" middle class was disproportionately concentrated, also had some good reasons to vote *against* the PT—their incomes grew at much slower rates than those of the poor during the Lula-Dilma years (Neri 2010, 2011b). With Dilma drawing votes predominantly from the upwardly mobile poor and Aécio from the tra-ditional middle classes, the electoral map in October 2014 was starkly divided: in the runoff, Dilma won with 72 percent of the vote in the poor Northeast, while Aécio won with 59 percent of the vote in the developed South. The regional skewing of the vote added yet another dimension of polarization to Dilma's subsequent decline and ouster: she maintained her strongest support in the Northeast to the very end of her presidency.

These patterns of regional and class voting are much less pronounced in legislative elections: the PT's congressional delegation elected in 2014 was actually slightly smaller than it was after Lula's breakthrough election in 2002. However, the presidency remains by far the most important prize in the po-litical system, and the PT's policies produced a "new constituency" (Zucco 2008): under Lula, poor voters quite correctly credited the federal govern-ment for the creation of new policies that reduced poverty and inequality. These policies allowed the PT to win the presidency four times in a row. Yet the fourth victory—Dilma in October 2014—was undeniably the least con-vincing, given not only the close margin but also the rapidly worsening mac-roeconomic indicators as the election approached (Brazil had experienced two consecutive quarters of contraction when voting got under way). Even leaving aside the corruption scandals that subsequently emerged, it is quite possible that, had the 2014 election been held only a few months later, Dilma and the PT would have lost power. In retrospect, this could have been a bet-ter long-term outcome for the party, given that the PSDB would have been saddled with Brazil's extended recession.

Michel Temer (PMDB) assumed the presidency at perhaps the most polarized political moment in modern Brazilian history. The reasons for the polarization were all closely connected to the impeachment of his predecessor and dominated the national discourse in 2015–2016. These included a cliffhanger 2014 election and the subsequent "loser's fatigue" on the part of the anti-PT parties; a massive corruption scandal and the ensuing finger-pointing; increasingly conflictual debates about macroeconomic policy; the regional and class divisions that were ingrained by more than a decade of rule by a leftist party implementing strongly pro-poor policies for the first time in the country's history; and open warfare between many traditional media outlets (mainstream newspapers and television networks hostile to the PT) and the new alternative media networks, cultivated both inside and outside the state apparatus by the PT and its allies. In decades past, these multiple tensions might not have intersected so quickly and so violently. However, Brazil's massive addiction to the Internet and social media (it is a top five country for both Facebook and Twitter usage) undoubtedly contributed to the increasingly acrimonious quality of political debate in the Dilma years, with both right and left intent on demonizing the other side through every digital means possible. This qualitative aspect of the current political crisis—the division of friends and families in ways unseen in decades—added a bitter edge to the Dilma impeachment and its aftermath.

The Economic Context

As noted earlier, Brazil's first two democratic governments (those of presidents Sarney and Collor) had poor socioeconomic performance. The nadir came between 1987 and 1993, when Brazil was plagued by low growth, astronomical hyperinflation, and record-high rates of poverty and inequality. But from the Plano Real (1994) through the end of Lula's second term (2010), it was commonplace to note the steadily improving policy performance of Brazilian governments (Table I.2). That performance declined throughout Dilma's first term and into the 2014 election. By the start of Dilma's second term, Brazil's economy was in full-blown crisis. The question facing the new center-right government of Michel Temer in 2017 is whether it can move beyond the crisis and preserve or restore the gains of the BRIC years.

Brazil's economy made important real strides from 2002 to 2012. Nominal and per capita GDP growths were solid, albeit moderate (on average 3.0 percent per year and 2.4 percent respectively). But other indicators tell a more impressive story, especially in two areas that have long plagued the country: poverty/inequality and macroeconomic performance. Income inequality as measured by the Gini coefficient, a widely used standard measure of inequality, improved from roughly 0.60 to 0.53—still leaving Brazil as one of

Table I.2. Policy Performance of Brazilian Governments, 1985–2014

President	Years	Mean Real GDP Growth Rate (%)	Mean Inflation Rate (%)	Mean Poverty Rate (%)	Mean Gini Coefficient of Income Inequality
Sarney	1985–1990	4.39	727.69	38.41	0.608
Collor	1990–1992	–1.26	1070.92	42.01	0.598
Itamar	1992–1994	5.00	1696.80	41.00	0.603
Cardoso	1995–2002	2.31	9.25	34.86	0.597
Lula	2003–2010	4.06	5.79	27.04	0.559
Dilma	2011–2014	1.60	6.17	16.11	0.529

Notes: For the first three presidents, terms were not coterminous with calendar years. We assign Sarney responsibility for 1985–1989 inclusive, Collor for 1990–1992 inclusive, and Itamar for 1993 and 1994. Figures are averages for presidential terms.
Source: Ipeadata (http://www.ipeadata.gov.br).

the most unequal countries in the world. Nevertheless, the situation for the poor improved dramatically. For example, indigence (defined as those earning below $1.25 per day) fell from 30 percent of the population to 7 percent. Unemployment fell from roughly 12 percent to under 6 percent, and for the first time in Brazilian history the country wrestled with the challenge of labor shortages. In those circumstances, real wages rose across the country, raising millions of Brazilians from poorer classes (designated Classes E and D) into a consuming middle class—Class C. Conditional cash transfer programs such as Bolsa Família contributed to the virtual elimination of hunger in Brazil, while school enrolments below eighth grade approached 100 percent of the eligible population.

Macroeconomic improvements were even more striking given the destructive roles of debt and inflation in Brazilian history. With successive governments committed to "inflation targeting" (essentially subordinating fiscal policy to the goal of maintaining inflation within targeted parameters), inflation averaged a mere 6 percent per year during the BRIC years. Public sector debt had fallen to 57 percent of GDP—a level much better than any of the rich European or North American democracies—while averaging a 2 percent primary budget surplus each year. Taking advantage of propitious external circumstances, Brazil found itself able not only to pay off dollar-denominated external debt but also to accumulate nearly $400 billion in reserves. Brazil's financial performance was so strong that the International Monetary Fund (IMF) asked the Brazilian government to contribute to the

European Stabilization Fund during the 2008–2009 financial crisis. This strong macroeconomic performance rested as well on years of improved regulation of the domestic banking system and cleaning up of insolvent state-owned banks, a process that had begun in the 1990s. By 2012 Brazil's banking system had one of the best ratios of non-performing loans to assets in the world—a stunning reversal of the financial chaos that had prevailed in the country during the "drunk" years (Porzecanski 2009).

These successes in social inclusion and macroeconomic performance accompanied Brazil's emergent strengths in agricultural production, and innovation in the agricultural sector, along with the rise of the *multilatinas*—the new crop of globally powerful multinational corporations coming out of Latin America generally and Brazil specifically. In the agricultural sector Brazil was the leading producer and exporter of goods like soy, meat, coffee, oranges and orange juice, and sugar along with non-agricultural commodities like gold or iron. Brazilian firms such as JBS Friboi became global leaders in food exports, while mining giants like Vale and construction powerhouses such as Odebrecht became major players in other parts of the developing world, especially Africa. Active support from Brazilian government agencies, particularly the National Development Bank (Banco Nacional de Desenvolvimento Econômico e Social; BNDES), helped propel these internationally competitive firms into world leaders (Amann 2009). In short, there was good reason to celebrate Brazil's achievements.

There were also good reasons to be cautious about the extent of the success. As of 2017, Brazil faces at least four distinct economic problems, one conjunctural and the other three reflecting longer-term issues with deeper historical root causes. The conjunctural issue is the most glaring one: Brazil's economy has contracted sharply and performance on all key macroeconomic indicators is deteriorating rapidly. Between 2013 and 2016, over 8 percent of Brazil's GDP vanished, a loss comparable in size to the economy of Peru. In brief, the macroeconomic balance achieved in the BRIC years came under strain. One of the key sources of macroeconomic success during the earlier period was because of China's rapid economic growth, its voracious consumption of commodities from around the world including vital Brazilian exports such as meat and iron, and the positive effect of Chinese commodity imports on prices. During the 2000s Brazil's commodity exports quadrupled in value, generating strong current account surpluses that supported the country's rising imports, paying down external debt, and financing expansionary programs to offset the global economic slowdown, such as Lula's Program for the Acceleration of Growth (Programa de Aceleração do Crescimento; PAC). However, slowing Chinese growth with continued imports of manufactured goods meant that the trade balance shifted in the Dilma years. By 2014 the country suffered from a current account deficit of over 3.5 percent. Unwilling or unable to cut spending, Dilma's government repeatedly shifted downward the primary surplus target for maintaining low inflation and then missed those new lower targets. By 2014 the primary surplus was projected at roughly 1.7 percent of GDP and falling. Pressure on spending came from things like obligations stemming from hosting the World Cup and the Olympic Games as well as commitments to the pension system, which despite a number of incremental reforms under previous governments continued to represent an unsustainable 12 percent of GDP. The Dilma government faced a fiscal squeeze requiring either politically difficult spending cuts or an increase in tax revenue. Tax increases were unlikely, given that the Brazilian tax burden had already reached an imposing 36 percent of GDP. By contrast, spending cuts depended on a greatly weakened president to muster political support for unpalatable options. Ultimately, Dilma's efforts to restore macroeconomic balance faltered in Congress and in the face of growing public antagonism.

The explosion of the Lava Jato scandal with the implication of Petrobras at the heart of the corruption, and the political paralysis that followed the impeachment charges turned a challenging conjunctural problem into a fullblown crisis. Petrobras had become the Dilma administration's key vehicle for public investment. The corruption scandal led to company losses and froze Petrobras's investment plans. The large-scale withdrawal of public investment in turn led to a sharp decrease in business spending and investment throughout the economy. Weakening investment led to both worsening unemployment and a sharp decline in consumer spending. The classic recessionary vicious cycle led to falling government revenues that further complicated efforts to balance the books in Brasília. In short, the corruption crisis helped fuel a process of dramatic reductions in private spending that multiplied the effects of reducing government expenditure. Yet, although these conjunctural problems are vexing and will challenge the embattled Temer government through 2018, they are not unresolvable. Ultimately addressing them depends on ending the political uncertainty that has crippled decision-making and led firms and households to put off investment and spending. In short, the Brazilian economy is not as weak as it appears.

Beyond the conjunctural crisis, three other issues are path-dependent, cumulative, and serious obstacles to long-term prosperity. Each will require medium-to-long-term responses from Temer and his successor. First, a critical shortcoming facing the Brazilian economy is the inadequate investment in infrastructure. Brazil funds only an estimated 25 percent of its actual infrastructural needs, and this threatens its overall competitiveness. For example, Brazil spends roughly 1.5 percent of GDP on infrastructure while the global average for upper-middle-income and wealthy economies is 3.8 percent of

GDP (*Economist* 2013). In large economies, the total value of the stock of infrastructure is 71 percent of GDP, while in Brazil it is 16 percent of GDP.

This manifests itself particularly acutely in transport. Bottlenecks in urban mobility are the predictable consequence of the PT's successes in fostering the growth of the new consuming middle classes. Between 2002 and 2012, the number of vehicles on Brazilian roads doubled while airports saw a rise from 35 million to over 85 million passengers annually. Inadequate investment in infrastructure has led to delays, deterioration of service, and high costs for users of transport systems with both political and economic costs. Transit fare increases were the trigger of the 2013 protests that brought millions of Brazilians into the streets. Economically, the expensive and slow transport system erodes Brazilian competitiveness even in areas of strength (García-Escribano, Góes, and Karpowicz, 2015). For example, while Iowa soy producers spend 9 percent of the value of their goods on transport, Brazil's highly competitive producers spend 25 percent, eroding their advantage in one of the strongest sectors in the economy. These infrastructural problems were decades in the making and will take years of investment to overcome. They are not a consequence of the Dilma government's policies or of her impeachment, and Temer's new government will not be able to resolve them during his term. However, crumbling infrastructure poses a substantial drag on Brazil's growth possibilities and forces politically difficult choices between long-term investment (with no short-term political gain) and immediate consumption (with limited long-term benefit but immediate political gain).

A second area of concern is the weakness of the manufacturing sector, due to both long-standing policy failings and relative policy neglect during the BRIC boom years—a decline that Brazilian entrepreneurs decried as "de-industrialization." The clearest signal of the decline in manufacturing has been its falling share of exports and of GDP since 2000. Orthodox market liberals dismiss these concerns and argue that it is a natural progression for a maturing economy (Oreiro and Feijó 2010). Others have been less sanguine, arguing that there is a cost to becoming increasingly dependent on commodity exports. The central concerns relate to the effect of the loss of manufacturing competitiveness, including the potential macroeconomic costs of rising import penetration. But, the most significant concern is that declining manufacturing contributes to an eventual loss of technological capacity and innovation. In effect, manufacturing matters for movement up the ladder of the "knowledge economy."

Proving conclusively that de-industrialization is occurring is a difficult undertaking. Yet even if one remains agnostic on this question, Brazil's performance as an exporter has presented cause for concern. On average and on paper, the picture appears very positive. From 2000 to 2011, exports doubled in value, reaching $256 billion. By 2012 Brazil was genuinely an agricultural superpower as the world's leading or second exporter of soy, sugar/ethanol, oranges and orange juice, meat, and coffee (Nassar 2009).

However, the story for manufacturing is quite different. In 2000 manufactured goods represented more than half the value of all exports and Brazil exported almost nothing to China. By 2012 commodity exports accounted for more than half the value with manufactured and semi-manufactured goods making up the rest, and China had become Brazil's leading trade partner. Yet the relationship was quite asymmetrical, as China overwhelmingly imported commodities from Brazil and exported manufactured goods back. Indeed, Chinese-manufactured goods increasingly became a leading competitor with Brazilian goods in both Brazil's domestic market and other Latin American markets. The net result for manufacturing changed markedly over the period. In 2005 Brazil's trade in manufactured goods ran a surplus of $8 billion equal to 1 percent of GDP. By 2011 the surplus had changed into a deficit amounting to 4 percent of GDP (Oreiro and Feijó 2010; Jenkins 2015).

Comparing Brazil's performance to other upper-middle-income competitors clearly reveals its failure to take advantage of the growth of the global economy in the 2000s. The period from 2000 to 2011/2012 was a highly propitious one for emerging economies and afforded considerable opportunities for improved economic performance. Brazil was not an exception and its exports increased an impressive 262 percent from 2000 to 2010 while high tech exports increased 36 percent. Yet, over the same period, the average export growth for the five BRICSA countries (Brazil, Russia, India, China, and South Africa) was 439 percent, showing that Brazil had been the least able among them to take advantage of global growth over the period. Focusing specifically on the country's relative performance on high tech exports also shows Brazil's status as a laggard. Over the period, the country's 36 percent stands in sharp contrast with India's 389 percent growth and China's 873 percent expansion. Expressed as ratios, in the year 2000 Brazil's high tech exports were 14 percent of China's and 290 percent of India's. By 2010 Brazil's exports were down to 2 percent of China's and only 80 percent of India's. Even if "de-industrialization" has not been occurring, the comparative data suggest that Brazil has not kept pace with key global competitors (Canuto, Cavallari, and Reis 2013).

As with the "de-industrialization" question, the exact causes for manufacturing weakness are subject to debate. The long stretch of rapid commodity export growth helped sustain an appreciation of the Brazilian *real* that weakened competitiveness. Indeed, one of the few bright spots of the conjunctural crisis is that it led to a depreciation of the real and the prospect of improved manufacturing competitiveness. Despite the improving exchange rate, industrialists still suffered from the inadequacy of the country's infrastructure as well as from heavy regulatory and tax burdens and the inadequacies of the education system.

The education system is the third major area of concern, both for present competitiveness and for Brazil's future capacity to compete on global markets (Bruns, Evans, and Luque 2012). The inadequacies of the education system lead to both the relatively low quality and the insufficient supply of skilled labor. Brazilian education has made impressive gains under the Lula and then Dilma regimes. Yet, that is still progress against a very poor baseline. The Bolsa Família has helped vastly improve school enrollments up to the eighth grade. But high school graduation rates remain low—roughly 50 percent. Brazil has one of highest dropout rates in Latin America and the highest rate of primary school grade repeaters (18.7 percent). The average of 7.2 years of educational attainment ranks below most of its global competitors as does its student-teacher ratio and the number of students at or below the lowest level of proficiency. All these problems, in turn, reflect in poor performance on the UNESCO's Program for International Assessment (PISA test) scores, with Brazil ranking below many of its competitors both inside and outside Latin America. The poor quality of labor shows up among factors like low labor productivity, serious shortfalls of skilled labor (the National Confederation of Industry estimates that Brazil has a shortfall of 150 thousand engineers), and comparatively low levels of skilled labor employment even in capital-intensive industries (Schneider 2009). Solving educational shortcomings takes time, resources, and political will. While there have been positive signs over the period of PT rule, the complexity of the problem and the inevitably slow pace of reform challenges Brazil's capacity to compete in higher valued added production.

The end result is that Brazil in 2017 presents a mixed profile. It is facing extremely difficult conjunctural circumstances. There is no guarantee that the Temer coalition will solve these challenges effectively; given the government's low public legitimacy and short time frame in which to act, expectations are (and should be) low. Yet the underlying problems are tractable, particularly if the political climate becomes more certain after 2018. At the same time, it is unwise to think only in terms of presidential administrations. The longer-term issues present deeper problems that will continue to challenge democratic Brazil well into the 2020s. Brazil's competitive position in the global economy depends on whether successive governments can address not only concerns at the micro level of competitiveness but also the way macro-level policies affect the micro environment.

Our focus on the bad news of 2013–2016 and the underlying causes can easily distract us from some other developments that are positive. Brazil has produced world-leading firms, backed by the BNDES. The country remains an agricultural power—with agriculture again supported by a key government agency, the Brazilian Agricultural Research Corporation (Empresa Brasileira de Pesquisa Agropecuária; EMBRAPA), that has played a critical role in fostering innovation, promoting the emergence of global leaders, and diffusing a Brazilian model of agriculture in other developing countries (particularly in Africa). Finally, the PT's two administrations have overseen improvements in social welfare that are unprecedented in Brazilian history. As with the political conjuncture, the mosaic of Brazil's economy defies simple categorizations. It is a giant complex economy with notable strengths and considerable weaknesses.

Lessons for Theory

The present volume, like its two predecessors, aims to offer a holistic, comprehensive appraisal of Brazilian democracy. One might legitimately question whether this is a realistic goal. After all, our focus is the political *regime*, which is a broad concept—perhaps too broad. What is the best way to approach it, and what is the most effective way of marshaling resources for collaborative research on an existing polyarchy (as opposed to a newly democratizing one) such as Brazil?

What we have learned in previous work is that to appraise the macropolitical, we must first engage the micropolitical. In adopting this approach, we have repeatedly endorsed the long-standing calls from scholars such as Philippe Schmitter (1992), Ben Ross Schneider (1995), and the late Guillermo O'Donnell (1996) to disaggregate the concept of democracy. In the 1990s O'Donnell and others argued that democratization theory was suffering from a host of problems, including tautology, teleology, and a poor understanding of the large category of intermediate cases between authoritarianism and consolidated democracy. A persistent problem was a tendency to work at too high a level of abstraction. In thinking about this specific challenge, Schmitter argued persuasively that democratic consolidation is a multidimensional process that operates at different speeds in different arenas. He advocated the disaggregation of the category of *regime* into several "partial regimes," each of which is organized around the representation of different social actors and the resolution of their conflicts: the electoral regime, the pressure regime, the representation regime, and so forth. Schmitter's method constitutes an actor-centric approach that aims for a deeper understanding of the patterned interactions that exist in and around discrete institutions and policy domains. This approach recognizes that partial regimes can "move at different speeds," and that change within them is neither uniform nor linear.

This line of thinking has several virtues that we have extolled in *Democratic Brazil* and in *Democratic Brazil Revisited*, and we remain committed to this theoretical approach. A clear advantage of Schmitter's "partial regimes" framework is that it provides a sober and practical approach to *empirical research* on democratic development, one that can organize middle-range research programs in an effective way. Given our preference for collaborative work with specialists in various subdomains of Brazilian democracy, we have organized the present volume into four sections that correspond roughly to Schmitter's electoral regime, policy-making regime, and representation regime, with the addition of new contributions on the separate domain of Brazil's regional and global projection.

The contributions to this volume confirm that a disaggregative approach is helpful in identifying both patterns and velocity of democratic change. Broadly speaking, each "partial regime" of Brazilian democracy displays uneven, nonlinear development that points to a fascinating combination of innovation, advances, and persistent challenges. For example, in the 1994–2014 period, Brazil's political institutions became more stable and settled on a relatively predictable pattern of coalitional presidentialism led by two programmatic formateur parties, the PT and the PSDB. Yet at the same time, public support for parties and Congress remained scandalously low, and the fragmentation of the party system has increased in every electoral cycle since 1990. In the policy-making sphere, the Brazilian state has increased its overall regulatory, accountability, and extractive capacity and has developed pockets of internationally recognized expertise in agriculture, diplomacy, social policy, and public banking. Yet some would argue that these "islands of excellence" float amidst an archipelago of mediocrity, in which many elements of the state apparatus continue to be used for clientelism and patronage or are indiscriminately horse-traded among political parties without any attention to efficiency. Arguably, the corruption and impeachment crisis is the result of the gap between these ongoing corrupt practices and the vastly improved capacity of the state to identify and prosecute individuals for engaging in them. In the domain of popular representation, Brazil has been an undeniable trailblazer in creating institutions of popular participation, and its extraordinarily differentiated civil society is robust at all levels. However, the protesters who took to the streets between 2013 and 2016 struggled to emplace their demands on the national agenda and to convert their incredible raw energy into effective and durable organizations.

Thus, the patterns of democratic development in Brazil are clearly fragmentary, uneven, and domain-specific, very often taking "two steps forward, one step back." In all of the partial regimes referred to above, there are myriad contextual factors operating at the micro level, factors that would be obscured or lost if we attempted a highly idealized, overgeneralizing characterization of Brazilian democracy as a whole. By focusing on actors, sectors, and institutions both separately and sequentially, we can place micro-level variables in their appropriate contexts and thereby illuminate some of the persistent challenges facing the world's fourth largest democracy. Focusing on micro-level variables and the nuances and complexities among them also helps us see Brazilian democracy for the complex mosaic it is and avoid the common tendency to see only the negative or the positive. In the "hangover" following Dilma's impeachment, Brazil is divided against itself and is currently confronting the deepest political and economic challenges of the New Republic. But it does so drawing on vital sources of strength. The only certainty is that Brazilian democracy will continue to unfold in ways that defy simple categories.

Overview of the Book

The present volume is organized into four sections, the first of which focuses on "The Democratic Context." In addition to the present essay examining the national mood and deep divisions at democracy's thirtieth birthday, this section features a second contribution by Oswaldo Amaral and Rachel Meneguello concerning the PT. At the time of Dilma's impeachment, the PT was by far the largest and best-organized left-wing party in the democratic history of Latin America. Although the PT had a long and frequently studied life as an opposition party between 1980 and 2002, Amaral and Meneguello argue, it was the experience of the Lula government (2003–2010) that defined the modern party. Economic growth and popular social policies guaranteed impressive levels of approval for the Lula government and expanded mass support for the party despite a series of corruption scandals that claimed several leading party figures. PT party identification rose notably in the Lula years and established the party as the only one in Brazil with a large and stable mass membership. Amaral and Meneguello claim that the PT deepened Brazilian democracy in two important "partial regimes": that of social inclusion and that of responsiveness of the state to the demands of varied social actors. Yet the PT as a governing party failed to overcome the political system's entrenched clientelism, corporatism, and patrimonialism. Indeed, the compromises made by the party under Lula and Dilma to govern under coalitional presidentialism led to the scandals of 2014–2016, created tensions within the organization, and triggered strong public reactions against corruption. Whether the party can recover from the crisis and whether Brazilian democracy can deepen as a result of the scandals remain vital questions for the future.

Chapter 2, by Benjamin Goldfrank and Brian Wampler, explores the tensions between the party base and the party as government. The authors ask how it was possible for the PT to both establish and empower the agencies charged with investigating and prosecuting corruption while simultaneously mounting a massive and elaborate corruption scheme. They argue that the answer lies in the schizophrenic nature of the party. On one hand, the dominant faction has focused on winning elections and governing with political alliances, both of which entailed the traditional clientelistic and patrimonial politics discussed by Amaral and Meneguello. On the other hand, establishing new institutions of participation, accountability, and transparency satisfied PT activists who were committed to the party's historic profile of clean and participatory governance. Ultimately, the newly strengthened agencies of oversight and accountability uncovered the workings of the Lava Jato and exposed networks of corruption that extended into all the major parties but that ironically also caught the PT's own leadership in the process. As a result, the PT and Brazil are standing at a crossroads, undecided whether to reform "politics as usual" or to weaken accountability institutions.

In Part II the focus is on "Policy Innovation and State Capacity in a Maturing Democracy." Chapter 3 by Matthew Taylor examines the critical issue of corruption and accountability. He reviews competing hypotheses about the sources of corruption in Brazil and undertakes a sober analysis of the country's national integrity system. A major obstacle to democratic legitimation in Brazil, Taylor shows, is the iterated cycle of "shock and disillusion" that occurs whenever a major scandal is uncovered: "the alarming recognition that something egregious has been going on under everyone's noses is quickly followed by the chilling realization that the perpetrators will probably get away with it." Although impunity is a serious and recurrent problem, Taylor argues that real gains have been made in improving the legislation and the accountability institutions that aim to curtail corruption. He ends on an optimistic note. While the Lava Jato scandal poses important challenges, the public agrees on the need for reform and the electoral arena is set to reward politicians who champion transparency.

In Chapter 4, Kathryn Hochstetler examines Brazilian environmental politics at two levels of analysis, domestic and global. In focusing on a domestic regulatory domain (environmental licensing) as well as on a key element of Brazil's approach to global governance (climate change negotiations), Hochstetler gives us two contrasting entry points into green politics. Domestically, internal battles over the environmental licensing of individual projects have been acrimonious and have shifted attention away from other necessary issues, such as the need for a comprehensive national energy policy. Globally, Brazil has been a positive force for South-South unity in debates about climate change, especially policies that would exact important concessions from developed economies in the North.

Chapter 5 turns to education policy. Marcus Melo argues that, although starting from a dismal baseline, educational indicators in Brazil have improved significantly in the twenty years of PSDB-PT governments. It is tempting to claim that it should be easy to raise educational performance when the starting point is so low, yet Melo argues that neither the low baseline nor the massive resources earmarked for education by Cardoso, Lula, and Dilma can explain the observed outcomes. Rather, it has been rising political competition and improved institutional oversight of subnational executives (governors and mayors) that have improved educational indicators. In addition to robust interparty competition, Melo credits audit bodies, NGOs, independent media, the judicial system, the public prosecutor's office, and regulatory agencies for pushing subnational governments to use their financial resources more effectively.

In Chapter 6, Wendy Hunter and Natasha Borges Sugiyama analyze what was perhaps the signature policy initiative of the PT years, Bolsa Família. In the most comprehensive analysis currently available of the positive, negative, and as-yet-unknown outcomes of the Bolsa Família, Hunter and Sugiyama conclude that the program has palpably improved the quality of Brazilian democracy—both directly, by reducing poverty, and indirectly, through knock-on effects in the domain of citizenship. The Bolsa has brought poor Brazilians into more routine and formalized contact with the Brazilian state, and it has also begun to emancipate them from traditional networks of coercion and clientelism. In short, Bolsa Família has undeniably turned many ordinary Brazilians into "citizens" for the first time.

The policy section of the book concludes with Chapter 7 contributed by Anthony Pereira, who examines Brazil's somewhat tardy initiatives in the area of transitional justice. The National Truth Commission that examined the human rights abuses of the military dictatorship (1964–1985) was established only in 2012, three decades after the controversial Amnesty Law of 1979. Pereira focuses on several factors that help explain both why Brazil was a laggard in the area of transitional justice and why it played catch-up in the PT years. These factors include the conservative nature of the transition to democracy, the legacy of the military justice system, the lack of leadership by prominent political parties, the decentralized nature of the Brazilian political system, the influence of cultural production, and international diffusion. The story of transitional justice in Brazil once again provides evidence that change within partial regimes need not be uniform or linear; after decades of slow movement or even utter inaction, the process accelerated rapidly in the Lula-Dilma era, culminating in "one of the largest reparations programs in the world," distinguished by its forward-looking focus.

The third section of the present volume, entitled "Politics from the Bottom Up," features two contributions on the political sociology of Brazilian democracy in the Lula-Dilma years. In Chapter 8, Maria Hermínia Tavares de Almeida and Fernando Henrique Guarnieri analyze the massive transformation in the Brazilian class structure that has taken place as a consequence of the PT's pro-poor policies. The authors stress the heterogeneity of the middle classes not only in terms of social composition but also with regard to their attitudes and beliefs. The new stratum of middle-income citizens is an extraordinarily diverse group: their political values and attitudes, as well as political identities, are endogenous to the sustainability of the social transformation itself. Their main common goal is to guarantee continuity of the consumption boom that began under Lula, an expansion that was fueled by minimum wage policies, conditional cash transfers (CCTs), and easy access to credit. The so-called new middle classes support these PT-led policies, but this sympathy in no way prevented people from taking to the streets to protest government actions of which they disapprove, whether corruption scandals or hikes in transportation costs.

In Chapter 9, Alfredo Saad-Filho takes a closer look at the massive wave of street protests in 2013. Similar to Almeida and Guarnieri's findings about the heterogeneity of the emerging Class C, Saad-Filho shows that the 2013 protests were themselves bewilderingly diverse. Those who took to the streets expressed a wide-ranging set of demands concerning corruption, public services, human rights, and sporting mega-events, among other issues. These movements also received supportive media coverage at a much earlier stage than other mass campaigns in recent Brazilian history, such as the Diretas Já campaign of 1983–1984 or the movement to impeach Fernando Collor in 1992. Both social and traditional media were important in the diffusion of the protests. Foreshadowing the division and polarization referenced in the editors' introductory chapter, Saad-Filho notes that the 2013 protests were the first since 1964 to have some elements expressing openly right-wing views. He traces this to the stagnation in income growth of the "traditional" middle class, for whom higher education is no longer a guarantee of economic privilege. Saad-Filho places a good deal of the blame for popular discontent on the PT itself—not only because of corruption scandals but also because the party failed to break cleanly with the neoliberal policies of the Cardoso years.

Brazilian politics focused on the many internal challenges prior to the victory of the PT. Brazil in the 2000s, however, became a global player with an increasing presence in international affairs. Therefore, the present volume concludes with a section on "Strategies of Global Projection." In Chapter 10, Sean Burges and Jean Daudelin provide a comprehensive overview of contemporary Brazilian foreign policy, focusing heavily on the institutional role of the Foreign Ministry (known informally as Itamaraty after the palace in which it is housed). Although there was a notable role for presidential summitry during the Cardoso and Lula years, Itamaraty still attempts to monopolize the foreign-policy-making process, even while recognizing that its diplomats do not possess the full technical expertise necessary for engagement on complex global issues. Itamaraty has a noted addiction to splashy but poorly institutionalized integration schemes and governance arrangements at both regional and global levels, a pattern that Burges and Daudelin see as an unnecessary distraction. Overall, despite a monopolistic and self-important foreign ministry, contemporary Brazilian democracy is still overwhelmingly focused on domestic issues, meaning that the political constituency necessary for deeper global engagement is still lacking at home.

Leslie Armijo concludes the volume with her essay on the "new developmentalism" model in Brazil, which she approaches via a case study of the National Development Bank (BNDES). Differently from the model of import-substitution industrialization (ISI) that dominated Brazil from the 1930s through the 1980s, the new developmentalism of the 1990s through the present has emphasized macroeconomic stability (low inflation), greater participation in global markets, and the reduction of domestic inequality. Both models emphasize the role of the state in promoting infrastructural development, and the BNDES has been important to each of the two models at different stages in its history. Given the immense role of this public bank in Brazilian development, Armijo develops the idea of a "public bank trilemma," which involves fascinating tradeoffs among the acquisition of expertise, insertion into the market, and delivery of policies according to democratic principles. Although these tradeoffs are also embedded in other mixed-capitalist, middle-income regimes, Armijo believes that the neodevelopmentalist consensus in Brazil is strong enough to overcome them. This has implications not only for the global projection strategies discussed by Burges and Daudelin but also for the current economic stagnation reviewed by the editors in the Introduction.

All in all, the twelve contributions in the present volume point to the need to appraise the macropolitical while dissecting the micropolitical. The expected thirtieth birthday party for Brazilian democracy was overshadowed by corruption and economic crisis followed by a polarizing impeachment trial only a year later, so the regime enters 2017 both weary and battle-scarred. After Brazil bathed in the adoration of the BRICs years, a correction was certain to occur sooner or later: the praise was always excessive. The sudden-onset malaise and the ensuing polarization in Brazilian society surprised many observers with its timing and intensity after 2013. Nobody predicted the exact events that unfolded. Nevertheless, as the contributors to the present volume have shown, democratic development in Brazil is still complex, vibrant, and fascinating across a wide range of actors, institutions, and processes.

THE DEMOCRATIC
CONTEXT

PART I

1

Oswaldo E. do Amaral and Rachel Meneguello

The PT in Power,
2003–2016

IN DEMOCRATIC BRAZIL: *Actors, Institutions, and Processes* (2000), William Nylen analyzed the role played by the Workers' Party (Partido dos Trabalhadores; PT) in the consolidation of democracy in Brazil. According to Nylen, the PT helped strengthen Brazilian democracy in three ways: first, by conducting itself as a loyal opposition that acted within democratic limits; second, by questioning the social and economic inequalities that existed in Brazil and proposing new, inclusionary public policies within the framework of a democratic regime; and third, by providing political activists with a nonviolent channel in which to challenge the existing political order (2000, 126–27). By 2000, in the wake of Luiz Inácio (Lula) da Silva's defeat in the presidential elections of 1989, 1994, and 1998, the PT had consolidated itself as the most important opposition party in Brazil. Two years later, Lula and the PT won the presidency for the first time and began the longest spell of single-party control over the Brazilian federal executive since the end of the authoritarian regime. However, after three complete terms, and the reelection of president Dilma Rousseff in 2014, the party faced its biggest political and institutional crisis. In 2016, after losing the party's support in the Congress and amid a strong economic recession, Dilma Rousseff was involved in the second impeachment process in the country since the end of the authoritarian regime.

What did twelve years in Brazil's Planalto Palace mean for the PT and for democracy in Brazil? What did this period represent for the Brazilian party system and for political competition in Brazil? What were the principal changes that took place within the PT during that period? A decade of PT presidency brought improvements in the quality of democracy in Brazil, although certain obstacles remain to the cementing of the regime's legitimacy among Brazilian citizens, as the economic and political crises in 2015–2016 clearly show.

There have been clear changes in the Brazilian party system between 2003 and 2016. While the Brazilian party system has stabilized over the past decade, it is still weakened because support for parties is not firmly entrenched in the electorate. Important transformations that occurred under the PT administrations, such as the significant reduction in national income inequality and the positive impact of poverty reduction programs, have proved to be important sources of political support during most of the PT's period in power, and PT governance has impacted on the perceptions Brazilians hold of democracy more broadly. The PT has also undergone transformations during its twelve years in power. Its organizational structure and programmatic ideology have evolved, and the party has experienced significant growth in its membership base and proved capable of maintaining a network of fruitful relationships between its leadership and social movements. However, it did not build mechanisms to prevent its leaders from involvement in corruption scandals connected to electoral campaigns. With regard to its programmatic scope, the PT opted to respond strategically to the dynamic of alliances fostered by coalitional presidentialism, even though these decisions resulted in political defections and a shift to the right. Organizational changes have been more gradual than programmatic ones, creating a source of tension inside the party during its period in power.

The Party System, 2003–2016

The Brazilian political system combines presidentialism, federalism, and a hybrid-norm electoral system that produces majoritarian and consociational arrangements in high magnitude districts. The resulting high number of actors contributes to a highly fragmented party system at the national level, allowing presidential elections to dictate the logic of party arrangements and political strategies (Limongi and Cortez 2010; Meneguello 2010). Furthermore, because the system relies on direct elections at the federal, state, and municipal levels, voters have the power to shape both executive and legislative electoral outcomes and can therefore dictate the character of the ultimate governing coalition.

What were the effects of twelve years of PT power on the party system? How

Table 1.1. Number and Percentage of Seats Obtained in the Chamber of Deputies (2002–2014), Principal Parties

	2002		2006		2010		2014	
	Seats	%	Seats	%	Seats	%	Seats	%
PT	91	17.7	83	16.2	88	17.2	70	13.6
PSDB	71	13.8	66	12.9	53	10.3	54	10.5
PMDB	74	14.4	89	17.3	79	15.4	66	12.9
PFL/DEM	84	16.4	65	12.7	43	8.4	22	4.3
PSB	22	4.3	27	5.3	34	6.6	34	6.6
PPB/PP	49	9.6	41	8.0	41	8.0	36	7.0
PSD							37	7.2

Source: Tribunal Superior Eleitoral (Superior Electoral Court).

did this period alter the patterns of political competition observed in Brazil? One way to answer these questions is to analyze the electoral performance of the PT between 2003 and 2014. In the three general elections in which the party participated while holding the presidency, the PT's performance at the national level was marked by stability. In the presidential elections of 2006, 2010, and 2014, Lula and then Dilma received, in the first round of votes, 48.6 percent, 46.9 percent, and 41.6 percent of the vote, respectively. As a result, both candidates had to compete in a second round of voting against Geraldo Alckmin (2006), José Serra (2010), and Aécio Neves (2014), all members of the Party of Brazilian Social Democracy (Partido da Social Democracia Brasileira; PSDB). In elections for the Chamber of Deputies during the same period, the PT received more votes than any other party in all elections but did not achieve significant growth and in fact declined relative to its performance in 2002. In that election the PT had received 18.4 percent of the vote and won 17.7 percent of seats in the Chamber. Four years later, the party obtained 15 percent of the vote and 16.2 percent of seats. In 2010, the percentages were similar: 16.8 percent of the vote and 17.2 percent of seats. In 2014, the party received 13.9 percent of the votes and obtained 13.6 percent of the seats (table 1.1), reflecting the increased level of party fragmentation in the lower house.

At the state level the PT's results were equally modest. In 2002 the PT held three of the country's twenty-seven governorships. In 2006, 2010, and 2014 that number rose to five. In the state legislative assemblies, the party held 147 assembly seats (13.9 percent of the total) in 2002; that figure fell to 126 seats (11.9 percent) in 2006, rose to 148 (14 percent) in 2010, and dropped back to

Table 1.2. Number and Percentage of Seats Obtained in the State Legislative Assemblies (2002–2014), Principal Parties

	2002		2006		2010		2014	
	Seats	%	Seats	%	Seats	%	Seats	%
PT	147	13.9	126	11.9	148	14.0	108	10.2
PSDB	139	13.1	152	14.4	123	11.6	97	9.2
PMDB	132	12.5	164	15.5	147	13.8	142	13.4
PFL/DEM	122	11.5	118	11.1	76	7.2	45	4.2
PSB	59	5.6	60	5.7	73	6.9	62	5.8
PPB/PP	93	8.8	53	5.0	48	4.5	51	4.8
PSD							75	7.1

Source: Tribunal Superior Eleitoral (Superior Electoral Court).

108 (10.2 percent) in 2014 (see table 1.2). At the municipal level, the party experienced substantial growth in the 2004 elections, achieving a 48 percent increase in the number of municipal council seats (*vereadores*) held and a 120 percent increase in the number of mayoralties (*prefeituras*) held, relative to the year 2000. In the elections of 2008 and 2012, the PT continued to gain seats, but at a slower rate. By the end of the period in question, after twelve years occupying the presidency, the PT held only 8.5 percent of municipal council seats and 11.6 percent of Brazil's more than 5,500 mayoralties.

Data on voting patterns in presidential and legislative elections shows the consolidation of two distinct competitive dynamics in the Brazilian political system. On the one hand, presidential elections have essentially become two-party contests. Since 1994 the PT and the PSDB have been the only parties whose candidates have garnered more than 25 percent of the presidential vote. The effective number of parties in the presidential elections of 2006, 2010, and 2014 were 2.4, 2.7, and 3.0, respectively. These numbers are consistent with the data from 1994 (2.7), 1998 (2.5), and 2002 (3.2). On the other hand, electoral competition for the Chamber of Deputies is quite open. In 2010 and 2014 only three parties (the PT, the PSDB, and the Brazilian Democratic Movement Party [Partido do Movimento Democrático Brasileiro; PMDB]) obtained between 10 percent and 20 percent of votes for the legislature. These numbers are similar to data from elections in 1990, 1994, 1998, 2002, and 2006. The result has been a Chamber of Deputies with a high—and increasing—level of fragmentation. The effective number of parties in the Chamber of Deputies was 8.5 in 2003, 9.3 in 2007, 10.4 in 2011, and 13.2 in

2015 — numbers that are broadly consistent with the data from 1991 (8.7), 1995 (8.2), and 1999 (7.1).

The restriction of viable presidential candidacies to the PT and PSDB between 1994 and 2014 reflects the Brazilian electorate's support for parties that offered strong leadership based on different visions for the country's development. The PT and the PSDB each led a partisan block with a distinct program. While the PSDB served as an organizing pole for Brazil's center-right parties, the PT played a similar role for the center-left. That dynamic has also played out at the state level, demonstrating the importance of presidential elections in shaping partisan alliances at all levels of the Brazilian political system (Limongi and Cortez 2010). The diversity of parties found in the Chamber of Deputies results from the Brazilian electoral system's combination of open lists with proportional representation in high magnitude districts. Worthy of note is the fact that stability in the effective number of parties competing for legislative seats is accompanied by consistency in the principal party actors present in the Chamber. Electoral volatility indexes, which measure the stability of voter behavior in successive elections, are thus another indicator of the consolidation of stable party dynamics. Data on volatility is available for congressional elections from 1990 onward. Volatility in the most recent elections was measured at 15.3 (1998), 14.9 (2002), 10.4 (2006), 11.2 (2010), and 17.6 (2014), a figure close to the average found in advanced industrial democracies (Mainwaring, Power, and Bizzarro, forthcoming).

Many scholars have observed that the Brazilian party system between 2003 and 2014 exhibited a growing stability (Limongi and Cortez 2010; Zucco 2011; Peres, Ricci, and Rennó 2011; Meneguello 2011; Braga, Ribeiro, and Amaral 2016). The routinization of democratic life, a general adherence to the rules of the game, the permanence of the same party actors and the emergence of a two-party cleavage in presidential contests all added predictability to electoral outcomes and conferred stability on the system more broadly. This is a positive development and indicates that the Brazilian party system is capable of processing demands and institutionalizing existing conflicts in Brazilian society. Furthermore, greater stability brings a greater capacity to coordinate political and electoral strategy within parties. These factors contribute to the stability of the democratic regime and help legitimize it.

However, increased stability has not translated into the firm entrenchment of parties within the electorate, as the data on party identification and loyalty indicates. With the exception of the PT, all Brazilian parties have had low levels of identification (figure 1.1). The PT, in addition to being an anchoring pole in the system of political alliances, is the only party that has garnered significant mass support in Brazil. The party, however, has been hit by the general crisis of representation that affected the whole party system between 2013

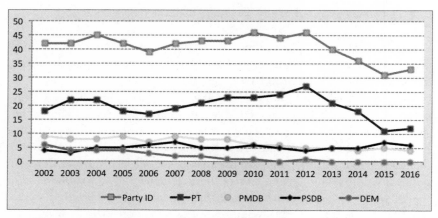

Figure 1.1. Changes in General Party Identification and Identification with the PT, PMDB, PSDB, and PFL/DEM, Brazil, 2002–2016 (%). *Source*: Datafolha.

and 2016. Identification with the PT has dropped from 27 percent in 2012 to 12 percent in 2016. For the PT, this crisis was more dramatic: the party lost one element of the ethical politics brand it had strived to build in the 1980s and 1990s, as its leaders were embroiled in corruption scandals. Furthermore, the party was unable to respond effectively to the economic crisis of 2015–2016.

The PT Government

The PT era ended in a very unpredictable way, combining economic and political crises, a polarized society, and the impeachment trial of president Dilma Rousseff. The PT administration, however, oversaw a number of well-known successes, especially between 2003 and 2013 when the PT government was responsible for the implementation of internationally lauded cash transfer programs, the expansion of employment, and increases in wages. Although to some extent improvements in the economy under the PT were a result of Brazil being insulated from the effects of the international financial crisis of 2008–2009, it is worth emphasizing that, by 2010, the PT had managed to significantly expand consumption in Brazil, including among low-income sectors of the population, who benefited from policies that brought higher wages and expanded the availability of credit. The emergence of what became known as the "new middle class"—the *nova classe* C—led to a rise in family income and consumption in previously marginalized sectors of the population. However, the economic success of the first decade in office came to an end in early 2014. The collapse of commodity prices, the economic slowdown in China, the rise in inflation, and a series of poor decisions regarding fiscal and investment policies drove the country into economic recession, with its GDP decreasing by 4.0 percent in 2015, and unemployment rising to 9.0 percent—the worst figure since 2009.

The PT also oversaw political successes resulting from programmatic deliberations. With regard to poverty reduction, the success of the PT government is indisputable: the expansion of Bolsa Família, which increased from 3.6 million beneficiaries in 2003 to 16.7 million beneficiary families in 2010, meant that a quarter of the Brazilian population received transfers from the program (Soares and Sátyro 2010).

While the first PT government (2003–2006) presided over only modest improvements in indicators of economic growth, it did oversee an important increase in the equality of income distribution. This resulted both from factors associated with the labor market, such as changes in the supply and demand of labor and real increases in the minimum wage, and from the improvement of social safety nets, particularly with the expansion of cash transfer programs such as the Bolsa Família program (Sergei Soares 2006). Social programs played a role in the substantial reduction in poverty that took place in Brazil between 2003 and 2006, when there was a 27.7 percent drop in the proportion of Brazilians living below the poverty line. By 2005 the poverty rate had fallen to 22.8 percent, and by 2006 it reached 19.3 percent. In addition, after 2004 there was a 6.6 percent increase in average income, which primarily benefited the poorest 50 percent of Brazilians, who experienced an average income increase of 8.6 percent. For middle and upper income brackets, the increases were 5.7 percent and 6.9 percent, respectively (Neri 2007).

Under Lula's second government (2007–2010), Brazil not only was the country least affected by the global financial crisis of 2008–2009 but also experienced significant reductions in its poverty rates. Relative to 2003, the percentage of Brazilians living below the poverty line decreased by an impressive 50.3 percent. Moreover, a 20 percent increase in average income between 2004 and 2009 made new levels of consumption possible and helped incorporate previously marginalized segments of the population into the market system; particularly notable is the fact that over 50 percent of the Brazilian population benefited from popular credit programs (Neri 2010, 2011b).

The reductions in poverty and increases in income that took place under Lula had a significant impact on public support for the PT government. A brief analysis of fluctuations in political support during the PT's time in power reveals certain trends in the relationship between the democratic regime and Brazilian society. The success of the PT government in defining an agenda centered on implementing wide-ranging social programs and a policy of prioritizing improvements in employment and income generated significant mass support from the beginning of the party's first presidential term.

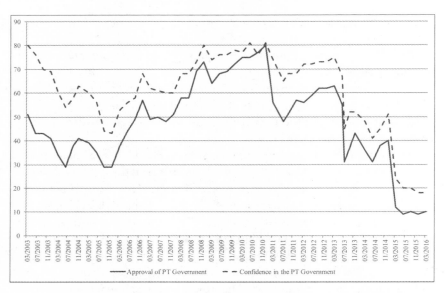

Figure 1.2. Changes in approval of and trust in the PT governments
(2003–2016) (%). *Source*: CNI-IBOPE Surveys and CESOP/Unicamp
Databases (http://www.cesop.unicamp.br).

Public opinion surveys show that improvements in economic and social indicators correspond with increases in public approval of and trust in the government. During the first two PT governments, public trust in the government was consistently high, particularly during Lula's second term. Notably, trust remained high even during a period of political crisis in 2005 that enveloped the PT in accusations of corruption, which reached prominent government figures. By March 2006 public trust had been fully restored, and by the end of Lula's second term in 2010, the government had the trust of 81 percent of the population.

Public approval of the government followed a similar pattern. During both of Lula's presidential terms, but particularly during his second, approval ratings were high. Although the government's approval ratings dropped as a result of PT corruption scandals, by the end of Lula's second term the party had the highest approval rating on record (80 percent of the population). The political capital that accrued from such high levels of public approval helped ensure a third PT term. At the beginning of Dilma's first term, both approval and trust remained high. In March 2013, 75 percent of Brazilians expressed trust in her government and over 60 percent gave her a positive approval rating. It was not until after June 2013—when a series of popular demonstrations demanding better public services and protesting against corruption took to the streets in many cities throughout the country—that her approval rating began to fall, stabilizing at around 40 percent. In 2015, with the deepening of the economic crisis, income reduction, the increase of unemployment, and the development of the investigations against corruption under the Lava Jato operation, the figures plummeted. In March 2016, only 10 percent approved of the PT government, and only 18 percent trusted it (figure 1.2).

It is important to remember that economic indicators have played an important role in determining levels of political support since the beginning of the post-1985 democratic period in Brazil. Studies on the determining factors of voting patterns in presidential elections suggest that since 1994, when the Plano Real changed voter expectations of government performance, a new pattern has emerged wherein a candidate's past performance and voter expectations about the candidate's future accomplishments constitute the strategic content of the vote. This strategic decision is oriented around the voter's individual interests and expectations of well-being and consumption—the so-called economic vote (Meneguello 1995; Balbachevsky and Holzhacker 2004). Under Fernando Henrique Cardoso's government (1995–2002), the state of the economy and levels of government approval were crucial determinants of election outcomes. But since the PT's presidential victory in 2003, partisan identification and political loyalty to particular candidates have also factored into voting decisions. The influence of partisan loyalty was especially clear in 2006, when national surveys taken before the beginning of the presidential campaigns showed significant loyalty to Lula across elections: 49.9 percent of voters interviewed believed that Lula deserved to be reelected in 2006, and of those, 64.7 percent had voted for Lula in 2002 (Desconfiança Survey 2006).

Survey data collected in 2006 and 2010 also suggests that political loyalty was a crucial factor in determining voting decisions for PT candidates. A survey conducted after the 2006 election found that 85 percent of voters who voted for Lula in the first round of voting in 2006 also voted for him in the first round in 2002. Furthermore, 80 percent of voters who chose Lula in the second round in 2006 also voted for him in the second round in 2002, and 92.4 percent of those who voted for Lula in the first round in 2006 also voted for him in the second round that year (ESEB Survey 2006).

Dilma Rouseff's presidential candidacy also benefited from high levels of political adhesion in PT voters. Although the extent to which popularity can be transferred from one candidate to another is clearly limited, the mass political support acquired by President Lula helped drive, in part, the continuation of high levels of partisan identification for other PT candidates. Survey data from 2010 shows a remarkable persistence in voter identification across candidates and elections: 62 percent of those who voted for Lula in the first round in 2006 also voted for Dilma in the first round in 2010, and 71 percent of voters who chose Lula in the second round in 2006 also opted for Dilma in the second round in 2010. In the presidential election of 2014, something similar happened: having voted for Dilma in 2010 increased the probability of voting for her again (Amaral and Ribeiro 2015). Many studies have suggested that Lula and the PT's electoral bases have shifted over time (Hunter and Power 2007; Soares and Terron 2010), but survey data from 2006 and 2010 indicates that adhesion to the government had a significant partisan component. In 2006 voter association with the PT correlated strongly with support for Lula: of the 49.9 percent of interviewees who supported Lula's reelection, 72 percent identified in some way with the PT. In 2010, 85 percent of interviewees who had voted for Dilma in the second round felt that the PT represented their way of thinking (ESEB Survey 2010). It is important, then, to emphasize that the bases of mass political support built by the PT in this period were sustained not only because of the success of PT economic and social policies but also because of party adhesion and voter loyalty to particular PT leaders.

This landscape had changed by the beginning of 2015, right after the presidential elections in which Dilma Rousseff won by a very small margin in the second round against Aécio Neves (PSDB).[1] The start of this administration was marked by the implementation of orthodox economic measures, exactly the opposite of what had been presented during the electoral campaign. Throughout 2015 Dilma lost support in Congress and was unable to stave off the economic downturn. It was against this backdrop that the opposition made its demand in December for an impeachment process to be admitted to the Chamber of Deputies, following the allegation that the president had unlawfully used state banks to finance the executive without seeking congressional approval. It is likely that the damage done by the economic crisis and the corruption scandals will affect support for the PT for a long time. However, we will only be able to measure the extent of the damage more precisely at the next general election, in 2018.

A More Democratic Country?

Although there was a decrease in levels of support for democracy during the final months of the PT administration, the economic growth and reduction in social inequality experienced in Brazil under most of the PT's rule affected the way that many Brazilians thought about democracy itself. Surveys on the values upheld by the Brazilian electorate suggest important shifts in the extent to which Brazilian voters perceived democracy as inherently valuable (Desconfiança Survey 2006; ESEB 2010; IPEA 2011). While support for democracy increased throughout the post-1985 period and peaked at 85 percent in 2010, a crucial question is whether Brazil has shed the characteristics often marking societies that have recently transitioned from authoritarian to demo-

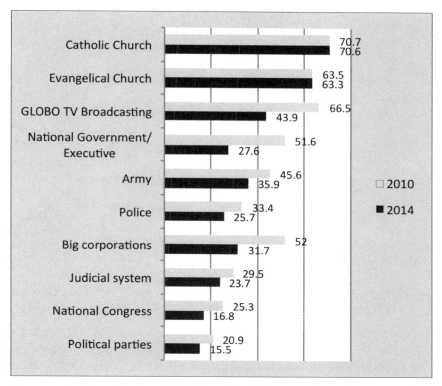

Figure 1.3. Positive evaluations of institutions, Brazil, in 2010 and 2014. *Sources:* Brazilian Electoral Surveys: Comparative Study of Electoral Systems, 2010, 2014.

cratic regimes. Such societies often support democratic norms but also, paradoxically, exhibit a tolerance for corruption, a lack of confidence in public institutions, and a continued acceptance of antiquated social norms (Moisés and Meneguello 2013). Although by the end of the second PT government most Brazilians viewed Brazil as more democratic than ever, particularly with regard to the expansion of social rights (ESEB 2010), there remained a lingering dissatisfaction with how public institutions functioned under democracy, suggesting a troubling failure to build institutions to mediate effectively between the Brazilian population and the democratic state. Data gathered by the ESEB 2014 survey in late 2014 confirmed this tendency and pointed to a growing dissatisfaction with institutions and the functioning of democracy (see figures 1.3 and 1.4).

However, since the beginning of its first term in 2003, the PT government identified several key policy areas that would drive a transformation in relations between the government and Brazilian society. The most important of these were efforts to reduce social and economic inequality and initiatives

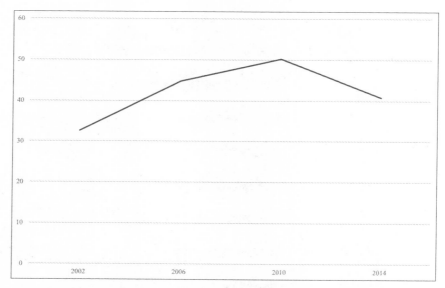

Figure 1.4. Satisfaction with the way democracy works in Brazil (%). *Sources*: Brazilian Electoral Surveys: Comparative Study of Electoral Systems, 2002, 2006, 2010, 2014.

designed to wipe out political corruption. To reduce social and economic inequality, PT governments advocated for social policies with a wide coverage that would incorporate marginalized groups and target the poorest Brazilians. Beginning with the *Fome Zero* (Zero Hunger) policy, which later became Bolsa Família, a variety of cash transfer programs acted as important intermediaries between the PT government and Brazilian society in general (see Hunter and Sugiyama, this volume). Such cash transfer programs encouraged Brazilians to view poverty and inequality as problems that a democratic state had a duty to solve.

Studies of democratic adhesion and legitimacy in Brazil, conducted in 2007 and 2010, have shown that social programs targeted at low-income populations are repeatedly cited by the Brazilian public as reinforcing positive perceptions of Brazilian democracy (Meneguello 2010; 2012b). A 2011 study that assessed the performance of democracy by asking citizens about their capacity to influence the government found that slightly more than half (52 percent) of interviewees considered themselves to have influence within the governmental sphere. This positive finding was accompanied by the even more noteworthy observation that, of all ethnic groups, Afro-Brazilians most frequently self-identified as having influence over the government. That fact would seem to vindicate PT policies directed at marginalized groups, in this case those directed toward Afro-Brazilians and implemented under Lula (Garcia and Silva 2014).

Improvements in the public's perception of the government's ability to respond to demands, however, have been accompanied by a deficit of egalitarian values in Brazil's political culture. Data from the same 2011 survey indicates that, in spite of the PT's insistence that reducing poverty is a function and duty of the state, a significant proportion of Brazilian citizens continue to view inequality as a natural phenomenon (23 percent) and consider individual effort to be the most important factor in overcoming poverty (33 percent). Social assistance, according to this perspective, is an act of charity and not a right, despite intense and ongoing efforts by the PT government to convince Brazilians otherwise (Garcia and Silva 2014).

Promoting integrity in politics was a central part of the PT's program during its time in opposition, and the PT's anti-corruption stance was presented as a fundamental difference between the PT government that took power in 2003 and its predecessors. Yet, as noted by Kingstone and Power in the introduction to this volume, corruption would become one of the most significant problems of the PT era. In recent studies of the PT in power, Hunter (2010) and Samuels (2013) emphasize that corruption scandals were one of the most strikingly negative aspects of the party's time in government. Irregularities in the use of public funds have marred Brazilian politics throughout the current democratic period—a simple search through the archives of Brazil's major newspapers shows that every government since 1985 has been accused of misusing public resources and of using illegal *caixa-dois* (second cash-box) funds to finance political campaigns—but the corruption scandals faced by the PT have marked a new low point in Brazilian politics. After all, since the 1990s the PT had branded itself as a party fiercely committed to rooting out corruption. In that sense the PT government was responsible for undermining the party's image as a uniquely corruption-free political organization within Brazilian politics.

The first scandal of the PT period, and one with strong damaging repercussions for the PT, was known as the *mensalão*. The scandal centered on accusations that the Lula government and the PT oversaw a bribery scheme designed to secure the support of federal legislators for the government's legislative agenda. During the investigation into the accusations, the PT's treasurer, Delúbio Soares, admitted that the PT relied on an illegal financing operation to fund its own electoral campaigns and those of its allies. The scandal ultimately resulted in the resignation of several prominent PT officials from both government and party positions, including José Dirceu, president of the party between 1995 and 2003 and subsequently chief of staff to the government; José Genoíno, then president of the PT; and Delúbio Soares and Silvio Pereira, the treasurer and secretary-general of the party, respectively. All left the PT, and Dirceu resigned from his government post.

Seven years after the allegations, the mensalão case was heard by the Supreme Court (Supremo Tribunal Federal) in a trial that lasted several months and was subject to unprecedented media coverage. Of the thirty-eight defendants accused of involvement in the scandal, twenty-five were convicted. The court upheld charges that political support had been purchased in the first years of Lula's government and found that the money for the bribes had come, in part, from public funds diverted from the Bank of Brazil and the Chamber of Deputies.

Two years later, a new wave of investigations would expose the promiscuous relationships between public funds, public works, party financing, and electoral campaigns. In 2014 the Federal Prosecution Service (FPS) started what would become the biggest corruption investigation in the Brazilian history: the Lava Jato operation. Under the aegis of this operation, the FPS discovered a web of corruption involving directors of the state oil company (Petrobras), political parties including the PT, PMDB, Popular Party (Partido Popular; PP), and building contractors. According to the FPS, throughout the whole of the PT administration, certain contractors had been overpaid for works at Petrobras, in exchange for generous contributions to electoral campaigns. As a result of this investigation, important businessmen and politicians, some of them from the PT, ended up in jail.

The mensalão scandal and the Lava Jato operation captured two major failings of PT governance. First, they showed that top-level government and party officials were willing to engage in corrupt practices despite a vehemently anti-corruption party rhetoric. Second, the scandal laid bare the limits of Brazilian institutional arrangements, in particular the challenges of coalitional presidentialism (Pereira, Power, and Raile 2011; Avritzer 2011). The need to build alliances within a highly fragmented congress may encourage corrupt practices, especially in a context where maintaining a governing coalition involves merging groups with distinct political and ideological profiles and different levels of access to executive power. The government may be incentivized to use illegal bargaining schemes as a way to maintain the delicate balance of power within a coalition. In addition, the revelation that the PT engaged in caixa-dois practices raises questions about the nature of Brazil's electoral institutions and the effects these have on the political system as a whole.

However much the mensalão scandal may have weakened the PT and forced Lula to distance himself from the party, the scandal did not significantly alter public perceptions of corruption. Although citizens identified corruption as a central public policy problem, surveys show that social acceptance of corruption is nonetheless widespread and that there is a general lack of understanding among the Brazilian public about how corruption impacts democracy (Meneguello 2011; Moisés and Meneguello 2013). The fact that corruption is seen as a fact of Brazilian political life may help us understand Lula's reelection in 2006 and the limited impact of accusations of influence-peddling leveled in September 2010 against Dilma Rousseff's presidential campaign.[2]

There are, however, indications that widespread tolerance of corruption may be waning. The mass demonstrations that took place across Brazil in June 2013 forcefully articulated the need for anti-corruption policies in Brazilian political life, as well as for reforms of the political system and improvements in government efficiency at all levels, especially with regard to public health and transportation. Survey data drawn from protests in eight state capitals shows that protestors identified changes in the "political environment" (65 percent), in the public transportation sector (53.7 percent), and in health policy (36.7 percent) as their primary demands.[3] The scale of the demonstrations—which included hundreds of thousands of people in major urban centers—conveyed a general sense of dissatisfaction rooted in multiple unfulfilled demands. The unfolding of the Lava Jato operation also had an impact on perceptions of corruption. A survey carried out by the Datafolha Institute in November 2015 found that, for the first time, corruption was identified by Brazilians as the country's main problem, having been mentioned by 34 percent of interviewees.[4]

The PT after Twelve Years in Power

Founded in 1980, the PT was initially regarded by political scientists as a "novelty" in Brazilian politics because of its history, its policy proposals, and its internal organization (Meneguello 1989; Keck 1991). The outsider status of the party, its strong links with organized labor and social movements, its centralized operating structure, and the priority it placed on aggregating interests all meant that the PT strongly resembled the quintessential "mass-based" party described by Duverger (1954). Beginning in the second half of the 1990s, the PT underwent both ideological and organizational changes. As the party came closer to winning the presidency, it moderated its rhetoric and drew nearer to the center of the political spectrum. Furthermore, it increasingly concentrated its organizational and financial resources on electoral contests, redesigned its organizational structure so as to streamline the management of party finances and grow its presence in the interior of Brazil, and became more flexible in constructing political alliances (Samuels 2004; Meneguello and Amaral 2008; Ribeiro 2010; Hunter 2010; Amaral 2011).

In 2003, upon taking charge of the federal government, the PT entered a new institutional environment wherein it was forced to respond to the dynamics of Brazil's political system, including coalitional presidentialism. After being elected to the Planalto Palace, Lula and the PT encountered a paradigmatic problem faced by presidential regimes within highly fragmented party systems: the need to build alliances to govern. Since 1990, no Brazilian president's party has achieved more than 25 percent of seats in the Chamber of Deputies. In 2003 the PT and its allies in the 2002 presidential election (the PL, PCdoB, PMN, and PCB) won just 25.3 percent of congressional seats among them.[5] One way of acquiring support and building coalitions is to divide the government by distributing ministries to allied parties through a delicate negotiation process. In Lula's case, there was an additional complication. Unlike all his presidential predecessors in the post-authoritarian period, Lula was elected by a party that was strong but internally divided and had spent its entire existence in opposition, which resulted in party demands on the executive that were unusually forceful and difficult to accommodate (D'Araujo 2011, 92).

The PT government's first cabinet (January 2003–January 2004) reflected these inter- and intra-party tensions. In an effort to maintain the unified support of the PT, the government allocated twenty of the total thirty-three ministries to the party. The PT's insistence on occupying the majority of ministries was the basis for Lula's decision to accept a highly fragmented cabinet that lacked the support of any other large party (Amorim Neto 2007; Pereira, Power, and Raile 2011; Samuels 2013). The PMDB, with 14.4 percent of seats in the Chamber of Deputies, was left out of the government. Instead, each of seven parties (the PSB, PDT, PPS, PCdoB, PV, PL, and PTB) was granted a single ministry.[6] The end result was a fragile support base (49.3 percent of nominal support in the Chamber of Deputies) that was incapable of guaranteeing victories in the Congress. However, the government did manage to pass a contentious social security reform with the support of the PMDB and other opposition forces (PFL-DEM and PSDB).[7]

Lula incorporated the PMDB into his second cabinet (January 2004–July 2005) by granting it two ministries. A larger nominal legislative majority (62 percent) came at the cost of a sizeable imbalance in the distribution of portfolios and public posts within the coalition, which generated considerable dissatisfaction (Amorim Neto 2007; Pereira, Power, and Raile 2011; Samuels 2013). That dissatisfaction came to a head with the emergence of the mensalão scandal in 2005.

The challenges of building a government exerted strong pressure on the PT and led it to adopt an increasingly flexible policy of alliance formation. In 2001, just under a year before the general elections of 2002, the party declared, at its twelfth National Meeting (NM), that political alliances in the following year should be formed with strong leftist and center-left parties that opposed "the Cardoso government and its neoliberal policies" (Partido dos

Trabalhadores [hereafter PT] 2001, 13). Although it was considerably more flexible than similar declarations made in the 1980s and early 1990s, the resolution of the twelfth NM still established clear ideological and programmatic limits for PT alliance formation. In the following year, the PT demonstrated an even greater trend toward flexibility by forming a presidential ticket with the Liberal Party (PL), a small right-wing party that represented business interests and was dissatisfied with the Cardoso government. In 2004, the PT fundamentally altered its process of alliance building by authorizing its Municipal Directorates to forge alliances with parties that formed part of the national governing coalition in that year's municipal elections. At the thirteenth NM, in 2006, the party affirmed that the same policy would be applied for the 2006 elections. In the party congresses of 2007, 2010, and 2011, the party maintained a flexible alliance policy at all levels of government (PT 2007, 2010, 2011). In 2010, for example, the PT declared the following: "The fourth National Congress believes that the principal objective of our party in 2010 is the election of Dilma Rousseff as president of Brazil. . . . To that end, it is necessary that the party seek alliances with all parties that support the current government" (PT 2010, 32).[8]

The ideological diversity of the government's congressional base during the Lula (2003–2011) and Dilma (2011–2016) administrations shows that the party definitively opened itself up to alliances with groups that spanned the ideological spectrum.[9] The determining factor in the building of electoral alliances became the need to support the government in the legislature, even if this meant making difficult ideological compromises. This increased flexibility with regard to political alliances is evidenced also by the coalitions formed by the PT at the state level in the general elections of 2002, 2006, and 2010. In this period, there was a notable increase in alliances forged by the PT and parties of the right (the PFL/DEM, PTB and PP) in state gubernatorial races. In 2002, just 4 percent of the alliances that the PT joined included a right-wing party. In 2006 and 2010 this percentage rose to 32 percent and 51.9 percent, respectively.[10] At the local level, similar trends emerged. In the 2000 elections, 20.2 percent of alliances formed with the PT also included at least one large right-wing party. In 2004 and 2008, that percentage rose to 42.3 percent and 54.6 percent, respectively (Meneguello 2012b).

The PT also underwent important programmatic changes. The retention of aspects of Fernando Henrique Cardoso's economic policies such as primary surpluses, elevated interest rates, and autonomy for the Central Bank created considerable tension within the party during Lula's first administration. Moderate factions, which made up a majority of the party, defended the steps taken by the government at the beginning of Lula's term and ensured the institutional support of the PT for the government. More radical party factions, however, openly criticized the direction the party was taking. Lula's social security reform in 2003 precipitated an eruption of criticism from PT deputies and party leaders who declared Lula a traitor to the PT's historical legacy (Meneguello 2005). Several PT members voted against the reform and, as punishment, were expelled from the party by the National Directorate in December 2003. Internal party factions linked to those leaders—and other party activists angered by the PT's increasingly moderate program—also left the party. Together they founded the Socialism and Liberty Party (Partido Socialismo e Liberdade; PSOL) in 2004.

After 2006 internal party turbulence and the tense relationship between the party and the government both eased significantly. The departure of party factions that were opposed to new PT policies increased the relative weight of more moderate factions. The continued drop in national income inequality and increases in employment levels (Neri 2007, 2010), longtime objectives of various groups within the PT, made it more difficult to level criticism against the federal government. In addition, the increased popularity of the government during Lula's second term offered a powerful incentive for groups within the PT to align their platforms with those defended by the government and moderate PT factions. This was especially important within an institutional context where the direction of the party was chosen directly by party members, independent of their level of activism. As a result the party's internal elections of 2007 and 2009 took place in an environment of limited factional disagreement. By the beginning of the first Dilma government, the PT was a considerably more ideologically homogenous party than during the Lula administration.

The PT's internal organization exhibited both change and continuity in this period, as work by Hunter (2010), Ribeiro (2010), and Amaral (2011) has demonstrated. During the Lula government the PT's membership rolls expanded considerably, and the party became more broadly represented across Brazil. In 2003 the PT was organized in 83 percent of Brazil's more than fifty-five hundred municipalities (counting both municipal directorates and provisional municipal councils). By 2009 the party had expanded into 96 percent of municipalities. It is interesting to note that the organizational difficulties the party faced in Brazil's northeast region were almost entirely overcome in this period. In 2003 the party was organized in 72.7 percent of cities in the Northeast. Six years later the party was present in 94.7 percent of northeastern municipalities.

The most significant growth in PT membership rolls occurred between 2003 and 2008. At the beginning of the Lula government the PT had just over 400,000 members—a rate of 3.6 members per thousand voters. By 2008 the party had become the second largest in Brazil in terms of membership, after the PMDB, with a membership of 1.4 million—a rate of 10.6 members per thousand voters. In subsequent years, the PT maintained that position. In 2012 the party had 1.5 million members and a rate of 11.0 members per thousand voters. It is important to note that the increase in PT membership between 2003 and 2008 took place largely in small and mid-sized municipalities and primarily in the northeast region, where membership doubled from roughly 180,000 to 360,000 (that is, from 5.5 to 10.1 members per thousand voters). It is beyond the scope of this chapter to assess the reasons for the PT's rapid northeastern expansion, but Amaral (2011) has shown that the party's improved organizational efficiency, the greater financial resources at its disposal, its ideological moderation, and the popularity of the Lula government in many regions of the country all combined to bring about a growth in membership across the nation. It is important to highlight the PT's uniqueness in this regard, especially as compared to European parties, which have registered decades of declining membership rolls (Van Biezen, Mair, and Poguntke 2012). Despite considerable expansions in membership and geographical reach, the organization of the PT also showed an important element of continuity in the period under discussion. The party had always been characterized by the inclusion of its base in decision-making and the selection of leaders. Since 2001 the selection of directorate members at all levels of the party has been by direct vote of all members who make regular dues payments and have been party members for at least a year. Since the PT assumed charge of the federal government, three Processes of Direct Elections (PEDs) have taken place. In 2005 and 2007 more than 300,000 members participated across three thousand municipalities. In 2009 more than half a million members cast votes in 4,300 cities across Brazil. In all three PEDs, voter turnout approached 40 percent of eligible members. If the PT has become similar to other Brazilian political parties in many respects, its participatory and organizational structures continue to set it apart. No other large Brazilian party utilizes a system of direct elections to choose its leadership at all levels. Furthermore, no other party is capable of mobilizing hundreds of thousands of members to participate simultaneously in party activities across the nation.

A further element of continuity is found in the PT's mid-level leadership. In the 1990s Leôncio Rodrigues found PT leaders to be predominately well-educated middle-class wage earners, typically public employees or union leaders (1997, 306). Survey data obtained by the Perseu Abramo Foundation (FPA) and by Amaral (2011) concerning party delegates attending PT National Meetings (NMs) and National Congresses (NCs) since 1997 show that this member profile has largely held constant. The PT that brought Dilma Rousseff to power was predominately led by Catholic males over forty years of age, with a personal income of at least five times the minimum wage and some university education. In 2006 the majority of party delegates were public sector employees; unfortunately, data on delegate employment is not available for 2007 and 2010 (see table 1.3).

Data on the participation of PT delegates in social movements also shows continued substantial overlap between PT membership and social organization activity. Every survey of party delegates (2001, 2006, 2007, and 2010) shows a social movement participation rate of at least 60 percent, whether the delegate is a state employee or a working professional. This suggests that actors in organized civil society continue to see the PT as a representative institution that is open to their demands and capable of furthering their policy proposals (Amaral 2011).

It is important to highlight that the sequence of corruption scandals involving the PT also showed the party's inability to build effective oversight mechanisms to monitor its leaders, especially during electoral campaigns. The future of the PT will depend on how the party reacts to the profound crisis affecting its leadership, and on the organizational changes it manages to implement. The PT's era of control over the Brazilian presidency raises important questions about the nature of party transformation more broadly. It is indisputable that the new institutional environment of the presidency exerted a powerful influence on the PT, causing it to further moderate its policy proposals and accelerating the speed of changes begun in the 1990s that nudged the PT ever closer to becoming an "electoral-professional" party (Panebianco 1988). However, it bears emphasizing that many of the PT's original characteristics are still preserved in its unique organizational structures. This suggests that different aspects of the PT were transformed at different speeds. In particular, organizational changes seem to have been more gradual than changes in ideological and programmatic profiles, creating an enduring source of tension within the party.

Final Considerations

The years of PT government changed the PT, the Brazilian political system, and the nature of democracy in Brazil. The years between 2003 and 2016 were marked by stability in political competition, especially at the national level. The characteristic features of the Brazilian party system that emerged in the 1990s were cemented during this "PT Era." Presidential elections continued to be, in effect, competitions between two parties (the PT and the PSDB), while the national congress remained relatively fragmented. The persistence of this pattern made coalitional presidentialism the preferred political arrangement and shaped the electoral growth of the PT even after twelve years in charge of the federal executive. This suggests that Brazilian democracy was robust enough to withstand the pressures exerted by the PT's ascension

	1997 11th NM	1999 2nd NC	2001 12th NM	2006 13th NM	2007 3rd NC	2010 4th NC
Table 1.3. Profiles of PT Delegates, 1997–2010 (%)*						
Employment						
State employee	33	49	44.3	54.3	–	–
Wage-earner	32	23	20.2	12.5	–	–
Professional	9	6	7.7	6.9	–	–
Self-employed	3	2	5.3	9.0	–	–
Education						
No schooling	–	–	–	0.1	0.1	0.2
Elementary	5	5	3.7	2.2	4.9	2.6
Secondary	21	22	13.0	16.0	19.0	16.6
University	62	57	64.7	68.1	65.7	70.3
Postgraduate	11	14	18.3	12.6	9.8	9.8
No response	1	1	0.2	1	0.5	0.4
Personal Income						
<2 min. wage	6	6	4.6	6.0	7.5	6.0
From 2 to 5 MW	14	9	11.8	19.1	25.5	19.6
From 5 to 10 MW	19	22	23.2	33.0	31.6	32.8
From 10 to 20 MW	27	34	34.3	26.4	24.3	27.8
Over 20 MW	28	26	23.7	13.4	10.3	11.9
No response	6	3	2.3	2.1	0.8	1.9
Age						
Under 25	5	5	3.5	4.3	1.7	2.9
25–30	13	9	8.6	6.9	6.3	8.9
31–40	46	41	40.4	29.5	27.1	24.8
Over 41	32	38	45.9	59.0	64.8	63.3
No response	4	6	1.6	0.2	0.1	0.2
Sex						
Male	80	77	71.7	75.6	80	70.8
Female	20	23	28.3	24.4	20	29.2
Religion*						
Catholic	57	59	58.7	62.7	66.5	59.5
Spiritism	5	3	2.1	6.1	5.2	5.1
Umbanda	1	-	0.5	2.8	1.5	1.0
Evangelical	2	2	1.4	9.7	8.4	7.0
No religion	30	31	33.4	24.5	22.2	24.9
Other	4	3	3.9	6.3	5.2	3.0
No response	1	2	0.7	0.2	0.3	0.7
N	(187)	(544)	(431)	(864)	(775)	(1103)

Note: * For 2001, 2006, 2007, and 2010, multiple responses.
Sources: Survey of PT/FPA Delegates 1997, 1999, 2001, 2006, 2007, 2010; *Amaral *2011 for data from 2006.

to the presidency in 2003. We have also shown how the performance of the Lula administration, in particular with respect to the economy and income redistribution programs, guaranteed substantial levels of approval for the government and expanded mass support for the PT at least until 2014, when new corruption scandals and the economic crisis marred the party's image.

The years of PT government have deepened two particular dimensions of Brazilian democracy: that of social inclusion and that of the state's responsiveness to the demands of varied social actors. From an institutional perspective, the stabilization of the structure of political competition meant that Brazil consolidated important advances with the establishment of stronger levels of support for democratic processes. The country is therefore unusual in Latin America where, in recent years, political trends have led to the election of candidates who do not necessarily strengthen democratic institutions and processes in their countries.

We have also argued that the PT positioned itself on the center-left of the political spectrum and adapted to the structure of the Brazilian political system by creating a flexible alliance policy that resembled those of other large Brazilian political parties. This process of accommodation and adaptation brought considerable resistance and ultimately precipitated the departure of many party activists who were dissatisfied with the new party style. In addition, the crisis that engulfed the party in 2015–2016 will surely play an important role in the relationship between leaders, party activists, and members in the near future.

The net impact of twelve years of PT power has been positive for Brazilian democracy but not sufficient to fundamentally change the Brazilian political system. Clientelism, corporatism, and patrimonial traditions continue to define relations between elites, parties, and the state, as the corruption scandals of the 2014–2016 period made very clear. The PT administrations also failed to overcome pervasive negative perceptions of Brazilian public institutions. Overcoming these challenges will be essential to the construction of a stronger and deeper democracy in Brazil in the twenty-first century.

2

Benjamin Goldfrank and Brian Wampler

Good Government and Politics as Usual?

The Schizophrenic Path of the Workers' Party

WHEN LUIZ INÁCIO "Lula" da Silva won Brazil's presidency in 2002, he and his Workers' Party (Partido dos Trabalhadores; PT) had most observers convinced that this was a watershed moment for the country's democracy. The victory of this former shoeshine boy, metalworker, and union leader symbolized to many the arrival to power of Brazil's excluded masses and the opportunity to put into practice the *modo petista de governar* (the PT way of governing), lauded as participatory, redistributive, and above all, transparent. Fourteen years of PT government and several astounding corruption scandals later, few illusions remain. The PT was gravely wounded by the scandals, starting with the so-called *mensalão* (monthly bribe scandal) in 2005. This scandal brought resignations and later jail sentences for the party's top leaders and members of Lula's cabinet as well as renewed calls for reforming Brazil's political institutions as multiple parties were caught taking bribes. Despite punishment for the mensalão's perpetrators, the PT's own efforts to strengthen participatory and transparency institutions, and the promises to clean house by Lula's successor, Dilma Rousseff, even larger corruption scandals followed, imperiling the PT's hold on the presidency and threatening its future.

From its inception in the early 1980s, the PT had stood for incorruptibility, refusing to accept the military's offer of indirect presidential elections during democratization, leading the charge for investigating corruption under President Collor, and emphasizing clean government at the municipal level, where the party was increasingly successful. Scholars of the country's notoriously weak party system regularly noted the PT's outlier status as virtually the only ideologically driven, internally democratic, and disciplined party. Lula's 2002 presidential campaign stressed the party's ethics and anti-corruption message. Its first commercial showed rats chewing on a Brazilian flag and the caption: "Either we finish them off or they finish off Brazil. Ciao, corruption—a campaign by the PT and the Brazilian people" (Markun 2004, 313–14). Just a few years later, when an aide to the PT president's brother was caught in Brasília's airport with a hundred thousand US dollars in his underwear, Lula's finance minister and chief of staff resigned, as did the PT's president, secretary-general, and treasurer, all tied to the mensalão scandal.[1] How did the PT move from a party that built its "party brand" on honesty and transparency to a party in which high-ranking officials were engaged in systematic forms of corruption? Further, why did the PT not switch course after the mensalão and limit the involvement of high-ranking officials in illegal political behavior?

Presidents Lula and Dilma tried to minimize the scandals in the press, saying that the PT had only done what other parties do, but this is precisely the point, as Gois argues: "In the end—and this is the mother of all issues—many people voted for the PT because the party did not do what the others do" (2005, 14). Why would the party put its hard-fought, vote-getting reputation for good government at risk? There are two disparate interpretations of the PT. On one hand, some observers highlight the modo petista de governar, which made the PT famous worldwide as an innovative party for the downtrodden that promoted the use of new democratic institutions, inclusive social policies, and more transparent implementation processes. The second interpretation, one its conservative opponents have long asserted, is that the PT's supposed ethical patrimony has simply been a farce all along; PT politicians used their access to state power (by winning elections) to divert public resources toward advancing the party's interests as well as their own.

The schizophrenic nature of the PT once in office is best exemplified by its strengthening of the state's oversight capabilities, building on its trajectory as a party of "good government," while simultaneously engaging in bribery and money laundering. Indeed, it is baffling that many high-ranking PT officials continued such illegal activities at the same time as the PT-led government invested in transparency and participatory institutions that improved monitoring of public resource allocation. The need for campaign resources to gain and maintain office held greater sway over PT officials than the fear that the newly strengthened transparency institutions would be applied to them.

Further, the initial use of illegal fund-raising activities by some high-ranking PT officials gave their political rivals power over them in three ways, making it difficult for the party to reverse course once its officials began to use corrupt practices. First, since ideologically distant parties were included in the governing coalition partly through kickback schemes, those politicians could threaten to reveal damaging information if the money did not continue to flow. Second, the prosecution of the PT's top officials following the mensalão scandal, including past party presidents José Dirceu and José Genoino, discredited the PT's ability to campaign on the claim that it would fight corruption. Third, political rivals working inside the state (such as prosecutors, judges, and police linked to opposition parties) were able to investigate and expose PT officials' involvement in wrongdoing.

Four interweaving strands of explanation help illuminate the PT's schizophrenic nature. These involve the rising cost of Brazilian elections, the strategic decisions of the party's dominant faction, the Campo Majoritário (Majority Camp), basic governing challenges faced by the PT, and finally, the establishment of new institutions that were designed to appeal to activists who sought to create new channels for participation and transparency.

The Rise of the PT

The activists who founded the PT in 1979 shared commitments to ending Brazil's military dictatorship, establishing democracy, and implementing some form of socialism. Unions, social movements, intellectuals, and progressive sectors of the middle class formed the base of the new party, which emphasized internal democracy regarding policy decisions, political orientation, and leadership selection (Keck 1992). From its early moments in local government, the party established a PT way of governing that also served as a party branding strategy (Goldfrank 2004; Nylen 2000). Although the PT gave minority factions the opportunity to influence their fellow party members, by the mid-1990s a dominant faction—known at the time as the Campo Majoritário—emerged under Lula, José Dirceu, and their allies in the state of São Paulo such as Celso Daniel and José Genoino. Internal democratic procedures encouraged minority factions to remain in the party because of a shared understanding that the PT represented a new way of conducting politics that would eventually change Brazil. While never explicitly defining the socialism it sought, the party maintained strong ideological commitments to the "inversion of priorities," which meant reorienting Brazil away from its historically unequal and exclusionary political and economic practices.

To transform Brazil, the PT long advocated a two-track strategy. The party emphasized both electoral politics and social struggle, conceived as building a grassroots movement capable of engaging in direct political action to advance PT causes. Over time Lula and the Campo Majoritário increasingly favored a focus on winning elections for executive positions over social movement-style activism (Freire de Lacerda 2002). Indeed, the PT's electoral fortunes improved steadily and dramatically at all levels of government from its first efforts in 1982 until recent elections, when popular support decreased (see table 2.1).

As the PT won office, its mayors and governors emphasized participatory decision-making as a means to invert priorities, appeal to social movement allies, demonstrate its commitment to honesty, and thereby build support by distinguishing itself from Brazil's myriad other parties. An exemplary case is that of Participatory Budgeting in Porto Alegre, which rests on the principles of deliberation, transparency, social justice, and direct citizen involvement in selecting policy outcomes (Abers 2000; Baiocchi 2005; Goldfrank 2007; Wampler and Avritzer 2004). More than two hundred PT mayors and even a few governors adopted Participatory Budgeting. The PT also succeeded in the 1990s at developing other innovative policies, such as Bolsa Escola, which — from its inception in Brasília — provided targeted funds to low-income families to reward and ensure regular school attendance. While PT federal deputies and senators, as members of the political opposition, continually demanded investigations into corruption by the ruling parties at the national level, subnational PT administrations illustrated that the party was capable of governing creatively and responsibly. By the time of the watershed 2002 election, public opinion polls suggested that Brazilians considered the PT the most honest political party by a wide margin, which was one factor among many in Lula's favor in his fourth run at the presidency (Goldfrank 2004, 207–8; Fundação Perseu Abramo 2006).

Campaign Finance, Official and Otherwise

To win the presidency, Lula needed money. Our starting point for examining the PT's unexpected descent into "politics as usual" is to note that running for election in Brazil was expensive in the 1990s, at least as expensive as in the United States (Samuels 2001, 33). An avowedly socialist party like the PT in an unequal capitalist country like Brazil could only raise comparatively small amounts of money. Given a law prohibiting union donations, the PT relied on the public funding available to all parties as well as on mandatory contributions by party members. For other parties, private corporations, especially in finance and construction, provided the most funds. This helps explain why PT candidates for federal deputy received eleven times less money on average than non-left candidates in 1994, and six times less in 1998 (our calculations from Samuels 2001, 39).

In the 1989, 1994, and 1998 presidential campaigns, the winning candi-

Table 2.1. PT Election Results, 1982–2014									
Election Year	1982	1986	1990	1994	1998	2002	2006	2010	2014
Governors	0	0	0	2	3	3	4	6	5
Federal Deputies	8	16	35	49	58	91	83	88	68
% of Chamber	2	3	7	10	11	18	16	17	13
Election Year	1982	1985	1988	1992	1996	2000	2004	2008	2012
Mayors	1	2	38	54	110	187	411	560	651
Mayors in Capital Cities	0	1	3	4	2	6	6	6	4

Source: www.tse.jus.br.

dates vastly outspent Lula. In 1994 when campaign contributions were first made public, Fernando Henrique Cardoso's donors gave his campaign more than twenty times as much as Lula, and the donation gap for the 1998 race was nearly the same (see table 2.2). Cardoso won easily in the first round of both elections. However, the 2002 campaign marked a major turning point, with Lula out-fund-raising all the other candidates, including Cardoso's intended successor, José Serra. In every election since 2002, the PT's presidential campaigns have raised more money than their opponents.

This official reversal of fortunes is interesting, of course. Yet more intriguing were the unofficial estimates of R$200 million in off-the-books donations (Attuch 2006, 16). Why did Lula's campaign coffers—official and otherwise—suddenly swell? The explanation lies in two converging trends at the turn of the century. On one hand, the PT had tried but failed to reform campaign finance laws banning union donations and desperately needed funding for the 2002 national elections, which the PT had a good chance of winning given the Cardoso government's unpopularity. On the other hand, the private firms that had previously spent money on keeping the PT out of office were watching the party's steady electoral growth and the public opinion polls and decided to finance not only Serra but also Lula as an insurance policy (Fausto 2005, 211; Attuch 2006). Attuch notes that the financiers gave equally to Serra's campaign and generally preferred to donate off the record (2006, 28–29).

Crucially, off-the-books contributions to Lula's 2002 campaign presaged the larger scandal, the illegal cash payments—or mensalão—to congressional allies during Lula's presidency. Like most parties, the PT spent more on campaigning than it raised and owed more than R$55 million for the presidential and governors' races combined (Attuch 2006, 37). In 2003 the PT's treasurer

Table 3.2. Presidential Campaign Donations and PT First Round Vote Share, 1994–2014						
Election Year	1994	1998	2002	2006	2010	2014
PT Candidate (in millions of current *reais*)	Lula, 3.1	Lula, 3.6	Lula, 26.6	Lula, 81.2	Dilma, 135.5	Dilma, 350.5
PSDB Candidate (in millions of current *reais*)	Cardoso, 77.3	Cardoso, 66.3	Serra, 18.2	Alckmin, 79.2*	Serra, 106.6	Neves, 226.9
Vote for PT Candidate (%)	27	32	46	49	47	42

Note: *Comitê Financeiro Nacional para Presidente da República PSDB- BR.
Sources: For 1994–2002 (Samuels 2006); for 2006–2014 (www.tse.jus.br).

began engaging in unusual financial transactions with a marketing executive whose firms secured loans to cover the campaign expenses of the PT, and soon thereafter, its allies. Drastically simplifying the story, the money trail operated like this: publicity firms took out loans for or with the PT; the PT used these to pay its 2002 national campaign debts and its 2004 municipal campaign expenses and to provide campaign funds to members of parties allied with the PT in Congress; and the publicity firms received contracts from federal government agencies, the funds of which they are assumed to have used in part to pay off the loans (see Flynn 2005, 1236–38).

Remarkably, despite the uproar regarding the mensalão, which included calls for Lula's impeachment, not only did subsequent national election campaigns follow the pattern of the 2002 race, with ever greater funds donated to the PT candidates (see Table 2.2), but corruption schemes similar to the mensalão continued as well. The largest of these is the so-called *petrolão*, in which Petrobras senior directors are alleged to have taken bribes to inflate costs for contractors (*empreiteiras*), who channeled parcels of those funds to lobbyists and money launderers, who in turn dispersed funds to politicians within the PT and its coalitional partners to cover campaign costs, among other things; to close the loop, those politicians appointed the Petrobras executives. It is worth pointing out that many of the contractors involved in the petrolão — such as Odebrecht, OAS, Camargo Corrêa, and Andrade Gutierrez — ranked among the top donors to the presidential campaigns of Lula and Dilma, and that, following the pattern from 2002, the same firms donated large amounts to the PT's rivals as well. The petrolão scheme helped all involved except for Petrobras itself, which in 2015, after the Lava Jato investigation uncovered the fraud, announced billions of dollars in losses to graft, saw its market value plummet, and faced class-action lawsuits from foreign investors.

In sum, from its mostly self-reliant and comparatively penniless position in the 1980s and 1990s, the PT's finances changed dramatically in the 2000s. In elections for all levels of government, the PT, like other parties, received large corporate donations, spent extravagantly on campaigns, and contracted debts, furthering the need for more funds. Yet campaign costs are not the whole story. To understand whether the PT had always engaged in corruption schemes and why it continued to do so even after the mensalão scandal broke, it is important to consider the role of internal party dynamics and factional politics.

Moderating (and Corrupting?) the PT

The party faction under Lula and Dirceu, which has led the PT for most of its existence, played a key part in transforming the party into one that could attract campaign contributions and win national elections. This faction, or coalition of factions, first called Articulação and later expanded to become the Campo Majoritário, has won all but one of the party's internal elections at the national level since 1984. Lula, party president during the 1980s and early 1990s, occupied a center-right position within the party from 1989 onward and consistently aligned himself with the right to ensure control. The left wing won the party's presidency only in 1993, leaving it in control of the disastrous 1994 general election, a humiliating loss for Lula. The alleged incompetence of the PT's left wing and Lula's vow to never again run for president without direct control over his campaign led to the 1995 internal party elections that dramatically reshaped the PT.

For those elections, Dirceu united center and right factions of the party to create the Campo Majoritário; he became the PT's National President and held that position for the next seven years. Dirceu used his victory to consolidate power, creating a "party within a party" to ensure loyalty to him, as well as building alliances at the PT's local and state levels to ensure that Lula's group would continue to control the party (Flynn 2005, 1254). Under the direction of Dirceu and over the left's objections, the PT (1) moved farther away from its grassroots social movement strategy, instead concentrating its energy and resources on winning elections for mayors, governors, and the presidency; (2) moderated its national campaign platforms; and (3) began entering into electoral coalitions with parties that previously had been vetoed as too corrupt, personalist, centrist, or clientelist by the PT left.

By 2002 Lula's campaign made the PT's transformation clear. Party militants waving flags at massive rallies and get-out-the-vote efforts were replaced by slick television spots and concerts. Lula did not mention revolution or socialism but, rather, respect for international contracts and IMF agreements. The campaign slogan was "Lulinha—paz e amor" (Little Lula—peace and love). As running mate, Lula selected the owner of one of Brazil's largest textile manufacturers, José Alencar, who brought his center-right Liberal Party (Partido Liberal; PL) into the PT-led coalition fronted by Lula.

While some see the PT's growing moderation and the ever-increasing dominance of the Campo Majoritário as results of internal party democracy (Samuels 2004) or successful party adaptation (Hunter 2010), other observers and PT insiders, especially on the left, claim that the Campo Majoritário's external and thus internal victories were aided by the same kinds of slush funds that apparently helped Lula's 2002 campaign (Flynn 2005; Moraes 2005; Wainwright and Branford 2006). In other words, they claim that the scandals that rocked Lula's administration were similar to the arrangements that had been used by the Campo Majoritário to consolidate its control of the PT. The more successful a faction's candidates were in winning executive offices (governors and mayors), and to a lesser extent, legislative offices, the more paid government positions the faction could offer its members and potential recruits from other factions, and in turn, the better it could perform in internal elections. This does not imply that the PT's emphasis on honesty and transparency was a "farce" but, rather, that the political group in control of the PT, the Campo Majoritário, was willing to use strategies previously rejected by the PT to consolidate its control.

As Moraes explains, Campo Majoritário leaders created a "parallel finance network" that "operated as an instrument of discrimination and internal privileges without the knowledge of the collective decision-making bodies," directing both official and unofficial resources to party moderates (2005, 196–97). This explanation echoes the complaints by critical PT leaders on the left. They claim that "the Campo Majoritário built its own political machine within the party to advance its aim of achieving more flexible policies" and that "some sectors of the party started to have incredibly well-funded campaigns" (Wainwright and Branford 2006, 21–22, also 23, 25–26, 33). Thus, Dirceu consolidated Campo Majoritário control to pull the party to the center, apparently utilizing similarly underhanded tactics to those that later would be used to carve out congressional majorities to support PT presidential agendas.

Evidence to support the critics' position includes the fact that the first corruption scandals linked to the PT emerged in municipalities governed by Campo Majoritário leaders. Many of Lula's 2002 campaign fund-raisers were already active in the PT's local administrations, especially in the state of São Paulo, where they engaged in the same sorts of financial practices for which they were later investigated (Attuch 2006; see also *Folha de São Paulo* 2005). Lower-level PT officials in municipalities appear to have been involved in financial transactions that gave them access to revenues from public and private bus companies, garbage collection, and bingo halls, which were sources of the PT's *caixa dois* (off-the-books slush fund) as well as more ordinary kickback schemes. Two key examples are the municipalities of Santo André and Ribeirão Preto. In Santo André the longtime mayor, Celso Daniel, was coordinating Lula's election campaign in 2002 when he was kidnapped and murdered, allegedly over a dispute regarding kickbacks from privatized bus lines (*New York Times* 2004). In Ribeirão Preto, a former advisor to then PT mayor, Antônio Palocci, was imprisoned temporarily in 2005 on charges of money laundering in transactions with bus companies and accused of over-billing for garbage collection services (*Folha de São Paulo* 2005). He implicated Palocci, who was ultimately forced to resign as Lula's finance minister in March 2006, because of these and related charges of operating a mensalão scheme as mayor (*Jornal do Brasil* 2006). And the very first corruption scandal during Lula's first term, "Waldomirogate," was associated with the Campo Majoritário. Dirceu's chief aide, Waldomiro Diniz, was caught on camera soliciting off-the-books campaign donations from a bingo hall owner.

Notwithstanding the mensalão investigations and eventual indictments as well as subsequent lesser scandals, the Campo Majoritário group, now called Construindo um Novo Brasil, continued to win internal elections. Several historical PT leaders abandoned the party over ideological, policy, or ethical differences; some formed a new party, the Party of Socialism and Liberty (Partido Socialismo e Liberdade; PSOL), and some, like Marina Silva, joined other parties. Yet most left factions stayed within the party and began calling for its refounding. The left factions generally garnered around 45 percent of the vote for the PT's national presidency, which gave them hope that they would win in some not-too-distant future. And they continued to engage in internal party battles to obtain government positions and increase the size of their internal voting blocs. With the PT's continued electoral success at all levels, the number of government positions to fight over constantly increased. Furthermore, the PT governments were delivering on many social promises (see Section 4 of this essay), and Lula's successor, Dilma Rousseff, was linked to none of the party factions and had vowed "a zero tolerance policy for corruption in her cabinet" (Balán 2014, 83). Dilma's independence from the factions gave her flexibility, but it also meant she had to pay careful attention to rewarding multiple groups to maintain their loyalty.

Governing Challenges

Lula and the PT ascended to the presidency in 2003 as a minority party in Congress with an ambitious policy agenda. Having met the challenges of a leftist party seeking campaign contributions and winning national power, the PT faced a set of four related governing challenges. It was the PT's response to these challenges that led high-ranking officials to be more closely involved in illegal practices; it was also the PT's continued efforts to build participatory

Table 2.3. Distribution of Cabinet Positions				
	Cardoso 2	*Lula 2*	*Rousseff 1*	*Rousseff 2*
Cabinet positions	21	35	37	31
Party of president	29%	60%	46%	29%
Party of coalition partners	47%	26%	35%	45%
Non-partisan	24%	14%	19%	26%

Sources: For Cardoso and Lula (*Amorim Neto 2007 cited in *Pereira et al. *2008); for Rousseff (personal communication with Amorim Neto and *Globo* 2015).

and transparency institutions that led these officials to be prosecuted by the state.

The first challenge faced by Lula—and later Dilma—was that they had to grapple with the PT's strong ideological and regional cleavages. Intense division within the PT meant that President Lula had to placate different internal factions to ensure party unity. Lula increased the size of the cabinet and also distributed far more seats to members of the PT than Cardoso had distributed to members of his party, the Party of Brazilian Social Democracy (Partido da Social Democracia Brasileira; PSDB). Lula's strategy became the blueprint for his two terms and President Dilma's first term. Although the PT held only 29 percent of the seats in the lower chamber during Lula's first term in office, they distributed 60 percent of the cabinet positions to PT officials (table 2.3).

The PT's distribution of cabinet positions to different PT factions meant that there were fewer seats for coalition partners. This helps to explain why the PT was induced to use the "monthly" payments scheme to generate support among congressional officials. The PT was unable to placate both PT officials as well as coalition partners, and there was a clear preference in Lula's two terms and Dilma's first term for the distribution of more positions to PT members. Only in her cabinet shake-up in 2015 did Dilma finally seek to reduce the number of ministers and PT prevalence.

The second challenge was that the PT needed to build support among congressional officials. This meant that the PT would need to work with political parties that had previously been bitter rivals—and even with specific individuals, such as Paulo Maluf and Fernando Collor, against whom the PT had once vigorously campaigned. When the PT first came to power in 2003, President Lula's challenge of building a stable voting coalition was somewhat greater than President Cardoso's challenge from 1995 to 2002 because there was a greater ideological and policy distance between the PT and other members of its coalition (PL, PP, PTB, PMDB) than had existed between the centrist PSDB and its key supporters (PFL, PMDB).[2]

To develop support within Congress, the PT followed the governing strategy established by the PSDB under President Cardoso, using what is now known as "coalitional presidentialism" to generate a stable voting majority (Power 2010). "The core insight of coalitional presidentialism is that presidents must behave like European prime ministers. Executives must fashion multiparty cabinets and voting blocs on the floor of the legislature" (Power 2010, 26). President Lula's magnetic personality made him ideally situated to play a central role in fashioning complex and stable voting blocs. Power identifies a "presidential toolbox" with four tools that help presidents to secure a stable voting majority in Congress: continual adjustment of the "size, heterogeneity and proportionality of the support coalition in Congress . . . , *plus* the use of pork (*budgetary clientelism*)" (Power 2010, 27). The "presidential toolbox" captures how the use of budget-based pork is a key institutional power at the disposal of the president. However, it has become increasingly apparent that the presidential toolbox concept needs to be expanded beyond budget-based pork to also include the allocation of well-positioned jobs that allow the jobholders to take advantage of their appointed positions for political gain and/or personal enrichment. A principal resource available to Brazilian presidents continues to be the allocation of strategically positioned "plum" jobs—from cabinet ministers to second- and third-tier management positions in the federal bureaucracy to executive positions in public companies such as Petrobras, BNDES, and Caixa Econômica Federal; Wendy Hunter estimates that the Brazilian president is able to distribute twenty thousand jobs (2010, 164).

The distribution of these jobs generates support for the incumbent president in three ways. First, the job provides a steady income to the individual. Although these wages are often a small amount of the larger budget, the ability to distribute jobs was extremely consequential for the PT because party members holding these jobs are often required to give 10 percent of their salary to the PT; these funds have long helped to sustain the party. Second, public officials use their positions to ensure that a small percentage of public resources are allocated through private companies back to the party to generate campaign resources. The mensalão and petrolão scandals are based on this scheme in which 1–5 percent of public contracts appear to be funneled back to party officials. Third, individuals holding these jobs could, if they wished, enrich themselves personally through bidding practices, allocation of contracts to political allies, and the like.

Initially, it appeared that many of the corruption scandals under the PT presidential administrations had more to do with redirecting public funds to politicians and political parties than with bribery for personal gain (Flynn

2005; Taylor this volume). The two largest corruption scandals under the PT's four presidential administrations, the mensalão and the petrolão (see Taylor this volume), were based on complicated money-laundering schemes in which public resources were captured by the PT, which then used those resources to build support in Congress or to strengthen its campaign efforts. The PT did not invent this kickback method of funding political campaigns, as there is ample evidence that President Cardoso (1995–2002) used a similar scheme (Flynn 2005, 1235). It is noteworthy that the PT's two earliest scandals—in the municipalities of Santo André and Riberão Preto, both in the state of São Paulo—concerned kickback schemes involving bus and trash collection companies contracted by PT administrations (Flynn 2005, 1241). In sum, the PT worked within the system of coalitional presidentialism to govern. This coalitional presidentialism involved budgetary clientelism, but it increasingly appears that it also included the use of well-positioned PT allies to continue the use of complicated kickback schemes. The PT adopted these schemes from the Cardoso administration, but it also appears that these schemes became more complex, which made them more difficult to unravel. It is telling that the two Brazilian reformist parties founded in the aftermath of the dictatorship, the PT and the PSDB, both used kickback mechanisms to sustain congressional majorities. The larger point here is that the PT moved away from its commitment to all aspects of the modo petista de governar and instead adapted much of the PSDB's economic program and its governing strategies to ensure consistent support in the national legislature. Often overlooked in the literature, the stability of coalitional presidentialism was partially based on the misappropriation of public resources to benefit parties and politicians.

The third challenge for the PT was to develop a positive working relationship with domestic and international capital so as to ensure the continuation of Brazil's economic stability. The PT's roots are situated in Marxist ideology, with an ill-defined commitment to socialism and social transformation. During the 1989 presidential campaign, Lula's political opponents tried to create fear that Lula was a Marxist revolutionary who sought to impose a Cuban-style communist regime on Brazil. In order to placate the financial markets during the 2002 presidential campaign, Lula committed to maintaining the fiscal austerity policies implemented by President Cardoso. In June 2002 Lula's campaign issued a statement promising that, if elected president, he would not employ capital controls, would not renegotiate the external debt, and would maintain the Cardoso government's financial commitments. This Letter to the Brazilian People (*Carta ao Povo Brasileiro*), derided as the Letter to Calm the Bankers (*Carta para Acalmar Banqueiro*) by its critics, seems not to have had a tremendous effect on foreign investors, though it caused a stir in Brazil. Lula essentially had committed his new government to following the economic strategy that had been developed by his predecessor. Thus, governing at the national level in a globalized environment dominated by neo-liberal ideas and institutions (IMF, Davos) strongly induced the PT to forge a close working relationship with the country's largest construction companies, banks, and agro-business.

The commodities boom and the rapid economic expansion during the 2000s made it easier for the PT to maintain better relations with important economic groups. The commodities boom allowed commodities exporters to expand, and it also greatly increased the revenues collected by the federal government. These revenues were used to fund an expansive infrastructure program (PAC) as well as the return of the developmentalist state (Schneider 2016). The economic boom thus helped the PT to maintain a stable voting bloc in Congress because there was tremendous growth in the federal budget as well as in the budget of nationally held companies, such as Petrobras. The Lava Jato investigation illuminated the close relationship between Brazil's largest construction companies and government officials. The PT was deeply implicated in a series of insider deals that involved large construction companies providing significant kickbacks to politicians of all leading parties. What is most noteworthy about these scandals is that the PT appeared to be no different from other parties; the PT thus traveled a long distance in twenty short years from a party brand of "honesty and transparency" to "politics as usual."

The fourth challenge for the PT was implementing its ambitious policy agenda. Over the course of four presidential administrations, the PT dedicated resources to implementing new social policies rather than addressing the institutional problems that made governing Brazil so difficult. For example, the trademark successes of the PT's government include the significant reduction of extreme poverty (mainly through Bolsa Família and wage increases), the expansion of the universal health care system (SUS) into previously underserviced communities (through initiatives like the Family Health Program and Mais Médicos), paying off the debt to the IMF to extract itself from foreign tutelage, expanding the federal university system (with new universities and increased enrollments), and the expansion of public participation mechanisms (see next section). However, when we consider significant institutional problems, such as the large number of political parties, the over-representation of rural states and regions, and the extensive corruption affecting all levels of government, it becomes clear that the PT did not focus on systemic political reforms.

Instead, Presidents Lula and Dilma worked within and through the existing system to secure support for—or at least acquiescence to—their social agenda. Without engaging in extensive counter-factual scenarios, given the historic animosity between the two parties that hypothetically might have aligned to pursue systemic political reforms, the PT and the PSDB, it seems highly unlikely that if Lula and Dilma had pushed for such reforms they would have succeeded. Furthermore, their social agenda would likely have been in jeopardy had they not added sweeteners to their coalition partners.

In sum, the PT's position as a minority party, without strong ideological allies in Congress, led top party officials to use a combination of budgetary pork distribution to secure the votes of non-PT congressional allies and the illegal reallocation of public resources to the PT and its allies to build support within Congress as well as for campaign purposes. The nearly decade-long economic boom generated abundant revenues that greased the wheels of this system, enabling Presidents Lula and Dilma to maintain consistent support within Congress. The weakening of the economy since 2013, in conjunction with the strengthening of the institutional capacity of the state to police corruption, dovetails with the declining support for Dilma's government. At the broader level, the dependency of the PT on this governing strategy precluded the ability of the PT to engage in broader political reforms but allowed for innovative social and even judicial reforms. Now we turn to how the PT's innovations help account for its continued ability to win presidential elections despite growing evidence of an abandonment of its core ethical principles. In terms of basic social dynamics, the PT changed Brazil.

Participation and Transparency

Given the mensalão corruption scandal prior to the 2006 election, as well as the beginning of the Lava Jato investigation into the petrolão scandal prior to the 2014 election, both of which suggest that the PT moved away from its commitment to clean government, how could the PT continue to draw support from progressive social movements? How can we account for the political base's apparent willingness to overlook the PT's transgressions? We argue that the PT's strong support for the expansion of social and political rights—alongside Brazil's generally positive economic performance for roughly a decade—can explain the PT's continued support. We focus here on the expansion of political rights during the 2000s.

The PT purposefully redesigned participation and transparency mechanisms, which created multiple opportunities for citizens to be engaged in the policymaking process while also strengthening oversight. Although the PT under President Lula abandoned its pledge to scale-up Participatory Budgeting, Presidents Lula and Dilma invested heavily in the building of a federal participation architecture, which allowed the social movement and civil society base of the party to be actively involved in building policy while also attracting additional supporters (Avritzer and Souza 2013). The PT thus eagerly sought to incorporate citizens and social movement activists into the broader participatory architecture. There were three institutional venues favored by the federal government: public policy management councils, policy conferences, and in a shift, "national level forums." While some scholars criticize the PT's national-level participatory institutions for lacking strategic importance and scope (see Gómez 2015), these venues provided policy and political resources for the government.

First, the policy councils are part of a federally integrated policymaking system that is organized around specific policy issues (such as health, environment, and education). Typically, councils are comprised of 50 percent civil society and 50 percent government members. Council members generally must approve the proposed budget for the policy area as well as approve a year-end report. Civil society representatives from municipal-level councils are then elected to a state-level council; from the state-level councils, civil society representatives are selected to serve on federal councils. This participatory architecture thus linked the federal government to civil society activists across the country. This provided a means for ongoing communication, which had a policy focus as well as a political focus. By 2015 there were over sixty thousand municipal-level councils, hundreds of state-level councils, and dozens of federal councils. The participation of over three hundred thousand civil society representatives in these councils allowed the federal government to connect to social movement and civil society activists. There is a growing body of evidence that the use of participatory institutions is strongly associated with improvements in human development (Touchton and Wampler 2014; Gonçalves 2014; Touchton, Sugiyama, and Wampler 2017). The use of participatory institutions is another extension of the accountability institutions implemented in Brazil since 1988; these councils allow for the exchange of information among citizens, community activists, and government officials, as well as for the additional monitoring of government actions.

The PT also invested heavily in public policy conferences. There is a long history of conferences being used in Brazil, but the PT elevated their use to a level not previously seen. Between 2003 and 2015, the federal government hosted nearly one hundred conferences, including many in new policy arenas such as public security, transparency, and communications (Avritzer and Souza 2013; Pogrebinschi and Samuels 2014). There were an estimated 9 million participants (it is impossible to know how many of the participants were counted more than once). The conferences were a great communication and mobilization resource for the federal government, as it was able to bypass the traditional media and directly connect with citizens and civil society activists. This enabled the PT to develop regular forms of communication with its base. In addition, Pogrebinschi and Samuels (2014) demonstrate that the conferences were positively associated with executive decrees issued by the president. Although we cannot definitely state that the government would not have adopted the decrees in the absence of the conferences, Pogrebinschi and Samuels's (2014) evidence suggests that the conferences were successfully used by the government to link citizen participation to government action. These actions thus helped to create a political space for civil society activists within the PT's governing agenda. The conferences are the best example of the PT seeking to reach out to civil society activists to generate direct engagement; the conference system connects citizens to government officials in an ongoing exchange. This, we believe, helps account for the PT's apparent ability to maintain ties to civil society even as it became a bureaucratized party.

Finally, the PT began experimenting with national-level policy forums that would better connect national-level policymakers to professional NGOs and experts who could contribute to ongoing policy debates. These forums represent the transformation of the PT from a neighborhood- and union-shop-level party to a party that inhabited a powerful executive branch. One forum, initiated by President Lula, was the Council on Economic and Social Development. The purpose of the Council was to bring together diverse economic and social leaders to debate Brazil's trajectory, yet it gained little traction and never became a strong entity that directly influenced presidential decision-making (Goldfrank 2011). Similarly, under President Dilma, the government created a national forum that was charged with deliberating over the federal government's four-year plan (2012–2015, 2016–2019). Such forums brought together policy experts representing civil society, unions, and private corporations in an effort to solicit inputs, and they represent an effort by the PT to incorporate a diverse body of experts into public deliberations. They symbolize the transition of the PT from a grassroots party that sought to be heard at the municipal level into a party that governed a country of 200 million residents. Nonetheless, there is little evidence that these councils directly influence policy outcomes.

In addition to the slow building of citizen-based oversight institutions like the policy councils, the investment in anti-corruption institutions also helps to explain the PT's continued support within civil society. The PT's schizophrenic actions in the presidency are nowhere better illustrated than in the fundamental contradictions between the government's efforts to strengthen anti-corruption institutions and the involvement of party officials in kickback schemes. During the Lula and Dilma administrations, three of the most noteworthy institutional changes include the strengthening of the General Controller of the Union (Controladoria Geral da União; CGU), the passing of the Freedom of Information Act, and a new law to combat money laundering.

President Cardoso created the CGU in 2001 to monitor the implementation of public works projects, and the PT strengthened it, in part through a national conference on enhancing the CGU's ability to fight corruption, the passing of a Freedom of Information Law, and the random selection of municipalities and states to be audited (Taylor this volume; Michener 2015). The institutional design of the CGU was a major advance over the design of the accounting tribunals, which are tied to the legislatures and form a legalistic body that focuses on close review of year-end reports rather than on curtailing and reining in existing corruption. The CGU, on the other hand, is actively involved in ensuring that municipal, state, and federal governments properly allocate federal resources. The CGU leads investigations on issues such as bidding, "ghost" employees and companies, and quality of implementation. At the municipal level, the CGU randomly selects fifty municipalities per year (out of 5,570) and conducts an extensive audit of each municipality's finances. Although the number is less than 1 percent of all municipalities, it creates the understanding that the federal government is more aggressively monitoring how municipalities spend resources. The CGU also receives complaints from citizens, which further allows it to identify wrongdoing (Teixeira et al. 2013).

More broadly, the great unknown, of course, is whether the PT was involved in corrupt activities to a greater extent than previous presidential administrations or if the federal state was finally equipped with the resources to investigate and prosecute allegations of corruption (see Praça and Taylor 2014; Taylor this volume). While it is hard to know whether the PT was more corrupt than prior governing parties or whether the state was much better than before at effectively policing illegal arrangements, it seems fair to conclude that the improved institutionalization of the state's oversight capabilities at least partially explains why the PT was ensnared in multiple corruption scandals, and why these scandals gained more prominence than similarly corrupt activities under prior administrations. What is baffling about the PT administrations is the continued engagement of many party officials in precisely those activities that oversight institutions were being strengthened to investigate.

President Dilma deepened the commitment to increased transparency by promoting the adoption of a sweeping Freedom of Information (FOI) Law as well as a critically important anti-money-laundering law. The former provides citizens the ability to gain access to basic data information using a formal request process that gives the government thirty days to respond. The FOI law had languished in Congress for years before President Dilma persuaded Congress to approve it (Michener 2015). The political push to approve the FOI was directly tied to Brazil's role as a founding member of the Open Government Partnership (OGP). Eight countries founded the OGP and the organization was initially led by the United States and Brazil. The first annual conference was held in Brasília in 2012 and was headlined by speeches by President Dilma and US Secretary of State Hillary Clinton. The leadership of President Dilma, the PT, and Brazil in this organization captures the efforts of some PT officials to promote policy reform: government officials used the OGP summit to push through the FOI legislation, which gave the Brazilian government more legitimacy within the OGP as well as internationally (Michener 2015).

The money-laundering law was approved by Dilma two months after the FOI law, in July 2012. Most significantly, this law made it illegal to conceal assets even when prosecutors cannot directly establish a link between the assets and criminal activity, made "dummy" companies and individuals equally liable as those directing the laundering process, and made plea bargaining an option for prosecutors to pursue. This combination has given the Lava Jato investigators the tools to follow the money trail in complex kickback schemes and get to the intellectual authors, including high-ranking business executives and party officials. Especially without plea bargaining (known as *delação premiada* in Brazil), it is unlikely that so many and such high-ranking accomplices would have been investigated.

Overall, the new or reinvigorated participatory institutions under the PT and its rhetorical and even legislative support for transparency and oversight combined with economic growth and improving social indicators to help convince the PT's base to continue voting the party into the presidency, at least through 2014. Dilma herself encouraged the notion that she was personally committed to fighting corruption, especially after the mensalão scandal, and was much more active than Lula or Cardoso in removing corrupt ministers from her cabinet during her first term (Balán 2014, 83–84). Initially this seems to have buoyed her popularity, but then the Lava Jato investigation and the economic crisis destroyed it in 2015. And, with her control over Congress in grave doubt, and impeachment proceedings looming, Dilma invited Lula into her cabinet in 2016, which was widely viewed as a move to help him avoid prosecution, thus shredding any credibility she had gained from her prior anti-corruption housecleaning.

Conclusion

Clearly, the PT moved far from its early roots as a party that sought to root out corruption and end the misuse of public resources. The PT has become quite schizophrenic, simultaneously engaged in some of the world's most innovative social, participatory, and transparency programs but also exploiting traditional presidential prerogatives of naming vast numbers of allies to key jobs, which were then leveraged to allocate resources to the party and to officeholders. It appears that the political need to raise campaign resources and create a stable voting majority in the national Congress had a greater influence over the behaviors of elite PT officials than the fear that the state would successfully prosecute these officials and than their interest in transforming Brazil's basic political institutions. Ironically, it was the PT's efforts to strengthen transparency institutions that help to explain how and why its high-ranking officials were successfully prosecuted for illegal activities. What is perhaps most baffling about the PT's governing strategies is the disconnect between the party's effort to improve transparency, participation, and accountability and its ongoing use of corrupt practices over the course of four presidential terms.

The PT obviously did not invent corruption in Brazil, but we must be mindful of the possibility that the absolute scale of the fraud was greater during PT administrations than other democratically elected governments because of the vast resources that were poured into the return of the developmentalist state during the 2000s and 2010s. Quite simply, the economic boom produced a volume of publicly available resources that had not seen since the late 1960s and early 1970s, when the government was controlled by the military. The bitter reality for many of the PT's most loyal supporters is that the PT behaved, once in power, in a similar fashion to political parties such as the PMDB, the PSDB, and DEM (previously PFL), as well as to military governments.

There are four interweaving strands that help illuminate the PT's schizophrenic nature. These strands are conditioned by external factors as well as internal features of the PT. Key external factors include the high cost of Brazilian elections and the basic governing challenges faced by the PT. Internal factors include the strategic decisions of the party's dominant faction (the Campo Majoritário), and the establishment of new institutions that were designed to appeal to activists who sought to create new channels for participation and transparency.

These interweaving strands also help us to illuminate how the PT might continue to shape Brazilian politics. First, political campaigns, especially presidential campaigns, are expensive. The PT desperately needed campaign donations from large business entities and not only altered its political and policy positions so as to place the party closer to the political mainstream to attract funding but also directed federal budgetary resources to maintain funding for the future (Boas, Hidalgo, and Richardson 2014). However, after the Supreme Court's 2015 finding that campaign donations by corporations are unconstitutional, political parties will need to find new ways to raise money, and public funding of electoral campaigns may become more important. The strengthening of transparency mechanisms may mean that parties will rely less on illegal contributions because there is a much greater risk that illegal actions will be successfully prosecuted. Thus, one important change we expect to see is that prominent campaigns (for the presidency, state governors, and senators) will be subject to more scrutiny and oversight, which will diminish the use of kickback schemes and increase reliance on public funding.

Second, the original Campo Majoritário group that directed the PT's move toward the center has lost many of its top leaders to jail or party expulsion. Lula and the PT itself have lost so much popularity that it is improbable the party will retain past levels of electoral support. It will prove difficult for Campo Majoritário leaders to maintain their hold on the PT, which could provide an opening for those sectors of the party that are less connected to the scandals. If Campo Majoritário leaders lose their grip on power, the PT may attempt to return to its roots as an ethical, reform-oriented party. The obvious danger for the PT is that its descent into "politics as usual" will make it very difficult for the party to regain, in the public's eye, its original brand of "good government."

Third, the PT's most significant governing challenge — its position as a minority party — meant that it needed to use the extensive budgetary and policy prerogatives of the presidency to build stable voting majorities. The dark underside of "coalitional presidentialism" is that presidents must find a variety of carrots to induce coalition partners to support their actions. Given the limited policy positions of most Brazilian parties, this has meant that presidents distribute personalistic benefits, including government jobs and campaign funds. It is likely that future presidents will contend with similar problems, but the exposure, in the Lava Jato investigation, of bribery networks reaching all the major political parties has renewed calls for a switch to a parliamentary system or, more minimally, at least to an internal reorganization of Congress.

Finally, the expansion of oversight and transparency mechanisms under the PT helps explain why so many PT officials working in the executive branch were caught involved in wrongdoing. The PT governments strengthened the very state institutions that caught PT officials. Going forward, researchers and activists will need to closely monitor the administrative and political support given to these institutions. If there is continued support for transparency, participation, and oversight institutions, we would expect that illegal use of public resources will diminish. If future governments weaken the new institutional arrangements, it is possible that there will be reentrenchment of "politics as usual." Given the PT's weakened party brand on the issue of clean government, there is now an absence of a credible political party that is willing to systematically lead this political effort.

The PT is obviously badly wounded by its immersion into politics as usual. The open question is whether voters will punish only the PT for its descent into politics as usual or whether they will reject all major political parties. Regardless, it is unlikely that the PT will be able to reposition itself as a party that appeals both to voters with its modo petista de governar and to businesses and political allies with its acceptance of politics as usual. Lula appears to have been a singular figure in his success in incorporating both of these governing strategies. If Brazilian basic accountability institutions are strengthened, we would expect to see the "ethical" side of the PT gaining strength within the party, which would suggest that it would lead the party away from traditional, corrupt practices. But if the accountability institutions are weakened, we would expect that the PT will remain mired in "politics as usual" and unable to present a coherent vision of change.

POLICY INNOVATION
AND STATE CAPACITY
IN A MATURING
DEMOCRACY

PART II

3

Matthew M. Taylor

Corruption and Accountability in Brazil

What we need at the moment is a profound institutional reform that eliminates from partisan electoral laws the roots and the causes of electoral corruption, that eliminates from Brazilian tax and criminal laws the foundations for electoral crimes, for corruption, and primarily, for impunity.

—Congressman José Dirceu

CORRUPTION—THE ABUSE of public office for private gain—has been a fixture of Brazilian politics under democracy. No presidential administration has escaped the taint of corruption, and perceptions of politicians as fundamentally corrupt are deep-seated in popular culture. Large scandals have contributed to this view, and a common thread runs from Collor's impeachment through the *mensalão* and Petrobras scandals that reached the highest levels of Lula's and Dilma's administrations: corruption is somehow intrinsic to the manner by which politics is done in Brazil, endemic to the political culture, and embedded in government institutions.

There are two problems with this common narrative: it both understates and overstates the problem. It understates the problem by focusing on high-level scandals while ignoring the equally important issue of bureaucratic corruption, corruption that does nothing to influence high-level policymaking or distort the electoral process. Such bureaucratic corruption is found routinely in the bribes paid to building inspectors, highway police, hospital purchasing agents, and other "street-level" bureaucrats. Bureaucratic corruption is as problematic as large-scale political corruption, given its effects on state capacity and the state's ability to deliver public services effectively and efficiently. Further, it frequently ties into larger scale political corruption, as the influence of corrupt networks finds its way up through the bureaucratic ladder and into political processes.

The second problem is that the pervasiveness of corruption in Brazil is often overstated. Brazil is no paragon of virtue, but it performs better in many international rankings than some of its Latin American peers. The country's score on Transparency International's 2015 Corruption Perceptions Index—which ranks countries from cleanest to most corrupt—lies just slightly below the world average and seventy-sixth out of 168 countries, marking it as less clean than Uruguay, Chile, Costa Rica, Cuba, El Salvador, and Panama, but cleaner than the rest of the Latin American region and other large emerging markets, such as Russia, India, and China.

What explains the simultaneous over- and understatement of corruption? In large part, both problems originate in the historical precariousness of accountability in Brazil. Corruption may not be as widespread as it appears in some of Latin America's worst performers. But the clumsiness of the state's efforts to police itself and the weakness of the courts in effectively punishing wrongdoers means that, when corruption is uncovered, it frequently causes a double shock. The alarming recognition that something egregious has been going on under everyone's noses is quickly followed by the chilling realization that the perpetrators will probably get away with it. Oversight has been weaker than desirable, allowing large-scale scandals to develop. Meanwhile, courts move too slowly to effectively punish the wrongdoers, and the legal structure offers too many loopholes for wrongdoers to evade punishment, feeding a politics of "permanent scandal" that threatens governability and institutional legitimacy (Filgueiras 2011, 144; Filgueiras and Aranha 2011, 380).

Recurring Corruption Scandals

Corruption scandals have marred federal governments of all stripes, without exception, since the return to democracy (see Power and Taylor 2011, 2). But two iconic events of the early 1990s have long offered the benchmark against which all subsequent cases are judged. These are the scandal leading up to Collor's impeachment in 1992 and the so-called budgetgate (or "budget dwarves") scandal of 1993. Collor's impeachment involved characters worthy of a popular TV *novela*. There was a glamorous young reformist governor elected to the presidency (Fernando Collor) after a campaign in which he promised to eliminate the public sector abuses of overpaid civil service "maharajahs"; a mysterious Rasputin-like campaign treasurer (P. C. Farias), whose behind-the-scenes machinations imperiled the president; and the president's brother (Pedro Collor) and driver (Eriberto França), whose testimony revealed the "sea of mud" in Brasília (Nêumanne Pinto 1992; Rosenn and Downes 1999). To add mystery and tragedy, Pedro would die of brain cancer soon after the impeachment, while P. C. Farias—after being captured in Thailand—would ultimately die in a murky murder-suicide alongside his mistress. At its core, however, this was a case of routine influence-peddling. Under-the-table donations collected by Farias had been used to pay for the campaign and were being used to finance the president's day-to-day expenses. The outcome was one all too common to Brazilian scandals: despite his impeachment by Congress, Collor was acquitted of criminal charges for lack of evidence and, a decade and a half later, returned to political life as a senator in 2007.

Less than a year after the impeachment, a Senate economist working on the congressional budget committee revealed systemic corruption by committee members. Representatives on the committee were writing exorbitant budget amendments benefiting NGOs tied to their friends and families, as well as drafting amendments that favored large construction companies, in exchange for a cut of the profits. The press, irreverent as always, dubbed the scandal the "dwarves' scandal" (*escândalo dos anões*), because so many of the implicated legislators were short of stature. Like Collor's impeachment, budgetgate proved that fact is often stranger than fiction. One of the most prominent members of the committee, congressman João Alves, defended himself from charges of illicit enrichment by arguing that he had won the lottery many hundreds of times. More tragically, the Senate economist was found to have ordered the murder of his wife, presumably to prevent her from revealing details of the multi-million-dollar scheme. Yet none of the six expelled deputies and not one of the four who resigned before they could be expelled was ever convicted in court. Several would later return to political life.

The "dwarves' scandal" led to a number of changes in the budget process, but these did not entirely halt the potential for abuse, as demonstrated by the so-called bloodsucker (*sanguessuga*) scandal of 2006, when congressional amendments were similarly used to purchase municipal ambulances at ludicrously overinflated prices (Praça 2011). Meanwhile, despite the changes in electoral finance rules implemented after Collor's impeachment (Speck 2012a; Mauro Campos 2009; Fleischer 1997), the scandals that embroiled the governments of President Lula and President Dilma demonstrate that campaign finance remains a murky business.

In mid-May 2005, just as President Lula's administration geared up for what looked to be a cakewalk to victory in the 2006 presidential campaign, a grainy film of an obscure political appointee aired on TV. The appointee, nominated by the Brazilian Labor Party (Partido Trabalhista Brasileiro; PTB) to the national postal service, was shown receiving R$3,000 to throw a public bid. In receiving the money, he spoke of his ties to the PTB's president, Congressman Roberto Jefferson, demonstrating that he was a man with influence. Soon after the tape aired, Jefferson ran to the floor of the Chamber of Deputies and then to the press to share his claims about corruption in the Lula government. Presumably he did so because he felt he was the target of a smear campaign by his erstwhile allies in the Workers' Party (Partido dos Trabalhadores; PT); if so, his revenge was devastating. Most damaging were allegations that the government had paid bribes to ensure the support of allied parties in Congress, used undeclared funds to pay off campaign debts offshore, and laundered money through advertising agencies to pay bribes and fund campaigns. The ensuing scandal—labeled the mensalão, or big allowance, by virtue of the stipends paid to lawmakers for their support—led to calls for Lula's impeachment, forced the resignation of the presidential chief of staff and the president of the lower house of Congress, drove the trial of thirty-eight alleged conspirators by the nation's high court, and led to the unprecedented conviction of twenty-five high-ranking officials and their associates.

Nearly a decade later, as Brazil headed into the 2014 electoral contest, prosecutors found evidence of corruption and money laundering at Petrobras. The ensuing investigation demonstrated corruption on a scale that dwarfs many of the world's largest corruption scandals, including the iconic *Mani Puliti* investigations in Italy in the early 1990s. Some of the money went to individual white-collar criminals, but a significant portion allegedly found its way into the coffers of political parties within the governing coalition. The investigation threw the Brazilian political system into turmoil, as a variety of previously prison-immune elites found themselves in jail: construction magnates, lawyers, Petrobras executives, bankers, and even a sitting senator were jailed. Taking advantage of new laws, prosecutors used so-called *delações premiadas* similar to plea bargains in US law to obtain testimony from nearly forty defendants, file more than a thousand charges against several hundred defendants, and recover several hundred million dollars in bribe payments.

These were not the only scandals of the PT's time in office, however, nor was the PT the only party tainted by accusations of corrupt practices associated with coalition management in Brazil.[1] Corruption is also not limited to the executive branch. The 2013 election, by secret ballot, of two members of the Party of the Brazilian Democratic Movement (Partido do Movimento Democrátic Brasileiro; PMDB)—Renan Calheiros and Henrique Alves—to preside over the Senate and the Chamber of Deputies drew widespread public opprobrium because of both men's alleged involvement in ongoing legal cases related to the misuse of public monies. Even before their election, political parties and Congress ranked among the public as the most corrupt institutions in Brazil (Transparency International 2010/2011). In 2016 the high court indicted the new Chamber president, Eduardo Cunha, but his counterpart in the Senate remained the scandal-prone Calheiros. The Judiciary, meanwhile, remains under suspicion in light of spectacular corruption cases that came to light in the 1990s and 2000s, including a judge's theft of nearly US$100 million from the construction of a labor court, and the widespread sale of judicial sentences uncovered by a police operation code-named Operation Anaconda. A former head of the National Judicial Council (Conselho Nacional de Justiça; CNJ), Eliana Calmon, herself a senior judge, in 2011 decried the prevalence of "bandits in togas," referring to the black cloaks her colleagues don on the bench.

Sadly, the prevalence of corruption may be even greater at the state and municipal levels. The vulnerability of Brazil's states is considerable, not least because of the existence of powerful criminal gangs such as the Primeiro Comando da Capital and Comando Vermelho, gambling rings like Carlinhos Cachoeira's politically influential group, and the considerable autonomy of subnational governments. To complicate matters, Brazil's lengthy border — totaling nearly seventeen thousand kilometers spread over ten neighboring countries — touches upon many nations marked by poor law enforcement and strong traditions of smuggling (such as Paraguay), and abuts the world's three largest cocaine-producing nations, Bolivia, Colombia, and Peru. Simple bureaucratic corruption is also pervasive, however, as seen in a major scandal that erupted in São Paulo during 2013. Revenue agents in the city government received bribes in return for not charging construction firms the requisite taxes, which cost the city more than US$250 million in forgone revenues over a decade (a similar scandal at the federal level came to light in 2015, with estimated losses in the billions of dollars through tax fraud).

Meanwhile, local politics are frequently dominated by family ties and political networks that can significantly weaken accountability by capturing oversight institutions like the state accounting tribunals (Tribunais de Contas do Estado) and state police forces, as well as credibly threatening reprisals against meddling journalists and prosecutors.[2] Brazil is not a safe place to be a journalist, especially in the less developed states such as Mato Grosso do Sul, Goiás, and Maranhão. Harassment, violence, and even murder commonly go hand in hand with corruption. In addition to journalists, prominent judges, prosecutors, and jail officials have all been killed in recent years.

These intimidation tactics are effective, and some states have essentially been transformed into organized crime fiefdoms, such as Espírito Santo in the 1990s and Acre and Rondônia in the 2000s. As Macaulay (2011) demonstrates, in such cases, the corrupt network first dominates at the municipal and state level, and its tentacles then slowly rise onto the federal stage. In Espírito Santo, for example, Macaulay notes that widespread corruption in the state assembly grew into a web of corrupt ties extending through electoral courts, state courts, police, and even the governor's office. A death squad served as muscle for the network, murdering an investigating judge, as well as other "inconvenient" meddlers. One leading state politician was elected to the national congress and was even serving as defense minister under President Cardoso when a congressional investigation uncovered his links to organized crime. Sadly, this is only one example of the "rhizomic" spread of corrupt networks (Macaulay 2011, 218), horizontally across the various branches of local government and upward vertically into federal politics.

Corruption is also pervasive at all levels of the civil service. Although Brazil's civil service—especially at the federal level—is well regarded for its professionalism, it is common knowledge that some "street-level" bureaucrats can be convinced to change their minds in exchange for a "small coffee" or a "little beer"; a speeding violation on the highway might thus be set aside or a difficult driver's test passed if the right driving school is engaged. The *cafezinho* and the *cervejinha* are never drunk in the company of the official, of course, but may find their way into a general pot of bribes. In some cases, it appears that this form of corruption is tied into broader political corruption. Some of the more lucrative postings in state civil police forces, for example, are reputed to have a "toll" associated with them; in exchange for turning a blind eye to brothels or gambling, payments are passed up the chain of command.

Corruption within law enforcement is particularly prevalent. Among many recent reports, there are allegations of payments to São Paulo police in exchange for their protection of gambling establishments (*Istoé* 2007), illegal payments to Rio police officials to run security for the Carnaval samba schools (*O Globo* 2013a), extortion of truckers by the Federal Highway Police (*O Globo* 2012), and the theft of more than US$1 million in confiscated criminal proceeds from the Federal Police headquarters in Rio (*Folha de São Paulo* 2005). Perhaps the most shocking, in Brazil's largest bank robbery, after a criminal gang burrowed into the Central Bank's vault in Fortaleza and stole a record R$160 million, many of the proceeds were stolen back by corrupt officers within the Civil Police, who kidnapped gang members and their families to ensure payment (Franchini 2011). Less than R$10 million of this Central Bank heist was ever returned to the government's coffers.

Surveys of civil servants find that a significant proportion—over one-third of federal government employees—report having suffered inappropriate pressures. More than one in five report having been offered a bribe, and more than one-third report that bribery in their agency is frequent or very frequent.

Strikingly, three of every five believe that accountability controls within the federal civil service are fragile, with the potential for corruption believed to be particularly high in bidding procedures, contract execution, and licensing (Filgueiras 2011). Given that the federal civil service is widely believed to be considerably less corrupt than most state-level bureaucracies, these findings are a sad reflection of the perceived pervasiveness of corruption among civil servants who are in a position to realistically evaluate its prevalence.

Popular perceptions are even more damning. Brazil leads Latin America in terms of popular experiences with corruption. Although only 23 percent of the population felt that bribing civil servants was necessary to obtain public services, more than a quarter (26 percent) had direct family experience with corruption in the previous year, a rate more than double the Latin American average of 11 percent (Latinobarómetro 2011, 64). More troubling still, perceptions that corruption is on the rise are evident in polls, and a majority (54 percent) say that government is ineffective in fighting corruption (as opposed to only 29 percent who thought it effective; Transparency International 2010/2011). Why is it that the Brazilian state is seen as so poorly equipped to tackle corruption, even though a strong majority (71 percent; Latinobarómetro 2011) believe the state could solve the problem of corruption if it tried to do so?

Impunity and Weak Accountability

When the mensalão scandal erupted in 2005, most Brazilians assumed that it would follow the same trajectory of many past scandals: a pyrotechnic display of sensational revelations and tawdry accusations followed by earnest vows from accountability agencies such as the Federal Police and the Ministério Público to do everything in their power to investigate, prosecute, and punish the guilty. Investigations would be undertaken and appropriate casework filed in the courts, where it would linger for years as the media lost interest, other scandals erupted, and the alleged wrongdoers went free. Most Brazilians assumed that the courts would never dare to convict the senior members of government implicated in the scandal, such as the president's chief of staff, José Dirceu, and the president of the lower house of Congress, João Paulo Cunha. President Lula had nominated a majority of the sitting members of the Supreme Federal Tribunal (Supremo Tribunal Federal; STF), after all, and the court had traditionally shown enormous deference to the executive branch, going so far as to absolve President Fernando Collor of corruption charges on a technicality, even after his impeachment by Congress in 1992.

Even if judges were willing to challenge the president, the vast privileges granted to politicians, the rights and protections guaranteed under the Constitution, and the slow and inefficient pace of the sclerotic courts would ensure that the case would fizzle out. Nearly three-quarters of those polled at the outset of the mensalão trial believed that the defendants should go to jail, but only 11 percent thought the court would convict (Franco 2012). The belief that impunity reigns is best expressed in the colloquial saying that most scandals "end in pizza," a disappointing mess into which most investigations of corruption have traditionally descended, neither proving nor disproving the charges, neither clearing nor convicting the alleged wrongdoers. The implicit belief was that the scandal would taper out and disappear into the vault of history as a vaguely troubling but never properly explained blot on the Lula government's achievements, much as his predecessors were sullied by similarly unresolved scandals, with neither conviction nor absolution forthcoming from the courts.

The public was thus mesmerized when the STF began deliberations on the mensalão scandal in August 2012. Its November ruling against twenty-five of the thirty-eight defendants, imposing sentences that would mean actual jail time and hundreds of thousands of dollars in fines for the most senior conspirators, was greeted as a crossroads for democracy. The presiding judge, Joaquim Barbosa, became a media favorite as a crusader for probity, willing to stand up to his colleagues in the court and to the political establishment outside it in the name of democratic virtue. The fact that Barbosa was a self-made Afro-Brazilian who had risen from working-class origins to become the most powerful judge on the highest court in the land added an element of human interest for members of a newly rising lower class facing both racial and economic barriers to their continued ascent. Barbosa's gruff and unyielding demeanor in his frequent tussles with opponents on the court made for dramatic television as he guided the case past a series of procedural roadblocks. By the end of the trial, Barbosa's visage adorned carnival masks and newspaper covers alike, but after a little over a decade on the court, Barbosa chose to retire early, in 2014, citing dismay and frustration with his colleagues.

In the Petrobras case, known as the Lava Jato or Car Wash investigation, the crusading prosecutors, led by Delton Dallagniol, and the judge at the center of the Petrobras investigations, Sérgio Moro, have similarly rocketed into the public consciousness. But they face pushback from criminal lawyers claiming prosecutorial overreach and judicial bias, as well as politicians reacting against harsher laws and punishments. Meanwhile, the cases they are supervising face potential reversal in the higher courts, and there is no guarantee that other judges or prosecutors elsewhere in the system would prove as tenacious in the face of powerful opponents.

There is no doubt that these two cases—the mensalão and Lava Jato—represent a major advance for Brazilian democracy. The courts have shown a willingness to challenge the ruling party; extraordinarily powerful political and business leaders have been convicted and are actually being sent to jail; the judiciary has challenged the other branches of government, who have indicated that they will comply with the court's decision; and courts have indicated that corruption may no longer be tolerated as a routine modus operandi of the political process. None of these outcomes would have been possible under the military regime that governed Brazil until 1985, suggesting that democracy has brought significant changes to the way institutions function and has placed limits on the power of Brazil's historically powerful executive branch.

Yet although the mensalão and Lava Jato trials are a watershed for all of these reasons, and a sign of the many improvements in accountability under democracy, they also highlight how much of a challenge corruption and impunity still pose to Brazil. An obvious reason is that they were very much the exception. In a review of the ten most salient scandals to hit Brazil in the past two decades, journalists at the *Folha de São Paulo* found that of 841 defendants accused in the affairs, only 55 had been convicted (6.5 percent), and only 9 (1.1 percent) had received a final unappealable conviction that would lead to jail time (Costa and Franco 2011).

Speaking solely about the mensalão case, since it has been concluded (unlike the ongoing Lava Jato case), it is clear that it was also far from a run-of-the-mill prosecution. As a high-profile case, it received expedited treatment in the courts. Even so, the case broke in 2005 and was not decided until seven years later, in 2012. Although they had been forced to resign in 2005, the officials who were convicted in 2012 spent many years freely circulating in the public eye and continued to play an influential role in the political and electoral process. When, after many years of delay, the most senior judges in the country took up the case, it nonetheless took four and a half months of deliberations, during the course of fifty-three sessions by the full STF, meeting en banc, to reach a decision. Even after a "final" conviction had been handed down in October 2012, the first defendants to go to jail did not do so until November 2013, and final sentencing motions continued into early 2014.[3] Most remarkably, this was far from being one of Brazil's longest trials.

This points to perhaps the most obvious problem of accountability in Brazil, the delay-ridden courts. Some of these delays are inevitable as part of the due process of law in a democracy. Indeed, many delays emerge from the laudable protections implemented to safeguard human rights in the aftermath of the authoritarian regime, such as the extraordinary habeas corpus protections created to shield against violations of basic liberty. Many defendants who can afford a good lawyer are thus able to remain free from prison until their cases receive a final decision with no possibility of further appeal.[4] Secrecy protections, including the right to bank secrecy and restrictions on access to trial documents, can also complicate prosecution and public disclosure.

In addition to these rights protections, however, legal formalism, a byzantine legal code dating to the 1940s, overloaded the lower courts, and the possibility of an almost endless stream of appeals and interlocutory appeals all tilt the judicial playing field in favor of defendants, creating an extraordinarily tough path to effective prosecution (see Taylor 2008). Even defendants who confess their guilt spend years and sometimes decades free before conviction. In the mensalão case, the STF made a decision that proved controversial in legal circles, to adopt a lower evidentiary standard to prove criminal intent; without it, obtaining the conviction of the alleged masterminds, such as José Dirceu, would have been unlikely.[5] And even in the rare cases of a conviction, statutes of limitation, rules on progressive imprisonment, and parole generally mean relatively short terms of imprisonment.[6] The results can be shocking: perhaps most notoriously, the 1993 murders of 111 prisoners by policemen putting down a riot at São Paulo's Carandiru prison have still not been resolved by the courts, more than two decades after the prisoners were shot in cold blood during what appears to have been a calculated massacre.

As damaging to the fight against corruption as the delay of the courts and the stringency of constitutional rights protections may be, the elitism of the legal code is often the harder pill for citizens to swallow. The legal code provides college graduates and senior officials with privileged treatment, such as special jail cells during trial, and includes rules forbidding suits against high officials in all but the highest courts.[7] At the federal level, seven hundred senior political figures are protected by special standing (known as the *foro privilegiado*), including all members of Congress and senior cabinet members, who can be tried only in Brazil's high court, the Supreme Federal Tribunal. A parallel system protects state governors and senior state judges, who can be tried only in the Superior Justice Tribunal (the nation's second highest court), and mayors, who can be tried only in their state's high court.

While at first blush it might seem that special standing should expedite trials by leapfrogging the delays inherent in the congested lower courts, a tradition of judicial deference has provided considerable protection to elected politicians. Under the 1988 Constitution, politicians could not be tried in the courts without express authorization from Congress. Not surprisingly, few cases against politicians found their way to the courts. A constitutional amendment approved in 2001 eliminated this protection, requiring only the notification of Congress, but the tradition of immunity has lingered on. The first politician to be convicted and forced to serve jail time by the STF—Congressman José Tatico—was sentenced only in 2010, a quarter century after Brazil's return to democracy, but the STF determined that his case had reached the statute of limitations and thus he could not be imprisoned.

Politicians such as Paulo Maluf—a former state governor and presidential candidate indicted by the Manhattan District Attorney's office, sentenced to a three-year jail term in France, and currently on Interpol's watch list—have used the country's laggardly justice system to their advantage to avoid conviction. Maluf has been a sitting congressman since 2007, a position that affords him special standing if needed. One state governor, who shot his predecessor in broad daylight in a crowded restaurant, played out his case in the STF for fourteen years. When sentencing was imminent, he resigned from office, thus losing his right to special standing and causing his case to begin all over again in a lower trial court. Like many defendants and plaintiffs, both he and his intended victim (who survived the shooting) died before the courts could reach a definitive verdict.

Meanwhile, as a court designed primarily to address constitutional issues, the high court is not well equipped to hear criminal cases. As of 2011, roughly one-fifth of the cases before the STF were criminal in nature. The mensalão case was a very big case, given the unprecedented number of defendants: the case file totals more than sixty-three thousand pages and the court heard more than six hundred defense witnesses. But the fact that this single case consumed four and a half months of the court's time during 2012 alone raises questions about the court's ability to effectively address the many outstanding corruption cases pending against politicians while also carrying out its duties of constitutional interpretation.

Further, a legal system that permits such impunity is clearly not functioning satisfactorily. But are the courts alone in bearing the blame for the pervasiveness of corruption in Brazil? What other factors contribute to the strange mix of corruption, scandal, and impunity under Brazilian democracy? Several mutually reinforcing answers have been suggested: culture, weak accountability institutions, and the mechanics of the political system chief among them.

Cultural Predisposition?

Brazil has been burdened by a variety of labels that point to its supposedly unique cultural predisposition to corruption. The so-called *jeitinho*, by which rules are bent to expedite or facilitate transactions, is frequently invoked to describe behaviors that may be either corrupt (e.g., a purchasing director who finds a way to privilege one competitor over another, despite a higher priced bid) or idiosyncratic but efficacy-enhancing (e.g., the civil servant who finds a way around rigid bureaucratic rules to expedite benefits to an elderly pensioner). Da Matta (1979) points to the existence of so-called *malandros*, or amiable rogues, who are able to leverage the jeitinho and bend the rules to succeed despite bureaucratic impediments and a rigid social structure. Brazil's tradition of cordiality frequently means turning a blind eye to malfeasance by others, while also ensuring low levels of interpersonal trust, even by Latin American standards.[8] At a broader, systemic level, influential Brazilian scholars have described society and politics as clientelistic and patrimonialist, with trust centered around family-based networks in a highly status-conscious and unequal societal hierarchy (Buarque de Holanda 1972; Carvalho 2008; Da Matta 1979; Faoro 1958; Nunes 1997).

But cultural explanations are dangerously broad, painting all Brazilians with the same brush, and slippery, in part because they so often are used to impart causal import to cultural phenomena that may only reflect the underlying material conditions governing Brazilian life. In a society marked by high income inequality, racial and socioeconomic barriers to advancement, family-centered trust networks, and weak institutions, it is perhaps not surprising that the notion of public good has not always been well formed, and that flexible rules have been prized over bureaucratic rigidity. More problematic still, these so-called cultural predispositions fail to explain the obvious changes in accountability in Brazil over the past generation, especially the important improvements that have taken place under democracy.

Weak Institutions?

A second answer is the weakness of accountability institutions. The Federal Police has historically been too small, too incompetent, and too corrupt to serve as an effective check on corruption, and in any case for much of its history was at the beck and call of the presidency. Oversight agencies such as Brazil's accounting tribunals (the Tribunais de Contas, at both the federal and state levels) were traditionally sinecures for retiring politicians, subservient to whichever parties were in power and thus unable to perform effectively. The media has been weakened as an agent of oversight by its domination in many states by politicians who own television and radio stations (illegally, under the Constitution), and the associated tendency of regional media to print stories from the large media markets (Rio and São Paulo, primarily), rather than conduct their own local investigations (Porto 2011). Congress, with its frequent convocation of congressional committees of inquiry (CPIs), has managed to fan the flames of many a scandal, but oftentimes with no effect in terms of providing evidence that would be useful to other accountability institutions. And although Congress has expelled nearly three dozen deputies since the return to democracy, its reticence to punish its own is legendary. Bureaucratic coordination, meanwhile, has been sadly lacking, with each of these institutions operating independently, and frequently at cross-purposes (Taylor and Buranelli 2007).

Institutional weakness, though, is an incomplete explanation if it does not refer back to the problem of an inefficient judicial system and the impunity it permits. Even relatively strong accountability institutions are weakened by the courts' inefficiency. The Prosecutorial Service (the Ministério Público, at both the federal and state levels), for example, has been well funded and given great autonomy but nonetheless had to survive in a world of perverse incentives, squeezed between poorly performing police investigators on the one side and the glacially slow courts on the other. The result is that many accountability agencies adopt second-best solutions: for example, the Federal Accounting Court (Tribunal de Contas da União; TCU) relies on fines and the administrative removal of corrupt civil servants so as to sidestep the courts (Speck 2011); other agencies such as prosecutors and police name and shame alleged culprits rather than undertaking lengthy and uncertain trials (Power and Taylor 2011, 255).

In a universe where corrupt politicians are seldom removed from office, or in which they are removed from office but remain free to participate in public life, there are few incentives for effective oversight and punishment, whether bureaucracies are strong or not. A member of the Federal Police might well be risking his career and a TCU minister might well be risking her cozy sinecure if they tangle with the wrong politician. Given that nearly a third of the sitting members of Congress in 2012 were defendants in ongoing legal cases (Sardinha and Góis 2013), and nearly 500 current and former mayors of Brazil's 5,570 municipalities are under investigation by the Federal Police at any given moment (e.g., O Estado de São Paulo 2012), this is not an unreasonable concern. Even when dealing with less powerful lower level bureaucrats, the incentives have not always been positive: a fired civil servant might challenge the decision in court, leading to a lengthy and costly trial, and could potentially even file a lawsuit against the public servants who worked to remove him or her from office. Judges have been notoriously difficult to unseat, with retirement at full pension the only possible punishment in most cases. The result has been a costly coexistence between corrupt and non-corrupt civil servants.

The Mechanics of Politics?

A third answer is the mechanics of Brazilian politics. The First Republic (1889–1930) was marked by *coronelismo*, machine politics whereby local power was held by so-called *coronéis*, landowners who were granted enormous autonomy to act as they wished locally, provided they supported the central government electorally (Leal 1977). The degree of regional autonomy has shrunk considerably over the past century, as a combination of military rule, economic and technological development, and a more efficient bureaucracy pushed the Brazilian state into the hinterlands. But as the examples of Antonio Carlos Magalhães (Bahia), Jader Barbalho (Pará), José Sarney (Amapá and Maranhão), Fernando Collor (Alagoas) suggest, Brazilian politics has not been exempt from regional power brokers and political dynasties that wield enormous power over state and local politics, especially in many of Brazil's less developed states. Da Ros (2014) demonstrates through exacting qualitative research that the judicial response to municipal corruption is highly influenced by state political dynamics, including political pluralism and legal mobilization, among other factors. Local influence and the ensuing impunity permits some power brokers to keep a powerful hand in national politics despite their unsavory records. Most notably, Collor returned to the Senate after having being impeached by a wide swath of Congress, including the Workers' Party, in 1992. And despite this historical conflict, he proved an important ally of the PT in power, alongside Sarney and other traditional politicians from the poor North and Northeast.

The cost of politics is also relevant. The electoral system, with its combination of large electoral districts and open-list proportional representation, generates a large number of candidates from a huge number of parties. As a result, elections are very expensive, even by international standards, and while the system of electoral courts has typically meant very transparent and clean voting procedures, campaign finance has not been marked by similar probity (Sadek 1995; Fleischer and Barreto 2009; Speck 2012a). Although there have been significant improvements in campaign financing, with the values declared by candidates doubling from 2002 to 2006 and again from 2006 to 2010 (Speck 2012b), problems remain. Of the ten leading campaign donors nationwide in 2014, half were construction companies dependent on government contracts. The use of a parallel set of books (the so-called *caixa dois*) has also been historically commonplace and is ingrained in the popular psyche. Indeed, one of the PT's defenses against the scandals of both Lula and Dilma presidencies was the argument that the scandals represented nothing more than a campaign finance violation. In other words, they were merely an innovative use of the caixa dois, rather than corruption per se.

Meanwhile, the legislative consequence of these electoral conditions is a system that is conducive to backroom negotiations. A central feature of the mechanics of contemporary Brazilian democracy is the system of coalitional presidentialism (Power 2010). As a rule, since the early 1990s, Congress has incorporated members from more than twenty parties, and no president's party has held more than one-fifth of all the votes. Given that so much legislation in Brazil has been constitutional in nature, a simple majority coalition has been insufficient to govern, and presidents have sought to create multiparty alliances that surpass the three-fifths threshold for constitutional amendments. Most presidents—with the exception of Fernando Collor, who rather ominously failed to assemble a strong party alliance—have been able to obtain this cross-party backing, usually managing to construct legislative coalitions that surpass 70 percent support.

The result has been a political relationship between presidents and Congress that is surprisingly effective (Figueiredo and Limongi 1999), but marked by *toma-lá, dá-cá* (literally, "take that, give this") bargaining over budget amendments, ministerial appointments, and political appointees within both the civil service and the state autarkies. That relationship has also spilled over into expressly illegal practices, as in the alleged purchase of congressional votes to approve the constitutional amendment permitting presidential re-election in the 1990s, or the stacking of political appointments within the bureaucracy, where recent research suggests that higher levels of political appointment are associated with higher levels of reported corruption (Bersch, Praça, and Taylor 2017). Coalitional politics carries over into state and local politics, where the politics of *é dando que se recebe* (literally, "it is in giving that one receives") prevail. With such large and heterogeneous coalitions, disputes between the parties are not uncommon—and with the constant bargaining required to sustain the coalition, the unearthing of skeletons in the closets of potential rivals is also far from unusual. But in the absence of significant opposition coalitions, scandals usually require a betrayal by someone from the inner sanctum, such as Pedro Collor or Roberto Jefferson, if they are to come to light. Even when these scandals do emerge, reciprocal protection is often the name of the game.

The Evolution of Accountability under Democracy

Despite these generally discouraging findings about both corruption and accountability in Brazil, it is important to recognize that since the return to democracy there have nonetheless been significant gains in the fight against corruption. At the broadest possible level, the underlying structural conditions that permitted corruption to flourish have improved markedly. Contested politics under democratic rule has created opportunities to remove corrupt politicians in ways that were unimaginable in the 1960s and 1970s, while democracy has enabled civil society to organize, mobilize, and challenge government in ways that would have been impermissible for the parents of most contemporary Brazilians. The stabilization of the economy in the wake of the hyperinflation of the 1980s and early 1990s required more stringent fiscal controls and a centralization of spending. Alongside lower inflation, economic stabilization implied greater budget transparency, providing citizens and accountability agencies with clearer insight into spending. The rise of the middle class, coupled with modest declines in Brazil's income inequality, has changed the scope of citizen demands while providing the wherewithal for greater civic engagement.

Together, these changes in structural conditions have led to incipient challenges to long-standing cultural "predispositions," such as patrimonialism and clientelism. Citizens have begun to contest these seemingly ingrained cultural practices and their associated syndrome of acquiescent deference toward authority, status, and class. Well-designed public policies have apparently begun to fracture the patronage ties that governed politics: the Bolsa Família, for example, was designed to reach the poor without passing through middlemen in state or local government, reducing the chances for clientelistic deference to those middlemen at election time. Increasingly, citizens feel empowered to challenge long-standing political dynasties at the state level, to monitor and report on local governments, and even to mobilize so as to change laws in ways that run counter to most politicians' wishes. The 1988 Constitution, despite its unwieldiness, has provided an important tool in this regard, allowing for popular initiatives—whereby petitions backed by signatures from 1 percent of the voting public become legislative proposals in Congress—and providing the institutional protections needed to guarantee effective public participation.

At an institutional level, these structural changes have enabled a variety of improvements to the accountability bureaucracy (for a more comprehensive discussion of this evolution, see Praça and Taylor 2014). Many accountability agencies have been created from scratch or been revamped in significant ways. The Ministério Público, a prosecutorial body organized into both state and federal units, was remodeled in 1985, providing it with unprecedented autonomy and operational independence from meddling politicians. The Cardoso government created, and the Lula government strengthened, the Comptroller General's Office (Controladoria-Geral da União; CGU), a federal oversight body with nearly three thousand employees whose primary goals are to defend public resources and increase transparency. The CGU has been particularly active in auditing state and municipal governments, as well as coordinating anti-corruption initiatives within the federal government. After many years as a tainted, politicized, and largely corrupt body, the Federal Police has been remade with strong leadership from the president and Justice Ministry (Arantes 2011). The Federal Police has grown by more than 55 percent since 2003, with five thousand new hires in the last decade and a large budgetary investment contributing to a proactive and powerful new role. Even the courts, which are a weak point in the accountability process, have worked to accelerate their efforts: the National Judicial Council established as a priority the resolution of the backlog of twenty-seven thousand pending administrative corruption trials by the end of 2013.

A flurry of new legislation and bureaucratic initiatives has significantly revitalized bureaucratic efforts against corruption. At the federal level, a national strategy for fighting money laundering and corruption—National Strategy for the Combat against Corruption and Money Laundering (Estratégia Nacional de Combate á Corrupcão e Lavagem de Dinheiro; ENCCLA)—has led to unprecedented cooperation between federal accountability agencies in choosing policy objectives and enhancing joint institutional efficiency. A number of new laws have been approved that demonstrate a desire to combat public sector corruption as well as being a means to facilitate the task (a comprehensive list is available in Cunha, Medeiros, and Aquino 2010).

Five recent laws stand out as particularly salient: the fiscal responsibility law (2000), a so-called clean slate law (2010), a transparency law (2011), the anti-money-laundering law (2012) and the anti-corruption law (2014).[9] The fiscal responsibility law constrains all public servants, at all three levels of the federation, to behave in fiscally transparent ways, with clear budgetary reporting requirements and harsh penalties for failure to comply. The Ficha Limpa, or clean slate, law, which has been upheld in court and went into effect during the 2012 elections, seeks to prevent criminals from running for office; a conviction in an appeals court bars candidates from running. The transparency law, meanwhile, follows a 2004 law requiring the rapid posting of all spending on a government Transparency Portal; under the new law, most government activities are subject to fairly stringent freedom of information rules, permitting citizens access to information that might otherwise be impossible to obtain. Although critics note that the law offers several tiers of secrecy—allowing for relatively long periods of restricted access to some documents—the legislation is nonetheless innovative in that it guarantees access to data in user-friendly formats and extends the new rules to lower levels of government as well as to state-owned enterprises (Michener 2011).[10] The anti-money-laundering law facilitates prosecution for these crimes, while the anti-corruption law offers the promise (still not entirely realized) of holding corporations and political parties responsible for crimes committed by their functionaries.

Civil society has worked closely with some government agencies to prioritize the fight against corruption. The CGU has an advisory transparency council, which includes representatives of agencies across the federal government; representatives from civil society, such as the Bar Association (OAB), the Brazilian Press Association (ABI), and the Confederation of Brazilian Bishops (CNBB); as well as from civil society organizations focused on corruption, such as Transparência Brasil and Instituto Ethos. In 2012 the CGU organized a national conference on transparency and social control (Conso-cial), aimed at bringing together civil society to discuss proposals on how to improve accountability. The conference came up with a lengthy list of eighty priority actions that should be undertaken in the fight against corruption. At the top of the list were public financing of electoral campaigns, the education of citizens on fiscal matters, strengthening the accountability bureaucracy, participatory budgeting, the weakening of Brazil's strict fiscal and bank se-crecy protections, and more rigorous laws against corruption, including lon-ger prison terms, larger fines, and accelerated judicial hearings in corruption cases.

Civil society has also been active on its own, often acting in ways that run counter to politicians' interests. The popular initiative instrument, for example, was used by a coalition led by the CNBB in 1999 to put forward a proposal to fight vote buying. With the support of 1 percent of the population, it was perhaps inevitable that the proposal against vote buying would be sub-sequently approved by Congress (Power and Taylor 2011, 290). This prompted the successful repetition of the initiative process in the case of the 2010 Ficha Limpa Law and, most recently, in a series of anti-corruption proposals spon-sored by the Ministério Público in 2015–2016. Even when politicians have not desired change, the ability of civil society to mobilize a significant block of popular support in favor of these proposals had a powerful persuasive effect on recalcitrant members of Congress. Meanwhile, at the local level, organi-zations like Amarribo Brasil (Transparency International's partner association in Brazil) have been active in forming and training citizen groups to monitor mayors and city assemblies, providing guidance on how to oversee public budgets, how to engage local government effectively, and in the worst cases, how to activate prosecutors and the media. Watchdog groups keep up pres-sure for oversight and reform.[11]

Finally, international agreements have led to important shifts in Brazilian law and institutions. Brazil is a signatory to the Organization of Economic Cooperation and Development (OECD) Convention on Combating Bribery, the Organization of American States' Convention against Corruption, and the United Nations' Convention against Corruption (UNCAC). As a signa-tory to the Organization of American States (OAS) and OECD Conventions, the Brazilian government has submitted to review on numerous occasions since 2002, receiving critical appraisal of its accountability processes from impartial external observers. One of the most important institutional implica-tions of the UNCAC has been the creation of specialized federal courts, in-cluding special courts for money laundering. Civil society organizations like Transparência Brasil, Movimento Voto Consciente and Amarribo have also been tasked with evaluating Brazilian compliance with the UNCAC treaty, ensuring oversight from below and helping these organizations to develop capacity of their own. Meanwhile, Brazilian prosecutors have used these treaty arrangements to obtain assistance from foreign governments in high-profile prosecutions. The international anti-corruption regime also has an effect on accountability within Brazil: several Brazilian companies and local affiliates of foreign firms have been targeted under Foreign Corrupt Practices Act (FCPA), while OECD criticism of Brazil's shortcomings has encouraged change. Most recently, at the OECD's urging, in 2014 Congress approved the previously mentioned anti-corruption law, increasing the liability of corporations for corrupt acts by their employees (Vaz Ferreira and Morosini, 2013).

The Complex Relation between Corruption and Democracy

Brazil finds itself in a curious situation with regard to corruption. Corruption is widespread in government, with practices that undermine the basic principles of democratic rule, including equality, justice, and responsiveness. Yet democracy itself has permitted a virtuous cycle of institutional improvement over the past generation, even as citizens struggle to comprehend the continued impunity with which recurring offenses are met.

There are at least three reasons that such gains may have happened under democracy. The first is the increased transparency brought by the democratic process, which has provided citizens with greater insight into the inner workings of the state, the freedom to demand change, and the ability to effect change when citizens are dissatisfied with state performance. This process may function through vertical, electoral accountability, but pressure from citizens may also have an effect in motivating horizontal accountability, as popular support for punishing the culprits in the mensalão arguably did in providing support for the STF's surprising decision in that case. The ability of Brazilians to mobilize through both formal and informal channels has become increasingly evident in the anti-corruption field in recent years, whether it is through the use of the popular initiative mechanism or the harnessing of social networks for protest.

Second, incumbents may strengthen accountability institutions in an effort to constrain their successors. This plays out in the story of Brazil's state accounting tribunals, which have frequently been strengthened when there was a possibility that rival parties might soon attain office (Melo, Pereira, and Figueiredo 2009). A similar political logic may have led to the creation of the CGU, which came about at a moment of likely transition from one party to another.

A third motivation may have to do with the need to oversee a heterogeneous political coalition. Under Brazilian coalitional presidentialism, the president's party seldom holds more than one-fifth of congressional seats, yet presidents have regularly managed to generate political coalitions that account for more than three-quarters of the legislature. In exchange, however, they frequently trade ministerial control for legislative support. Better functioning accountability agencies, in other words, may be a means of policing the members of the alliance to impose limits on the worst abuses. When scandal hits, furthermore, governments may have no choice but to pay lip service to accountability improvements aimed at curtailing a recurrence.

Whatever the causes, Brazil's accountability framework appears to be moving in a positive and increasingly self-sustaining direction. It will face important challenges in coming years, including the immediate challenges posed by the gigantic Petrobras scandal, as well as dealing with the backlog of corruption cases accumulated over the past two decades. But the public appears to be in agreement on the need for improved accountability, an abundance of new ideas for reform are germinating within civil society, electoral gains are possible to politicians who champion improved transparency, and the apparent gains from effectively fighting corruption are becoming increasingly evident. It is no exaggeration to conclude that the corruption panorama has shifted enormously, and in a largely positive direction, over the space of the past generation.

4

Kathryn Hochstetler

Environmental Politics in Brazil

The Cross-Pressures of Democracy, Development, and Global Projection

ONE OF THE Lula government's first initiatives in 2003 was to bring "light for all" (Luz Para Todos). The government made universal electrification part of the larger campaign for a "Brazil without Misery" (Brasil Sem Miséria), on the grounds that Brazil's remaining electrical exclusion was associated with locales that had low scores on the Human Development Index and low levels of family income (Portal Brasil 2011). The Brazil without Misery initiative was called a citizenship program, meant to be an engine of civic, economic, and social inclusion. With electricity, voters could read a newspaper or watch campaign coverage on television, students could complete their homework, and public safety would be enhanced. Over the first decade of the twenty-first century, almost all Brazilians gained electrical service, including those in the rural Amazon whose coverage had lagged most seriously.[1]

The Workers' Party (Partido dos Trabalhadores; PT) governments have, however, brought another set of related developments to the rural Amazon: the return to building big hydroelectric plants. Much of this electricity is transferred to the national grid and powers industry and consumers across the country, including those previously "electrically excluded," while the negative effects of deforestation and displacement remain in the region. Amazonian citizens have resisted the plants, challenging the massive Belo Monte project all the way to the Human Rights Commission of the Organization of American States.[2] There, they argued that the Brazilian government refused to carry out adequate democratic consultation; that its building of the dam despite local resistance constituted a serious human rights violation; and that local peoples *and* environments would not survive the project (Hochstetler 2011).

These two stories show why environmental issues inevitably rank high on any listing of the governing challenges that remain even for a consolidated democracy that is emerging as a global socioeconomic role model. While there is no simple opposition between environment and development, there are many difficult tradeoffs to balance. Environmental issues are often presented as common or public goods—no one can be excluded from clean air, no one can have clean air if all do not—but there are usually very concrete distributional effects of both environmental problems and solutions that create concerns about environmental justice (Acselrad, Herculano, and Pádua 2003). These will oppose some citizens against each other or may pit consumers and residents against industry. Another classic debate of environmental democracy is between citizens, who might decide that the Belo Monte plant is their worst electricity option, and technical experts like those in the Ministry of Mines and Energy who decide it is the best of the possible alternatives (Ministério de Minas e Energia 2010).

Brazilian environmental politics and policy in the twenty-first century can be examined with a focus on two topics. The first topic, environmental licensing, introduces the major actors and institutions in Brazilian environmental politics. It also demonstrates the routine processes of everyday environmental planning in Brazil and how these are related to recent developments in both democratic consultation and the return of a more active and developmental state. The second topic, climate change, can give insight into Brazil's changing role in global environmental governance. Since 2009 Brazil has engaged in global climate negotiations in partnership with the BASIC (Brazil, China, India, South Africa) emerging powers. While other countries around the world watch and prod them for action, these countries have been weighing whether they are ready to take on more significant global obligations. Largely domestic developments have made Brazil the most inclined of the four to take climate action. Both topics illustrate the ways in which Brazil is balancing old and new political and economic models, at home and abroad.

Environmental Licensing

Environmental issues hit the front pages and Twitter feeds when there are crises: protesters blocking a dam in the Amazon, an explosive gas leak in a factory, and the like. Environmental Impact Assessment (EIA) usually has a much lower profile, but a much greater effect on the overall environmental quality in a country. It often lies in the background of even the headliner events. EIA is, at least in principle, a means of preventing environmental damage by using scientific analytical techniques to predict the impact of proposed projects, consider alternatives that might prove less damaging, and propose strategies for compensation for unavoidable damage. Brazil has required licensing of activities that are likely to have an environmental impact at the federal level since 1986, with some earlier state level requirements. As the licensing process has developed since then, it has become an unwieldy hybrid of technocratic analysis by governments, firms, and scientists, on the one hand, and the primary site where the broader social impacts of economic initiatives can be debated and possibly blocked, on the other. This means that environmental licensing presents a classic instance of the "technocracy-democracy" dilemma, where the two different rationales for policy action often conflict (Dahl 1985). The two sides of environmental licensing in Brazil can be examined using recent licensing experiences in the energy sector as examples (for more detail, see Hochstetler 2011; Hochstetler and Tranjan 2016).

The Technocratic Side of Environmental Licensing in Brazil

Brazil is one of a small number of Latin American countries that created its environmental institutions on a timetable of its own choosing, establishing a national environmental agency in 1973 (Hochstetler and Keck 2007). A National Environmental System followed in 1981, and environmental issues gained ministerial status for the first time in newly democratic Brazil in 1985. A year later, the Brazilian environmental bureaucracy created one of the earliest environmental licensing requirements in the region (second only after Colombia). Brazilian EIA reflects longer experience and more qualified analysts than that of its South American neighbors, although it still shows many gaps in quality. The Brazilian Institute of Environment and Renewable Natural Resources (Instituto Brasileiro do Meio Ambiente e dos Recursos Naturais; IBAMA), an agency in the national Ministry of the Environment, evaluates multistate and complex projects, while state licensing agencies handle smaller projects (Hochstetler and Keck 2007). The focus here is on the federal licensing process, as state and municipal processes are generally similar in form while differing substantially in their capacity to carry out those processes well (IBAMA 2009; Sánchez 2012).

IBAMA issues environmental licenses in three steps, at the planning, installation, and operational stages of a project. Firms are required to provide an Environmental Impact Study that they or a contractor have prepared, which IBAMA then evaluates and may license, reject, or ask to have revised. The documents of a single EIA can run up to thousands of pages per project; some in São Paulo's environmental agency library occupy an entire library shelf and more. Brazilian EIA regulations require analysis of not just narrowly environmental but also social impacts, so analysts from many disciplines— from anthropology to geology and zoology—are involved. Since 2006 every IBAMA licensing document is published on its searchable website, including original terms of reference, IBAMA's correspondence with the preparers of EIAs, modified versions of the EIAs, and reports of consultations.[3] The state of São Paulo and some others also post EIAs online, a very unusual practice in a region where almost all EIAs are constructed on paper and commonly available only through whatever (often minimal) public information request processes exist.

Brazil has had graduate programs to train environmental impact analysts since the 1980s, and undergraduate programs since the 1990s (Sánchez 2010), and has professional associations and publications for the sector. Those trained in environmental licensing often move between specialized consulting firms that prepare EIAs, the governmental agencies that evaluate them, and firms that conduct their own impact assessments. Petrobras, for example, conducts much of its own impact analysis while using some specialized contractors. It maintains a highly trained internal assessment team that even engages in basic scientific research to establish baseline data against which impacts can later be measured. In 2003 IBAMA had just three or four permanent licensing analysts and about one hundred consultants, but Marina Silva oversaw a significant process of professionalization of the agency during her time as Minister of Environment (2003–2008) (Abers and Oliveira 2015). Working in IBAMA's environmental assessment division has become an increasingly high-pressured occupation, with close public and legal scrutiny of environmental licensing and many contentious cases. The 1997 Environmental Crimes Law makes individuals criminally responsible for environmental degradation, including EIA analysts who knowingly license damaging projects, a prospect that contributes to their anxiety (IBAMA 2009).

In the Brazilian context it is not unusual for development projects to linger in the licensing process for years or even decades, although it is also possible for potentially hazardous projects to move through quickly and with minimal discussion (Hochstetler 2011). For recent large hydroelectric plants, the charges for avoidance, amelioration, and/or compensation for environmental and social impacts amounted to 12 percent of total project cost, on average. Social costs averaged 83 percent of the total added cost of $113 per kilowatt installed (World Bank 2008, 10, 26). Projects may be significantly changed through the course of the environmental licensing process, with IBAMA's technical teams responsible for adjudicating between the expressed concerns of firms, scientists, and ordinary citizens, all of whom have a place in democratic Brazil's licensing process.

Even this summary of the "technical" side of licensing in Brazil makes it obvious that this is a highly contentious process. The World Bank and Brazilian firms and business journalists are heavily critical of the "regulatory risk" that licensing represents for Brazilian projects, while environmentalists are equally critical of the fact that most projects eventually are approved (Hochstetler and Keck 2007; World Bank 2008). Understanding this contentious process requires a focus on the ways that citizens and elected politicians have directly influenced the direction of environmental licensing in recent years.

The Politics of Environmental Licensing in Brazil

Over the course of the Lula and Dilma administrations, the Brazilian state once again came to play a larger role in the economy, with numerous initiatives like the Program for the Acceleration of Growth (Programa de Aceleração do Crescimento; PAC), the World Cup, and the Olympic Games spurring state investments in infrastructure and industrial projects. Petrobras's discovery of large oil and gas fields deep off-shore in 2006 added to this project agenda.[4] These initiatives join more routine projects to upgrade and expand the country's energy and sanitation systems. The national development bank BNDES arranged approximately three hundred project finance loans in the energy sector alone from 2004 to 2012 (Hochstetler and Montero 2013). Each of these projects and initiatives forms part of the PT's larger developmental vision, where state spending and investment join with private economic activity to propel more and better-quality economic growth. Both Lula and Dilma have made such projects part of their election campaigns, touting them as the cornerstones of an increasingly powerful country, traveling to ceremonial construction openings, and inaugurating finished projects. The payoff schemes documented in the Lava Jato operation gave individuals personal and partisan reasons to support the projects as well. The broad preference for industrially grounded growth creates considerable challenges for those seeking greater environmental protection.

In the first years in office, Lula and his then Minister of Mines and Energy, Dilma Rousseff, sought to loosen and simplify the rules for environmental licensing. Marina Silva, as Minister of Environment for much of Lula's two terms as president, resisted most of the changes, losing battles on specific projects but actually strengthening the licensing arm with the hires mentioned above and by backing her analysts against political pressures (Abers and Oliveira 2015; IBAMA 2009). Silva decided to run for the presidency on the Green Party (Partido Verde; PV) ticket in 2010, running a surprisingly strong campaign despite the party's historic weakness. Her personal appeal won her nearly 20 percent of the vote, sending Dilma into a second round against José

Serra and pushing her to take a more measured set of environmental stances as presidential candidate and president than those of her years in the cabinet (Hochstetler and Viola 2012).[5] As an economist with extensive experience in the energy sector, Dilma had leaned heavily toward building large infrastructure projects.

While she was in office Dilma's technocratic orientation has given considerable scope to her Minister of Environment, Izabella Teixeira, to carry out practical reforms grounded in Teixeira's doctoral studies on EIA. While Lula spent his last years trying to circumvent environmental licensing altogether (asking that all World Cup projects, for example, be allowed to avoid the process), Teixeira has led efforts that reform with a scalpel. One particularly important effort involves working with actors representing municipal, state, and federal governments to develop criteria defining which level handles which projects. This process is meant to free IBAMA from working on numerous small projects that are not really in its jurisdiction so it can concentrate on and more speedily address the large and complicated projects that are. Teixeira has also led a change in the licensing of petroleum extraction, which considers the environmental impact of a whole auction block rather than individual wells—a recommendation direct from her dissertation (Teixeira 2008). Environmentalists continue to be strongly critical of her efforts to speed up the EIA process through steps like asking for less information. Even the fastest processes are too slow for many in Congress, who have tried at least twelve times recently to pass legislation that would speed licensing (Pêgo et al. 2016, 11–12). Cutting the time allowed for community consultation is a favorite tactic in these so-far failed bills.

Beyond their overall orientation of the EIA process, elected officials and their political appointees at IBAMA and the Ministry of the Environment also sometimes weigh in on individual projects. The technical teams make recommendations to the politically appointed leadership, who retain the ability to override their recommendations. While the political appointees rarely do so, they have been influential in some particularly contentious cases, including removing members of IBAMA's licensing staff who resisted licensing particular projects. Reportedly, two different ranking figures within IBAMA resigned over their opposition to the Belo Monte plant, and licenses were granted after technical staff said that important conditions had not been met (Bratman 2015, 68).

Given all of this activity, environmental licensing was regularly on the front page of business news sources like *Valor Econômico* throughout the PT governments. Specific projects like the licensing of the Belo Monte hydroelectric dam or the Angra 3 nuclear plant, both originally conceived under the military government of the 1970s, were widely covered by the news sources of ordinary citizens as well. Local residents, indigenous populations, and environmental movements have all played roles in shaping the outcomes of these projects, in ways that they could not have done in earlier years. Their opportunities to participate and the scope and limits of their influence provide an additional window into environmental politics in a democratic and rapidly developing Brazil. It is worth noting that the overall rates of contentiousness are lower than one would think based on the news, as 71 percent of electricity plants built from 2002 to 2012 faced no notable opposition from environmental licensing, the Prosecutorial Service (Ministério Público; MP), or mobilized community activists (Hochstetler and Tranjan 2016).

Citizen participation was included in environmental licensing in Brazil since its beginning in 1986. Part of the EIA process involves writing a report of the assessment in language that is accessible and publicly available. Public consultation is not mandatory for every project but is required for projects in indigenous areas and is done for many initiatives. A comparatively well-organized and extensive environmental movement can also mobilize allies in many social sectors given the broad scope of the licensing process. For example, IBAMA's licensing documents show that 4,417 people attended thirty hours of public hearings on the Belo Monte dam. They included environmentalists, indigenous peoples, church groups, local residents, human rights activists, and others (Hochstetler 2011, 360). The limited evidence available suggests that more typical consultations are pro forma and lead to few concrete results (Abers 2016).

Concerned citizens gain more influence in the licensing process through their ability to activate the MP, which is charged with defending collective rights like environmental and consumer issues. Federal and state-level MPs can freely investigate situations that they believe might violate the law, and they can either demand Voluntary Conduct Agreements to bring the violator (typically a firm or state agency) into compliance or take the violator to court. They may challenge the original terms of reference of an EIA, argue to have an assessment moved to a different level of government, or challenge the quality of the EIA in some other way. To give some idea of the MP's level of activity, the São Paulo Ministério Público alone handled 36,859 environmental cases from 1984 to 2004 (McAllister 2008, 98–99). The presence of the MP means that all actors carry out the licensing process in full awareness that their decisions are likely to be closely scrutinized and may end up in court, as the Belo Monte plant did eighteen times from 2001 to 2010, with more cases since (almost half of these decisions were higher courts reversing the injunction of a lower court).

Many of the Belo Monte cases included charges that the consultative processes, especially of indigenous populations, were inadequate, no matter how many people came to IBAMA's hearings (Hochstetler 2011). Amazonian activists won a decision from the Inter-American Commission on Human Rights of the Organization of American States in April 2011 that agreed with this assessment of inadequacy. The Brazilian government reacted angrily, saying that the Commission should act only when there had not been internal opportunities for participation, which it had provided. In their standoff, they embodied one of the classic dilemmas of environmental licensing, as expressed by a former president of the International Association of Impact Assessment: "Proponents of projects often expect IA [impact assessment] to make opposition go away; opponents of projects expect IA to prevent change from happening in their back yard" (Fuggle 2005, 1). No democracy, including Brazil, has found a clear solution to this dilemma, which is another expression of those that opened this paper (McAdam and Boudet 2012).

The governmental response has included efforts to streamline processes and to ask for less information from proponents, both of which tip the balance in such standoffs toward proponents of projects. Proponents also have a great deal of structural power from the ways in which their projects fit into large government and public visions of economic development. Lula's last Minister of Mines and Energy, Edison Lobão, fumed that the country's energy future was a "hostage of the whims" of the Ministry of the Environment (*Folha de São Paulo*, January 4, 2010). But the governmental response also has included initiatives like the one in 2005 to make all licensing materials public. As explained by a participant, IBAMA's logic was that the process would benefit from having negative feedback from potential opponents earlier rather than later, and that offering more information could avoid the many conflicts that originate in misunderstandings and rumors (IBAMA 2009). These are the instincts of responsiveness and transparency. Similarly, the National Indian Foundation (Fundação Nacional do Índio; FUNAI), the federal indigenous agency that was quick to say there had been adequate consultation in the Belo Monte case, has also announced that it will require environmental reports to be in highly accessible Portuguese or translated into indigenous languages and will require earlier consultation with indigenous populations, all demands in the case at the Commission on Human Rights (*Valor Econômico*, April 12, 2012). Given the many actors and preferences involved, environmental licensing is likely to continue to be an activity where contentious balances must be re-struck every day.

The National and International Politics of Climate Change

Stepping up to a larger scale, addressing the problem of a warming global climate is one of the most difficult challenges facing human beings today. Among the many reasons for the intractability of the issue is that the causes of climate change are deeply and widely embedded in essentially every economic activity (Roberts and Parks 2007). Brazil has come to be one of the most important countries in global climate change politics, although it would often prefer a lower profile. In the international politics of climate change, Brazil has coordinated its positions with China, India, and South Africa as the BASIC coalition since 2009. None of these emerging powers has been legally obligated to reduce emissions by current climate treaties, notably the 1997 Kyoto Protocol, but all are under increasing pressure to act, as their emissions have risen with their economies. Of the four, Brazil has undertaken some of the most substantial domestic initiatives to reduce emissions, although China is catching up. I argue here that both Brazil's advances and retreats in addressing its climate emissions stem more from shifting political coalitions at home than the impact of global negotiations. This section presents evidence for these claims.

Brazilian Global Warming Emissions

Brazil's annual contribution to the emission of greenhouse gases (GHG; carbon dioxide, methane, and nitrous oxide) that create climate change is currently 4 percent of total global emissions. This is well below the current contributions of China (24 percent) and India (7 percent), but Brazil's smaller population makes it a much weightier contributor to emissions per capita. On a per capita basis, Brazil and South Africa are closer to the levels of wealthy industrialized countries while the others are much lower (Viola 2010). The BASIC countries prefer to think of emissions in historical rather than current terms, however, with Brazil going back to 1850 to calculate that developing countries will catch up with the historical emissions of developed countries only in the twenty-second century (BASIC Experts 2011). Brazil stands out from almost all countries with industrial development in having about 80 percent of its emissions in 2005 originating in agriculture and land use and land use change, especially deforestation, rather than the energy and transportation sectors that dominate the emissions of the others (Ministério de Ciência e Tecnologia 2010). Brazil's reliance on non-fossil fuel sources in its energy sector, notably hydropower and biofuels, contributes to this result.

While there has been no full inventory of Brazil's GHG emissions since 2005, it is known that this balance is shifting. For one, new studies of emissions suggest that Brazil's hydro energy sector may not be as carbon-neutral as it was once thought to be (e.g., Cullenward and Victor 2006; Scharlemann and Laurance 2008) and the discovery of extensive off-shore oil reserves may prove tempting to use at home (Hochstetler 2011). Even more significantly, Brazil has greatly improved its control over Amazonian deforestation, with annual deforestation rates dropping over 80 percent between 2004 and 2012,

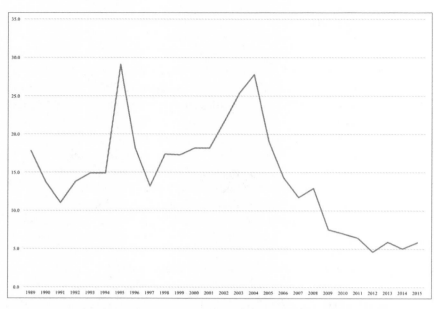

Figure 4.1. Deforestation in the Legal Amazon Region of Brazil, 1989–2015, in Thousands of Square Kilometers. *Source*: http://www.obt.inpe.br/prodes/prodes_1988_2015n.htm.

although the annual rate has been essentially flat after 2012 (see figure 4.1). Deforestation in the *cerrado* region—the savannah region of central Brazil, where large export-oriented crops like soybeans are concentrated—fell only after the 2008 recession. Satellite monitoring since 2005 and an array of policy and political initiatives generated these improvements. The Amazonian declines came even in the context of economic growth and have had important effects on the domestic politics of climate change as well as Brazil's emissions profile and its international negotiation stances (Hochstetler and Viola 2012).

Brazil in BASIC and the Global Politics of Climate Action

Brazil has played an important role in global climate governance since its inception. The UN Framework Convention on Climate Change (UNFCCC) was negotiated and signed as part of the UN Conference on Environment and Development, hosted by Rio de Janeiro in 1992. Brazilian negotiators took credit for making sure that the economic needs of developing countries were considered in the convention (Brazilian Delegation 1993). Five years later, they led a coalition of developing countries that codified that principle in the Kyoto Protocol, which charged only an "Annex 1" of developed countries with obligatory reductions of GHG emissions (Johnson 2001). In the first decade of the negotiations, Brazil clearly positioned itself as a developing country, articulating a strong discourse that divided the world into two camps, with developed countries seen as those responsible for causing and solving climate change and developing countries painted as innocent victims.

The United States never accepted this characterization and refused to join the Kyoto Protocol in large part because it carried no obligations for large and quickly growing developing countries like China (Roberts and Parks 2007). After 2005, Brazil, China, India, and a small cast of other "emerging" countries were regularly pulled into special side negotiations that were meant to pressure them into more climate action as befitted their growing economic weight and increasing emissions. At the 2009 climate negotiation in Copenhagen, Brazil, China, India, and South Africa surprised observers by embracing their status as emerging powers and negotiating together as the BASIC coalition (Hallding et al. 2011).[6] While presenting themselves as a distinct group, they have retained a foot in the developing world, remaining members of the G-77 of developing countries and claiming to speak for the interests of the rest of this group (Hochstetler and Viola 2012).

The Copenhagen meeting was the high point of BASIC coordination and influence. The meeting was intended to negotiate and adopt an international agreement that would create emissions reduction obligations for a much larger group of countries than those committed under the Kyoto Protocol. In the final days, however, BASIC country leaders sat down with President Barack Obama and a small group of others to jettison the existing treaty text and replace it with a sketch of a system of voluntary national commitments—a move that Brazilian president Lula said he had not experienced since his labor negotiation days (Lula da Silva 2009). For participants who expected a conventional treaty of mutual obligations and oversight, the Copenhagen Accord was a big disappointment, and negotiators failed to adopt it officially until the next year's meeting in Cancún. Many explicitly blamed the BASIC countries for the result (e.g., Dimitrov 2010).

For the BASIC countries, the result was a reasonably good outcome. It fit their insistence that the developed countries' historical responsibility for climate change meant that late developing countries like them should have different kinds of obligations. Voluntary emissions reduction aims that they set themselves also meant they retained national control over their development choices, perhaps the most important feature of the Copenhagen Accord for them. Independent analyses of Brazil, China, and India have all found a remarkable disjuncture between the level of climate action these countries were willing to undertake at home (comparatively high) and the level of climate action these countries were willing to commit to internationally (comparatively low) (Conrad 2012; Hochstetler and Viola 2012; Vihma 2011). Once developed countries agreed to a new stage of emissions obligations under the

Kyoto format at the 2011 Durban conference, however, Brazil and South Africa became willing to contemplate additional international agreements that China and especially India still resisted.[7] India was "left isolated, and fighting its own corner" at Durban (Hurrell and Sengupta 2012, 472), and India and China joined with other climate action resisters at the Doha negotiations in 2012 as often as they did with Brazil and South Africa. In 2015 Brazil was the only BASIC member to join the "High Ambition Coalition" that brokered a successful agreement, although bilateral meetings of the US Obama administration with Brazil, China, and India led to breakthrough climate action commitments for all involved. All of these developments suggest a need to look more deeply into the national politics of climate action in Brazil, since its BASIC negotiation partners clearly do not set its national positions.

The Domestic Politics of Climate Action in Brazil

In the first decade of global climate discussions, Brazil was an enthusiastic champion of climate action—by others. Brazil struggled with environmental problems like deforestation and air pollution that are closely related to climate change but, with a very few exceptions, resisted framing them in those terms. Some environmental activists in both state and society made the link but found few echoes in national politics or in Brazil's negotiation teams from Itamaraty. After 2000, however, the political base of domestic climate activists began to grow, as several different groupings began to prefer climate action for self-interested reasons, even if they were not conventionally environmentally concerned. The previously mentioned national electoral competition between Marina Silva and Dilma Rousseff again provided a critical impulse for a stronger Brazilian commitment to climate action, just as Brazil began to work with the BASIC countries (for an extended version of this argument, see Hochstetler and Viola 2012).

During the 1980s global activists spotlighted the rapid rates of deforestation in the Brazilian Amazon. While foreigners talked of the Amazon as the "lungs of the world" and made the link to the global climate, the predominant Brazilian response was a nationalist claim to Amazonian territory and the right to develop it as Brazilians wanted (Kolk 1998). Even at the peak of this discourse, many Brazilians in environmental groups, indigenous communities, and state agencies did want to reduce the deforestation rates and sought national and international allies to that end (Hochstetler and Keck 2007; Keck and Sikkink 1998). Since the Rio conference, the Brazilian public has expressed strongly positive orientations toward environmental action, seeing global environmental problems as serious and warranting action. Brazil often stands out in comparative national surveys for its levels of environmental concern, a stance generally supported in the Brazilian media (Hochstetler and Viola 2012, 764). These developments, the process of hosting the 1992 Rio environment conference, and the use of foreign assistance as both carrot and stick, brought the Brazilian government to a more cooperative stance on Amazonian deforestation by the mid-1990s (Kolk 1998). As Figure 4.1 shows, however, deforestation was still far from controlled and would remain this way for some time. Anti-deforestation initiatives were not justified in the name of climate change at this point.

Domestic efforts to address climate change itself were more sporadic and oriented to the state level. São Paulo, where long-standing environmental leaders Fábio Feldmann and José Goldemberg were State Secretaries of the Environment during the 1990s and 2000s, respectively, was the most engaged. Feldmann linked transportation and air pollution initiatives to GHG emissions reductions as early as 1995 (Hochstetler and Keck 2007; Lucon and Goldemberg 2010). Goldemberg and his California counterpart Alan Lloyd launched a joint "No Reason to Wait" challenge to their national governments in 2005, identifying ways in which the two countries could learn from one another, with strategies that promoted economic advances while reducing climate emissions (Reid et al. 2005).

The broader base of support began to grow as Brazil brought its Amazonian deforestation under control after 2005. While a full account of this development is beyond the scope of this chapter (see Hochstetler and Viola 2012; Nepstad et al. 2009), it reflected a series of changes in the Ministry of the Environment under Marina Silva's leadership. Regular satellite monitoring meant that deforestation could actually be tracked, including by the public on a website that allows anyone to compare satellite images from month to month. Silva, who grew up in the Amazon region as a rubber tapper, rebuilt relations between the national and state governments that allowed for stronger federal oversight. A series of smaller policies changed the microincentives of the Amazon's occupants. Changes in the Forest Code between 1996 and 2006 strengthened the legal framework, provoking a backlash after 2010 as traditional rural elites tried to reassert their prerogatives. They were locked into a show of force and counter-force with Dilma through multiple rounds of drafting, redrafting, vetoes, and yet more drafts. The final version gave impunity for past deforestation and contained other clauses that have contributed to the previously mentioned leveling off of deforestation rates rather than the prior sharp declines.

Traditional understandings of how to make money from the forest may conflict with new strategies. Brazil has received extensive support for Amazon protection since 1992 (Kolk 1998), which continues with renewed commitments by countries like Norway. The new controls over deforestation also moved many Amazonian governors and mayors to demand that Itamaraty and the national government support global plans to set up the REDD+ (Reducing Emissions from Deforestation and Forest Degradation) program. The Amazonian governors formed a coalition in 2009 to demand that Brazil support this mechanism (Nepstad et al. 2009), and Itamaraty finally conceded at the Copenhagen conference. Conceived as a mechanism to allow developing countries to receive foreign funds for maintaining forests, REDD+ awaits definitive international implementation, and expectations vary (Angelsen 2012).

At about the same time, industry groups joined the climate action coalition. After watching the US House of Representatives approve a climate bill in Obama's first year in office *with* a clause that included border carbon taxes on the products of countries that did not control emissions, three different industry groups on climate formed. As the 2009 Copenhagen conference approached, they developed a variety of platforms and positions, but all of them were oriented toward pushing the Brazilian government to take action on climate change (Viola 2010). They believed they might actually gain an advantage over their BASIC allies by adopting stronger action on climate change and avoiding the border carbon taxes Europe has also discussed.

Marina Silva also decided in the middle of 2009 to run for the presidency, and she made environmental issues and administrative probity centerpieces of her campaign. All of these developments gave environmental issues, and climate change in particular, a rare central role in electoral politics (Hochstetler and Viola 2012). The three candidates competed to push hardest for action, and all three attended the Copenhagen negotiation. Presidential candidate José Serra, then governor of São Paulo, pushed through a strong state law on climate change that became law right before the Copenhagen meeting (Lucon and Goldemberg 2010). Lula's preferred candidate, Dilma Rousseff, attached herself to the national climate law that was passed right after the meeting. Silva, then a senator, pushed to have Brazil's international voluntary commitment to reduce 2020 climate emissions by 36.1 percent—38.9 percent below what would otherwise have been written into the law. That clause failed, but the drop in deforestation meant that Brazil had already largely met its pledge by the time it was made, since the country had set 2005 as its baseline year. As already noted, deforestation has continued to fall since, but the many conflicts and tradeoffs associated with environmental licensing indicate that further drops may not come as easily, and indeed they have not since 2012.

As Brazil fell into economic stagnation and then crisis after 2012, environmental issues took a backseat. Dilma's narrow reelection win in 2014 and her subsequent struggle to manage the political fallout and polarization of the corruption trials put them further off stage. Expectations for Brazil's pledges — its Intended Nationally Determined Contribution (INDC) to climate action, in the language of the United Nations—in the pivotal Paris climate negotiation session of 2015 were correspondingly low. The eventual INDC won praise for Brazil as the only developing country to have a countrywide absolute target for emissions reductions, although activists noted that the specific promises again mostly codified laws and policies already in place. The Paris agreement itself was the fruit of an unusual alliance of developing and developed countries that called itself the High Ambition Coalition. Brazil's decision to break from its Chinese and Indian partners to join the coalition was seen as a critical step in achieving the agreement (King 2015).

Conclusions

As should be clear, the environment is a good topic for seeing the complexity of what it means for Brazil to be simultaneously a democracy, undergoing rapid development at home, and an emerging global power. Actors who favor large-scale industrial development and rapid economic growth continue to have strong structural power in Brazil and are central to the PT's governing coalition. Brazil also has many actors who favor greater environmental protection, however, and they have some institutional and political points of access to decision-making. Environmental choices pose genuine quandaries that pit the interests and values of some citizens against others, require complex thinking about the relative priorities of multiple social aims, and ask fundamental questions about the place of expertise and participation in democracies. These are not issues that are ever fully resolved, and there are no magic solutions. They require hard political work on a permanent basis. Compared to its counterparts in the Latin American region and its fellow emerging powers, Brazil appears comparatively thoughtful and resourceful in its approach to these dilemmas, although its choices are far from perfect.

One of the most problematic features of Brazilian environmental politics is that so many of the largest issues are debated mostly in quite narrow fights over the environmental licensing of individual projects. Brazil has not had anything like a serious national-level discussion of its energy options, for example. Beyond specific siting questions, would Brazilians want more nuclear energy if it meant fewer large hydroelectric dams in the Amazon? Would they rather have the cheaper electricity rates Dilma has offered or a less precarious and less wasteful energy system? How do those choices square with the 92 percent of Brazilians who said in 2010 that they believe global environmental problems are very serious?[8] How should the rights of those without electricity be balanced against the rights of those who currently live where electricity might be generated? Electoral democracy does not appear to easily deliver such debates or the answers to them.

In environmental issues, Brazil has been an emerging power for several decades now. Once considered an environmental reprobate for its uncontrolled deforestation, Brazil began the transition—quite deliberately—to positive contributor by hosting the UN Conference on Environment and Development in Rio de Janeiro in 1992 (Kolk 1998). Over the last two decades, the nation has contributed many ideas and proposals, especially ones that would require action by developed states. In this most recent stage, it has allied with other emerging powers that face equally if not more complex challenges in reconciling environmental and developmental aims. Their national challenges are repeated on the global scale, and their national resolutions will have a significant impact on global environmental outcomes, including in the core area of climate change.

5

Marcus André Melo

Checking the
Power of Mayors

Explaining Improvements
in Brazilian Educational
Outcomes

IT IS DIFFICULT to overstate Brazil's progress in the area of education. Indeed, up until the current political and economic crisis it had become commonplace to extol the country's achievements in this area. Although current educational indicators lag behind countries with similar per-capita incomes—and even poorer countries—there has been a great deal of praise for the relative improvements in the standard of Brazilian education. Recent evaluations have pointed to Brazil as a role model in areas such as evaluation and monitoring—a contrast to the abysmal state of these areas twenty years ago. What is driving these changes in education, on a political and institutional level? The first thing to note is that there has been great continuity in the agendas of Cardoso, Lula, and Dilma. Apart from the fact that there was some programmatic consensus (these administrations shared basic social democratic ideas about social policy and redistribution), I claim that much of the continuity stems from a number of common issues they had to address. An empirical and analytical exploration of the underlying causes of policy continuity in the area of education will focus on the influence that political and institutional checks on education spending have had on recent progress in the area of education. These accountability reforms in education have been crucial for tackling local corruption—and consequently for the improvements the country has witnessed in the last fifteen or so years. However, the scale of irregularities in the sector is substantial.

After a decade of scholarship on accountability, it is now commonplace to distinguish institutional checks on executives from citizens' evaluations of incumbents' performance in elections. While the former involve horizontal mechanisms such as oversight by audit institutions, parliaments, and judicial institutions, the latter is a vertical mechanism whereby citizens can retrospectively sanction wrongdoing and underperformance and reward rectitude and good performance (O'Donnell 1998; Mainwaring and Welna 2003; Przeworski, Stokes, and Manin 1999). An integrated analysis of the role of horizontal checks and electoral competition on the use (and abuse) of educational funds in Brazil inspires several questions. How do checks on educational spending impact education policy outcomes? As expected, democratization led to the emergence of a political market in which politicians respond to a newly empowered electorate (or more technically, the median voter). Have electoral incentives and political competition shaped how educational funds are spent or captured by politicians?

The Cardoso and Lula governments faced two important dilemmas when they embarked on a series of reforms not only of education but also in other areas of social policy. First, in a federal country the national government relies on the support of subnational governments to implement its programs. Although primary education and secondary education are not functional responsibilities of any level of government, the constitution of 1988 mandates that primary education is to be provided by the municipalities with the financial and technical assistance of the federal government and of the state (Article 30). Reforms thus required the cooperation and coordination of many institutional actors. The first dilemma was how to implement reforms that might affect subnational governments and at the same time secure the cooperation of these governments. Instead of implementing command and control measures designed by the central government, these changes required the introduction of incentives to encourage subnational political actors—teachers, unions, and particularly mayors—to pursue the same agenda as federal-level reformers.

The second dilemma consisted of mobilizing new resources and transferring them to lower levels of government while minimizing what have come to be known in the jargon of transaction cost economics as "agency losses." This can be described as a delegation dilemma: an attempt to reconcile the transfer of power, on one hand, with holding on to some degree of control, on the other. The first part of this equation—mobilizing new resources—was relatively simple when growth resumed at the end of Lula's first term of office. But the crucial task was the second: putting in place regulatory structures and accountability institutions to check social expenditure.

Both Cardoso and Lula faced the same basic dilemmas, and their governments differed little in terms of the strategies adopted. Contextual factors also mattered, not only the fiscal constraints facing each administration but also political constraints. Despite the dismally poor quality of education in the country the outcomes of the reforms have been very positive, and Brazil has been praised for its progress in every single aspect of education. The focus here is on these two dilemmas and the specific strategies designed to deal with them. The first dilemma—building a structure to align the interests of municipalities and the federal government—led to the introduction of FUNDEF under Cardoso (1997) and the FUNDEB (2006) at the end of Lula's first administration, which Dilma's government then continued.[1] The second dilemma—how to both transfer resources and control expenditure—involved creating evaluation mechanisms and audit institutions. The resources earmarked for education transferred from the federal and state governments to municipalities are vast, totaling R$100 billion (roughly US$50 billion at the time of writing) annually. The risk involved in this policy has thus been considerable.

This chapter includes four sections. After the introduction, the second section provides some basic information about the country's progress in education. The third section considers the first important dilemma: how FUNDEF and FUNDEB resulted in the realignment of the incentive structure for mayors. The fourth section focuses on supervisory institutions—the Federal Audit Body (Controloadoria-Geral da União; CGU) and state court tribunals—as well as the crucial role of public opinion and political competition. Overall, checks on local (meaning state and municipal) corruption were strengthened considerably over the past two decades. High-level corruption involving federal government procurement and political financing has expanded considerably and become institutionalized, as evidenced by the *mensalão* and *petrolão* scandals. In other words, both the incidence and the level of exposure of corruption have increased. Local level corruption, however, appears to have diminished. Several factors have contributed to this outcome, including the fact that federal checks on municipal corruption were strengthened, while the checks on state-owned enterprises and federal entities were weakened (Leite 2010).

Progress in Education under Cardoso and Lula

For a long time when observers sought an educational underperformer, Brazil was the usual suspect. A collection of essays from the mid-1990s famously referred to education reform in Brazil as an "opportunity foregone" (Birdsall and Sabot 1996). Indeed, in comparison to other countries, the indicators were dismal: in 1990 Brazil lagged far behind middle-income Latin American countries. Less than 40 percent of children nationally completed the eight grades of primary school, compared with an average of 70 percent in Latin America and 95 percent in the Organization of Economic Cooperation and Development (OECD) countries. Only 38 percent of children were enrolled in secondary schools, compared with over 70 percent in Argentina and Chile, and 91 percent in the OECD countries. The average level of schooling in the labor force in 1990 was only 3.8 years, compared to 7.9 in Argentina and 8.1 in Chile (Bruns, Evans, and Luque 2012). Fewer than 20 percent of primary school teachers in Brazil had a higher education degree.

In the wake of the reforms under Cardoso (1995–2002) and Lula (2003–2010), the improvements have been remarkable, and some educational experts have argued that Brazil has in fact become an international role model in some important areas within education (such as evaluation and monitoring). Hanushek, Peterson, and Woessmann (2012) show that Brazil was one of the top performers in improving education quality worldwide between 1995 and 2009. In Brazil, test score performance has improved annually at a rate of about 4.05 percent of a standard deviation. The country ranks third in a sample of forty-nine countries for the annual growth rates in student achievements in mathematics, reading, and science. From 1990 through 2010, the increase of the educational attainment of the Brazilian labor force was one of the fastest on record, and secondary school enrollments have grown faster and are now higher than in any other Latin American country (Bruns, Evans, and Luque 2012, 3–4). Basic education spending in Brazil reached 4 percent of gross domestic product (GDP), above the OECD average. Other impressive gains include improvements in primary school completion rates and preschool coverage. In the period from 1992 to 2009, economic activity among seven- to fifteen-year-olds fell by more than half, from 18 percent to less than 7 percent, while school attendance rose from 85 percent to 98 percent in 2013 (ILO 2011). The system has also become more equitable: the number of years of schooling completed by children in the bottom quintile of income distribution has doubled, from four to eight (Ter-Minassian 2013). A recent World Bank report claims "in key areas such as assessing student learning and educational performance monitoring, Brazil in 2010 is not only the leader in the LAC region but a global model" (Bruns, Evans, and Luque 2012, 3).

Can Brazil's surprising relative gains be explained entirely by the fact that its absolute levels were so low in the past? This is intuitively plausible but untrue. In their book on education in northeastern Brazil, Harbison and Hanushek found that in the early 1990s, only about 40 percent of teachers had completed primary education themselves (1992). However, in a recent multi-country comprehensive comparison of progress in test scores, this argument is refuted. In a detailed assessment of test score performance, Hanushek,

Peterson, and Woessmann (2012) found no evidence for the perspective that they label "catch-up theory," namely, that growth in student performance would be easier for those countries or subnational units that were originally performing at a low level than it would be for those originally performing at higher levels. The causal mechanism would be that poor performers might be able to copy existing models at a lower cost than high performers can innovate, leading to a convergence in performance over time.

If Brazil's initial appalling educational levels do not explain the ensuing progress, what could? A common alternative argument is that there has been a boost in educational expenditures and this is reflected in performance. However, more resources seem to be only one factor explaining the improved performance. As Ter-Minassian has argued: "Total public spending on education has risen in recent years to a level (over 4.7 percent of GDP) that is higher than the average for countries of similar per-capita income. More significantly, spending per student is significantly higher in Brazil than in countries of comparable (or even higher) per-capita income with higher learning achievement scores (e. g. Korea and Chile)" (Ter-Minassian 2013).

What explains Brazil's improvements? Rather than providing an answer to this open empirical question, I claim that institutional and political factors might each be playing a role. By exploring the possible institutional determinants of change, I suggest they form part of the answer. Despite controversies about specific findings, there is some consensus that the reforms undertaken under Cardoso and deepened under Lula explain much of the improvement in education in Brazil.

Delegation Dilemmas in Education

In a stylized principal-agent setup, delegation dilemmas are typical of transactions between actors whereby power (or resources) is delegated from the principal to the agent. A variety of problems arise in such settings, problems ranging from hidden information (the principal cannot observe agents' behavior) to moral hazard (post-contractual opportunism leads agents to cheat when they see an opportunity of holding up the principal). Thus, in the context of educational decentralization, schools, teachers, or mayors may deviate from their expected behavior after devolution of power or resources takes place. Mayors have incentives to use education funds for other purposes that better serve their individual interests. School directors may refrain from implementing directives for improving school quality. Lack of transparency and information asymmetries make it possible for agents to misbehave.

Massive decentralization of funding is associated with high risks of agency losses. Unless oversight mechanisms are put in place, deregulation can produce poor outcomes. Decentralization of education and health in Brazil involved transferring 1 percent of GDP to subnational governments: a transfer of resources on a scale unparalleled in Latin America (Ferraz and Finan 2011; Leite 2010). Bruns, Filmer, and Patrinos (2011) estimate that in developing countries, at least 30 percent of centrally allocated education funds fail to reach their intended destination. Reinikka and Svensson (2005) estimate that up to 80 percent of funds are diverted before they reach schools in Uganda. Ferraz and Finan (2011) found irregularities in 35 percent of the municipalities randomly audited in Brazil, which would represent roughly 0.1 percent of GDP.

The most recent CGU audit provides a comprehensive picture of corruption in basic and secondary education. In 2013, 41 percent of bids with FUNDEF funds ($40 billion) showed evidence of fraud (Controladoria-Geral da União 2013). In addition, evidence of wrongdoing was shown in 42 percent of disbursements, and 14 percent of audits revealed illegal non-identified withdrawals (*saques na boca do caixa*) from FUNDEF accounts. Finally, 58 percent of audits had irregularities in the uses of FUNDEF resources. More significantly for the analysis of checks on the use of FUNDEF funds, in 33 percent of the municipalities audited, the ad hoc participatory commissions did not monitor the FUNDEF accounts as required by law (Controladoria-Geral da União 2013).

A host of mechanisms can be put in place to minimize the agency losses that result from the misuse of funds. They typically involve increasing information ("identifiability") on outcomes and some accountability mechanism to sanction performance. But they also involve ensuring that agents benefit from the collective outcomes. The delegation dilemma involved in decentralizing resources is that the "decentralization contract" between a higher-level unit of government and a lower unit is "incomplete," as it cannot include all possible contingencies involved. But some institutional arrangements can be put in place to minimize the extent of agency losses. Randomized audits of educational expenditures may serve the purpose of deterring mayors from misappropriating funds. Transparency and the empowerment of actors (parents' groups, among others) also mitigate agency losses. For the case of educational expenditures, Zamboni (2012) found experimental evidence that the random nature of audits deters mayors from engaging in corruption. While this would not affect the poor use of funds, this does prevent deviations.

Realigning Incentives, from FUNDEF to FUNDEB

Although there are advocates of a centralization strategy in the area of basic education in Brazil, there is virtually a domestic consensus built over time that is supported by the international epistemic community that education should be a responsibility of the municipal level of government. An isolated crusader for converting primary education teachers into federal civil servants has been Cristovam Buarque, Lula's first Minister of Education (January 2003–January 2004). In his view the Ministry of Education would have a strong regulatory hand, as is the case with the successful university system. By centralizing recruitment and regulating pay and careers, the Ministry of Education would make it possible to overcome problems of qualifications, pay, recruitment, quality, and regional imbalances in educational outcomes. Buarque's solution to agency losses was centralization. However, Buarque's model is inconsistent with the political interests of many politicians and is at odds with the country's constitutional federal structure.

The alternative model was to decentralize educational financing, converting mayors and other local actors into educational stakeholders. This strategy was encapsulated in the creation of the FUNDEF, which was based on the principle that money would follow the students. Because tax assignment is defined in the Constitution, this strategy involved amending the Constitution. In December 1996, Congress passed Constitutional Amendment 14 and approved the Lei de Diretrizes Básicas (LDB), the complementary law on basic guidelines for education. Proposed by the federal executive, FUNDEF represented an ingenious device created by the Cardoso government to change the incentive structures that were built into the provision of basic education in Brazil. This program was supported through a combination of freeing up existing funds and shifting funds from other programs, as well as through administrative reforms associated with changes in incentives to enhance the quality of services and extend their coverage.

The Constitution of 1988 contained provisions for hard-wiring resources for education. It determined an increase in the resources set aside by the federal government to 18 percent and established a level of 25 percent of net tax revenues for the subnational governments. For the federal government, Article 60 of the temporary clauses of the Constitution required that, for a period of ten years, 50 percent of the equivalent of the 18 percent of revenues was to be allocated to literacy programs and to universalize the coverage of primary education. This proposal was resisted by both the planning and finance bureaucracies and by legislators closely associated with these circles.

In the late 1980s and 1990s, the centrality of education to development became a recurrent issue in the public agenda. From business interests to social movements, a consensus emerged on improving the quality of education.[2] In the 1990s, Cardoso's commitment to reforming education was reflected in the fact that he appointed one of his closest economic advisers to the post of education minister, as well as in the new recruitment pattern for the key positions at the ministry, and the thorough reform of its organizational structure. Cardoso was committed to insulating the educational sector politically. The key policy issue was how to improve education and promote decentralization of the sector.

A key challenge in the new strategy was the low pay of teachers. In many schools in the rural Northeast, the pay scale was below the minimum wage. With resources hard-wired in the Constitution, the challenge was then how to make sure that teachers were paid better. In 1989 there was a Parliamentary Inquiry Commission on the earmarking of resources for education (the "Calmon amendment"). The Commission found that states spent less than 20 percent of the constitutionally required educational expenditures on salaries. It was widely agreed that teachers' exceedingly low pay and lack of training at the subnational level was one of the main reasons for the low quality of education (Harbison and Hanushek 1992).

FUNDEF mandated that, for ten years, at least 60 percent of the 25 percent of the subnational resources ring-fenced for education was to be spent on the payment of teachers actively involved in classroom activities and on teacher training programs. It also mandated the creation of career structures for teachers. The resources required for raising pay and training were to come from a specific fund (or more appropriately funds since, in fact, each state had its own fund). These funds were financed by incorporating 15 percent of the FPM (the intergovernmental transfers from states to municipalities), 15 percent of VAT paid in the state, and a supplementary contribution from federal government taxation (Castro 1998). These sources represent over 90 percent of the fund revenue, and their respective shares vary significantly across the states. The federal top-up grant is the equalizing element that ensures some element of equal redistribution in the system. This is the amount necessary to help those municipalities whose spending levels fall below the national minimum per capita spending set in the country's annual budget law. All transfers to and withdrawals from FUNDEF were automatic and were formula-based. The law required that FUNDEF accounts were monitored by ad hoc FUNDEF commissions, which included extensive participation by representatives of teachers' unions.

FUNDEF's most important innovation was related to the mechanisms that governed the allocation of resources from the fund. These resources were distributed according to the number of pupil enrollments at each level of government. This produced a revolution in the incentive structure of education. Mayors actively engaged in attracting pupils because this would lead to more transfers from the fund. In addition, the FUNDEF innovation encouraged decentralization from states to municipalities because there would be negative transfers in some municipalities if educational services were provided by the states. The new incentive structure produced two important results: it created strong incentives for municipal governments to expand coverage in their territories, and it encouraged municipalities to take over educational services provided by the states. The municipalities in which primary education was provided mostly by the state governments had to make a compulsory contribution of a minimum of 25 percent of their revenue to FUNDEF but would not be able to draw any resources from it.

More importantly, the capitation principle introduced by FUNDEF undermined existing political bargaining in the process by transferring discretionary funding from central government to municipalities.[3] The old practice of vote buying through educational resources was weakened in the process and remained in use only through the so-called budget amendments that congressmen could approve in the annual budget. Resources were transferred to schools on the basis of pupil enrollment numbers rather than through political bargaining involving mayors and federal and state governments.

As indicated, the FUNDEF mechanism represents a highly successful initiative implemented by the Cardoso government, which led to the further decentralization of education in Brazil. This had a positive effect on actual enrollment rates rather than on just an expansion of the school network. Mello and Hoppe (2006) found that the lower the proportion of students enrolled in the state—rather than the municipal—school network, the faster the increase in enrollment. The initiative also helped improve working conditions and salaries of teachers, particularly in the most remote areas (the average salary increase was of almost 12 percent in one year, but in some cases salaries doubled or tripled). The proportion of so-called lay teachers (teachers without formal qualifications from teaching colleges) in municipal systems was reduced significantly, and the increase in coverage has also been noteworthy.

Education expenditures across all levels of government in Brazil increased in the period 1995–2000, from 4.2 percent to 5.6 percent of GDP. The net enrollment rate at the primary level increased from 89 to 96 percent in the period 1996–2001 (World Bank 2002). Municipal governments accounted for 34 percent of public primary education enrollment in 1996, but for 54 percent of enrollment in 2001 (see figure 5.1). Municipalities as a group spent nearly R$24 billion on education in the year 2000, nearly twice what they were spending, in real terms, in the year 1995 (World Bank 2002). Conversely, in the states where primary education was already decentralized to the municipal level (as was the case in most of the northeastern states, Rio de Janeiro, and Rio Grande do Sul), the rules meant that there would be a redistribution of resources from the state to the municipalities, and particularly to smaller and peripheral municipalities.[4]

There was a good deal of policy continuity between the Cardoso and Lula administrations regarding educational financing. The Workers' Party (Partido

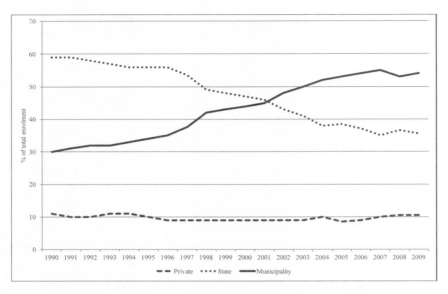

Figure 5.1. Primary Education Enrolment by Provider, 1990–2009.

dos Trabalhadores; PT) had been highly critical of FUNDEF, but rather than dismantling the scheme, the Lula administration reauthorized and expanded it to cover pre-primary and secondary education and raised the per capita funding levels. The changes to FUNDEF took four years—a period during which the Fome Zero initiative became the centerpiece of the government agenda—this window of opportunity stemmed from the fact that the FUN-DEF legislation essentially had a sunset clause. Article 5 of Constitutional Amendment 14 modified Article 60 of the Constitution, with the stipulation that the fund would be valid for ten years. Created in September 1996, FUN-DEF would thus expire in September 2006—four months before the end of the last year of Lula's first administration.

Law 11,494 of September 2006 transformed FUNDEF into FUNDEB (Rossinholi 2008). The new law addressed many flaws of the old scheme: its coverage, which was limited to primary education (grades one to eight), the low levels of funding by the federal government, and the absence of national minimum spending levels. Indeed, the fiscal constraints associated with the *real* crisis facing the Cardoso administration during his second term in office limited the federal government transfers. FUNDEF had revolutionized incentives for education by restructuring existing funds and sources, but without increasing federal funding for the educational sector. During Lula's second term of office, there was a significant expansion of funding (see figure 5.2). Much of the expansion resulted from the increase in municipal spending

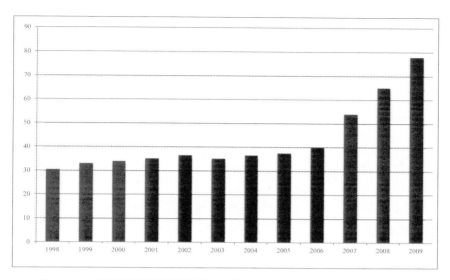

Figure 5.2. FUNDEF/FUNDEB Expenditure, 1998–2009 (in billions of reais).
Source: Brazilian National Treasury.

(that is, from municipalities' own expenditures on education, as opposed to those associated with discretionary transfers) (figure 5.3).

FUNDEB did not mandate a very clear delineation of jurisdiction between the states and municipalities. However, it kept in place an incentive scheme that punished municipalities that did not specialize in primary education. Education financing in Brazil maintains the same system of distributing resources that reflects the traditional overlapping distribution of jurisdictions in the area (Castro 1998). Under FUNDEB, the share of FPM channeled to the fund rose from 15 to 20 percent. FUNDEB extended the equalization scheme to cover nursery services and preschool, as well as secondary education (grades nine to eleven). In addition, it included minimum levels of per capita funding for enrollment in education programs for indigenous and quilombola communities, as well as youth and adult education. As outlined in Martins's (2012) detailed comparative study of the extensive bargaining associated with the legislative approval of FUNDEF and FUNDEB, the latter was marked by extensive legislative participation, which meant that the initial proposal was significantly modified. In the case of FUNDEF, the opposition parties offered great resistance, which included two appeals by the PT to the Supreme Court. However, there is no fundamental discontinuity between the two schemes.

The evidence reviewed thus far suggests that FUNDEF prompted mayors to attract more pupils; but did students in the schools that were transferred from state to municipal jurisdiction perform better? In a countrywide

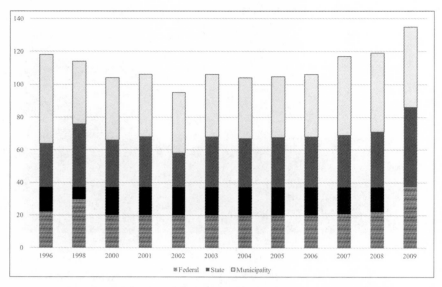

Figure 5.3. Consolidated Education Spending, 1996–2009 (in billions of reais).
Source: Brazilian National Treasury.

study, Ceneviva (2011) found that the extensive municipalization that took place between 1998 and 2009 was not accompanied by improvements in the educational attainment of the schools that were transferred from the states to the municipalities. Using data for the SAEB/INEP administered exams, Ceneviva compared the difference in students' school performance at two different times, comparing three groups of schools: those that were already under municipality control at the time of the SAEB exam; those that were under state control for both the SAEB exam and Prova Brasil; and those that migrated from state to municipality control between the two tests (treatment group).[5] The author found no difference in the quality of education between the groups, which suggests an overall improvement in the country, irrespective of the schools' institutional type.

By raising minimum spending levels in basic education, however, FUN-DEF/FUNDEB has significantly increased overall education spending, both in real terms and as a share of GDP. Indeed, basic education spending in Brazil doubled between 1995 and 2008, rising from 2 to 4 percent of GDP. Although there was a decline in educational spending as a share of social spending during Lula's first term, there was a significant increase during his second term of office. The FUNDEF/FUNDEB reforms have transformed Brazilian education by stimulating an overall increase in basic education spending, and by improving the equity of spending across municipalities, states, and regions in the country.

Despite its overall improvement, much remains to be done in education. Brazilian students lag behind their OECD counterparts by a gap of nearly one hundred points (20 percent) in PISA scores in math, science, and reading. Brazilian scores in these tests also lag behind Chile, Mexico, and Uruguay. In 2012 only 27 percent of students attained the expected proficiency in language and 17 percent in mathematics. Repetition rates are high and preschooling is deficient. School facilities in poorer and more remote rural areas remain inadequate. States also differ in the extent to which they offer monetary rewards for test outcomes and teacher performance, and there is little accountability for school directors. Finally, actual teaching activities account for a small share of classroom activities, due to a disproportionate share of classroom time being spent on routine or administrative activities (Ter-Minassian 2013).

Two important issues remain unaddressed in the education agenda. The first is the quality of educational outcomes. Having universalized access to primary education through FUNDEF/FUNDEB, the quality of educational provision remains the single most important issue. Second, recent dynamism in the labor markets has undermined gains in school attendance. Between 1995 and 2003, there was an increase of 15 percent in school attendance for those aged between fifteen and seventeen. From 2003 to 2011 this figure fell to just a 2 percent increase. The corresponding figures for those in the eighteen to twenty-two age bracket are a 7 percent increase in 1995 to 2003 and a 5 percent decrease from 2003 to 2011 (Menezes Filho 2012).

Institutional and Political Checks on Educational Spending

The second dilemma that both Cardoso's and Lula's governments had to grapple with was how to strengthen controls and to create accountability mechanisms to make sure that the funds transferred to municipalities were actually spent on education. In 2002 the Cardoso government transformed the existing Secretaria Federal de Controle—the internal audit body in charge of monitoring public expenditures and making sure that financial rules were followed in the public sector—into the CGU. This measure was carried out alongside the enactment of the Fiscal Responsibility Law (FRL) in 2000, which imposed a host of requirements for transparency, monitoring, and reporting for subnational governments in Brazil. The existing Tribunais de Contas Estaduais, or state audit tribunals, were mandated to oversee compliance with the FRL. They were also charged with monitoring the spending of FUNDEF/FUNDEB funds.

There is evidence that the strengthened checks on mayors have led to a decline in corruption in education spending. In addition to better institutional controls, there is also evidence that societal accountability has improved with regard to education, and underachievement in education has acquired an un-

Table 5.1. Summary Data on Randomized Audits of Municipalities by CGU (1-14)			
	Category	N	%
Area	Health	11,935	27.8
	Education	9,212	21.5
	Social development	5,836	13.6
Level of government	Prefectures	33,400	77.9
Justification	Partly justified	435	1.0
	Not acceptable	19,889	46.4
	None	21,807	50.9
Target of audit	Execution of project or public work	11,412	26.6
	Bidding process	7,011	16.4
	Managerial aspects of existing goods or equipment	6,378	14.9
	Rendering of accounts	5,072	11.8
Findings	Irregularities	23,327	54.4
	Improprieties	15,714	36.6
Total		42,876	

precedented visibility. In the past there was virtually no credit claiming in the area of education. Education had low political saliency, and politicians had few incentives to invest politically in the sector by attracting funds for schools or sponsoring innovations that might improve quality. Since the mid-1990s, the federal government has claimed credit for education outcomes.

The gap between spending allocated to education at the source and funds actually spent on service delivery on the ground largely explains the low impact of spending on educational attainment (Bruns et al. 2012). In Brazil, the diversion of funds within the educational sector is substantial, but there is indirect evidence that increased monitoring may be going some way to reduce it (Zamboni 2012). Using CGU data, Mendes (2004) estimated that between 13 and 55 percent of FUNDEF funds showed evidence of irregularities. In turn, in a study of 790 municipalities, Ferraz and Finan (2011) found that 35 percent of funds showed evidence of corruption. Melo, Leite, and Rocha (2012) found evidence of corruption associated with education spending in 21 percent of municipalities (with 27 percent showing evidence of corruption in

Table 5.2. Findings of Randomized Municipal Audits Carried Out by the CGU		
Audit Finding	*Irregularity*	*Impropriety*
Equipment not found	2,224	
Documentation missing or with irregularities	1,629	
Irregularities in bidding	1,081	
Deviation of funds	884	
Missing or irregularities in invoicing	752	
Failures in project execution		2,036
Lack of or inefficiencies in monitoring		999
Lack of stock control		731
Lack of infrastructure		644
Lack or shortage of qualified personnel		454

health spending; see table 5.1), in an analysis of 42,876 municipal audits. In this study Melo, Leite, and Rocha found 9,212 irregularities in the education sector, of which about 55 percent represent serious wrongdoing (equipment purchased but not found, overpricing, embezzlement, etc.). A striking number of serious irregularities were found. For example, the auditors found that 2,200 pieces of equipment supposedly purchased—including motor vehicles and computers—were missing (see table 5.2).

Corruption can largely explain low educational standards as well as the recent improvements in such standards. Since 2003 CGU has carried out audits of municipalities—at a rate of sixty per month—randomly selected from across the country. A multidisciplinary team of federal auditors spends one week in situ to complete the audit. The selection process is based on a lottery, monitored by a private external independent body—KPMG—and open to the public.

Ferraz and Finan (2011) found that corruption significantly affected the quality of municipally provided education. Municipalities with detected corruption were much less likely to have adequate school infrastructure or to provide in-service training to teachers. In these municipalities teachers and school directors were more likely to cite a lack of resources as a principal concern. In municipalities where irregularities were found, test scores were on average 0.35 standard deviations lower (a dismal outcome by global standards), and failure and dropout rates were higher.

In order to investigate if institutional checks in a state affect corruption in municipal schools, Melo, Leite, and Rocha (2012) estimated an econometric model and found evidence that the quality of state institutions (including state audit courts and the local judiciary) matters. The authors use a hierarchical model where the variable "Checks index" is a state-level variable and corruption is a municipal-level variable. They found that where state audit courts are stronger and the judicial system is better there is less corruption, even when controlling for human development and per capita income. In this study the authors use *irregularidades* (irregularities) as a proxy for corruption and utilize data from the education sector. Irregularities are distinct from *impropriedades* (improprieties), which involve some form of infringement of due procedures not necessarily involving misappropriation of resources. These impropriedades include, for example, use of food not fit for consumption (with an expired best-before date) in school meals. The types of irregularidades found range from supposedly purchased nonexistent equipment to fraud in competitive bidding. Thus the data used is an accurate measure of corruption and does not reflect lack of institutional capacity, which is more associated with improprieties.

To test the impact of institutional and political checks on the incentives for committing irregularities, Melo, Leite, and Rocha use the index devised by Alston, Melo, Mueller, and Pereira (2009) to measure the quality of checks within Brazilian states. This index includes principal component analysis of scores for audit bodies, NGO density, independent media, judicial system, the public prosecutor's office, and regulatory agencies. The study also considers the effect of a competitive political environment on corruption on education. In other words, the study tests for horizontal and vertical accountability mechanisms in the education sector. The results confirm not only that better checks reduce corruption but also that increased political competition is associated with less corruption (although very close electoral races are associated with increased levels of corruption).[6] In other words, better accountability mechanisms have an impact on the occurrence of corruption. In political monopolies (municipalities where the same elites, usually linked through kinship ties, wield political control and face no opposition), irregularities occur at a much higher rate. The micro-foundation for this finding is that self-enrichment is the dominant driving force where the likelihood of denouncement by political rivals is low. But corruption rises when competition is fierce: in the context of a tight electoral race, the diversion of educational funds during elections may serve to tip the balance.

The study thus shows the nonlinear effect of political competition. The finding that at both low and high levels competition generates incentives for corruption is surprising and has substantive significance. For each 10 percent increase in the margin of victory there is an increase by a factor of 1.119 in the expected number of instances of corruption. A 30 percent margin increases the number of instances of corruption by approximately 34 percent. A 50 percent margin gives a substantial predicted increase in the number of irregularities, from 6.2 to 9.8. The authors also explored how access to the judiciary affects the corruption associated with mayors with regard to education spending. Municipalities that are also the seat of a judicial body (the variable labeled "Town with District Court") indeed tend to have less corruption according to model five, corroborating Zamboni and Litschig (2006).

Interestingly, the conditional effect of political competition on corruption is positive: in states with better institutional environments this effect is reduced. The substantive interpretation of this result is that political competition degenerates into predation in states such as Rondônia, where institutions are weak, there is no traditional entrenched elite, and consequently fierce political competition. The substantive interpretation of this finding is that mayors in states such as Rondônia or Alagoas, where the local judicial branch, the public ministry, and audit court are less effective than those in, for example, Santa Catarina or Pernambuco, are not constrained in their behavior. Conversely, where checks are stronger, mayors are deterred from engaging in corruption because the likelihood of being caught is not trivial.

In sum, in contrast to the conventional wisdom holding that good governance follows from political competition, this study concludes that political competition in contexts of weakly institutionalized environments lead to predation and low accountability. The virtuous combination is political competition and strong checks. In other words, horizontal and vertical accountability interact in complex ways to generate good policy outcomes. Much of the heterogeneity in education outcomes may have institutional foundations: we can expect much higher diversion of funds in states with weak institutions than in states with robust institutions.

The evidence reviewed thus far suggests that gains in educational achievement may have come from better checks. Vertical accountability is at play, but in the states with weak institutions, strong political competition is associated with predation rather than with improvement. Horizontal and vertical accountability mechanisms seem to combine to produce better outcomes. There is experimental evidence that municipal audits have a deterrent effect. Under Dilma's administrations, the municipal audit program was partially discontinued. Overall, the CGU's checks on local (state and municipal) corruption had been strengthened under Lula. By contrast, high-level corruption involving federal government procurement and political finance expanded considerably under Dilma and has become institutionalized. Local corruption, however, seems to have diminished. The incentive structure facing PT governments contributed to this outcome. The federal government claims credit for punishing mayors but incurs reputation losses when corruption is found in federal bodies. This might explain why federal checks on municipal corruption strengthened—with the corresponding positive impact on education—while the checks on state-owned enterprises and federal entities weakened.

Conclusion

Starting from a very low base, educational indicators in Brazil have improved significantly over the last two decades of stable democratic rule. Neither this very low base nor the expansion of resources earmarked for education seems to fully explain Brazil's sustained and rapid improvements in this area. I have explored the hypothesis that the strengthening of checks along with electoral incentives account for a significant part of the progress in the area. The scale of the diversion of funds in education is massive and the improvements in horizontal checks combined with the electoral incentives for politicians' performance in the area are at the bottom of the underlying transformation experienced by the sector. This is not tantamount to stating that education is Brazil is performing adequately—far from it—but, rather, it suggests that there is a new, politically and institutionally driven, dynamic that has put the sector on a promising track. Much of the relative improvement in education stems from the new incentive structure that was implemented in the 1990s and 2000s, as well as the operation of political markets under a vibrant democracy. The reform agenda for education is challenging, but for the moment there is no institutional reform proposal under discussion, aside from the rules for sharing the revenue the newly found pre-salt oil. Recent experiences suggest that funneling more resources to the sector without a massive sectoral overhaul may result in waste and rent seeking rather than further significant improvements in education.

6

Wendy Hunter and Natasha Borges Sugiyama

Assessing the
Bolsa Família

Successes, Shortcomings,
and Unknowns

HIGH QUALITY DEMOCRACIES meet the basic needs of their citizens. This is because functioning democracies respond to citizen demands by providing a minimum degree of social protection. For much of Brazil's history, during periods of both authoritarian and democratic rule, social exclusion has been the norm. Whether in the form of direct exclusion through the disenfranchisement of the illiterate population or indirect exclusion in the form of corporatist politics that benefits only a narrow group of formal sector workers, Brazil has a legacy of social, political, and economic exclusion that renders it a society with huge social inequalities (Hunter and Sugiyama 2009). The challenge associated with creating a democratic society where all citizens are extended meaningful citizenship has been pressing. Surprisingly, despite the long-standing need to address poverty and inequality, many of the advancements in this regard have been relatively recent. Brazil's signature poverty alleviation program under Presidents Lula and Dilma, the Bolsa Família (the Family Grant) contributed to expanded citizenship against the broader backdrop of Brazilian social policy.

When Lula began his presidency in 2003, Brazil faced significant social challenges, including high rates of indigence and poverty and dramatically high rates of economic inequality. Approximately 15 percent of the population lived in extreme poverty and approximately one-third of the entire population

(36 percent) lived below the poverty line (Ipeadata 2013). Brazil was also well known for its dramatic rates of income inequality. For instance, in 2001, Brazil had the highest rate of income inequality in the region, with a Gini Index that was higher than that of Bolivia and of Haiti (World Bank, *World Development Indicators*).[1] These figures were particularly troubling given the country's ascendant position in the global economy. Poverty and its pernicious effects on human capital formation would emerge as crucially important, both developmentally and politically. For a country that started the millennium with diplomatic aspirations to lead the hemisphere and the global South more generally, its lagging social protection system represented a sore spot. At the same time, President Lula's own personal history, with poor origins in Brazil's Northeast, and the Worker's Party (Partido dos Trabalhadores; PT) left-of-center platform elevated the need to address poverty alleviation and brought it to the political forefront.

Lula's focus on the basic needs of all Brazilians initially prioritized the issue of hunger and nutrition. The creation of the program Fome Zero (Zero Hunger) reflected his campaign promise that every Brazilian would be able to eat three meals a day. Despite the initial fanfare of Fome Zero, the program never emerged as a large-scale flagship social program (see Hall 2006). Disagreements among technocrats over program design and the merits of its focus, as well as administrative entanglements over the leadership of Fome Zero, were early indications that the program was off to a shaky start. At the same time, in 2003 federal technocrats also launched the Bolsa Família program. It would consolidate existing federal programs put in place under Lula's predecessor, Fernando Henrique Cardoso, including Bolsa Escola, Bolsa Alimentação, and Vale Gás (Melo 2008; Sugiyama 2012). The Bolsa Família would follow the program design of Bolsa Escola, which included conditionality requirements of its beneficiaries. For example, in exchange for monthly cash grants, beneficiaries would need to ensure that their children maintained regular school attendance. These programs initially operated in conjunction with one another, but over the course of Lula's first administration the policy aims of Fome Zero would be incorporated into the Bolsa Família. The Bolsa would emerge as Lula's single most important social policy achievement. The program has endured through three full administrations and continues under Dilma Rousseff's second term. Today, nearly 14 million families (about 55 million individuals) receive a family grant.

The Bolsa Família has garnered tremendous attention in the international development community, and it is widely regarded as one of Brazil's most important social policy advances in the last ten years. With favorable policy evaluations and significant attention from international development agencies, the Bolsa, along with Mexico's PROGRESA/Oportunidades Program, have emerged as models that have spread throughout the developing world (Fiszbein and Schady 2009). In Latin America alone, eighteen countries have adopted conditional cash transfer (CCT) programs (see Sugiyama 2011). To put this trend in perspective, over 25 million families (about 113 million people, or 19 percent of the region's population) are recipients of such grants (Cecchini and Madariaga 2011, 7). Brazilian officials have hosted many foreign visitors, including bureaucrats from African countries, who are interested in learning about the mechanics of operating the Bolsa Família. Given that CCTs are now firmly entrenched as a linchpin in the model for social protection and human capacity building, we need to know more about the opportunities they open up and the limitations they entail. We also need to acknowledge the extent to which Brazil's "successful model" can translate to other country contexts. Surely countries have different needs and capacities and therefore "one size" may not "fit all." For example, if there is an inadequate supply of schools and clinics, it is not reasonable to try and address the demand for such services through a conditional cash transfer program. Similarly, countries with low administrative capacity cannot reasonably hope to run a program that requires the complex coordination necessary for the level of means testing and monitoring carried out in Brazil.

What do we know about the effects of the Bolsa Família? To address this question, we draw on policy evaluations of the program and our own research on the experiences of recipients of the Bolsa in the Northeast. Our analysis focuses on the contributions of this new policy model to the alleviation of poverty, creation of human capital development, modernization of the bureaucratic state, and citizenship development among the poor. We caution, however, that despite the merits of the program, CCTs need to be analyzed for what they cannot do. For this reason, we include a discussion of the shortcomings of the program and its design as well as the need for further evidence about the program's full promise.

First, we contextualize the Bolsa Família within the broader Brazilian social policy context. It is important to have perspective on the relative importance of the Bolsa, given other social spending priorities. We provide details on how the Bolsa Família works and why it has become politically important. Then we detail the findings to date on the contributions of the Bolsa Família. Specifically how and how much the Bolsa Família has contributed to poverty reduction, human development, innovations in the federal management of social services, and citizenship acquisition? We explain some of the shortcomings of focusing on the Bolsa Família to address the needs of the poor. Specifically, a focus on alleviating childhood poverty leaves out other features of human capital formation that are also crucial, including the need for quality primary education and the capacity building of mothers. As one might expect with a relatively new social policy, only time will tell whether the Bolsa has contributed to improving outcomes in the long term. Thus we then lay out the questions that call for future investigation.

The Emergence and Evolution of CCTs

In order to gauge the relative importance of the Bolsa Família on Brazil's existing social welfare model, we provide a brief historical perspective on the state's approach to social protection. Brazil has a long history of federal social welfare investments, initially focused on social insurance, that date back to the 1920s.[2] The earliest social safeguards against illness and death targeted workers in particular sectors of the economy, namely, railroad workers and, later, other formal sector employees. Under Getúlio Vargas in the 1930s, Brazil's social welfare state would expand further and reflect a Bismarckian model, where formal sector workers would participate in social insurance schemes that included financing from the government, employers, and employee payroll contributions. In return, workers received generous federal pensions, health insurance, death benefits, and unemployment insurance. This corporatist model benefited formal sectors of the economy, civil servants, and the military but left out informal urban workers and rural sectors, in other words, those who were most in need of social protection by the state (Collier and Collier 1991; Huber 1996; Malloy 1979; Weyland 1996).

While the overall pension system has generally exacerbated income inequality (Hoffman 2003), the federal government did take some measures to incorporate informal workers and extend social insurance protections. Most notably, during the military period (1964–1985), the government created a non-contributory rural pension for agricultural workers, FUNRURAL. This policy represented one of the most equity-enhancing and pro-poor measures of the corporatist state (Weyland 1996, 10). While the absolute sum of these pensions is modest (typically, one monthly minimum wage), it has been one of the best social policies in directing cash assistance to families living in dire poverty (Schwarzer and Querino 2002). Subsequently, the Continuous Cash Benefit (Benefício de Prestação Continuada; BPC), a non-contributory program for elderly and severely disabled persons whose incomes per capita are less than one-quarter of a monthly minimum salary, has also gone far to assist those living in abject poverty (Medeiros, Britto, and Soares 2007, 7; citing IPEA 2006).

In addition to social insurance, federal and state authorities have made long-standing investments in the areas of health and education. While the poor are the primary consumers of health care and primary education, as they cannot afford to opt out of a public system, the Brazilian state has historically prioritized its resources in ways that are regressive and that privilege the interests of middle- and upper-class sectors (Hunter and Sugiyama 2009). Through much of the twentieth century this has meant that health care spending was dedicated disproportionately to the social insurance agency, INAMPS, where expensive contracts to hospitals and physicians reinforced the corporatist model (Arretche 2004; Weyland 1996). Federal spending in education also directed resources disproportionately to higher education as opposed to primary education, reflecting the priorities of modern state-building and the interests of elites (Hunter and Sugiyama 2009). Primary education, which is arguably the most important social investment for lifting children out of poverty and building future citizens, was left to local governments that had varying degrees of fiscal capacity to manage primary schools.

Given the need to address the shortcomings in public health and basic education, it is not surprising that the Constituent Assembly (1987–1988) took on the issue of social sector reform. After democratization, the health system would undergo profound change with the establishment of unified funding for health, called the Unified Health System (Sistema Único de Saúde), and the integration of federal services through the Ministry of Health. The education system would also see reforms, albeit more modest ones, that clarified intergovernmental responsibilities among municipal, state, and federal authorities and that reallocated federal resources to produce more equalizing funding streams to poorer states (Draibe 2004; Sugiyama 2012, 78–85). Brazil's democratic constitution laid out an impressive list of social rights and obligations for its citizens, including the right to health care and compulsory education. Yet, the heart of the challenge for Brazil has been not only to fulfill the promise of expanded access but also to offer quality schooling and health services.

The Brazilian state has spent a large share of its GDP on social benefits, whether social insurance or spending on education and health, yet most of these investments have not prioritized the needs of large segments of the poor and destitute (Hunter and Sugiyama 2009). Until the creation of the Bolsa Família, federal spending on poverty alleviation measures took piecemeal form. Small programs, particularly subsidies, were common despite the fact they are generally considered by economists to be economically inefficient (see Fiszbein and Schady 2009). For instance, the Ministry of Education had a school lunch program, the Ministry of Health had voucher programs for nutritional supplements for pregnant women and children, and the Ministry of Energy had a voucher program for the purchase of household gas. Prior to the establishment of the Ministry of Social Development and the Fight Against Hunger (MDS), the agency responsible for social assistance (the Ministry of Social Assistance) was relatively weak and underfunded. Social assistance was primarily the purview of local governments, and it was common for the

wives of governors or mayors to take on "charitable" causes as part of their responsibilities as first lady. In many instances, the distribution of private goods
(food baskets, household appliances, home-building supplies) contributed to
patron-client relations and the politics of clientelism (e.g., vote buying). The
whole field of social protection (*assistência social*) lacked a unified mandate,
direction, and governing structure.[3] As part of this picture, social work as a
profession was underdeveloped and social workers were few and far between.

The introduction of the Bolsa Família thus marks both continuity and
change within the overall federal social welfare model. On the one hand we
see continuity, as the structure of government spending and its overall regressive nature has not changed significantly (Medeiros and Souza 2015). Spending on pensions still represents the largest share of all social expenditures and
vastly outweighs other social policy priorities, for example. Budgetary information from the Ministry of Planning is illustrative. The 2012 budget called
for R$400 billion in funds for Previdência Social (pensions) whereas only
$19.3 billion (R$18.7 billion in grants) went toward the Bolsa Família (Ministério de Planejamento 2011). While the Bolsa has garnered considerable attention and its share of the budget has grown over time, its overall share of the
federal budget is relatively small and represents just 0.5 percent of GDP (*The
Economist* 2010).[4] In other words, the Bolsa Família is an "add-on" program
that has not dismantled the overall social welfare model. The need to improve
sectors such as education and health remains evident.

Without a doubt, however, the introduction of a large-scale poverty relief program represents a significant change. On a symbolic level the Bolsa
Família represented the first time that a Brazilian president made poverty relief a political priority. The Bolsa Família is strongly identified with Lula, who
made it his flagship program while he was in office. On a substantive level,
the program has brought new resources to poverty reduction and contributed
to important gains for the poor.

Several features of the program represent real innovation and are worth
previewing here. To begin with, it is the first federal program to bridge traditional sectoral divides by requiring complex coordination across ministries,
including the MDS and the ministries of education and health. In this way
the Bolsa represents a more integrated approach to poverty relief and human
capital development. Second, the federal government has emphasized that
the program is a "social right" and has promoted it as such through its publications and outreach. This is a marked departure from previous social policy
designs. Previously, social initiatives of the federal government were more
likely to fall prey to clientelist machines at the state and local levels. Poor
people were treated as clients who received benefits as "favors" in exchange
for votes on election day. Programs associated with the ministries of health

and education were typically subject to such a political dynamic (Ames 1987). With the Bolsa Família, however, an emphasis was placed on avoiding political intermediaries and building a sense of social inclusion and agency for recipients. Our research suggests that beneficiaries have internalized this message.

The Bolsa Família is designed to alleviate both short- and long-term poverty by ameliorating conditions for the poor while also building human capital to alter the intergenerational transmission of poverty. Poor and indigent families are eligible to participate if they fall below an income threshold (R$140 per capita). Mothers are typically the designated beneficiaries of a household; they receive a bank card in their name (along with a secure PIN) and are charged with meeting the "co-responsibility" requirements of the program; namely, their children must be enrolled in school and must attend school regularly (85 percent of the time), and both mothers and their children need to maintain basic health care requirements. For instance, pregnant women must have regular prenatal checkups, and it is recommended that, after birth, they breastfeed their infants. Children are required to get regular vaccines and receive checkups to ensure that they are meeting nutritional targets. Failure to comply with the conditionality requirements of the program can lead to a suspension of benefits.[5] The MDS has periodically updated its formulas and adjusted the value of the cash grants. Today, the cash sum varies according to the composition of the family—age and number of household members—and their monthly income per capita. The payments can range from R$32 to R$306 depending on family profiles.[6] In 2015 the average benefit was R$167 (Gazola Hellman 2015).

The Bolsa has expanded considerably since its initial introduction. In December 2003 there were 3.8 million families (15.7 million individuals) in the program, and by 2006 the number of families had nearly tripled (Lindert et al. 2007, 18). During the presidential campaign of 2010, both Dilma Rousseff (PT) and José Serra (Partido da Social Democracia Brasileira; PSDB) promised to keep the program in place. Since Rouseff's inauguration, the program has continued to expand and now reaches over one-quarter of the total Brazilian population. Much of the expansion has focused on a new effort—Brasil Sem Miséria (Brazil Without Extreme Poverty)—to improve targeting, resources, and services for families living in extreme poverty. Thus, Brasil Sem Miséria focuses on families with monthly incomes per capita below R$70. The Brazilian government estimates that 16.27 million Brazilians find themselves in conditions of extreme poverty (Falcão and Viera da Costa 2014, 88).

While the concept behind CCT programs is fairly straightforward, the program is administratively complex to deliver.[7] The Bolsa requires seamless coordination between local and federal authorities. This is a major feat, given Brazil's decentralized governance structure (over fifty-five hundred auton- omous municipalities), local governments' uneven administrative capacity, and the country's unequal regional development. For beneficiaries, local gov- ernments are important because they are the "gateway" (*porta da entrada*) into the program. Applicants must apply at locally administered offices where municipal personnel enter their family's data into a federal database. The doc- umentation requirements for application are fairly extensive. Mothers need to present several legal documents for themselves, including a state issued identity card (Registro Geral; RG), and a federally issued taxpayer identifica- tion card (Cadastro de Pessoas Físicas; CPF) or voter registration card (Título de Eleitor).[8] They also need to present birth certificates for all their children. Local street-level bureaucrats are responsible for monitoring compliance with beneficiaries' co-responsibility requirements. Applicants to the Bolsa present their information to local authorities, who in turn enter data into a *Cadastro Único* (or unified registry). The Cadastro is a vast database with information on all program applicants and is designed to reduce "slippage" and duplica- tion of benefits. The MDS established the Cadastro in an effort to safeguard the program's resources (Lindert 2007). Once all the local information is sub- mitted, the MDS determines entry into the program. Federal authorities take into account information on poverty by municipality and family data in order to target resources accurately. Along with information on each family's need, federal authorities utilize census poverty maps in order to establish municipal quotas and to target resources accurately (Barros et al. 2010).

The Bolsa Família has generated considerable interest among scholars given its high political visibility, size and scope, and its beneficiaries' poten- tial to sway elections. After all, with compulsory voting the large numbers of *bolsistas* have the potential to turn electoral outcomes. Most research has focused on the program's effects in presidential politics and has documented the electoral rewards that Lula enjoyed in his reelection as a result of the pro- gram (Fried 2012; Hunter and Power 2007; Licio et al. 2009; Zucco 2008). A few others, including Fenwick (2009) and Montero (2010) have also explored the connections between the national program and gubernatorial elections. Our research has focused on the perspectives of the poor themselves and how they view the program, interact with the state, and experience empowerment. One line of inquiry examines whether the Bolsa renders the poor more vul- nerable to local clientelism, such as vote buying, or has the capacity to build citizenship (Sugiyama and Hunter 2013; Hunter and Sugiyama 2014). Our findings based on case studies in the Northeast suggest that the Bolsa Família has remained remarkably insulated from subnational political malfeasance, thus representing a significant departure from other historic examples of federal poverty relief, which frequently became enmeshed in local patronage networks.

Positive Outcomes Associated with the Bolsa Família

There are many positive outcomes known about the Bolsa Família and several shortcomings and limitations. Some of the results or "dependent variables" involve "hard" or objective and fairly readily quantifiable measures. Other dependent variables are of crucial importance but fall into less clear-cut or easily measurable categories. These involve perceptions and norms held by Bolsa Família recipients about the program and its contributions to broadening people's sense of social inclusion and political autonomy. In addition to the positive contributions and limitations of the program, there are numerous unknowns. Time will bring forth evidence on these matters.

Below we survey the results on select dimensions. Our goal is to report the major findings on these outcomes. There are numerous debates on the "hard" outcomes, many of which revolve around methodological issues. Analysts with much more technical knowledge than we have are better equipped to sort out the controversies on such outcomes. Our main contribution rests in examining and analyzing some of the more sociological outcomes, those related to questions/feelings of social inclusion, political autonomy, and self-worth among beneficiaries.

Two cautionary notes are in order before proceeding. Because the program did not roll out from scratch (several transfers had been implemented independently and were folded together) there is no ready longitudinal comparison ("before" vs. "after") to be made in evaluating the program's effects. Furthermore, because it rolled out relatively quickly, the situation did not lend itself to making hard and fast cross-sectional comparisons—that is, controlled comparisons between people enrolled in the program vs. those not enrolled.

Poverty Reduction

Brazil has made significant strides in poverty reduction in recent years. According to Soares (2012, 21), in the last decade and a half the percentage of the population in poverty fell from 26 to 14 percent, and the numbers in extreme poverty decreased from 10 to 5 percent, with the most significant drop being from 2003 to 2009. In the Northeast, the poorest area of the country, where the Bolsa Família (along with Brazil's noncontributory pension program) has penetrated the most, poverty fell from 40 to 22 percent over the same years (cited in Hall 2012). Similarly, a study by the Fundação Getúlio Vargas shows that the number of Brazilians with incomes below the equivalent of $440 a month has fallen more than 8 percent a year since 2003 (*The Economist* 2010). According to an MDS analysis, poverty has declined substantially from nearly 24 percent in 2003 to less than 10 percent in 2011 (Souza and Osório 2013). Extreme poverty itself has also declined, from 8 percent in 2003 to 3.4 percent of the population in 2011.

Without a doubt, the Bolsa Família has contributed significantly to the reduction of absolute poverty among those Brazilians in the lowest income rungs. Given that income from the program can make up the single largest income stream among families in situations of extreme poverty, it is hard to imagine that the Bolsa, known for its broad coverage, would not have had that result. The question remains, however, what role or part that income from the Bolsa Família has played in this trend. Notable increases in the minimum wage, the expansion of the Brazilian economy in the first decade of the twenty-first century (in no small part due to the commodities boom, which had positive repercussions on the north and northeast regions), and the increased formalization of the workforce have also contributed to decreasing poverty rates. Studies do suggest, however, that the Bolsa Família has played a notable part in absolute poverty reduction. For example, Soares, Souza, Osório, and Silveira (2010) show that the Bolsa Família, in one decade, was responsible for a 16 percent and 33 percent fall in poverty and extreme poverty, respectively. Similarly, a study by the Fundação Getúlio Vargas estimates that about one-sixth of the poverty reduction experienced by Brazilians since 2003 can be attributed to the Bolsa Família (*The Economist* 2010).

Inequality Reduction

Alongside reductions in poverty, income inequality has been decreasing in Brazil for somewhat over a decade. While inequality levels in Brazil remain among the highest of any country in the world, the Gini coefficient has fallen steadily. For example, in Brazil's major cities alone, the Gini coefficient fell by 7.6 percent to 0.534 from 2002 to 2009 (Hall 2012; citing IPEA 2009 study). According to Soares and Silva (2010) the Bolsa Família was responsible for a 16 percent fall in inequality that took place between 1999 and 2009. The high coverage and unusually accurate targeting of the program explains this good performance. In a different cut at the problem, which captures an earlier time period, Soares, Ribas, and Osório (2010) begin with the finding that the Gini index for Brazil fell by 4.7 percent from 1995 to 2004. They estimate that the Bolsa Família (and its predecessor programs) were responsible for 21 percent of that fall (before 1995 there were no federal CCT programs in Brazil, so there is confidence that 1995 is a baseline year).

School Enrollment and Attendance

School enrollment and attendance have also increased in Brazil, and the Bolsa Família has exerted some positive impact on these results, although scholars differ in their assessments of the program's role. A major longitudinal study by the International Food Policy Research Institute (IFPRI) shows higher school attendance (4.5 percentage points) by beneficiary children (in an aggregate sample of children aged from six to seventeen years) compared with nonbeneficiary children (Gilligan and Fruttero 2011). The positive effects of the Bolsa Família program on school attendance and enrollment rise markedly when looking at the Northeast alone and when separating out older children. In the IFPRI study, among children of that age group, the impact in the Northeast was that the Bolsa Família lifted enrollment by 11.7 percentage points.[9]

Clearly, the Bolsa has larger effects on keeping children in school after age fourteen. For example, girls in rural areas of the age cohort from fifteen to seventeen are 22.5 percentage points more likely to attend school if their family receives the grant (De Brauw et al. 2015, 313). Similarly, the grant slows the entry of boys into the labor market by one and a half years (Gilligan and Fruttero 2011). The same researchers found that Bolsa Família increased school participation among boys aged from fifteen to seventeen (Gilligan and Fruttero 2011, 311). The fact that CCTs typically exert more impact among older children is due not only to baseline attendance rates being higher at the lower grades but also the diminished control that parents tend to have over them (absent the monetary incentive of staying in school) and the greater income possibilities that older children have (compared to their younger counterparts) in the labor market.

Child Labor

The jury is still out on how much the Bolsa Família has reduced child labor. Needless to say, since the informal sector is where most children work, it is exceedingly difficult to document who is working and how many hours they are putting in. This is especially true given the rural areas where most child labor takes place. The most conservative and cautious assessment is that the grant program has decreased but by no means eliminated child labor. This is partly because attending school for four hours a day does not preclude working in the remaining hours. One study by the Brazilian census bureau (Instituto Brasileiro de Geografia e Estatística; IBGE) estimates that between 2009 and 2011, the number of children who worked fell by 14 percent. That same report, however, estimates that there are still 3.7 million child workers in the country between the ages of five and seventeen, with male youth being the most at risk. Roughly seven hundred thousand are thought to be under fourteen years of age, which is the legal cutoff point for child labor in Brazil. At least two-thirds of all children and youth who are deemed to work unacceptably long hours and/or in worrisome conditions do so in agricultural activities (as cited in *Economia-IG* 2012).

Nutrition

The Brazilian Institute for Social and Economic Analysis (Instituto Brasileiro de Análises Sociais e Econômicas; IBASE), a leading nongovernmental organization, has found that the Bolsa Família program has contributed to notable improvements in nutrition (IBASE 2008). In one study, the body mass index was significantly better among beneficiary children than poor nonbeneficiary children (Soares 2011). In another study, children from families who received the Bolsa were considerably more likely to have normal height and weight for their age than those from low-income nonbeneficiary families. The result pertains for children after the first twelve months of life (Paes-Sousa, Santos, and Miazaki 2011). These outcomes no doubt reflect a broader shift in consumption patterns among beneficiary households. Although the Bolsa Família does not seem to have significantly affected aggregate levels of household consumption, it has increased expenditures notably on food, education, and children's clothing (Soares, Ribas, and Osório 2010).

We also know that rural malnutrition among children under five in the arid parts of the Northeast has dropped from 16 percent to under 5 percent since 1996 (*The Economist* 2010). Food purchased from income coming from the Bolsa Família has probably played a part in this. Nonetheless, some of the physical effects of malnutrition are still disturbingly evident among young children even in beneficiary families (Soares, Ribas, and Osório 2010). One hypothesis about this concerns the failure to monitor children's growth through regular visits to a health center, even though such visits are a condition of the program. As with vaccinations, health facilities are a requirement for the program to work as it should, but they are not always available. Needless to say, the program cannot function well independent of investments in other areas.

Health

Evidence is somewhat mixed on health outcomes. An IFPRI study found that the Bolsa Família increased the use of prenatal care somewhat (1.5 visits on average) on the part of pregnant mothers (Gilligan and Fruttero 2011). In addition, the program has increased the likelihood (by 12–15 percentage points) that a child in a beneficiary family will receive all seven required vaccinations by six months of age (Gilligan and Fruttero 2011). There is also evidence of improvement in the form of longer gestations and less premature births, 14.1 percentage points higher for beneficiary pregnant women than nonbeneficiary ones (Tapajós et al. 2010; as discussed in Soares 2011). A nationwide analysis of under-five (years of age) mortality found that deaths attributable to poverty-related causes such as malnutrition and diarrhea decreased as Bolsa Família coverage increased (Rasella et al. 2013). Yet on some health outcomes, studies have found less improvement than one might expect given how much the MDS has advertised the need to engage in preventive health care and make use of Brazil's public health care system (Soares, Ribas, and Osório 2010). Similar to what is suspected about why so much malnutrition still goes undetected, many analysts think the lack of a greater impact suggests that supply-side deficiencies (an insufficient number of clinics and health professionals) might constitute an important constraint.

State Modernization and Citizenship Building through the Unified Registry and the Provision of Identity Documents

In many countries, including Brazil, the introduction of a CCT was accompanied by the implementation of a single national registry (the Cadastro Único) charged with collecting information on the socioeconomic characteristics of low-income people, in order to know where risk and vulnerability reside. In addition to facilitating the identification of beneficiaries and helping to monitor the conditions of the poor, the goal is to reduce duplication and fraud and increase efficiency. The analysis of Cadastro Único data should allow technocrats to design better policies and programs for at-risk populations. Inclusion in the Single Registry does not imply entitlement to the Bolsa Família. There is a quota by municipality and it is the MDS that runs the selection process, calculating the per capita income within the family, which includes household income, pension benefits, and other earnings.

In order to gain registration in the Cadastro Único, applicants provide essential documents that are markers of citizenship. The Bolsa Família has provided an incentive for low-income Brazilians to acquire identity documents, beginning with a birth certificate. Participation in the program requires that the central beneficiary, typically the mother of the family, present an identifying state document, the RG, and one of two federal identification documents, either the CPF or a voter identification card. Additionally, all the children need to have birth certificates. Aside from being necessary to apply for the Bolsa, document acquisition will enable poor Brazilians to gain access to other social programs and government benefits, including the BPC, the country's non-contributory pension for old age and disability. In short, identity documents are a foundation of citizenship. As development practitioners note, lack of proper documentation is one of the most important barriers the poor encounter in the exercise of citizenship rights (Harbitz and Tamargo 2009). Although having identity documents always increased the life chances of an individual, until the Bolsa provided an immediate concrete cash incentive to acquire them, many poor Brazilians did not surmount the (numerous) obstacles to getting them, foremost among these being cost and time. Likewise, until the demand for documents became pressing, the Brazilian state did little to facilitate the supply. The introduction of the Bolsa thus put into motion an increased demand, which has been met by greater supply (Hunter and Sugiyama forthcoming).

A study by Inter-American Development Bank consultants Wong and Turra (2007) and our numerous interviews with federal Bolsa Família administrators and municipal directors from fieldwork conducted in 2009 and 2011 suggest the role of the CCT in bringing about this positive outcome. Wong and Turra attempted to ascertain the effect of the Bolsa Família on the level of birth registration through an indirect measure. For the year 2006, the year that the program expanded significantly in Brazil, the authors compared the present age of Bolsa Família registrants in the North to the age they were when they first received their birth certificate. Of those program beneficiaries who were five years old or older, only 21.7 percent had received their birth certificate in their first year of life (a time when the program had not yet been rolled out). By comparison, 39.6 percent had received it after their fourth birthday. This can be interpreted as a group that probably obtained the birth certificate specifically for the purpose of enrolling in the Bolsa Família. Wong and Turra also recorded in the year 2006 how long different age cohorts within the population of Bolsa recipients in the north region had a birth certificate. The question posed to beneficiaries in the year 2006 was How long have you had a birth certificate? For those in the four-to-five-year age cohort, 7.3 percent had a birth certificate for one year or less, suggesting the relevance of the Bolsa as an impetus to late registration.

Interviews we carried out with federal administrators and local Bolsa Família coordinators on two fieldwork trips in the Northeast (in 2009 and 2011) revealed further the crucial linkages between the program and the provisioning of documents. Once it became apparent that low-levels of document possession, particularly the birth certificate, would be a challenge for Bolsa applicants, other federal agencies, notably the Ministry of Justice, stepped up their registration campaigns in remote regions underserved by notary publics or *cartórios* (Garrido 2011). The Bolsa Família program not only spurred federal agencies but also local governments into action. Since registration for the Cadastro Único takes place at the municipal level, local administrators bear the brunt of day-to-day challenges that applicants encounter. All of the municipal Bolsa Família coordinators we spoke to acknowledged that the presentation of basic documents poses a real challenge for the poor. For this reason, one of the frequent duties for social workers is to provide the poor with information on how to acquire them (Centro de Referência de Assistência Social 2011).

In sum, the Bolsa Família program motivated registration for essential documents in several ways. With application requirements that demand the presentation of numerous documents, the lacuna in legally identifying documentation emerged as a considerable challenge for effective targeting. At the same time, the poor had a very concrete incentive to obtain these documents. The program is well known and is often the catalyst for the poor to seek out services (Cordeiro 2011). Federal agencies and Bolsa Família's street-level bureaucrats have made considerable efforts to address the long-standing barriers that have hindered the poor's ability to fully realize their citizenship rights.

Gender Empowerment

One of the common questions asked in the CCT literature concerns the effect of cash transfers on women's autonomy and empowerment. Most CCTs target grants to mothers. In 2010, for example, 92.5 percent of all Bolsa Família beneficiaries were women (Constanzi and Fagundes 2010, 267). The general assumption is that CCTs empower women. On the one hand, it stands to reason that targeting the grants to mothers gives women a degree of autonomy and power—from their male partners and from local politicians—that they would not otherwise have. On the other hand, there are major questions that remain. Even apart from the notion that CCTs reinforce gender stereotypes, what prevents men in the household from appropriating the Bolsa Família funds? Does the grant fundamentally alter a male-dominated power dynamic? And who in the family takes the children to schools and health clinics and meets the other conditions? More research needs to be done to ascertain whether the Bolsa Família empowers women. Like most of the outcomes assessed, it probably does under some conditions and not others, and among some groups of women and not others. Here we report some preliminary findings.

Walquiria Leão Rego and Alessandro Pinzani's recent qualitative study of female Bolsa Família beneficiaries in the poorest regions of Brazil (in the states of Minas Gerais, Alagoas, Piauí, Maranhão, and Recife) captured the effects of the program on their lives (2013). Through a series of interviews carried out between 2006 and 2011, the authors find the grant had effects that went far beyond their monetary value. Women gained a sense of liberty, autonomy, and dignity. The result was that the program empowered women who previously felt "invisible." These findings are similar to those by Hunter and Sugiyama (2014) who observed that the Bolsa Família increases feelings of agency despite stringent conditionality requirements.

One important recent finding from the IFPRI survey is that participation in the Bolsa Família increases the share of women who report exclusive control over contraception by 10 points (De Brauw et al. 2014). This result was especially marked in urban areas (some rural areas did not show the result at all). It also seems that when a woman's initial status is lower than that of her male partner (measured by comparing their respective educational levels), the impact of the Bolsa is greatest in boosting her autonomy over contraceptive choices. The same IFPRI study found that (especially in urban areas), women reported greater autonomy in making decisions about household purchases that affect the children and the household, including consumer durable items. Brandão, Dalt, and Gouvêa (2008) noted that beneficiary mothers reported an elevated sense of status due to their new source of regular income and newfound status as consumers. They enjoy better credit for consumption in the local markets and are no longer in as much debt with local shopkeepers, thereby experiencing liberation from all the negatives that the historic situation of indebtedness brings with it. A four-community study by Suárez and Libardoni (2008) finds the Bolsa Família to be important for bringing rural women out of social isolation and their interacting more frequently with teachers, nurses, and social workers, all part of the state network necessary to run the program. Coming out of isolation and interacting with service providers is regarded as a positive step for the integration of the poor over time. The authors report some evidence for lower rates of domestic violence with the income streams going to mothers. As with the IFPRI study, the authors see an enhanced status of women in the family as a result of the program and yet reserve judgment about the degree of change that has taken place.

Social Inclusion and Political Autonomy

Beyond the material gains that poor Brazilians have experienced as a result of the Bolsa Família are less tangible advances. Our own fieldwork in three locations in Brazil's Northeast—two municipalities in Pernambuco and one in Bahia—suggests that many Bolsa recipients have subjectively felt more socially included as well as more autonomous from local patronage networks as a result of the program. The details of our fieldwork and associated findings are reported elsewhere (Hunter and Sugiyama 2014; Sugiyama and Hunter 2013). Here we report some of the highlights on both dimensions.

Studies of the welfare state in western Europe and the United States often underscore the importance of building a sense of social inclusion among poor people who have long lived on the margins. If their integration is important for a country's economic ascent and for the legitimacy of its democracy they cannot continue to feel ignored and excluded. The design of social protection programs, the discourse that surrounds them, and how street-level bureaucrats interact with those enrolled in them influence greatly how low-income individuals view themselves as well as their government. Notably, two key features of the Bolsa Família—that it is means tested and that it subjects recipients to conditions and monitoring—might be expected to have stigmatizing effects that would militate against feelings of enhanced social inclusion. Interestingly, however, we did not pick up such a reaction among the people we surveyed (fourteen hundred individuals) or in the eleven focus groups we contracted. When asked whether they were proud or ashamed (or neither) to be recipients of the program, the overwhelming majority reported being either proud (75 percent) or neutral (18.8 percent). Very few people reported any feelings of stigma (1.6 percent). In an open-ended question about the origins of the program, most people noted the personal background of Lula—a hardscrabble childhood in Brazil's Northeast—and his outreach to them through the Bolsa Família as a meaningful bridge to the government. One elderly man even exclaimed that until Lula came along and promised all Brazilians three meals a day (and ultimately delivered on the promise) he never believed in the country's democracy. With faith restored (or created for the first time) presumably he will become a more participatory and engaged citizen. As for the subjective effects of the conditionalities, we heard almost no one discuss them as suggestive of paternalism or government heavy handedness. Perhaps the persistent efforts of the MDS to describe the program as a right (for everyone who qualifies) influence this result. It is also the case that the failure to carry out the conditionalities tends to be seen by program administrators less as a reason to cut off a family immediately (there are four steps that precede a definitive termination) and more as a red flag that something is awry on the home front that is preventing a family from rising to the occasion. Social workers from the CRAS network are charged with investigating why a family is falling between the cracks (Centro de Referência de Assistência Social 2011)

As for enhancing people's sense of political autonomy, our fieldwork suggests that the Bolsa Família has largely avoided the clientelistic games that are often entailed in municipal co-administration of a large federal program. Whereas most people believe there is vote buying in their city (65 percent) and more than one-quarter report receiving a vote-buying offer in the last election (28.3 percent), only 14.9 percent thought that the Bolsa Família was used for vote buying (Sugiyama and Hunter 2013). As a result, people feel less subject to the "favors" of local politicians and the perceived need to trade votes to obtain these goodies. We credit the MDS's commitment to a rights-based social policy, thoughtful policy design (namely, the direct transfer of funds to recipients and the provision of bureaucratic mechanisms for solving problems instead of having people work through political brokers), and strong technocratic capacity as important in structuring social provisioning in ways that have avoided shenanigans and empowered ordinary citizens. The Bolsa is a prime example of how institutions can work toward "good government." Whereas many people we polled admitted that the age-old practice of "selling their vote" is alive and well in many parts of the Northeast, the Bolsa remains outside of the trading currency. In other words, it is unavailable to local politicians seeking to use state resources to attract votes.

We are convinced that the beginnings of a rights-based understanding of social policy is underway and, with it, the political liberation from local patronage machines. If the Bolsa Família continues to be implemented in a strict bureaucratic fashion using clear eligibility criteria, and if it continues to keep funds out of the subnational political channels, it may well help free poor Brazilians from thinking that securing social assistance depends on supporting local political machines. This can only be a step in the right direction if Brazil is to become a more programmatically based democracy.

Shortcomings and Limitations of the Bolsa Família

As part of the human development aspirations of the Bolsa Família, program conditionalities stimulate demand for health and education facilities. The hope of many educators and health professionals was that the program would stimulate a greater supply of services in these sectors, and also services of higher quality. So far, there is no evidence that either quantity or quality has improved as a result of the Bolsa Família program.

As long as schools are available to attend and if monitoring prevails, it stands to reason that the Bolsa Família program should induce more young people into school. Yet higher attendance rates say nothing about whether more learning takes place, which would require indicators that measure the quality of the education the students receive. Also, attending school also does not necessarily mean advancing in school. In fact, one study reported that children benefiting from the Bolsa Família are almost 4 percentage points more likely than nonbeneficiary children to fail to advance in school (Soares, Ribas, and Osório 2010). This should not come as a surprise since many such students have been out of school for a while (or have never attended). Hence, they are likely to have difficulty keeping up with those who have had more consistent and regular attendance. Even if this is true, however, children who have been induced into school through the Bolsa Família program are probably learning more than they would be doing otherwise.

Finally, we see missed opportunities in the program design to work with

Bolsa Família mothers to improve their life chances and human capital development. In many ways, the Bolsa conforms to the conventional wisdom in the development literature that shows that directing resources to mothers, as opposed to fathers, better ensures that resources make it to their children. Not only do mothers tend to prioritize their children's basic needs when making household spending decisions, they also are more likely to have primary custody of their children. Thus, mothers are in a better position to monitor their children's educational attendance and comply with the various health requirements of the program. As Molyneux notes (2006) mothers in CCTs often appear to be instruments of the state's development project. Brazil's CCT focuses conditionality almost entirely on the welfare of children and has not sought to leverage access to mothers or parents to further the life prospects for adults or empower women.[10] Mothers in the Bolsa Família program are relatively young. In 2010, nearly half (47.3 percent) were under thirty-four years of age (Constanzi and Fagundes 2010, 267). As a group, their levels of educational attainment were very low; 12.3 percent were illiterate and 65.1 percent had not completed their basic primary schooling. The educational profile of beneficiaries is particularly troublesome if one considers the prospects for parents once their children leave the household and age out of eligibility for the cash grant. All to say, the Bolsa's near exclusive focus on the next generation misses an opportunity to develop complementary policy initiatives—such as literacy courses and educational training—that can result in the more immediate advancement for women. Clearly, not only federal designers understand this issue. The closer one gets to the ground, the more evident it becomes that unless they are given some rudimentary job skills or vocational training, women beneficiaries will be vulnerable to falling into (perhaps even greater) poverty when their children leave the house and their Bolsa checks either diminish greatly or stop coming altogether (Suárez and Libardoni 2008).

Unknowns
Potential Trade-Offs

Another potential drawback of the popularity of social assistance programs like the Bolsa Família concerns the trade-offs entailed. Highly targeted cash transfers typically cost less money, are easier to pass politically, and pack a more immediate electoral punch than structural reforms in sectors like education and health, which frequently stir up powerful interests like provider unions. Is the Bolsa Famíia crowding out spending in traditional ministries like education and health, where fundamental quality-enhancing reforms would have a far greater chance of lifting the life prospects of poor children? Anthony Hall raised this potential problem several years ago (2008) as well as more recently (2012). In 2008 he wrote of early signs that the Bolsa "may be contributing to a reduction in social spending in key sectors such as education, housing and basic sanitation, possibly undermining the country's future social and economic development" (Hall 2008, 799). More recently, he referred to research on social spending in Brazil that suggests that the rise in non-contributory social welfare schemes has been accompanied by falling per capita investment in several key social sectors at all levels of government (2012, 36). How would we determine if the Bolsa's advance is taking place at the cost of funds spent elsewhere? A first (rough) cut into the issue would be to examine whether expenditures for other purposes fall as spending on the Bolsa rises. An examination of the trajectory of federal social spending between 1995 and 2010 does not suggest an inverse relationship between social assistance, which includes the BPC and the Bolsa, and spending on other key social ministries, although admittedly education rises more than health. Education, health, and housing rise over this period, albeit not as steeply as spending on social assistance (Castro et al. 2012, table 1). They increase as a percentage of social spending and of the gross national product and in absolute terms. It could be, however, that they might have experienced higher increases in the absence of the Bolsa's tremendous appeal. A closer look at how the new allowances are being spent in those ministries—whether on regressive or progressive purposes—is also in order. It would be lamentable if funds allocated to the Bolsa were used to cover the poor while spending in the traditional social ministries focused disproportionately on higher income sectors. In any event, without further investigation, it is difficult to know how federal social spending would have evolved in the absence of the Bolsa Família.

Future Life Prospects

While federal officials have designed a well-regarded CCT program, there are important questions that have yet to be answered. First among them is the question What is the exit strategy for families? In other words, how long will families remain in the program and what happens to families in the long term? We need to know what becomes of adult recipients when their children leave home and their presence no longer "counts" toward the income formulas for the grants. As the program has prioritized children and their human capital development, what will become of the parents? Given that most of the investments and conditionality requirements have focused on the children, we should be concerned with the prospects of poor women. Will they be able to enter into an increasingly competitive labor market that increasingly demands high skills of its workforce? Or will the market render them future dependents of their children? Time will tell.

Conclusion

We conclude that the Bolsa Família represents a step forward for a country whose welfare state long excluded the poorest of the poor, those in the informal sector who had not been among those in the occupational categories privileged by the Vargas era labor reforms. The story of the Bolsa Família is that of a steady gradual advance that has proceeded one step at a time. From the inception of the Bolsa Escola to the improvements made over time with the Bolsa Família, incremental learning and piecemeal adaptations have marked the CCT's evolution. Although the Bolsa Família represents an "add-on" to a configuration of social policies marked by the endurance of many highly regressive features, it is nonetheless part of a broader move to recognize and incorporate the truly destitute and marginal. It has not only brought such people into more routine and formalized contact with the Brazilian state but also made them feel more socially included and independent of local political networks. In short, such people are closer to enjoying the benefits of citizenship than before. What we have witnessed is the steady upward direction of the policy's march, which conforms to the image of progress in Brazil occurring one step at a time instead of by leaps and bounds. The economic downturn and need for fiscal austerity will likely lead to greater scrutiny of poverty alleviation spending, even though the Bolsa is a relatively inexpensive program when compared to other social spending. In a highly charged political scenario, programs that operate effectively and that can demonstrate positive outcomes like the Bolsa Família may indeed weather the storm.

7

Anthony W. Pereira

Progress or Perdition?

Brazil's National Truth
Commission in Comparative
Perspective

The error of the dictatorship was to torture and not kill.
— Federal deputy Jair Bolsonaro, August 7, 2008

The government's project for the Truth Commission could disappoint
many who hope it will deliver the definitive gesture against the coup-
mongering [golpista] sectors of society. Nonetheless, the commission is
an undeniable step forward.
— Gabriel Landi Fazzio, September 24, 2011

We look to the future. We don't look in the rear view mirror.
— Adhemar da Costa Machado Filho, March 15, 2012

ON DECEMBER 10, 2014, the Brazilian National Truth Commission (NTC)
issued its report, the result of two and a half years of investigation. Its formal
brief was to research the state's responsibility for grave human rights violations
from September 18, 1946, to October 5, 1988, although its principal focus was
the dictatorship from 1964 to 1985. The commission heard the testimony of
1,116 witnesses and produced a three-volume report consisting of 1,193 pages.
The report, part of a process of transitional justice that began in the early
1990s, identifies 434 people who were killed by the dictatorship (including
210 disappeared).

The report reaches two main conclusions. These are that the violations of
human rights under the dictatorship were the result of state policy, and that

the 377 perpetrators of human violations named in the report (or at least the 191 of them who were still alive) should not benefit from the Amnesty Law and should be held responsible in a criminal, civil, and administrative sense. The report, signed by all six members of the commission, also made twenty-nine recommendations, most of which were aimed at curbing contemporary human rights violations (Comissão Nacional da Verdade 2014).

How does the NTC report compare with others released in Latin America over the last three decades? Does the NTC represent a break with the prior pattern of Brazilian transitional justice? And what are the implications of its work? The Brazilian case is important because the country is an outlier in a region that has seen the most transitional justice activity in the world since the late 1970s. Latin America innovated in the use of, although it did not invent, the truth commission, and has been the location of more than half of the domestic human rights trials in the world since 1980 (Sikkink 2011, 22–23, 139). The Truth Commission is also a potent illustration of a major theme of the current volume, that is, the deep divisions in Brazil's democracy. Loathed by its critics as a waste of time and money, seen by many of its supporters as too long delayed and not vigorous enough, the NTC provoked strong feelings and revealed the extent of polarization within Brazil's political system.

The chapter proceeds as follows. First, it summarizes some of the important characteristics of the transitional justice process in Brazil, and the role of the NTC in that process. This section emphasizes the distinctiveness of the Brazilian approach to transitional justice compared to that of others in Latin America, and the extent to which the NTC can be seen as representing either continuity or a break with the prior pattern. The second section argues that two factors weigh heavily in accounting for the combination of continuity and change found in the Brazilian case: the conservative and gradualist regime transition of the late 1970s and 1980s, and the transnational pressures in favor of transitional justice in the 1990s and 2000s.

The implications of the Brazilian NTC are discussed in section three. This section examines the approach of Sikkink (2011), who argues that the significance of the NTC lies primarily in whether it can provide a springboard to a criminal trial or trials of perpetrators in Brazil, and that the lack of trials up to now helps explain the relatively high levels of state violence in Brazil's democracy. Assessing the impact of the NTC's work in terms of trials is questionable, given the level of violence and human rights abuses in democratic Brazil. Furthermore, the section argues that the data used by Sikkink in her statistical analysis is of insufficient quality to draw the inferences that she draws from them. The chapter concludes by suggesting some alternative ways of thinking about potential impacts of the NTC, including the implementation of some of the reforms recommended in the report.

The NTC and Brazilian Transitional Justice

Transitional justice, in the words of Paul van Zyl, represents "an attempt to build a sustainable peace after conflict, mass violence, or systematic human rights abuse" (Van Zyl 2011, 45). Transitional justice usually refers to attempts made during or quite soon after the transition from an authoritarian regime to a democratic regime, or from war to peace, although there is some debate in the literature as to how to delimit this transitional period. Common mechanisms of transitional justice include trials of perpetrators of human rights abuses, truth commissions to investigate the past, and reparations programs to compensate victims and family members of victims (Minow 1998). These mechanisms represent an attempt "to establish a moral and political break with a repressive, non-democratic past" (Barahona de Brito 2011, 22).

During the transition away from authoritarian rule in Brazil, unlike in Argentina and Chile, transitional justice was not on the political agenda. The general amnesty passed during the dictatorship (Law Number 6,683 of August 28, 1979) was upheld. Brazil adopted what Sikkink calls the "impunity model" (Sikkink 2011, 13). Informal discussions among Brazilian politicians ensured that during the first civilian government after military rule — that of President José Sarney (1985–1990) — no transitional justice institutions were established. In Argentina, in contrast, there were trials, a truth commission, and reparations, while in Chile there was a truth commission and reparations.

This pattern changed in 1991, when a committee was created in the lower house of Congress to monitor the identification of political prisoners' remains discovered in the Perus cemetery in São Paulo (Meyer 2012, 256). In subsequent years, reparations in Brazil came in two waves. In 1995 the Cardoso government created the Special Commission on the Politically Killed and Disappeared (Pereira 2000, 227). This commission was originally housed in the Ministry of Justice but now resides in the Ministry of Women, Racial Equality, and Human Rights. The commission responded to requests from family members, examined the cases of several hundred persons killed or disappeared during the dictatorship, ruled that the state was responsible for many of these, and awarded compensation to family members in those cases.

The Amnesty Commission in the Ministry of Justice, created in 2001, operated on a much wider basis than the previous commission.[1] It responded to the claims of people who had lost their jobs, been tortured, gone into exile, been persecuted, or in other ways suffered under the repression by the authoritarian regime. It eventually created an archive of seventy thousand cases and paid billions of reais in compensation, in one of the biggest reparations schemes in the world. Its opponents called these payments "bolsa ditadura" (the dictatorship allowance, with a reference to Bolsa Família, the conditional

Table 7.1. Chronology of Main Transitional Justice Events in Brazil, 1964–2014	
Year	*Event*
1964	A military coup d'état installs a dictatorship in Brazil.
1968	The military regime decrees its Fifth Institutional Act, ushering in the most repressive period of the dictatorship.
1974	President Geisel announces a "slow, gradual and sure" liberalization.
1979	The Fifth Institutional Act is repealed.
1979	Congress approves an amnesty that frees political prisoners (except those convicted of "blood crimes"), allows the return of political exiles, and creates impunity for state agents suspected of violations of human rights.
1982	Direct elections for governors take place.
1985	Civilian politician Tancredo Neves is indirectly elected president, in Congress, signaling the end of the dictatorship.
1985	Congress approves an amnesty for those political prisoners convicted of "blood crimes."
1985	The Archdiocese of São Paulo publishes *Brasil: Nunca Mais* (Brazil: Never Again), a report on the use of torture by the dictatorship.
1988	Congress approves a new constitution.
1989	Brazilians vote in the first direct presidential elections since 1960.
1991	The lower house of Congress establishes a committee (*comissão externa*) to monitor the search for remains in the Perus cemetery in São Paulo.
1992	Families of victims begin to gain access to the archives of the political police, the DEOPS, in several states.
1995	The Special Commission on the Politically Killed and Disappeared is created. It subsequently evaluates several hundred cases, compensating the families of those victims judged to have died as a result of state action during the dictatorship.
2001	The Amnesty Commission is created. In the ensuing years, it examines thousands of cases of human rights violations, including cases of torture and unfair dismissal from employment, creating an archive documenting the dictatorship's repression.
2010	Brazil's Supreme Court upholds the 1979 Amnesty Law, by a vote of 7–2.
2010	In Gomes vs. Lund, the Inter-American Court of Human Rights rules that Brazil's 1979 Amnesty Law is incompatible with the American Convention on Human Rights, which Brazil has signed. In the court judgment of the case, brought by family members of guerrillas disappeared in Araguaia, the judges ruled that Brazil had violated the family members' right to information (article 13), its duty to investigate (article 8), and the plaintiffs' right to access to a court (article 25).
2011	Legislation to create the National Truth Commission is passed by Congress and signed by President Dilma Rousseff.
2012	The National Truth Commission is created.
2014	The National Truth Commission releases its report, in December.

Table 7.2. A Comparison of Some Truth Commissions in Latin America

Country	Period Investigated	Number of Years Investigated	Year of Publication of Report	Years between the Date of Publication and the Period Investigated
Argentina	1976–1983	7	1985	2
Brazil	1946–1988	42	2014	26
Chile	1973–1990	17	1991	1
El Salvador	1980–1991	11	1993	2
Guatemala	1962–1996	34	1999	3
Haiti	1991–1994	3	1996	2
Panama	1968–1989	21	2002	13
Paraguay	1954–2003	49	2008	5
Peru	1980–2000	20	2003	3
Uruguay	1973–1982	9	1985	3

Note: In the Guatemalan case, there were two truth commission reports. This table uses the report by the Commission on Historical Clarification.

cash transfer program for low-income families), while its managers and supporters saw it as "the linchpin of transitional justice in Brazil" (Abrão and Torelly 2011, 443).

The reparations program took place despite the amnesty law remaining intact. The amnesty was interpreted within the Brazilian judiciary as applying to all crimes committed by the dictatorship's security forces prior to that date. The Supreme Court upheld this interpretation in April 2010, in a ruling that argued that the amnesty played a foundational role in the transition to democracy. The Brazilian approach to post-transitional justice up to 2012 was thus not that of holding trials but, rather, of carrying out discrete, state-led investigations in response to requests from victims and family members of victims, and paying compensation where appropriate.

The creation of the NTC in 2012 led to an upsurge in transitional justice work in Brazil. Dozens of other truth commissions were established during this time, in universities, state and municipal legislatures, and civil society groups. The NTC signed letters of cooperation with twenty-eight of these other commissions in 2012 (Torelly 2015a, 21). The NTC itself had powers that neither the Special Commission nor the Amnesty Commission were granted, for example, to request classified documents, to compel witnesses to testify, to hold secret hearings, to name individuals and institutions responsible for human rights violations, and to make official recommendations to the government (Torelly 2015a, 11). The main events in the Brazilian process of transitional justice can be seen in table 7.1.

The NTC represents a ratcheting up of the Brazilian state's commitment to transitional justice. While the principle that the Brazilian state was responsible for the human rights abuses of the dictatorship was established in legislation in 1995, the NTC report can be seen as the definitive fulfillment of that obligation (Pagliarini 2015, 3). The Brazilian approach to transitional justice is distinctive in many ways. One concerns the sequence of its measures. Whereas in Argentina, Chile, and most of the other Latin American cases, truth commissions established the evidentiary basis for reparations programs, in Brazil, that pattern was reversed, so that reparations programs provided the basis for the creation of a truth commission. And the Brazilian reparations program is extensive, covering many different types of damages, not just loss of life and torture.

Second, the NTC report came very late, twenty-six years after the end of the period it investigated (1946–1988). In most other Latin American countries, truth commissions released reports two or three years after the end of the dictatorship or war. As table 7.2 shows, the average for Argentina, Chile, El Salvador, Guatemala, Haiti, Paraguay, Peru, and Uruguay is 2.6 years (Hayner 2011, 256–61). In Panama, the period was twenty-one years, while in Brazil it was longer than in all the other cases, at twenty-six (Hayner 2011, 256–61). The Brazilian Truth Commission also had the second-longest historical period to investigate compared to its Latin American counterparts—the forty-two-year period between 1946 and 1988. Third, partly because of this long time lag, the documentary evidence gathered and drawn upon by the NTC is vast compared to that of most other truth commissions in Latin America, comprising no fewer than 60 million documents, according to NTC member Paulo Sérgio Pinheiro (Pagliarini 2015, 3). While this archive is no doubt still only a selection, and one that excludes many incriminating documents that have been destroyed or passed into private hands (especially those concerning the armed forces), it is nevertheless a significant future resource for researchers and a strength of the NTC.

Fourth, Brazil is the only country in Latin America, with the exception of El Salvador, where an amnesty passed by an authoritarian regime has not been partially or entirely overturned. Fifth, there has still not been a criminal prosecution for human rights abuses during the dictatorship that has led to a conviction, despite the NTC's rather surprising recommendation that the amnesty law should not be applied to any of the 191 living perpetrators it named in the report.[2] Sixth, the Brazilian armed forces have still not issued a statement in which they disown, apologize for, or otherwise distance themselves from the human rights abuses of the authoritarian period.[3] This is very different from the armed forces of Argentina and Chile. Seventh, Brazil is also distinctive in that the doctrine of legal continuity, which sees the 1988 Constitution as deriving from the prior legality of the authoritarian regime, is still influential and was invoked by the Supreme Court in its 2010 decision on the amnesty (Torelly 2015b, 41). Finally, there has not been a great deal of institutional innovation in Brazil after regime change. This is unlike in Argentina and Chile, where major reforms of the judiciary took place under democracy.

The NTC had an opportunity to increase the official total of victims of regime repression but chose not to take it. In the chapter on the indigenous in its report, for example, the NTC mentions 8,350 indigenous victims and declares, "the real number of indigenous killed in the period could be exponentially greater" (Comissão Nacional da Verdade 2014, vol. 2, text 5, 205). However, none of these indigenous victims was included in the official total of victims of regime repression, in a decision that reinforces Brazil's traditional social hierarchy. The same marginalization occurred with the report's treatment of the peasants killed during the dictatorship.

Overall, the Brazilian approach to transitional justice is still, in comparative terms, moderate, gradual, non-confrontational, and conservative. This is captured in a statement by Senator Randolfe Rodrigues (PSOL, Amapá), when discussing his resolution in Congress on December 17, 2013. The resolution, which was passed, annulled the congressional session of April 2, 1964, that declared the presidency of Brazil open, thus paving the way for the military regime. In doing so, the resolution posthumously restored the mandate of the deposed President João Goulart. Senator Rodrigues declared that the action "is not against anyone. It is a revolution in favor of the history of Brazil" (quoted in Foreque and Falcão 2013). The resolution was symbolic and confined to the margins of "history" rather than impacting upon contemporary political conflicts.

The Brazilian trajectory of transitional justice has, thus far, been marked by more continuity than change. This outcome was predicted by Nino (1996, 126–27), whose checklist of factors likely to induce or inhibit transitional justice included six positive and five negative factors. Brazil scores low on four of the six positive factors: it did not experience a rupture with the previous authoritarian regime; it had a high degree of legal continuity across the regimes; it did not have a large number of victims of lethal violence (the official number of politically killed and disappeared under authoritarian rule in Brazil is in the 400+ range, compared to 3,000–5,000 in Chile and 20,000–30,000 in Argentina [Pereira 2005, 21]); and it did not have leaders interested in transitional justice during and immediately after the transition. (It did have heinous abuses, and social identification with victims of those abuses.) Similarly, Brazil had all but one of the five negative factors. It had a gradual, consensual transition; a long gap between the height of repression and the transition; social identification with the perpetrators of abuses; and strong cohesion among the perpetrators. There was not a broad diffusion of responsibility for the human rights abuses, although even that factor could be said to exist, if one considers the armed forces' institutional commitment to an official history that portrayed the 1964 coup and subsequent regime as necessary for saving the nation from communism. If we accept Nino's theory and conclude from his calculations that Brazil is a "least-likely" case of activist transitional justice, we are still left with the task of explaining that outcome.

Brazil's Regime Transition and the "Justice Cascade"

According to the legal scholar Ruti Teitel, the critical approach to transitional justice denotes "a maximally transformative legal repertoire aimed at repudiating prior regime policy." The restorative approach "draws normative force from a return to the state's prior legacies" and the residual approach aims to preserve as much as possible of the preexisting legal order (Teitel 2002, 210). In Brazil in the 1990s, a combination of domestic and transnational pressures shifted the country into a more activist phase of transitional justice, but one that looks residual compared to the critical approach taken by reformers in Argentina, and the restorative approach taken in Chile.

Historical institutionalism helps to explain this outcome. In historical institutionalism, "the basic point of analytical departure is the choices that are made early in the history of any polity. . . . These initial policy choices, and the institutionalized commitments that grow out of them, are argued to determine subsequent decisions" (Peters 2005, 19–20). For historical institutionalists, "There will be change and evolution, but the range of possibilities for that development will have been constrained by the formative period of the institution" (Peters 2005, 76; see also March and Olsen 2009; Sanders 2006; Smith 2008).

The sequence by which Brazil arrived at the "impunity model" was the 1979 amnesty, the 1982 gubernatorial and congressional elections, the 1985 indirect presidential election, the Constituent Assembly formed in the 1986 elections and operating in 1987 and for most of 1988, and the 1989 direct presidential elections. Throughout this process, opponents of the dictatorship had good reason to accept the framing of the debate in which they were involved. That framing excluded transitional justice.

The nature of the regime transition is key to explaining the Brazilian outcome. In Pinto's words, "The type of democratic transition is the most operative predictor for an explanation of the form of transitional justice in a democratization process, particularly in its punitive aspects" (Pinto 2011, 5). Brazil's transition was gradualist and pacted, with the avoidance of *revanchismo* (revenge), or any attempt to prosecute perpetrators of human rights abuses under authoritarian rule. It may well be that Brazil's informally pacted transition, in the long run, provided more guarantees of impunity to those perpetrators than did the more formally negotiated and constitutionalized transition in Chile. Once prosecutors successfully established that disappearances were ongoing crimes not covered by Chile's amnesty of 1978, hundreds of trials took place in that country, something that has not occurred in Brazil.

Brazil's transition was unusually slow and gradual. The military regime announced liberalization in 1974, and this proceeded in a zigzag fashion throughout the 1970s. A movement in favor of amnesty for political prisoners put pressure on the regime, while regime leaders allied with members of the moderate opposition in Congress to engineer a conservative transition that preserved important prerogatives for the armed forces. In 1979 Congress approved an amnesty that triggered the release from prison of all political prisoners save those who had been convicted of "blood crimes" (homicide and attempted homicide) and allowed exiles to return home. In addition, the amnesty provided blanket immunity to all state agents suspected of having been involved in killings, disappearances, and torture. The few remaining political prisoners incarcerated in Brazil were released in a separate amnesty in 1985, after a civilian president, Tancredo Neves, had been elected in an indirect election in Congress. (Neves died before he could assume office and his vice-presidential running mate, José Sarney, took his place.) In subsequent years the country moved toward constitutional, formal democracy with popularly elected presidents, a transformation that was more or less complete by 1990.

Throughout this transition, the armed forces retained considerable influence, and their desire to avoid investigations into the human rights abuses of the past and block any attempts at justice for victims of the dictatorship's repression was generally respected (Bethell and Castro 2008). The result was a transition marked by an almost complete absence of the transitional justice mechanisms seen elsewhere. There are several features of the Brazilian regime transition that constrained subsequent approaches to transitional justice. First, as the NTC report shows, the military regime maintained a high degree of control over the process. President Ernesto Geisel (1974–1979) saw Spain, a country that adopted and maintained the "impunity" approach until very recently, as a model for Brazil to follow. In southern Europe, Spain engaged in much less transitional justice than Greece, Italy, or Portugal, while in South America, Brazil did less than its neighbors Argentina, Chile, and

Uruguay, which all held trials of the perpetrators of human rights abuses carried out under their dictatorial regimes (Pinto 2011, 8).

Second, the transition involved informal, secret discussions between leaders about how no *revanchismo* was highly desirable. Third, the publication of *Brasil: Nunca Mais* (Arns 1996), a book researched and published under the auspices of the São Paulo archdiocese of the Catholic Church with support from Protestant churches, filled a gap and made it easier for the state to do nothing.

Fourth, the costs of a critical approach to transitional justice in Argentina became apparent just as Brazil entered its regime transition. Argentina experienced four junior officer rebellions between 1987 and 1990, partly in protest at the trials that had taken place under the Alfonsín government. (The last rebellion took place under President Menem.) These rebellions were amply covered by the Brazilian media and reinforced the conservative position that impunity was safer for a new democracy than trials or truth commissions. In Argentina itself, they led eventually to the U-turn under Alfonsín, which stopped trials. Fifth, Brazil was in the midst of a severe economic crisis during its regime transition. Inflation was accelerating and external debt had reached unsustainable levels, resulting in a moratorium on debt repayment in 1987. This absorbed the attention of politicians and made it harder to put transitional justice on the political agenda. Sixth, there was no party equivalent to the Radicals in Argentina or the Socialists in Chile, both of which had campaigned on the need for some kind of transitional justice.[4] Seventh, ex-president Emílio Garrastazu Médici, the man who had presided over the worst period of repression during the Brazilian dictatorship, died in 1985, depriving activists of an obvious target. In Argentina, in contrast, nine members of the juntas that had ruled the country from 1976 to 1983 were alive, and prosecuted, in 1985. These factors help to explain the non-confrontational, low-key, compensatory nature of Brazil's transitional justice. A transition in which the military controlled important elements of the process, an informal pact that was all the more durable for being informal, a *jeitão* or arrangement among Brazilian rulers that allowed for total impunity and selective amnesia, was a major feature of this and other Brazilian regime transitions.[5]

Authoritarian legacies are "all behavioral patterns, rules, relationships, social and political situations, norms, procedures and institutions either introduced or patently strengthened by the immediately preceding authoritarian regime" that endure in the democracy (Pinto 2011, 3; citing Cesarini and Hite). For our purposes, institutional arrangements are key—and in the institutional realm, "the more institutionally durable and innovative the authoritarian regime, the greater the potential influence of authoritarian legacies" (Pinto 2011, 3; citing Cesarini and Hite). In the words of Barahona de

Brito and Sznajder (2011, 153), "The more prolonged and institutionalized a dictatorship, the harder it will be to stigmatize the social groups and institutions that participated in the old order." Brazil's gradual and slow transition preserved many authoritarian legacies. The structure and procedures of the state military police forces—their constitutional status as reserve forces of the army, their organization in barracks, their militarized tactics in dealing with protestors and criminal suspects—make a good example of an authoritarian legacy, albeit one that is as much a legacy of a particular pattern of state formation as it is of the authoritarian regime of 1964–1985.

This rapid sketch helps to account for the endurance of the impunity model in Brazil until the early 1990s, and the relative timidity of the institutional innovation in the 1990s and early 2000s, when low-key commissions were established that were oriented to reparations—but not the naming of perpetrators. This change can best be accounted for by what Sikkink calls the justice cascade: the combination of domestic and transnational pressures to act in some way to address past human rights abuses. The justice cascade includes the international human rights "revolution" that gained strength in the 1970s and again after the end of the Cold War, strategic organizing by human rights organizations, and the transnational movement for transitional justice, including international courts, domestic courts claiming universal jurisdiction, and domestic courts. The justice cascade reached an important juncture in 2010, when the Inter-American Court of Human Rights ruled against Brazil in the Gomes Lund case. The court ruled that the Brazilian state had a duty to the family members of Guilherme Gomes Lund, a guerrilla fighter disappeared and killed in Araguaia in 1973, to provide information about his death. This led to the creation of the Truth Commission, an institution that had been proposed as early as 2009.

The ceremony to formally inaugurate the Truth Commission reflected the transnational nature of the justice cascade. The ceremony began with a speech by Amérigo Incalcaterra, the regional representative of the UN High Commission for Human Rights. The representative read a letter from the UN High Commissioner for Human Rights, Navi Pillay, in support of the creation of the NTC. The Truth Commission was constructed in response to both domestic and international audiences, and its formation has been influenced by domestic and transnational networks.[6] But what can we say about the role of international factors in shaping Brazil's transitional justice outcomes? Such factors have been important, if not preponderant. International NGOs such as Amnesty International and the International Center for Transitional Justice have applauded what they see as progress (see, for example, Wilcken 2012; González 2012). Actors have looked to influences outside of Brazil to put pressure on the Brazilian government. Admittedly Brazil is less influenced by international trends than some other, smaller countries. Its judiciary also tends to believe that its national legal tradition overrrides international obligations, or it is simply unaware of international law, so this factor should not be overemphasized.

The cultural sphere is also part of the justice cascade. As in the international context, production in the cultural arena facilitated the eventual emergence of a more activist policy in the area of transitional justice in Brazil. Atencio (2014, 4–9) argues that, in the 1990s and 2000s, important and popular memoirs, television series, plays, and memorials reminded the Brazilian public of the authoritarian past and produced "cultural memory cycles." In these cycles, cultural production became linked to policy innovations in the public sphere, allowing groups and individuals to press for new mechanisms of transitional justice such as the Truth Commission. To borrow the language of social movement theory, cultural production helped to "frame" debates about human rights in ways favorable to those pressuring for transitional justice. (For a discussion of frames, see Tarrow 2011, 140–57.)

In the words of Atencio (2014, 277, 281), "cycles of memory have a significant impact on memory struggles in Brazil over the long run. Each turn of the cycle produces its own 'returns' or yields. . . . [T]he impact of these cycles is neither unidirectional nor linear. A cycle may not lead to a single outcome, but rather to multiple, contradictory ones." Even when official policies toward the past were low-key and modest, cultural works raised questions about Brazil's regime transition, and whether justice in relation to human rights abuses could be considered "unfinished business" on the country's democratic agenda.

Wilson (2001, 19), writing about the South African truth commission, suggests that these commissions occupy a "'liminal' space betwixt and between existing institutions. . . . During the period of liminality, the core moral values of society would be restated and internalized (it was hoped) by those participating in the process. . . . [T]he ritualized and moral features of transition were the result of the failure of secular mechanisms (such as law) to deal with conflict in society." In the Brazilian case, the core failure of the law lay in the contradiction between the 1979 amnesty and international human rights treaties signed by Brazil, which did not recognize the legitimacy of amnesties in cases of crimes against humanity. The NTC was created, in part, to bridge this contradiction.

The Significance and Impact of the NTC

The significance of the 2014 NTC is contested. A full understanding of the impact of the report must await the passage of time, and much depends on what is expected of the report. Criticisms abound. As Barahona de Brito (2011,

28) reminds us, "the 'truth' of some commissions may be very partial," and their impact limited. Truth commissions serve different purposes in different political contexts. Steve Stern suggests that truth commissions can produce new information, open up debate, promote justice, and enhance the understanding of the past, but they can also be used to produce an official story and close the door to any further activity in the realm of post-transitional justice (Stern 2004).[7]

The NTC report caused anxiety in some circles, because it argued that the named living perpetrators of human rights abuses should be made responsible at the criminal, civil, and administrative level. It could therefore trigger additional challenges to the 1979 amnesty. These challenges could come in one of at least three forms. First, the Supreme Court could decide to hear a case that once again challenges the constitutionality of the Amnesty Law. Although the court voted seven to two to maintain the amnesty in 2010, it is always possible to reverse a previous ruling, and the composition of the court has changed in recent years (justices are required to retire when they reach the age of seventy). Second, Congress could repeal the amnesty, as its counterpart in Uruguay did in 2011. Third, a judge could respond positively to one of several prosecutorial briefs currently in Brazilian courts, which argue that the disappearances that took place during the dictatorship are "continuing crimes" and therefore not subject to the amnesty.[8]

Many supporters of the Truth Commission make explicit the link between the task of historical memory and the demand for punishment. For example, on April 9, 2012, the congressional Commission for Memory, Truth, and Justice heard eight people testify in favor of the Truth Commission. Seven of the eight in their testimony mentioned the importance of ending the amnesty (Passos 2012).[9] Amnesty International researcher Patrick Wilcken ended his 2012 article on the Truth Commission with the hope that "Brazil will at last follow in the footsteps of its neighbors, revoke the Amnesty Law and start the long-overdue process of judicial reckoning." He hoped that this would "serve as a catalyst for urgently needed reform of Brazil's police forces and prison system," warning ominously that the Truth Commission could be "Brazil's last chance to back out of the historical bunker in which it has entrenched itself" (Wilcken 2012, 78).

Sikkink makes a strong argument in favor of the view that the NTC report should lead to trials. In her commentary on the NTC report, she wrote, "The key test of the truth commission's impact, then, is whether it can provide not only a public acknowledgement to victims and a record for collective memory, but also spur the Brazilian state to hold offenders accountable. Yet virtually every other country in the region has either overturned or circumvented its amnesty law in order for prosecution to proceed—making it hard to believe Brazil won't ultimately follow suit" (Sikkink and Marchesi 2015, 6).

Sikkink believes that human rights trials matter. She analyzed approximately one hundred countries that experienced a transition to democracy between 1974 and 2000. Sikkink finds that those countries that had human rights trials had a better record of enforcement of human rights. This is because the trials deterred would-be perpetrators, and they also communicated norms of respect for human rights. Sikkink quotes Joachim Savelsburg, who wrote that "Law steers collective memory . . . directly but selectively" (Sikkink 2011, 173).

Sikkink argues, "if Brazil had carried out human rights prosecutions, it might have a seen a reduction in the level of violence" (2011, 187). In the aggregate, "The level of repression decreases as the number of years with human rights prosecutions increases in a country. If a country were to move from the minimum (zero) to maximum possible number of prosecution years (twenty), this would bring about a 3.8 percent decrease in the whole repression scale" (184). She argues that truth commissions have a similar, although less powerful impact. "The fact is that a truth commission being present also contributes to improved human rights protection in transitional societies. Our model shows that a truth commission brings about a 0.19 point decrease in the repression score and a 0.43 point decrease in the long term" (184). In other words, "punishment matters but . . . truth telling matters as well" (185).

Sikkink's work is an interesting attempt to quantify the impact of trials and truth commissions on human rights, but the inferences from her data are flawed. Her large-N data set does convincingly show that human rights trials do not destabilize new democracies or lead to military coups, as Meyer (2012, 278) argues. But her data are not persuasive in showing that trials or truth commissions in and of themselves reduce state violence. One problem is omitted variable bias. The variation could be explained by any number of independent variables that Sikkink and her colleague did not examine. Second, the statistical work rests on coding of both independent and dependent variables that is based on impressions gleaned from largely qualitative reports. These data are given the veneer of rigor through coding but the statistical variation found—3.8 percent—is too slim to be relied upon, given the margin of error on which the coding is based. This is a good example of the danger Hopkin (2010, 298) warns of when he writes, "One of the principal claims of quantitative analysis is that numbers can provide a more objective understanding of phenomena than anecdotal, one-off descriptions of events. However, much data used in quantitative political science is [*sic*] qualitative data, coded into numerical form."

This can be seen in Sikkink's independent variables of "human rights prosecutions" and "cumulative human rights prosecutions." For the former, she codes each country with a 1 or 0; a country is given a 1 if it held any kind of human rights trial in that year. The measurement of this variable is crude. It does not take into account whether one trial took place or hundreds, nor does it differentiate between the trial of a head of state and that of the lowliest prison guard. Cumulative human rights prosecutions refers simply to the aggregate number of years with trials, for a maximum of twenty and a minimum of one. In Latin America, the average score was seven, while for the world as a whole, it is under three (Sikkink 2011, 180).

The measurement of the dependent variable—the enforcement of human rights—is even more problematic. Sikkink uses the Cingranelli and Richards (CIRI) physical integrity scale, a measure from zero to eight, based on US State Department Country Reports on Human Rights, in which zero is the worst (widespread abuse of human rights by the state) and eight is the best (widespread respect of human rights by the state). This kind of measure lumps together many different kinds of state violence and involves difficult coding decisions. Sikkink cross-checks the CIRI physical integrity data with the Political Terror Scale (PTS), an index in which zero is the best score (broad state respect for human rights) and five is the worst score (widespread state abuse of human rights). Sikkink claims that "Our findings were basically the same whether we used the physical integrity index or the PTS" (2011, 181). This may be true for the aggregate data, but checking the scores for Brazil reveals widespread discrepancies in the two measures. Table 7.3 compares the scores for selected years (the PTS was converted to an eight-point scale for purposes of this comparison).[10]

There are a number of disturbing aspects to the change in these scores, as well as the discrepancies between them, given that they are treated as reliable, objective indicators in Sikkink's analysis. This is especially the case because both indices use the same raw material, the US State Department Country Reports on Human Rights. These reports are not systematically quantitative but are essentially anecdotal, mixing quantitative and qualitative data and interpretations. Converting these reports into numerical scores is highly arbitrary. For example, it is hard to imagine what could have changed on the ground so much in Brazil to justify the drop in Brazil's physical integrity score from the relatively high 5 in 1983 (when a military dictatorship was still in power) to 2 in 2006 and 2011. Second, the PTS index goes through a completely different trajectory from the physical integrity scale, declining from the relatively high 4.8 in 1981 to 1.6, before rising again in 2011. Third, the gap between these scores is huge from a statistical point of view, raising doubts about Sikkink's claim that human rights trials increase the probability of a decrease in state human rights abuses by 3.8 percent. Claims with this level

Year	Physint	PTS
Table 7.3. Comparison of CIRI Physint and PTS Scores for Brazil, Selected Years		
1981	4	4.8
1983	5	4.8
1985	5	3.2
1987	4	1.6
1991	4	1.6
1996	4	1.6
1999	4	1.6
2003	4	1.6
2006	2	1.6
2011	2	3.2

Sources: CIRI Human Rights Data Project at www.humanrightsdata.com/p /data-documentation.html and Political Terror Scale at www.politicalterrorscale.org.

of precision do not seem to be appropriate when the degree of variation in coding is this large.

The compilers of these indices themselves recognize the problem. The managers of the PTS published an article in which they point out the wide discrepancies between PTS and CIRI scores, despite the use of the same source material, and criticize the CIRI for claiming "a level of precision that is not possible given the source data from which both data sets are coded" (Wood and Gibney 2010, 367). This characterization could be made about both data sets, in a dispute that appears to have as much to do with academic entrepreneurialism and turf protection as it does about the measurement of human rights abuses.[11]

Therefore the argument that a few human rights trials would lower the level of state violence in Brazil, a vast, diverse, and violent country with an average of more than fifty thousand homicides each year, is not convincing. This does not mean that normative arguments in favor of human rights trials do not have resonance. It is hard to object to trials of perpetrators. However, making such trials a sine qua non of transitional justice may be misguided in the Brazilian case. Possas and Bastos make a good case for another approach. They write that "justice in courts is usually the first and most prominent of demands; . . . [but justice can also be viewed as an effort to] consolidate in the country a culture that values life and human rights, and to prevent the possibility of those abuses ever happening again. . . . For these reasons it seems that it is possible to refer to justice latu sensu, meaning the broader transitional justice, and a justice strictu sensu, related to the punishment/accountability dimension" (Possas and Bastos 2015, 27–28).

Many of the NTC's most important recommendations have to do with justice latu sensu, especially in preventing future human rights abuses, and this sets it apart from most other truth commission reports. In Argentina's *Nunca Más* report, for example, the authors conclude that "The facts presented to this Commission in the dispositions and testimonies speak for themselves" (CONADEP 1986, 446) and go on to make four recommendations, three of which concern backward-looking, reparative justice. In the Chilean Rettig Report, the authors spend fifteen pages on proposals for reparations to the victims' families before turning to the prevention of human rights violations (Comisión Nacional de Verdad y Reconciliación 1993, 837–86). In the NTC report, in contrast, only eight of the twenty-nine recommendations concern redressing the impact of past human rights abuses, with the others all seemingly designed to provide more possibilities of justice to contemporary victims of state violence.

This seems entirely appropriate in a country that has become such a violent democracy. Table 7.4 compares the number of lethal victims of human rights abuses listed in Latin American truth commission reports with the number of homicide victims in those countries in 2012. As one can see, in all the other countries listed (Argentina, Chile, El Salvador, Guatemala, Paraguay, and Peru), the victims of authoritarian violence outnumber the homicide victims of 2012, by factors that range from 4:1 in Argentina to 15:1 in Paraguay, with the average being 8.3:1. In Brazil, by contrast, the homicide victims in 2012 outnumber the official tally in the truth commission by a ratio of 116:1. This points to another singularity of the Brazilian process of transitional justice. It is taking place in a context in which the violence of the present outweighs the violence of the past, at least by these measures.

It may be objected that the NTC report's official statistic on victims is an undercount. As we saw earlier, the commission chose not to include indigenous people and peasants in the official tally. But the discrepancy would still exist, even if these other victims were added. It could also be said that what is relevant is state violence, not violence as a whole.[12] In this regard, the recent report of the Brazilian Forum of Public Security should be considered. The Forum's eighth annual report, released in November 2014, claimed that in the five-year period 2009–2013, the police in Brazil killed 11,197 people (Forum Brasileiro de Segurança Pública 2014, 6). This is almost certainly an undercount, given the prevalence of police officers in death squads.

Given this state of affairs, other factors that could enhance justice latu sensu

Table 7.4. Number of People Killed and Disappeared, as Listed in Truth Commission Reports, and Victims of Homicide in 2012

Country	A. Number of Killed and Disappeared Identified in Truth Commission Report	B. Year of Truth Commission Report	C. Number of Homicides in Country in 2012	Ratio of A to C
Argentina	8,960	1985	2,237 (2010)	4:1
Brazil	434	2014	50,108	1:116
Chile	3,428	1991	550	6:1
El Salvador	27,000	1993	2,595	10:1
Guatemala	42,000	1999	6,025	7:1
Paraguay	9,923	2008	649	15:1
Peru	24,000	2003	2,865	8:1

Sources: Hayner 2011, 256–71; Fleitas, Ortiz de Rozas, and Flom *2014.

would seem appropriate. These include recommendations such as abolishing the 1983 national security law, abolishing the police practice of using *autos de resistência* to justify executions, and strengthening the state's human rights institutions, including the police ombudsmen. Since most state killings of citizens are carried out by the military police, the NTC's recommendations concerning the state military police are particularly important. These include transforming them into civilian forces by abolishing their constitutional status as army reservists, abolishing their special jurisdiction in state military courts (to which all crimes except intentional homicide and attempted homicide are referred), and integrating them into the civil police. In the words of the NTC, the military attributes of the military police are "incompatible with the exercise of public security in a democratic rule of law, which should focus on attending to the citizen" (Comissão Nacional da Verdade 2014, vol. 1, pt. 5, ch. 18, 971). The prospects for seriously building on the work of the NTC by implementing some of its recommendations look poor, as the NTC report was released at a time of economic recession and political turbulence. Basic matters of governance, such as creating a stable majority in Congress, have been difficult in the second presidential term of Dilma Rousseff. Unlike earlier truth commissions, the NTC has used modern social media to communicate with the public. It placed videos on YouTube, created a Facebook page, and used Twitter and FeedBurner. The YouTube videos, which mostly showed members of the public testifying to the NTC, had over half a million hits. The NTC report is also freely available online. Therefore there could be a gradual process by which the NTC findings influence memories of the dictatorship and perceptions of Brazilian transitional justice. As Glenda Mezarobba, one of the NTC staff members, writes, the copious documentation of the NTC is an important counterpoint to the previous silence of the state about the human rights abuses of the dictatorship and makes denial of the existence of those abuses less likely (Mezarobba 2015, 356). This is significant in itself. But expecting a short-term reaction to the NTC report, in terms of popular mobilization and pressure for reform, seems unrealistic.

Conclusion

There were many obstacles to transitional justice in Brazil that have gradually been overcome, leading to the creation of one of the largest reparations programs in the world from 1995 to 2012. The creation of the NTC was another step in that process; it came about through a combination of domestic and international factors. A historical institutionalist approach that takes the sequence of events seriously can best account for Brazil's singularity in the area of transitional justice.

The Brazilian NTC report is unusual because its recommendations focus so heavily on forward-looking measures designed to curb future human rights abuses. This is appropriate in a country in which contemporary violence looms so large in relation to the violence of the dictatorship, compared to other countries in the region. The NTC is a "liminal institution" designed to reconcile the contradiction between Brazil's 1979 Amnesty Law and its ratification of major international human rights treaties. Despite the importance of the NTC, it has not changed the basic pattern of transitional justice in Brazil, which is gradual, moderate, and non-confrontational. This is consistent with a historical institutionalist emphasis on the impact of defining moments—in this case, the regime transition of the late 1970s and 1980s—in constraining later political choices.

The NTC could come to be seen as representing a major shift in the Brazilian approach to transitional justice, but only if some of its recommendations for reform are implemented. Whether there are trials of perpetrators is less important than some of these other reforms of the police and criminal justice system. As Laurence Whitehead reminds us, democracy is an open-ended, context-dependent, socially constructed entity (Whitehead 2002). If there is anything that the history of transitional justice has taught us, it is that the struggle for democracy and human rights is never over.

POLITICS FROM
THE BOTTOM UP

PART III

Maria Hermínia Tavares de Almeida and Fernando Henrique Guarnieri

Toward a (Poor) Middle-Class Democracy?

Upward Mobility and Politics under Lula and Dilma

What does it mean to be in Class C? A computer, mobile phone, car, mortgage, house, bank credit, in general, and productive credit, in particular, being a freelancer or an employer, having a private social security plan, and a university degree, private schooling, health insurance, life insurance. But above all, having a work document (carteira de trabalho) is perhaps what best represents the rise of a new Brazilian middle class.

— Marcelo Neri, 2009

Once, travelling to New York was fun, but, if your building's janitor can go there paying R$50 per month, what is the fun now?

— Danuza Leão, *Folha de S. Paulo*, November 25, 2012

IN THE LAST fifteen years millions of Brazilians have risen out of poverty, and this has greatly increased the number of those in the middle income bracket. The press, the government, and some specialists have praised the transformation of Brazil into a middle-class society and have emphasized the changes in consumption patterns, as more middle income earners have been able to access a greater number of high-quality goods and services. These changes are real and are visible even to the most inattentive observer, sitting in one of the airports now crowded with new travelers who have replaced slow long-distance bus journeys with air travel, or waiting in one of the interminable traffic jams due to the exponential increase in the number of cars in every Brazilian city and town. While these changes are indisputable, their nature, depth, and consequences—social as well as political—are controversial.

The (Third) Great Transformation of Modern Brazil

In the 1950s, under the first and limited experiment in democracy (1946–1964), urbanization, industrialization, and the modernization of labor laws led to a previously unheard of movement of mass social and political inclusion, with millions of Brazilians leaving rural areas in search of a better life in the cities. In the 1970s, under an authoritarian military regime (1964–1984), strong economic growth created a new wave of social inclusion, as the population became predominantly urban and industrial employment thrived—shaping a society as mobile and modern as it was unequal. Then, from 2002 to 2012, some 30 million people rose out of extreme poverty. This time the transformation combined upward mobility and the reduction of inequality, under a fully competitive democratic regime.

In a decade, the middle-income stratum swelled to include the majority of Brazilian society, approaching 100 million people.[1] According to SAE estimates (2012b), in this ten-year period, 21 percent of the poor left the lower stratum and acceded to the middle one, while 6 percent of the latter climbed their way to the upper stratum. A set of conditions and policies seem to account for this progressive change. Contrary to conventional wisdom, huge cash transfer programs, dramatically enlarged under Lula's government, although important, are not the sole explanation for this dramatic process of upward mobility.[2] The expansion of formal employment, combined with the rise in wages and salaries, has played a far more significant role. The market, rather than the state, was responsible for the rise of a significant portion of the Brazilian poor. Demographics also played its part, as the dependency rate decreased. Based on econometric models, SAE estimates that the changing rate between adults and children explains around 20 percent of the upward mobility; cash transfer programs account for 30 percent; and access to jobs and the increase in mean pay for employed workers account for 10 percent and 40 percent, respectively (SAE 2012b). The expansion of personal loans by public and private credit institutions has also been identified as playing an important role in the process.

If the fact that the middle class has increased in size is undisputed, its interpretation has given rise to huge controversies. Neri (2008, 2011b), the specialists of the SAE, and Souza and Lamounier (2010) have all lauded the expansion of the middle class and the advent of a middle-class society, with specific patterns of consumption, work opportunities, education, entrepreneurship, and aspirations. In contrast, Souza (2010) and Pochmann (2012) argue that the process is one of an enlargement of the upper echelons of the working class, whose living conditions have improved only through the imposition of an overextended working day. This upgrading, they argue, requires significant investment in public services in order to become sustainable. In an intermediate position, Oliveira (2010) emphasizes the *gap* between Brazil's so-called new middle classes and their counterparts in the developed world, not only in terms of mean income but also with regard to education, cultural habits, and patterns of consumption. There is no doubt that Oliveira's analysis is correct. In 2011, while Brazil was the seventy-seventh country in the ranking of Gross National Income (GNI) per capita with US$11,500 (at purchasing power parity), the equivalent figure was US$58,900 in Norway, US$48,890 in the United States, US$36,970 in the United Kingdom, US$35,860 in France, US$31,930 in Spain, and US$30,290 in South Korea (World Bank 2012).

Given that the mean income in Brazil is not particularly high, those in the middle income bracket are significantly closer to poverty than their counterparts in the developed world. We are not talking about the middle classes of US suburbia as depicted, for instance, in the television series *Desperate Housewives*. We are not talking about the middle classes as portrayed in British sitcoms on the BBC. We are not even talking about what Brazilians used to call the "traditional middle class," whose members were typically public servants and highly educated professionals, or the more recent middle classes born out of the so-called economic miracle of the 1970s, both predominantly white and both mimicking the behavior of those in the upper tier. The middle income stratum being described as the new Brazilian middle class differs from previous ones in terms of both color and education: it is half black and mulatto (51 percent), is predominantly urban (89 percent), and works in the formal economy (56 percent). Only 7 percent of its heads of family have university degrees—30 percent have some secondary education while 51 percent have four or less years of schooling.[3] Its expansion, between 2002 and 2012, resulted fundamentally from the incorporation of blacks and mulattoes (75 percent), of families from urban areas (86 percent), from the Northeast (34 percent) and Southeast (36 percent), whose heads attended school for four years or less (64 percent) (SAE 2012a).

How sustainable is the position of those who have recently exited poverty? While critics of the official euphoria warn that this reversal of fortune is a threat, since those who are now out of poverty have not gone far away and strongly rely upon the job market and public credit, other commentators think that the "new middle class" is investing in promising, future-driven assets—the improvement of education for the present and future generations (Neri 2010) as well as entrepreneurship (Souza and Lamounier 2010; SAE 2012b).[4] The SAE's specialists are also optimistic. They believe that the value attributed to education and a more cautious behavior regarding savings and family indebtedness reflect an increasing capacity to plan for the future (SAE 2012b, 32).

However, the extent of change should not be underemphasized. The expansion of the middle-income group is part and parcel of a deep process of societal democratization through consumption that seems to be permanent. In a sense, it is a Tocquevillian process of democratization, one that begins to erode previous social barriers between groups and to challenge established hierarchies. In no other place has this social transformation been better captured than on Brazilian TV soap operas whose plots, locations, and characters increasingly depict the dilemmas, settings, and lifestyles of the new middle classes. The consequences for Brazilian political life are not clear; perhaps it is too early to assess them. There is some evidence available on how middle income earners perceive democratic values, electoral competition, and political life.

Middle of the Road Attitudes towards Democracy and Diversity

There is a long established intellectual tradition that connects the middle classes to democracy. Different strands of modernization theory claim that there is a positive correlation between democracy and the middle classes, and three different arguments have developed to support this. First, the rise of the middle classes, as a correlate of economic development, provides a buffer between the upper and lower classes, avoiding the political polarization that is conducive to either oligarchic despotism or plebeian revolution. The existence of a large middle class would work to moderate political conflict. Second, because of their autonomy from the dominant elites, the middle classes, as they strive for expanding political participation and political competition, contribute to political pluralism. Finally, as they tend to be more educated and better informed, the middle classes would favor political moderation, a necessary condition to the stability of democracy (Lipset 1959; Almond and Verba 1963). In brief, there is a strong link between the existence of a vibrant middle class and a democratic political culture, based on values of pluralism, political competition, and moderation. Compelling as they may be, these structural explanations underestimate, to a certain degree, the heterogeneity of the middle classes and of their attitudes and beliefs. The middle income stratum is a diversified group; the political values and attitudes, as well as political identities, of its members are contingent on its specific process of expansion, as much as on the political agents that mobilized these people in the first place.

How Do Brazilian Middle Income Earners Relate to Democratic Values?

When presented with the traditional survey question about their preferences regarding political regimes, members of different income strata differ significantly regarding their support for democracy (table 8.1). Although a majority of Brazilians prefer a democracy to a dictatorship, there is still a minority who

Table 8.1. Preference for Political Regime, 2008 (% of Respondents)					
	Lower	*Lower-Middle*	*Middle*	*Upper-Middle*	*Upper*
Democracy	58	61	70	71	78
No preference	28	25	16	14	5
Dictatorship	14	13	15	15	17

Note: N=3386.
Source: Datafolha 2008 PO-3474.

would rather live under an authoritarian regime, and significantly, more than one-quarter are indifferent. Results like these have been consistently observed in distinct surveys, conducted over the last twenty-five years, placing Brazil below average in rankings of popular support for democracy in Latin America.

In Brazil, endorsement of democracy increases steadily with income: the upper strata are more convinced of the advantages of democracy over authoritarianism than the lower strata. Disaggregating the middle-income group into three brackets, we can see that the lower-middle-class attitude to democracy is very close to that of the poor, while the upper-middle-class standing is not too far from that of the upper class.[5] In short, the middle income earners are not a homogeneous group in terms of attitudes toward democracy. Around 40 percent of the lower middle stratum—a sizeable minority—do not prefer a democratic regime over other possibilities. It is not possible to positively identify that these have been recently incorporated into the middle-income group, but most probably, the contribution of newcomers to this group is not insignificant. In a previous article using Datafolha survey data, we found that support for democracy usually included a positive attitude toward legislative independence and civil and political rights, such as freedom of the press, political organization, union activity, and industrial action (Almeida and Oliveira 2010, 112).

Another way of relating the middle classes to democracy stems from studies on the sociocultural transformation of mature capitalist societies. In this tradition, the middle classes are not seen as the ballast of stable democracies but, rather, as the agents of a new democratic agenda focused on postmaterialist issues such as the environment, minority rights, respect for cultural, ethnic, and religious diversity, tolerance of different lifestyles, and individual behavior. Inglehart (1977) described this as a silent revolution (it has become rather noisy nowadays), propelled by the middle-class youth in developed countries.[6] According to this explanation, the middle classes would be agents of a process of deepening and enlarging democracy beyond the nation-state toward global issues, such as protection of the environment and disarmament;

beyond the materialist agenda of wealth distribution toward cultural issues, such as recognition of ethnic, cultural, and religious diversity; beyond the public sphere toward private and intimate choices such as divorce, abortion, same sex marriage, and drug consumption.

This agenda has spread to Western and Asian developing countries and has become ingrained in the public debate. In Brazil, as elsewhere in Latin America, women's rights including abortion, same sex marriage and the right for same sex couples to adopt children, affirmative action for black people and native Brazilians, protection against police violence, and decriminalization of marijuana consumption all became important and contentious political issues promoted by advocacy movements. While some of them, such as affirmative action, have been absorbed by political parties and translated into public policies, other more sensitive issues have been manipulated through negative propaganda during electoral campaigns.

Would Theories of Middle Class Support for Postmaterialist Demands Hold Up in Brazil?

Datapopular in 2012 conducted a survey on the social tolerance of members of different income strata (table 8.2). The majority of Brazilians, irrespective of their social class, seem tolerant of different races, religions, and individual behaviors. Nevertheless, there is considerable variation depending on the issue at stake. Professing different religious beliefs is highly tolerated, but a significant minority discriminates against atheists. Diversity of sexual behaviors and preferences seem generally accepted. Women can use provocative clothes, men can use cosmetics; the Gay Pride march in São Paulo, perhaps one of the biggest of the world, is attended also by heterosexual families and their children; and LGBT people tend to be accepted by a majority across all classes. But abortion and drug consumption are widely opposed. Once more, the middle-income group stands in the middle of the road, between a more tolerant upper class and a more prejudiced lower class. As a matter of fact, only in regard to homosexual behavior do the Brazilian poor seem significantly more tolerant than the middle and the upper strata.[7]

Political Preferences and Electoral Behavior

When asked to position themselves on a scale from 0 to 10, where 0 is "left" and 10 is "right," those in the lower and lower-middle classes tend to position themselves more to the right (around 7.0), while those in the upper-middle and upper classes are more centrist, with positions around 5.4 and 5.8 respectively (ESEB 2010).[8]

The majority of Brazilians do not identify with any of the more than twenty registered parties. A post-election survey conducted in 2010 by the Estudo

	Intolerance (%)			
Characteristic	All classes	Lower class	Middle class	Upper class
Different color	1.7	2.8	1.6	0.9
Different religion	2.4	3.2	2.4	1.3
People who do not believe in God (atheists)	35.8	41.1	36.9	25.9
Overtly sexual women	8.1	10.7	8.1	4.9
Older women married to much younger men	9.5	11.7	8.6	8.6
Older men married to much younger women	10.1	12.9	9.6	7.7
Homosexuals	9.6	6.7	11.2	9.4
Men who care about their appearance, who depilate and use beauty creams	11.2	9.9	11.3	12.4
Women who have had an abortion	36.7	42.8	38.2	24.4
Former drug users	18.0	22.9	16.3	15.8
Drug users	58.1	59.9	58.4	55.1

Table 8.2. Tolerance of Otherness, Measured by Percentage of Those Who Dislike People with the Following Characteristics

Note: Numbers in bold show statistically significant differences from those for the middle class.
Source: SAE *2012. Based on Datapopular survey 2012.

Eleitoral Brasileiro (ESEB 2010) shows that just 40 percent of respondents identified a political party that represented their way of thinking. There is little difference between classes, although the upper-middle-class response was slightly above the mean, with 44 percent of respondents identifying themselves with one of the parties. Nevertheless, although results from surveys on party identification vary considerably, there is evidence that party identification has declined in the last few years.

Among those who identify with a party, 63 percent expressed a preference for the PT, followed by the PSDB (14 percent), the PV (9 percent), and the PMDB (7 percent).[9] The poorer the respondents, the more likely they were to identify with the PT. Members of the upper class identify far more with the mean with the PSDB (31 percent), and the PV finds its strongest support among the middle class (lower-middle 12 percent, upper-middle 14 percent).

Half of the respondents say they would vote even if voting were not mandatory. The propensity to vote increases with income as does participation in unions and social movements. Institutional political participation in Brazil, measured by affiliation to unions, political parties, or participation in social movements, is very low, barely surpassing 10 percent. As we will suggest below, some new forms of political participation are emerging with the help of those in the middle income strata.

The new and older middle classes participate in an institutionalized political arena, structured during the transition from authoritarianism to democracy and fully consolidated in the 1990s. The transformation of both the population and the electorate into a predominantly middle-income group has not had a significant impact on the basic terms of political competition. At the national level, in presidential disputes, an extremely fragmented multiparty system converged around two parties (the PT and the PSDB), which headed two broad electoral coalitions, one from the center to the left and the other from the center to the right. The competition is centripetal, and both poles are variations on a moderate social reformist agenda, combining a commitment to monetary stability with action to promote economic growth and poverty reduction. Both try to label the other as corrupt. In almost all elections, a third centrist candidate has been present on the first-round ballot, attracting votes from a minority that is discontented with both dominant parties.

The preferences of different income classes for electoral coalitions, as measured by surveys conducted just before the first round of a succession of presidential elections, show that, from 1989 to 1998, the percentage of people intending to vote for Lula (the left-wing coalition candidate) remained stable at around 25 percent and did not vary too much between social classes (table 8.3). In 2002, the center, represented by candidates Ciro Gomes and Anthony Garotinho, took on greater significance, and preference for Lula rose to around 40–50 percent, although this support remained independent from social class. Only in 2006 did income appear to become relevant for voters in determining ideological preference: support for Lula decreased among the upper class (from 50.4 to 37.9 percent), increased slightly in the upper middle class (from 44 to 48 percent) and greatly increased among lower- and lower-middle-class voters (from 50.2 to 70 percent among the former and from 44.6 to 58.4 percent among the later). In 2010, 58.7 percent of the lower class, 46.8 percent of the lower-middle class, 41 percent of the upper-middle class, and 35.8 percent of the upper class declared their intention to vote for Dilma Rousseff.

In short, the middle-income group has always been divided in terms of

Stratum	Ideological position of candidate supported	1990	1994	1998	2002	2006	2010
Table 8.3. Voter Ideological Preferences (as Expressed in Pre-presidential Election Opinion Polls; in Percent of Respondents)							
Lower	Right	67	59	60	21	30	28
	Center	8	7	9	29	0	13
	Left	25	34	31	50	70	59
Lower-Middle	Right	61	62	62	22	40	33
	Center	8	7	10	32	1	20
	Left	31	30	29	46	58	47
Upper-Middle	Right	56	64	58	20	48	36
	Center	6	5	10	36	4	23
	Left	38	31	32	44	48	41
Upper	Right	58	64	60	18	55	40
	Center	13	4	12	31	7	24
	Left	29	32	28	50	38	36

Source: Datafolha: 1990 PO-1750, 2002 PO-3228, 2006 PO-3370, 2010 PO-3493.

political preferences. Although the preferences of the lower-middle class have been closer to those of the lower income class, and have followed, to a certain extent, its turn to the left, it was not until 2006 that a majority of this group declared they would vote for the PT and its center-left coalition. In 2010, less than half expressed a preference for Dilma only two days before elections.

In a recent survey carried out with a sample group of middle-class people, around 60 percent of respondents reported an improvement in their lives over the past ten years. This perception was strongest among lower-middle- and mid-middle-class respondents (table 8.4). This same survey shows that 33 percent of those who reported experiencing some improvement in their lives—and who supported a political party—supported the PT. This figure is seven percentage points higher than the mean support for the PT in the sample group (26 percent).

In the ESEB 2010, respondents were asked to report the class that they believed they belonged to both that year and eight years earlier. Using a re-

Table 8.4. Perceptions of Change in Living Standards over the Past Ten Years (Percent of Respondents)			
	Lower-Middle	Middle	Upper-Middle
Improved a lot	22	24	22
Improved a little	43	43	35
Stayed the same	8	12	14
Worsened a little	18	14	22
Worsened a lot	9	8	7

Source: Datapopular 2016, for the project "Middle Income Groups and Politics in Brazil."

gression model, we found that the best predictor of vote choice in 2010 was the individual's vote cast in 2006, but a perceived improvement in social status had an impact of 16 percent in the probability of voting for Dilma. In any case, translating perceived improvements in individual and family situations into support for the current government is not an automatic move. It depends on how those affected explain their upward mobility, and on the importance they attribute to governmental policies in comparison with their own individual efforts to improve their situation.

Narratives about succeeding due to hard work, family commitment, and individual abilities abound in qualitative research data.[10] People attributed the improvements in their lives mainly to their own efforts, to the support of their families, or to God (see figure 8.1). These same people attributed any decline in their living standards to the government or to economic conditions.

It is interesting to note that the lowest-income group showed the biggest increase in support for the candidates from the left. This is the group that did not rise up to join the new middle class and even includes people who experienced a decrease in income. On the other hand, perceived interest and instrumental reasoning may not be the only mechanisms leading to political support for the PT government under both Lula and Dilma. Descriptive representation (Pitkin 1967) can also be helpful in explaining the support for the PT candidates among low- and lower-middle-income earners. After all, Lula's personal trajectory is one of successful upward mobility. Qualitative interviews with middle-income families, conducted during the 2010 presidential election, have shown that respondents admired Lula "as a fighter who overcame his very difficult life circumstances" or someone who "had achieved his goals and, although he was working class, became the head of state" (Almeida, Pereira, and Mignozzeti 2011). In addition, the life stories of several PT leaders and activists parallel those new members of the middle classes. They come

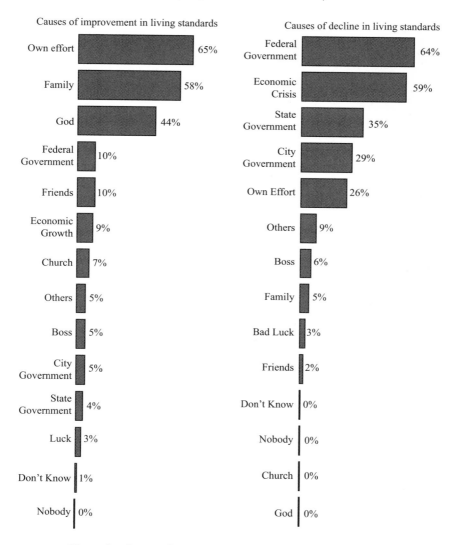

Figure 8.1. Causes of improvement and decline in living standards

from the same social milieu and share their levels of education, tastes, and aspirations of social mobility.

Shortly before the 2014 elections, both the PT government and the opposition apparently became aware of the political importance of emerging middle-income groups and began trying to address this in different ways. Under Lula's administration, the Ministry of Education implemented an array of policies intended to expand the access to higher education for those coming from low-income families, although these policies have mostly benefited lower-middle- and middle-class families. The PROUNI, an ingenious scholarship program, allowed students access to private universities. The expansion of the federal university system and the unification of access procedures have expanded enrollment in free public federal higher education institutions. More recently, Dilma signed into law a proposal approved by Congress that imposes extensive affirmative action measures on all federal universities.

From 2005 to 2012, 1.6 million students were granted PROUNI scholarships, and more than two hundred thousand students each year or 25 percent of all students that have applied for the ENEM—the test that is used in the selection to some universities. The federal government created fourteen new federal universities spread across 237 municipalities. Since 2012 all federal public universities must reserve 50 percent of their places to students who have been through the public high school system, with proportional quotas for black, mulatto, and native Brazilian students depending on the state population.

Under Dilma, the Secretariat of Strategic Affairs created a research project aimed at proposing public policies specifically intended to meet the needs of and the challenges faced by those in the middle-income strata, in terms of "professional qualification, funding for education, access to credit, financial education, real estate financing" (SAE 2012a). The SAE also proposed public policies aimed at supporting small entrepreneurs. Although fighting poverty continued to be central to the policy agenda and the political rhetoric during the third PT term in office, there was also an increased awareness of the importance of addressing the new middle classes.

The same is true for the opposition. In May 2012 Fernando Henrique Cardoso published a controversial article arguing that it would be pointless for the PSDB to try to compete with the PT for the support of the poor, and therefore, it should address and win the support of the new middle classes. Cardoso addressed the issue in terms of values. He proposed to mobilize a middle-class identity clustered around the ideas of honesty, decency, and self-made social improvement.[11]

Although Cardoso may have believed his party could appeal to and mobilize the emerging middle-income groups around ideas of public morality and republican democratic government, the discourse—and sometimes the policies—of other PSDB leaders has been tinged with more conservative colors. While the governor of São Paulo state presents himself as being tough on crime and tough on drugs, the former mayor of São Paulo city—who has also stood as a presidential candidate—has presented himself as pro-life and opposed to same sex marriage.[12] Of course, these discourses were not aimed solely at the middle classes. Opposition to abortion and demands for criminal violence and drug consumption to be curbed are issues that cut across class boundaries. Nevertheless, they are also particularly sensitive issues among those in the middle-income bracket. In brief, the government and the opposition have acknowledged the political importance of middle-income earners, and while the government has tried to appeal to their heads (and their pockets), the opposition has fumbled its way toward their hearts.

Like a Thunderbolt from a Clear Sky

Just as government and opposition were beginning to recognize the political importance of the new middle classes and looking for ways to gain their support as party followers and voters, this group suddenly emerged as active participants in the mass street demonstrations that plunged Brazil into political turmoil. What began on June 6, 2013, in the city of São Paulo as a tiny march called by a little-known student group and involving two thousand young people protesting against an increase in bus fares—the Free Fare Movement (Movimento Passe Livre)—soon spilled over into a wave of political protest. Peaceful rallies as well as pitched street battles between demonstrators and police forces paralyzed the city of São Paulo, then Rio de Janeiro, Brasília, and several other state capitals and major Brazilian cities. It became the largest mass movement Brazil had ever experienced.[13] Using social media platforms such as Facebook and Twitter to convoke the meetings and instantly convey information, the demonstrators had no recognized leaders, with no formal organization, and made a broad range of contradictory demands.[14] But beyond the cacophony of disparate watchwords, there were repeated demands for better urban and social services—better transportation, education, health care, and security—and these were as significant as the protests rejecting political corruption and the traditional political elite. Also important was the rejection of what had come to be considered as excessive and inexplicable expenditure on the 2014 FIFA World Cup. Criticism of this expenditure came hand in hand with demands for "FIFA-quality education," "FIFA-quality healthcare services," as the high standards for the construction of stadia and sports facilities for the World Cup were contrasted with the poor quality of social services.[15]

The demonstrators came from diverse social strata and political affiliations: middle-class students and professionals mingled with an urban mob; progressives and moderate and extremist left-wing activists marched side by side with right-wing punks; LGBTQ sympathizers stood with homophobic thugs.[16] Inspired by Huntington, Fukuyama (2013) described the Brazilian rallies, which he compared to other recent uprisings in the world, as "the middle class revolution," an expression of feelings of alienation from the ruling political elite and frustration regarding the failure of society to "meet their rapidly rising expectations for economic and social advancement."[17]

Table 8.5. Motivations for Participating in the Avenida Paulista Demonstrations (São Paulo, June 2013; Figures Express Percentage of Respondents)

Motive	Income (in minimum wages)					
	Less than 2	2 to 5	5 to 10	More than 10	Refuse to answer	Don't know
Better transportation	4	4	5	6	0	0
Better public services (education, health care, social security)	24	27	22	16	7	33
Against excessive expenditure and/or corruption	40	32	38	38	28	22
Against politicians and/or the government	12	8	6	8	14	11
Pro-gay rights	2	3	1	2	7	0
Pro-change in general	10	16	22	13	14	33
Against abusive taxes/ Pro-tax reform	2	2	1	1	0	0
Against violence and police repression	0	1	1	0	0	0
Other	6	10	4	10	21	0
Refuse to answer	2	2	2	1	0	0
Total	100	100	100	100	100	100

Source: Datafolha 2013 PO-813692.

We do not have enough information to make broad generalizations like Fukuyama's. Nevertheless, the results of two opinion polls conducted by Datafolha during the demonstrations of June 17 and June 20 in São Paulo seem to confirm the predominance of middle-income participants (around 57 percent in the June 20 rally) with a range of different occupations.[18] These people offered a long list of possible motives for their decision to crowd onto the streets of São Paulo (see table 8.5).

There is significant fragmentation and dispersion of motives for protest. Nevertheless, demands for better public services, a hatred of corruption, and rejection of institutional politics were shared motives in getting protesters out onto Brazilian streets. Demands for improvements in public services seemed to have greater importance for the lower-middle classes than for the middle and upper sectors of the middle-income group. At first glance, the wave of demonstrations engulfed the political system. Approval ratings for all governmental officials from the president of the nation to the mayors of state capitals plummeted; confidence in government at all levels, which until then had seemed fairly solid, simply melted away. Nevertheless, as long as small groups of demonstrators still occupy the streets, it will be impossible to accurately assess the consequences of these movements for the political system. Divided and diverse in their opinions and demands, the middle-income groups have become a political presence that, from now on, no party dares neglect.

9

Alfredo Saad-Filho

The Economic Context of Social Protests in 2013

THE MASS MOVEMENTS that erupted in June 2013 were the largest Brazilian protests in a generation; they signaled the onset of a new wave of political polarization and social conflict in the country. These movements had a distinctive social, economic, and political character, which stands in sharp contrast to the mobilizations that took place between 1977 and 1985, which led to the collapse of the military dictatorship, and those preceding the resignation of President Fernando Collor in 1992 (they would also stand in contrast to later demonstrations taking place in 2015 and 2016, but these are outside the scope of this chapter).[1] While the earlier movements were narrowly focused around the demand for democracy, in the first instance, and the ouster of a president who was widely regarded as both corrupt and incompetent, in the second, the 2013 protests expressed a diverse set of demands concerning public service provision, governance, corruption, human rights, international sporting events, and religious matters, among other issues. These movements also received supportive media coverage at a much earlier stage than previous mass campaigns. Finally, while the earlier movements expressed left-wing transformative demands through the language of civic rights and democracy, the 2013 demonstrations reflected conflicting social, economic, and political agendas including—for the first time since 1964—extreme right-wing views.

The 2013 protests were symptomatic of the rupture of the political hegemony of the PT and the expression of a confluence of dissatisfactions that became increasingly intense in later months. Examination of the first wave of protests, in 2013, is essential for our understanding of later developments in Brazil. These dissatisfactions derived from the social, economic and political developments that took place in the country during the neoliberal period in general and, more specifically, during the federal administrations led by the Workers' Party (Partido dos Trabalhadores; PT) including the presidencies of Luiz Inácio Lula da Silva (2003–2010) and Dilma Rousseff (2011–2016). They include perceptions of missed opportunities for faster growth and rising income, distorted patterns of employment and fiscal spending, chronic dysfunctions in the political system, including perceptions of widespread corruption, and unexpected shifts in social hierarchies and income distribution.

President Lula

Lula was elected president of Brazil in 2002 by an "alliance of losers": a coalition of heterogeneous social groups that had in common only the experience of losses under neoliberalism (Morais and Saad-Filho 2003, 2005). These groups included the organized working class, the internal bourgeoisie, large segments of the traditional oligarchy, and assorted sections of the middle class and the informal workers.[2] This collection of supporters had few objectives in common beyond more expansionary macroeconomic policies and some redistribution of income, and this group was certainly not committed to a transformative economic program. In order to avoid a fourth consecutive electoral defeat, after his failed presidential bids in 1989, 1994, and 1998, Lula's campaign centered on a diffuse discourse about "change," but the candidate studiously avoided committing his administration to specific goals or even processes of change. In addition to this, several weeks before the election, Lula circulated a "Letter to the Brazilian People" stating that his government would respect contracts (i.e., service domestic and foreign debts on schedule) and enforce the policies that the preceding Cardoso administration had agreed with the International Monetary Fund (IMF). In sum, in 2002 Lula neither sought nor received a mandate to introduce policy changes leading to a break with neoliberalism—quite the contrary.

Once in power, Lula's administration maintained the neoliberal macroeconomic policy "tripod" introduced by Cardoso in 1999 after the crisis of the *real*. This included inflation targeting enforced by a virtually independent central bank, floating exchange rates supported by (essentially) free international capital flows, and fiscal restraint expressed by large primary government budget surpluses (for an assessment, see Saad-Filho and Mollo 2002,

2006). In order to further secure his credibility with financial markets, Lula appointed to the central bank a prominent member of Cardoso's Social Democratic Party (Partido da Social Democracia Brasileira; PSDB), with carte blanche to raise interest rates to the level required to secure low inflation. The executive also raised the primary fiscal surplus target from 3.75 percent of GDP to 4.25 percent and cut fiscal spending by almost 1 percent of GDP. The real minimum wage was virtually frozen for two years, and the government pushed through Congress a harsh reform of pensions and social security that had eluded Cardoso's government, partly because of the firm opposition by the PT and its left-wing allies.

The conservative credentials of Lula's "early" policies were tempered in two ways. First, the government significantly expanded the federal social assistance programs. For example, the administration consolidated four existing programs into the new Bolsa Família, in 2003, and expanded program coverage from 3 million families to 14 million (one-quarter of the country's population) in 2014 (see, for example, Mattei 2012).

Second, the Lula administration appointed a large number of left-wing political, trade union, and NGO representatives to the federal administration and the state-owned enterprises (SOEs). More than one hundred trade unionists took up these high-level posts; in turn, they appointed several hundred subordinates with a similar background (Boito 2003; Singer 2010). These personnel changes inevitably aligned the material interests of the leaders of many social movements with the government's political agenda and the interests of the state bureaucracy, effectively "nationalizing" some of the most combative sections of civil society.[3] At the same time, however, these appointments changed the social composition of the Brazilian state. For the first time, poor citizens could recognize themselves in the bureaucracy and relate to friends and colleagues who had become "important" in Brasília. This change in the composition of the high levels of the administration greatly increased the legitimacy of the state; it also committed key sectors of the administration to the government's policy agenda.

In mid-2005 Lula's government was virtually paralyzed by a furious political and media offensive triggered by the *mensalão* corruption scandal, involving allegations that government officials paid deputies and senators a monthly stipend in exchange for their votes in Congress. The string of charges related to the mensalão led to the resignation of the president's Chief of Staff, the president of the PT, and several high-ranking federal officials. The scandal triggered a catastrophic loss of support for the PT. After twenty-five years of almost uninterrupted growth, the PT reached 25 percent of voter preferences in early 2005; after the mensalão, these rates fell by half. Lula was close to being impeached, and his bid for reelection seemed close to collapse. Despite these grave setbacks, Lula's share of first-round votes reached 49 percent in October 2006 (up from 46 percent in 2002), and he maintained his second-round share at 61 percent.

This remarkable recovery was due to the transformation of Lula's base of support: he lost most of his residual support among the middle class after the mensalão but won comfortably among first-time voters, beneficiaries of transfer programs, poor women, low earners, and the unorganized poor. Their backing can be traced back to the distributive programs introduced in Lula's first administration: Bolsa Família, university admissions quotas, the formalization of the labor market, mass connections to the electricity grid (the Light for All program [Luz Para Todos]), and a 48 percent real increase in minimum wages since mid-2005, which triggered automatic increases to most pensions and benefits. For the first time, support for the PT became inversely correlated with income (Marques et al. 2009; Singer 2009). In households earning more than ten times the minimum wage (roughly, the traditional middle class), PT support fell from 32 percent in 2002 to 17 percent in 2006. Between August and October 2005, the number of voters with a university education rejecting Lula jumped from 24 percent to 40 percent; 65 percent of these voters chose the opposition candidate in 2006. In 1997 the PT had 5.5 million "high income" and 3.1 million "low income" supporters, and only 17 percent of the party's supporters earned less than twice the minimum wage. In 2006 the PT had only 3.3 million "high income" supporters but 17.6 million "low income" supporters, and 47 percent of its supporters earned less than twice the minimum wage (Singer 2010, 96–97).

The transformation of Lula's support base was part of a structural realignment of Brazilian politics. On the side of the PT governments, we observe most of the internal bourgeoisie and the organized and informal workers.[4] The opposition (that is, prior to Dilma's impeachment in 2016) drew its strength from the alliance between the neoliberal bourgeoisie and the middle class, bound together by a vitriolic mainstream media.

This political transformation was supported by a significant policy shift in Lula's second administration. The government introduced heterodox neo-developmentalist economic policies, which were juxtaposed with the neoliberal "tripod" (Morais and Saad-Filho 2011, 2012). This policy inflection included a more ambitious regulatory and planning state, higher levels of public sector investment, and a significant expansion of development loans through the National Development Bank (Banco Nacional de Desenvolvimento Econômico e Social; BNDES), as well as larger transfers and more ambitious welfare programs. These policies were associated with a marked upturn in macroeconomic performance and job creation, in the favorable context of the global boom of the mid-2000s; they also supported an unprecedented reduction of inequality in the country. It is well known that the Brazilian economy had performed poorly since the transition to neoliberalism in the early 1990s. The average real per capita GDP growth rate between 1995 and 2002, during the presidency of Fernando Henrique Cardoso, was only 0.75 percent per annum. In the first Lula administration, between 2003 and 2006, these rates reached 2.4 percent. They improved further in his second administration, between 2007 and 2010, to 3.5 percent, despite the adverse impact of the global crisis in 2009 (income growth rates declined sharply afterward, to 3.2 percent growth in 2011, around zero in 2012–2014, and contracted by 3.8 percent in 2015).

Brazil's growth surge in the mid- to late 2000s was driven by consumption and state-led investment, especially by Petrobras and Eletrobras. Investment centered on the government's "Growth Acceleration Program" (Programa de Aceleração do Crescimento; PAC) and the initial outlays to develop the country's new pre-salt offshore oilfields. These investment projects were both accompanied by a large housing program, Minha Casa Minha Vida (My House, My Life), and supported by increased funding for education, health, and other public services, in addition to the expansion of the civil service after many years of restraint. The government also supported, both diplomatically and through BNDES, the expansion and transnationalization of selected domestic firms (known as "national champions"). These include Itaú and Bradesco (banking), Embraer (aviation), Odebrecht (construction), Vale (mining), Inbev (beverages), Gerdau (steel), and Friboi and Brazil Foods (processed foods) (Boito 2003).

In turn, consumption expanded because of the rapid rise in the minimum wage, the increase in federal transfers to pensioners, the unemployed, and the disabled, and the quadrupling of personal credit, which rose from 24 percent of GDP to 45 percent, while mortgage lending expanded from R$26 billion in 2004 to R$80 billion in 2009 (Pochmann 2011). Despite these aggressive spending initiatives, the fiscal deficit remained stable and the domestic public debt declined from 55 percent of GDP in mid-2002 to around 40 percent in 2010. This was largely because of the rapid growth of GDP, the increase in fiscal revenues due to economic growth, and the program of labor market formalization, which brought in new social security contributions.

President Dilma

Lula's approval rate reached 90 percent toward the end of his second term. He handpicked and secured the election of his successor, former Chief of Staff Dilma Rousseff, who won 56 percent of the vote in the second round. Dilma was a technocrat; she had never fought an election before and had no personal base of support. Having been anointed by Lula, she inherited both his supporters and his opponents. Unsurprisingly, the voting pattern in 2010 closely mirrored that of the 2006 elections: Dilma won in the poorer states in the north and northeastern regions and in most of the Southeast, except São Paulo state. In each state, her vote was concentrated in the poorer areas and among the least educated voters. Her main rival, from PSDB, won in São Paulo and in the richer states in the "arch of agribusiness" across the South and the Center-west and, nationally, among higher income and more educated voters.

After Dilma's inauguration in January 2011, the government further expanded its social programs, with the aim of eliminating absolute poverty, and tilted economic policy slightly further toward neo-developmentalism, but without formally abandoning the neoliberal tripod. Monetary and exchange rate policies were aligned more closely with the government's industrial policy, in order to limit the current account deficit and support the internalization of strategic production chains. Real interest rates fell to their lowest levels in twenty years (from an average of 22 percent in Cardoso's first administration, to less than 3 percent under Dilma), and the Central Bank started to extend the maturity and lower the costs of the domestic public debt. In a significant departure from the earlier focus on the manipulation of interest rates, the government introduced successive rounds of tax rebates in order to stimulate production and control inflation. The government also forced private operators to reduce electricity prices. Finally, the administration sought to attract private investment into infrastructure and transport through offers of concessions, public-private partnerships, and regulatory changes. This was done in order to bypass budgetary constraints and legal limitations to state spending and to commit domestic capital to the government's investment program.

Despite these policy changes, the Brazilian economy experienced a significant slowdown under Dilma, with GDP growth rates nosediving in her ill-fated second administration. It became clear that the government had failed to kick-start a virtuous cycle of growth driven by private investment, despite the increase in fiscal spending, higher levels of investment by the public sector and state-owned enterprises, loans by state-owned banks, and the profusion of tax rebates and fiscal incentives on offer. The country also experienced a deteriorating balance of payments due to the continuing slowdown in Brazil's main external markets (China, the European Union, the United States, and Argentina), sluggish commodity prices, and aggressive devaluations and export-led recovery strategies in several large economies. Moreover, low interest rates in the leading economies followed by quantitative easing policies triggered large flows of capital to Brazil in the early years of the global crisis. This led to the appreciation of the *real* and further worsened the country's competitive position. As a result, the country's current account deficit rose from 2.1 percent of GDP in 2011 to a peak of 4.3 percent in 2014.

This worrying trend was tempered (if this is the right word) by the reversal of capital flows in 2012–2013, anticipating the unwinding of quantitative easing in the advanced economies. Their reversal triggered a crash in the São Paulo stock exchange, which tumbled from 62,000 points in January 2013 to 46,000 in July, and led to a rapid devaluation of the *real* between May and June. For these reasons, as well as the weak food crop season that followed, inflation edged up in the first months of 2013.

Under severe pressure from the media, the financial markets, its parliamentary base, the middle class, and most economists, the government reaffirmed its commitment to the inflation target regime and signaled to the Central Bank that it was time to start raising interest rates; at the same time, the Ministry of Finance announced cuts in public spending in order to purchase "credibility" from the financial markets. Although wage income and the level of employment remained stable, the cycle of sustained improvements in living standards was suspended. These policy adjustments are symptomatic of the narrow limits of government power in a globally integrated middle-income economy.

In the first months of 2013, the media and the opposition were trumpeting the "failure" of every aspect of government policy, and the "imminent threat" of runaway inflation. Their negative campaign shifted the popular mood, and Dilma's popularity fell by eight to ten percentage points, although this fall is from the extraordinary level of 70 percent, never before achieved by any Brazilian president in their third year in office.

The government's economic difficulties were compounded by political limitations. Lula was a charismatic leader, and he excelled at the conciliation of differences. Dilma lacked these virtues (Morais and Saad-Filho 2012; Saad-Filho and Morais 2014). Although she is an accomplished manager, she is said to be abrasive and intimidating toward her subordinates, and in its early years her government turned away from entrepreneurs, trade unions, left-wing NGOs, and the Landless Peasants' Movement (Movimento dos Trabalhadores Rurais Sem Terra; MST) in order to pursue an increasingly technocratic agenda. This generated a sense of despondency even among her strongest supporters; in turn, Dilma became isolated from the organized support base of her administration. After ten years in federal office, the PT seemed to have political hegemony without the substance of power; at the same time, it seemed to engage in the same dirty political games as everyone else, which undermined the party's historical claim to hold the moral high ground.

Social Policy and Distribution

The pattern of growth under Lula and Dilma unquestionably supported the reduction of poverty and inequality in Brazil across a broad spectrum of measures. In the 2000s, 21 million jobs were created, in contrast with 11 million during the 1990s. Around 80 percent of those jobs were in the formal sector, which expanded from 45 to 51 percent of the workforce.[5] Significantly, around 90 percent of these new jobs paid less than one and a half times the minimum wage, in contrast with 51 percent in the 1990s. Unemployment fell steadily, especially in the lower segments of the labor markets, reaching, in 2014, less than 6 percent of the workforce for the first time in decades. After a long period of stagnation, average real wages grew 4.2 percent per year between 2003 and 2012, and real per capita household income grew 4.6 percent per year. The real minimum wage rose 72 percent between 2005 and 2012 (8.6 percent per year), while real GDP per capita increased by a more modest 30 percent during that period. Rising minimum wages lifted the floor of the labor market and triggered simultaneous (constitutionally mandated) increases in pensions and federal transfers.

Inequality declined significantly for the first time since records began in the 1950s. The Gini coefficient fell from around 0.60 at the turn of the century to 0.53 in 2012, while the income ratio between the top 10 percent and the bottom 40 percent fell from 23 to 15. Between 2001 and 2011 the income of the poorest 10 percent rose, on average, 6.3 percent annually, in contrast with 1.4 percent per annum for the richest 10 percent (Barros, Grosner, and Mascarenhas (2012, 15). Incomes rose by 42 percent in the poorer Northeast of the country, as compared to 16 percent in the Southeast; more in the periphery than in the center of São Paulo, and more in rural than in urban areas. Female income rose by 38 percent, compared to 16 percent for men (60 percent of the jobs created in the 2000s went to women), and the income of blacks rose 43 percent compared to 20 percent for whites (Bastos 2012; Morais and Saad-Filho 2011; Pochmann 2010, 640, 648; Pochmann 2011, 38; Pochmann 2012, 32; Tible 2013, 68).

Poverty declined rapidly. The country had 60 million poor people in 1993 (41 percent of the population) and the same number again in 2003 (35 percent of the population).[6] Poverty subsequently fell rapidly, to under 30 million poor people (15 percent of the population) in 2012. The number of extremely poor individuals touched 29 million in 1993 (19 percent of the population), and 26 million in 2003 (15 percent), but fell to less than 10 million in 2012 (5 percent). The proportion of poor households fell from 35 percent in 1993 to 28 percent in 2003, and to 12 percent in 2012.

Federal social spending increased 172 percent in real terms (125 percent per capita) between 1995 and 2010, rising from 11.0 percent of GDP to 15.5 percent (16.2 percent in 2011) (Castro et al. 2012, 29; Chaves and Ribeiro 2012, 11). These growth rates were especially rapid after 2003. Higher spending permitted the creation of new social programs, including Bolsa Família, as well as the expansion of existing programs through larger payments (two-thirds of which are fixed at one minimum wage and rose in real terms by 130 percent), and an increase in the number of beneficiaries from 14.5 million to 24.4 million (with 77 percent of citizens above the age of sixty receiving benefits). However, informal workers remain largely excluded from social security coverage, including maternity pay, sick pay, and pensions in case of retirement, illness, or death (Castro et al. 2012, 14).

Higher wages, a more equal distribution of income, the expansion of social programs, and the growing availability of consumer credit benefited tens of millions of people. For the first time, many poor people could visit shopping centers, fly across the country, and buy a small car. For example, the number of automobiles in circulation rose from 42 million in 2005 to 81 million in 2013.[7] The number of passengers transiting through Brazil's sixty-three largest airports rose from 96 million to 135 million (Infraero 2016). However, rising incomes at the bottom of the pyramid were not accompanied by improvements in infrastructure, which led to a generalized perception of deterioration in the quality of urban life.[8]

The Social Movements

On June 6, 2013, the radical left Free Fare Movement (Movimento Passe Livre; MPL) led a small demonstration demanding the reversal of a recent increase in public transport fares in the city of São Paulo. A parallel increase had taken place simultaneously in Rio de Janeiro. The MPL demonstration on São Paulo's main thoroughfare was attacked by the police and criticized in the media for its unrealistic demands and the ensuing "vandalism" and disruption of traffic. In the days that followed, the MPL returned in larger numbers, and the police responded with growing brutality. Several journalists were wounded. Media alacrity due to the victimization of journalists inflamed the generalized revulsion at the police because of their perceived clumsiness and overreaction. São Paulo's transport fare protests quickly became the main national news. Political confusion soon followed, fueled by overlapping responsibilities and political rivalries across the municipal, state, and federal administrations.

In the following days, the mainstream media changed sides and started to support the movement overtly. The protesters were now portrayed as expressing the energy of youth and a popular rejection of the country's dysfunctional political system. Under the appearance of coverage, the mainstream media effectively called people to the streets and sponsored the multiplication of their demands, away from public service provision and toward a new focus on corruption and the country's political dysfunctionality. The media also claimed that the movement was non-partisan, but it was at risk of being captured by the far left. The mobilizations exploded: in less than two weeks, more than one million people took to the streets in hundreds of cities.[9]

In common with recent mass protests elsewhere, the Brazilian demonstrations in 2013 were highly heterogeneous, including a variety of groups and movements with unrelated demands concerning, inter alia, the FIFA 2013 Confederations Cup and the 2014 World Cup, gay rights, drugs policy, compulsory voting, abortion, religious issues, public spending, privatizations, Dilma Rousseff and the PT, and (for a small fringe) the call for a military coup. The focus of media coverage was firmly on corruption, against which everyone felt they could march together. The demonstrations were organized primarily through television and social media. Most demonstrations had no clear leaders and involved no speeches. Groups would form spontaneously on Facebook or Twitter,[10] advertise their events on the television, meet somewhere and then march in a random direction, depending on decisions made on the spot by unknown people.[11] Brazil experienced a "Facebookization of protest," in which anyone could come up with a personal statement about the state of the nation and offer potential followers an original remedy (Saad-Filho 2014). Marches would often merge or split up for no clear reason; some would disperse peacefully, while others were led by "Black Blocs" or unknown groups aiming to confront the police, damage commercial property, and occupy public buildings.[12]

Since "all politicians are corrupt" (a message endlessly, if subliminally, repeated by the media for many years), some marches were proclaimed to be "party-free," and left-wing militants and trade unionists were harassed by thugs. These thugs were often wrapped up in the national flag and tended to use the slogan "my party is my country," which received support from anti-political demonstrators. There was growing speculation of a plot to create an atmosphere of chaos in order to justify a military coup.

On June 19, the federal government pushed São Paulo and Rio de Janeiro to reverse the recent transport fare increases, with the offer of tax breaks and the threat of leaving them alone to sort out the mess otherwise. Their surrender was followed by speedy reversals of planned toll increases in São Paulo state and electricity price rises in Paraná. The success of the MPL placed public services at the top of the country's political agenda. However, at that point the demonstrations were out of control, and their middle-class and anti-government edge had become prominent.

In response the MPL announced that it would withdraw from the streets, and on June 21, a large number of trade unions, leftist parties, and social movements met in São Paulo to agree on a list of demands and send an open letter to President Dilma. They also proclaimed a national day of mobilizations on July 11, around issues of immediate interest to workers, primarily concerning wages, pensions, and working hours. The federal government called a meeting in Brasília to propose a "national pact," including a call for constitutional reforms, and started a health program that brought thousands of (mainly) Cuban doctors to Brazil to work in the most deprived municipalities.

The demonstrations deflated rapidly, with the exception of the national strikes on July 11. The mass movement of June was succeeded, for a few days, by scattered mobilizations of small numbers of people, often with a heavy presence of anarchists and hooligans, and then these in turn also fizzled out. Rio de Janeiro was the only exception. There, the mass movement morphed into a political offensive by the PT and radical left parties against the state governor—a member of the center-right Brazilian Democratic Movement Party (Partido do Movimento Democrático Brasileiro; PMDB) and, nominally, an ally of Dilma Rousseff—as part of the positioning of those parties in advance of the elections in October 2014.

Sporadic protests emerged over the course of the following year, illustrating the persistence of discontent with the economic slowdown, the inability of municipal, state, and federal administrations to address the country's problems of housing, health, education, transport, and other public services, and sectoral demands by key categories of workers, especially in the transport sector and the civil service. In the background, there was continuing speculation that there would be explosive protests in the run-up to the FIFA World Cup, in June–July 2014. These destabilizing reports were circulated as part of a relentless campaign against Dilma Rousseff's administration. Symptoms of imminent political and economic crisis in the country included the (undeniable) slowdown of growth and perceptions of rising inflation, economic mismanagement, widespread corruption, and the eagerly anticipated disintegration of the government's base of support in Congress.

This campaign was ramped up in early 2014, anticipating the continuing deterioration of the macroeconomic variables and the expected systems failures in the run-up to the World Cup. It was widely reported that the infrastructure would be unable to cope, that most stadiums were white elephants, that they would not be ready on time, and—unsurprisingly—that the contracts to build them were tainted with corruption. In the last month before the World Cup, the Brazilian media (with the foreign media in tow) speculated aggressively about the flaws in the country's preparation and the inevitability of a social outburst during the tournament.

In the end, nothing major happened. The stadiums were ready, the infrastructure was imperfect but coped with the demands of the Cup, and the protests were small. The most significant conflicts prior to the World Cup were strikes by several categories of workers, especially in the transport sector, and the emergence of demands by urban homeless movements, which cleverly projected their historic claims onto the World Cup in order to maximize their leverage. Grudgingly at first, Brazil was eventually gripped by one of the most successful World Cups in recent decades (at least until the national squad buckled in the final leg of the tournament).

Lessons from the Movements, Anticipating a Bleaker Future

The protest movements in 2013 shed light on the social consequences of the economic slowdown in Brazil, the multiple shortcomings of public service provision, the failings of the PT, and the political vulnerabilities of the Dilma administration even three years prior to her impeachment. A detailed examination of the protests suggests four key determinants, which may also help to frame their long-term implications. First, the protests were symptomatic of the political isolation of the government from the middle classes and the mainstream media, at two levels. On the one hand, Lula's government brought into the federal administration hundreds of left-wing political, trade union, and NGO cadres. The ensuing changes in the legitimacy of the state were called a "democratic revolution" by some analysts (such as Wu 2010). This may or may not be an exaggeration, but it was symptomatic of a new relationship between citizens and the state. Conversely, these developments increased Lula and Dilma's distance from large swathes of the middle classes, the traditional bourgeoisie, and financial market interests, which used to have almost exclusive access to the state administration. To their chagrin, the Brazilian middle classes and large sections of the traditional elites realized that—at least temporarily—they could not drive Brazilian politics on their own.

On the other hand, the PT administrations between 2003 and 2016 delivered significant improvements in social welfare and income distribution. These gains by the poor were accompanied by significant losses by the middle classes. In contrast with the creation of millions of low-paid jobs, approximately 4.3 million jobs paying more than five times the minimum wage were lost during the 2000s (compared to the creation of an additional 950,000 such jobs in the 1990s). The implication is that "good jobs" for the middle class have become scarcer, and that education no longer guarantees a high income. In sum, the middle classes lost both income and status during the PT years and feel alienated from the political system. Although these groups are relatively small, internally divided, and politically unstable, they are influential because of their economic power, privileged access to the media and social movements, and widespread ideological influence.

Second, the movements also suggest that the achievements of the PT administrations raised expectations faster than incomes: in this sense, the PT became a victim of its own success. The emerging poor want to consume more, larger masses of people want social inclusion, and both want better public services. The middle classes oscillate between indifference and hostility to the poor, but they would also like to benefit from good public services—as long as they are not asked to pay higher taxes. The outcome is that, while the middle classes are confused, exceedingly angry, and disorganized, the workers are unhappy for different reasons, marginalized, and also disorganized. This recipe for political volatility foreshadowed the extreme polarization visible during the impeachment proceedings of 2016.

Third, the 2013 protests reflect, in part, the limitations of the government's hybrid economic policies, which include the neoliberal policy tripod imposed by Fernando Henrique Cardoso's administration after the 1999 *real* crisis, and the neo-developmentalist policy "twist" introduced in Lula's second administration. Under favorable global circumstances, this hybrid macroeconomic policy framework and the greater legitimacy of the state that followed Lula's election disarmed the political right and paralyzed the radical left. However, the good economic times could not last. The economy was bound to decelerate during Dilma's administration following the boom years in the mid-2000s and Brazil's highly successful bounce back in 2010. However, GDP growth tumbled far more drastically than had been expected, the current account deficit increased, and the media sponsored a near panic in early 2013 because of the supposed threat of runaway inflation. Although inflation had barely touched the upper band of the government's target range (between 2.5 percent and 6.5 percent per annum), the Central Bank suspended its effort to reduce real interest rates in order to attend to the emergency. These adverse developments were, ultimately, due to the country's poor export growth (due, in turn, to flat commodity prices, stagnant advanced economy markets, and the economic slowdown in China), rapidly rising imports, and volatile capital flows induced by quantitative easing (and, later, its reversal) in the advanced economies. In response, the *real* fluctuated from around R$1.80 per US dollar in 2010 to R$1.60 in early 2011, to R$2.10 in 2012, R$2.35 in 2013–2014; it declined further in subsequent months, fueling the perceived threat of inflation.[13]

The government responded to these pressures with credit restrictions, spending cuts, and delays to public investment, which helped to drain the economy's sources of growth. The recession made it increasingly difficult to sustain the government's attempt to reduce inequality without directly hurting established privileges. These tribulations were magnified by a relentless media campaign suggesting that the government was out of touch, that corruption was more prevalent than usual, and that the economy was spiraling out of control. These economic difficulties were compounded by the government's political limitations in Congress, where the PT and its reliable allies have never controlled more than around one-third of the seats. This has made it impossible for Lula and Dilma to govern without alliances with undisciplined centrist parties and unsavory individuals, which must be managed under the gaze of a hostile media and the scrutiny of an unfriendly judicial system.

These difficulties were compounded by the contradictions in the modality of growth favored by the PT administrations. For example, faster economic growth in the 2000s, the distribution of income, and the wider availability of credit and tax breaks to manufacturing industry triggered the explosive growth of automobile sales, while woefully insufficient investment in infrastructure and public transport led to traffic gridlock in many large cities. Rapid urban development and the diffusion of durable household goods have overwhelmed the electricity, water, and sanitation systems, leading to power cuts and repeated disasters during the rainy season. Lack of investment condemns large cities, especially in São Paulo state, to permanent fears of water scarcity. Public health and education have expanded, but their quality is widely perceived to be poor. There has been virtually no progress on land reform, condemning millions to a life of marginality while agribusiness prospers. In this sense, the Brazilian protests were *not* primarily due to the perception of losses, except by the middle classes (who poured into the streets en masse, but only in the second phase of the movement). Instead, the protests were motivated by demands for the improvement of services that are already available, but that have become unsatisfactory in the light of the growing expectations of the poor majority. As the economy stagnated and social and distributive conflicts picked up, the government found it difficult to juggle the ensuing pressures and started to show signs of running out of steam.

Fourth, the 2013 protests and their aftermath revealed a profound disconnect between many social groups and their structures of representation (state institutions, political parties, the media, trade unions, NGOs, and so on). These structures were demonstrably unable to channel discontent and address conflicts between social groups, which is deeply problematic for Brazilian democracy in the longer term. Thus, the 2013 demonstrations and their sequels have tended to be against politics as a whole (instead of expressing a rejection of specific administrations or political leaders). Many demonstrated against Dilma and the PT, and Dilma's approval in the opinion polls slumped after June 2013. However, no one demonstrated *for* neoliberalism, Cardoso's economic policies, or the PSDB. No one demonstrated for socialism either, suggesting that, although discontent is high, radical left anticipations of an imminent revolutionary breakthrough were wide of the mark. In sum, the

Brazilian protests show that, without organization, dissatisfaction—however legitimate, widespread, and deeply felt it may be—tends to be fruitless and that spontaneous mass movements by a mixed social base fueled by unfocused anger can be destabilizing without being constructive. In sum, the Brazilian protests express a confluence of dissatisfactions. They center on both the expansion of citizenship—which has been too slow to satisfy the "emerging poor" and too rapid and indiscriminate for the traditional middle class—and the slow rates of economic growth, which have been attributed to the persistence of the neoliberal straitjacket imposed by Cardoso in 1999 or, conversely, to Lula and Dilma's misguided attempt to loosen up these neoliberal policies.

The profound differences across these dissatisfactions were veiled by the strident media campaign against corruption and political dysfunctionality in the country. The media has promoted a trite and highly abstract consensus against corruption and political distortions, fed by studious leaks and spectacular actions of the Public Prosecutor and the Federal Police. In the meantime, the artificial opposition created between endless scandals, which everyone opposes, and the vacuous notion of a nation united in its desire for a "clean" political system obscure the underlying causes of social dissatisfaction. These contradictory demands and expectations could probably be managed politically if the Brazilian economy was growing, but its unprecedented contraction makes every grievance more urgent and every constraint tighter. This is a recipe for structural instability and political volatility, with limited scope for the emergence of widely accepted institutional and economic policy reforms.

At a further remove, the inability of large social groups to find appropriate channels of representation has led to the "lumpenization of protest."[14] Political protests tend to become disarticulated because of the erosion of the middle class, changes in the employment patterns of formal and informal workers, and the institutional limitations of political parties, trade unions, and NGOs. In these circumstances, when social protests eventually emerge they tend to be unfocused, destructive, and individualistic and include disparate social groups with poorly articulated and sometimes conflicting demands. These are vulnerable to capture by more powerful and better-organized social groups.[15] In contrast, "traditional" protest movements (for example, those taking place during Brazil's democratic transition) were associated with the creation and consolidation of organizations and movements that accumulated experiences of success as well as failure and developed increasingly sophisticated practices.

In Brazil and elsewhere many social groups and large segments of the younger population are disorganized and distrustful of structures of representation that, from their point of view, are ineffective. At the same time the diffusion of direct modalities of web-based communication tends to reduce the perceived need for representation, including by the traditional media. Instead, individual aspirations and desires tend to be articulated directly and expressed in an unmediated form. When groups organized in this way appear in the "real world," they tend to perform a spectacle that can be relayed back to their "friends" in the ether, creating incentives for the individualization of demands and the personalization of the means of delivery through humor, colorful disguises, and so on. Facebook becomes the world, and the world is what appears on Facebook. Unsurprisingly, then, the Brazilian demonstrations were media-friendly, and many demonstrators were more intent on taking pictures than demanding well-defined political reforms. In this sense, *social protest was not only lumpenized: it was also Facebookized.*

The lumpenization and Facebookization of protest, underpinned by the disarticulation of traditional social structures and their institutions of representation and collective action, are limited at three levels. First, the aggregation of spontaneous demands does not directly promote social organization or support the emergence of cogent, ambitious, and historically informed programs of social change. Instead, they foster simplification and "common sense," that is, the formulation of demands in the broadest terms (for general acceptability—and more Facebook "likes"). These are naturally framed in the language of "rights" (to transport, housing, work, health, education, drugs, abortion, self-expression, and so on) and, closely related, claims for "respect" for any self-identified group (women, gay people, teachers, truck drivers, ethnic minorities, inhabitants of specific neighborhoods, and so on). In other words, the decomposition of traditional social structures under neoliberalism and the nearly simultaneous emergence of web-based forms of communication tend to channel social discontent toward a universalist ethics that elides the social divisions in modern societies and supports "spontaneous" demands based on minimum common denominators. In turn, common sense demands can rarely be transformative, which makes it difficult to address the needs they ultimately express.

Second, direct representation and "horizontality" (the lack of hierarchies within the movement) foster individualism and structural disorganization. Disorganized dissatisfaction tends to explode and then evaporate, however. That is, spontaneous mass movements with a mixed social base and fueled by unfocused anger can be destabilizing but are rarely constructive, and they have great difficulty supporting alternative institutions or forms of social organization.

Third, the need for organization, delegation of power, and compromises within the movement and with outside institutions suggests that successful social movements are predicated on the creation of collectivity *in practice*.

This means talking and doing things together, more than interacting through web-based media. Twitter and Facebook are good ways to exchange discrete morsels of information, but they do not allow the exchange of ideas and the formation of the personal and collective bonds of trust that are essential to sustain long-lasting social movements.

Conclusion

The protest movements in Brazil in June 2013 seemed straightforward on television. Millions of poor people were showing their fury, having finally realized that the country's flawed political system was unable to deliver decent public services despite faster economic growth, Brazil's promotion from economic basket case to emerging powerhouse, and the rapid increase in private consumption. If I live in one of the BRICS and can now borrow my way to happiness, why does it still take me three hours to get to work, why is there no sanitation in my street, why are my child's teachers on strike again, why do I have to fear the police, why are they building fancy stadiums in cities without football teams, and why are all politicians thieves? The brutality of the police repression against the initial demonstrations in São Paulo invited a simplistic analogy with the "Arab Spring" and with the Gezi Park protests in Istanbul and suggested that political decency and respect for human rights are irrepressible universal values.

On closer inspection, the roots of the movement were shown to be complex and often contradictory. The wave of protests emerging in mid-2013 was the outcome of deeply felt needs and repeated disappointments that cannot be understood simply through the newspaper headlines. The protests were, first, associated with historically unmet needs for public service provision and long-standing perceptions of corruption and political dysfunction in Brazil. However, the long-standing nature of these needs leaves unexplained the timing and form of the demonstrations. In addition to this, these persistent needs cannot be directly related to the social composition of the demonstrations, which included a disproportionate number of relatively educated and well-paid middle-class participants—that is, many protesters were complaining about public services they do not actually use.[16]

Second, the protests were driven to a considerable extent by the mainstream media. It is essential to appreciate that *all* mainstream newspapers and television chains shifted, almost simultaneously, from minimizing and criticizing the protests to supporting the demonstrations stridently under the appearance of "coverage." This was replicated by the media coverage of the expected mobilizations against the World Cup, in mid-2014. Despite these expectations and the apocalyptic predictions that key parts of the infrastructure either would not be ready in time or would be unable to cope, the protests failed almost completely to materialize.[17] Media opposition to the World Cup was abruptly reversed days before the event. Nevertheless, the confrontational attitude of the country's main newspapers and television stations persisted throughout the 2014 election campaign, and worsened during the Lava Jato scandal and Dilma's impeachment proceedings in 2015–2016. Given the weakness of the political parties of the right, it was the mainstream news media that took up the mantle of the opposition to the PT after the mid-2000s.[18] The administrations led by Lula and Dilma are routinely measured against the highest possible standards. In contrast, the Cardoso government and the state and municipal administrations led by the PSDB are treated leniently, despite allegations of vast corruption within the privatization program of the 1990s, the blatant economic mismanagement in the run-up to the collapse of the *real* in 1999, and large corruption scandals in the states of São Paulo and Minas Gerais.

Media opposition and middle-class hostility feed upon each other. They can be explained, in part, by the attachment of the media to the finance-friendly neoliberal program pursued by Lula's immediate predecessor and the loss of both income and social status by the middle class during the PT administrations.[19] They also relate to the disastrous loss of economic dynamism in the country and the political fractures among the powerful domestic sectors that drove Lula's economic policies, and which Dilma was unable to keep on side (Boito 2012; Morais and Saad-Filho 2012).

Finally, the protests were mediated by the disarticulation of the working class under neoliberalism and the emergence of new forms of web-based communication that allow millions of people to exchange information instantly and to mobilize at short notice. This has contributed to the explosive yet diffuse nature of the Brazilian protests and their rapid evaporation at the end of June 2013; a similar cycle took place in 2015. These protests show that, although the political right can mobilize large masses of people (as was also shown in Brazil in 1964 and, subsequently, in France under de Gaulle, Chile under Allende, and Venezuela under Chávez and Maduro, among other examples), these political groupings do not currently have a cogent political program in Brazil. This limitation, combined with the genuine advances made by the poor and the workers during the last decade, drastically reduces the space for the articulation of a right-wing political program. The impasse remains: the radical left has no traction; the reformist left led by the PT could not deliver growth or address the deeply felt dissatisfactions of millions of poor and middle-class people, and the extreme right must hide in order to prosper.

The protests opened a new phase of political contestation in Brazil. New

actors emerged, and they started to articulate their views and needs in a much more overt manner than had previously been possible. Yet their dissatisfactions were often contradictory: more social inclusion or the return of elite influence? Higher wages and benefits or lower taxes and greater competitiveness? Political reform or business as usual? These deadlocks have no easy resolution, and they are likely to make the next decade in Brazil at least as interesting as the previous one.

STRATEGIES OF
GLOBAL PROJECTION

PART IV

10

Sean Burges and Jean Daudelin

Democracy
Postponed

A Political Economy of
Brazil's Oligarchic
Foreign Policy

THE EBBS AND flows of pressure to democratize Brazil's foreign policy hold considerable implications for Brazil's Ministry of Foreign Affairs, Itamaraty, which claims a monopoly over the formulation and practice of the country's diplomacy. There are distinct questions of the democratic character of Brazilian foreign policy and the extent to which it is monopolized by Itamaraty (Lopes 2013). Just as a state's monopoly over the means of violence tells us little about a country's democratic nature, the monopolization of diplomacy by a foreign ministry provides scant insight into the political character of a country's foreign policy.

We make five related arguments. First, Brazil's deepening insertion in the global strategic and political economy has led both to a certain democratization of its foreign policy and to a weaker hold by Itamaraty over policy formulation and implementation. In particular, the opening of the Brazilian economy implied that the lives and interests of a growing number of people were affected by the outside world, and foreign policy suddenly mattered for them in very concrete ways. A degree of engagement resulted, from both the private sector and the public, which opened up the range of interests foreign policy was meant to defend and promote. At the same time, the greater public relevance of foreign policy increased its political appeal, leading several of the country's successive presidents, in particular Fernando Henrique Cardoso and Luiz Inácio Lula da Silva, to take from Itamaraty a much larger share of foreign policy-making and diplomatic activities than before.

Second, by global standards and in spite of the opening just mentioned, Brazil remains relatively insulated from the vagaries of world affairs. The stakes at play in domestic politics still dominate electoral contests and make foreign policy issues a transitory and minor political side note at best. As a consequence, broad-based public engagement in international affairs remains limited and democratization pressures weak. The result is a policy regime best characterized as "oligarchic," although at times interest engagement either narrows even further—or conversely, broadens—creating both monarchic and democratic "moments."

Third, the pressures on Itamaraty's monopoly resulting from Brazil's deeper global insertion have been reinforced by the peculiar institutional forms of the country's engagement. For the most part, Brazilian diplomacy has invested in a broad range of poorly institutionalized regional and global multilateral mechanisms. Effective policy through such channels calls for the mobilization of political capital that diplomats can rarely muster, creating a space that could best—and sometimes, only—be occupied by the country's presidents.

Fourth, the growing technical requirements of international policy-making has forced the generalists, who overwhelmingly dominate the Ministry, to rely on the expertise of other government departments or even outside think tanks and specialists. This further weakens Itamaraty's monopoly. In areas such as trade and investment, the private sector is running several steps ahead of the government, creating more coordination challenges not just for Itamaraty but also for increasingly internationally engaged departments such as Finance, Agriculture, and Development, Industry and Trade.

Fifth, in spite of these structural, institutional, and technical pressures, Itamaraty's hold over foreign policy remains quite strong. To a certain extent this is due to successful resistance by a powerful subsection of Itamaraty's senior staff tightly focused on a defensive bureaucratic posture. Through the end of President Dilma Rousseff's first term in office these influential policy-makers successfully mobilized the Ministry's substantial prestige and general expertise to maintain their dominant position, an achievement greatly facilitated by the relatively marginal place of foreign affairs in Brazil's broader policy arena.

This chapter unfolds in three steps. The first briefly outlines the theoretical framework, which proposes to look at the institutional and political mechanics of foreign policy-making and implementation as a policy regime, that is, as a more or less institutionalized system of rules and norms that organize the activities of the social actors involved in policy-making and implementation. We then turn to the evolution of Brazil's "insertion" into international strategic structures and the global political economy. We map out a few key democratic and monarchic "moments" over the last thirty years of Brazilian foreign policy and documents broader public engagement in foreign policy, namely, slow moves toward a fuller, albeit never fully realized, democratization of the regime. Finally, we look at the implications of the changing structural and institutional environments of foreign policy for Itamaraty's monopoly over the means of diplomacy, especially in recent years. It illustrates the main ways in which these dynamics have weakened the relative position of Itamaraty in Brazil's foreign policy regime, and its grip over the country's external engagement. Given its scope, this argument is by necessity somewhat impressionistic. It relies on relatively few key examples but we feel that they clearly demonstrate how structural constraints and freedoms linked to the country's changing global strategic and economic insertion have played out very concretely in everyday foreign-policy-making, affecting both the scope of interests it represents and the range of actors that play a key role in it.

Democracy and Foreign Policy

Following Adam Przeworski, we understand democracy as the institutionalization of uncertainty for all social interests (Przeworski 1991). Democracy is an arrangement whose institutional makeup—normative and organizational—ensures that the outcome of the political process protects no single actor's interests in particular. Broad social engagement is a necessary condition to the democratic character of a given policy regime because the involvement of the few would likely lead to less uncertainty, or none at all, for their own interests.

Such broad engagement rarely happens in the real life of policy-making. The relevance and impact of most issues are simply too narrow to justify the significant investment by the large number of actors that would be implied in substantive and direct engagement. We thus propose a lower threshold and consider policy regimes democratic when a space exists for direct engagement, for open and public debate, when some congressional as well as public engagement effectively takes place, and where the content of this debate in turn does influence the formation and implementation of policy. This would include regular media and public mobilization around an issue on a potentially mass basis or, within a more formalized context, through institutions such as congressional committees or other consultative bodies that routinely convene and directly engage policy-makers.

Even in well-established democracies, foreign policy development and implementation is typically not very democratic, or at best only episodically so. Still, when international challenges of critical importance emerge, broad and fierce public engagement sometimes results, creating democratic

Policy Change	Year(s)
Rapprochement with Argentina	1985–1986
Unilateral trade liberalization	1989–1990
Establishment of Mercosul	1993
Signature of the Non-proliferation Treaty	1996
Opposition to the FTAA	1994–2000
South American "pivot" (first South American Presidential Summit)	2000
Southern "pivot" (major investment in relations with Africa and Asia)	2003–2006
Establishment of the India-Brazil-South Africa Forum	2003
Recognition of China as a market economy	2004
Establishment of UNASUL	2004
Involvement of Brazil (with Turkey) in defense of Iran's right to develop civilian nuclear program	2007
Brazilian support for the admission of Venezuela in Mercosul	2006
Creation of the Community of Latin American and Caribbean States (CELAC)	2010

Table 10.1. Key Policy

"moments." For most countries, most of the time, such moments are rare, and foreign policy remains a side issue, the preserve of specialists and of special interests. As a result, it is not a particularly democratic policy field. This also stems in part from the fact that the discussions and expertise involved are often esoteric, making the implications of the policies debated unclear for social interests—and engagement, direct or indirect, less likely. Foreign policy making also usually takes place in spaces, physical or virtual, that are not truly open and whose access is in fact typically restricted.

In other words, foreign policy making is usually oligarchic, conforming to a policy regime where all interests are *not* submitted to the rule of uncertainty, even in well-established democracies (Daudelin 1995). The one major exception among significant international players is probably the United States, where Congress and the president, for good or ill, *regularly* engage in very public foreign policy debates that reverberate widely through the media, and where a range of interest groups feed a lively and broad-based discussion of foreign policy. The situation in Brazil, by contrast, is much more typical

Developments under Democracy				
Presidency	*Electoral Theme*	*Public Consultations*	*Congressional Debate*	*Public Debate*
José Sarney	No	No	No	No
Fernando Collor de Melo	No	No	No	Yes
Itamar Franco	No	No	Yes	Limited
Fernando Henrique Cardoso	No	No	Yes	Limited
Itamar Franco, Fernando Henrique Cardoso	No	Limited	No	Limited
Fernando Henrique Cardoso	No	No	No	Limited
Luiz Inácio Lula da Silva	No	No	No	Limited
Luiz Inácio Lula da Silva	No	No	No	No
Luiz Inácio Lula da Silva	No	No	Limited	Limited
Luiz Inácio Lula da Silva	No	No	No	Limited
Luiz Inácio Lula da Silva	No	No	No	Limited
Luiz Inácio Lula da Silva	No	No	Limited	Limited
Luiz Inácio Lula da Silva	No	No	No	Limited

of the general trend. A number of significant changes in the country's foreign policy or in policies that profoundly affect its global insertion (e.g., trade liberalization) have taken place since the end of the 1980s without the issues ever becoming electoral themes, without broad-based formal public consultations, with limited congressional inputs, and in the absence of broad public debate (see Table 10.1). Even in those rare instances where open public consultation does take place, the foreign policy elite, and Itamaraty in particular, keeps close control of the process. This was demonstrated during the 2014 public consultations resulting from foreign minister Luiz Alberto Figueiredo's call for input on a possible foreign policy white paper. Tellingly, the public presentations and discussions were conducted in the large formal meeting halls of the Itamaraty Palace in Brasília, not in regional centers away from the capital. Perhaps even more significantly, two years after completion of the consultations, there was little word about the existence of even a draft white paper based on those discussions, much less rumor of its release.

Two caveats suggest that the "baseline" political character of a policy regime does not tell its whole story. The first concerns the rapid changes that sometimes affect the social relevance or breadth of a given issue. Political and policy regimes, even stable ones, have "uncharacteristic" moments where elected presidents or prime ministers behave and act like monarchs, or during which massive mobilizations support the policy decisions of autocratic rulers. To take an extreme and no doubt polemical example, the invasion of the Falklands by Argentina's military regime should probably be seen as a profoundly democratic moment when a broad range of social sectors converged in support of a decidedly undemocratic government's decision. The strong emphasis with which Cristina Kirchner, by no means an apologist of the military regime, seized upon the Malvinas as a major tenet of her foreign policy underlines the continuing strength and breadth of its appeal.

By contrast, one can also think of many "quasi-monarchical moments" in the foreign policy of Lula when little else but his own views and interests appear to have been at play (Table 10.1). One case with significant adverse repercussions for Brazil's manufacturing sector was Lula's decision to seek Beijing's support for a permanent Brazilian seat at the UN Security Council, by recognizing China as a market economy. Very clear objections to this policy were raised not only by Brazil's industrial elite but also in Brazil's Senate Foreign Relations and National Defence Committees, because market recognition makes it almost impossible to take anti-dumping action against China in the World Trade Organization (WTO). A more familiar quasi-monarchical moment was Lula's May 2010 attempt, with Turkey, to broker a way out of the Iranian nuclear enrichment impasse, a policy for which there was virtually no domestic constituency outside of small pockets in the Workers' Party (Partido dos Trabalhadores; PT) hard-core and some old-guard corners of the military.

Second, the monopoly of the means of diplomacy is but one possibility on a whole continuum of concentration of control over foreign policy development and implementation, and a priori, there is no reason to think that an authoritarian policy regime is necessarily monopolistic or that a democratic one necessarily involves a fragmentation of policy praxis. On the contrary, while many dictators are fond of foreign travels and activism, diplomats and foreign ministers often play important roles along state leaders in very closed regimes: think for instance of Andrei Gromyko, who led the the USSR's Ministry of Foreign Affairs between 1957 and 1985. Conversely, extensive engagement around foreign policy decisions can take place while policy formulation and implementation, including complete control over international negotiations, remain firmly in the hands of the diplomatic corps.

These two parameters—democracy and monopoly—could be combined to create a two-dimensional matrix that defines four ideal-types of policy regimes. For the sake of simplicity we will look at each of those parameters separately here, assessing the democratic character of a policy regime and the location and degree of concentration of institutional control over it. We then organize and classify a few key policy "moments" of recent years from the standpoint of the breadth of the social and political engagement and the degree of fragmentation of policy-making that they involved.

A Superficial Economic and Strategic Insertion

A series of structural factors have historically helped to insulate and preserve the monopolistic and oligarchic tendencies in Brazilian foreign policy. In spite of its large population, cornucopia of resources, and often ballyhooed "continental size," Brazil has never been much of a player internationally. For most of its history Brazil has played no significant role in the main currents of global affairs. Between the consolidation of its frontiers early in the twentieth century and its push for subregional integration in the 1980s, Brazil has also not had a concerted or sustained presence in regional politics. A self-centered gentle giant with population centers concentrated along an Atlantic coast that lies thousands of kilometers away from most of its Latin neighbours, Brazil has mostly turned its attention away from the continent.

The overwhelming presence of the United States and Washington's credible claim to strategic prominence over the whole hemisphere have understandably preoccupied the country's political, military, and foreign policy establishment (Almeida and Barbosa 2006; Bandeira 2004; Crandall 2011; Hirst 2005; Smith 2010; Spektor 2009; Van Eeuwen 2010). In practical terms, this has not been very consequential, as the United States' direct relevance in Brazilian politics and for its economy has been limited, except perhaps in a paradoxical way (Smith 2010). America's strategic umbrella over the hemisphere has provided a de facto security guarantee against extra-regional intervention that has allowed Brazil to get away with remarkably limited investments in defence and national security.

One country that has historically preoccupied Brazil is Argentina, although its importance has both changed over time and diminished overall. Up until World War II, Argentina was recognized as a true strategic threat (Bandeira 2003; Medeiros and Ferraz 2010; Spektor 2002, 2004; Vidigal 2010), a status it progressively lost, with the last nail in this coffin being the nuclear agreement that committed both countries to terminating their atomic weapons programs. Argentina's importance for Brazil has become significant on the economic front, although it too has been declining in relative terms since the mid-1990s (interestingly, in keeping with the launch and development of the Mercado Comum do Sul; Mercosul). Today, trade with Argentina represents a small proportion of Brazil's GDP—1.5 percent in 2012—and it only matters because much of it, contrary to the rest of Brazil's other exports, is

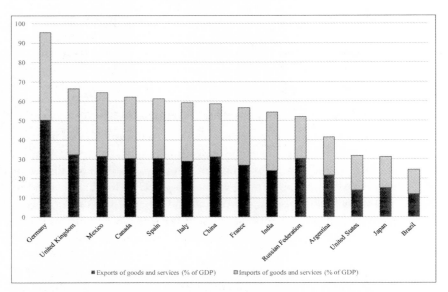

Figure 10.1. Trade as Percentage of GDP (2011), Largest World and
Latin American Economies. *Source*: World Databank.

made up of manufactured products, which is consequential for Brazil's belea-
guered industrial sector.

Traditionally, Brazil's most important external vulnerability has been its
dependence on imported energy, primarily oil. Although Brasília had a limited capacity to act on this through foreign policy, what could be done was
done swiftly. The giant Itaipu hydro project was quickly negotiated with tiny
Paraguay and has proved to be critical to national energy security, still supply-
ing 17 percent of Brazil's electricity in 2013. Guaranteeing oil and gas supplies
proved much trickier and was essentially immune to diplomacy. For much
of the last fifty years, Brazil was doomed to be a "taker" in the global energy
game and to a certain extent subject to the political vagaries of otherwise
marginal countries such as Bolivia, a central source of natural gas from the
late 1990s on (Hollanda 2001). This element of insecurity has eased in recent
years thanks to massive offshore oil and gas discoveries that have effectively
insulated the country from a global energy landscape that, anyway, does not
look very challenging anymore.

Brazil's economic health depends in part on access to foreign markets for
its products. That dependence has been increasing in recent years, but at just
27 percent of GDP the portion of trade in Brazil's GDP is still very small by
global standards (see Figure 10.1). Moreover, Brazil's import and export matrix have become remarkably balanced with, on average for the last decade,
about one-fifth each in Latin America, the United States, the EU, and China.

Finally, a significant—and increasing—proportion of its exports is made up of primary goods, both minerals and agricultural commodities, whose prices were at historical highs during the 2000s and, in spite of recent declines in global mineral prices, retain very good long-term prospects on the agro-industrial front (Veiga 2007).

Access to capital is similarly unproblematic. Domestic investment is to a large extent state-driven and significant in scale (see Armijo in this book; Hochstetler and Montero 2013). The size of an internal market, increased by deepened social reforms, the relative stability of Brazil's economy, and the potential of its primary goods export sector, made the country a magnet for domestic and foreign private investment through the 2000s, a situation that should return once the political conflicts emerging in second Dilma presidency and beyond are resolved—which, admittedly, could take time (Brainard and Martínez-Díaz 2009). Furthermore, sound and relatively prudent economic policy over the last two decades has drastically reduced the priority given to rich countries' treasuries and international financial institutions in the calculations of Brazilian decision-makers, which they used to dominate. As post-2014 events demonstrate, Brazil's economy is not recession proof, or immune from external shocks, but its fate is truly in the hands of its own government. Lastly, while Brazilian companies have lately become quite active on global markets, these activities have been dominated by a small number of firms such as the mining giant Vale and construction combines such as Odebrecht, which often finance their operations with internal resources that in some cases have been earned and held outside of Brazil. These holdings remain relatively small in size when put in a global context, and they are of minor importance to the country's economic performance (see Figure 10.2). In sum, Brazil's peculiar and privileged insertion in the global strategic and political economies, anchored by relatively inelastic global commodity export demand, makes foreign policy largely irrelevant to the country's economic stability and strategic safety.

Democracy and Democratic Brazil's Foreign Policy

In such a context, sustained engagement with foreign policy issues by broad sectors of Brazilian society and politicians does not make much sense. Unsurprisingly, therefore, foreign policy has played a marginal role in the country's political life. Outside of an op-ed page debate between secondary players, it continued virtually absent from electoral discussions during the 2014 presidential election and it has gained only episodic prominence in congressional debates. An interesting window into such marginality is the absence of controversy or debate surrounding the nomination of a foreign minister in Dilma Rousseff's first cabinet: whereas all other cabinet and senior administrative

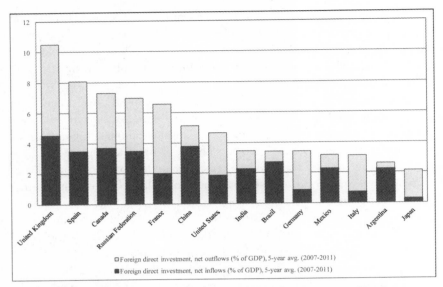

Figure 10.2. Total FDI flows as percentage of GDP, largest world and Latin American economies. *Source*: World Databank.

positions were claimed—sometimes forcefully—by the various parties of the governing coalition in exchange for political support, no one demanded Itamaraty. Dilma was left free to pick Antonio Patriota, an experienced diplomat with extensive international experience most recently as ambassador in Washington, but without public profile and, from a policy standpoint, an unknown quantity: what he thought about the country's foreign endeavors and positions simply did not matter to the public or the political forces represented in the Brazilian Congress and a fortiori for the public at large.

Three caveats must be introduced at this point. The first is that Brazil's strategic and economic insertion, while still relatively superficial, has been deepening in recent years (Vigevani and Cepaluni 2009). A doubling of the weight of exports as a proportion of GDP matters and implies that trade issues are likely to draw more interest—and *interests*—than in the past, although the change has more to do with rises in the price of commodities than in the physical volumes shipped. The second caveat is that, while little if anything is seen to be immediately at stake in foreign policy for Brazilian society as a whole, much is often at play for selected social, political, and economic sectors. For example, the ever-influential agricultural interests and the huge engineering firms—the *empreiteiras* whose global presence has been expanding very significantly in recent decades (Fleury and Fleury 2011)—have noticed a change from Lula to Dilma. During the Lula years these firms could rely upon their president to act as door opener and their government as something of a facilitator. These support mechanisms largely disappeared as Dilma eschewed foreign policy in favor of domestic concerns. Lastly, even in the context of an essentially stable strategic environment "things happen," from regional or local crises to policy decisions by neighbors or significant global players, which create conjunctures that affect broad interests. These caveats imply that, while Brazil's foreign policy has remained essentially oligarchic over the last twenty years, it has also been poked by "moments" during which social engagement, be it practical or symbolic, became broad enough for such episodes to be deemed "democratic." There were also moments in which foreign policy appeared to obey little more than the whims of the "reigning" president, and we propose to call such moments "monarchic."

An Oligarchic "Situation"

The most important element in Brazil's foreign policy landscape over the last three decades has certainly been the country's reengagement with the world. The military regime did have a clear foreign policy, and its peculiar modalities of strategic alignment and non-alignment were aptly characterized as "responsible pragmatism" (Lima and Moura 1982; Spektor 2002, 2004). However, it is difficult to negate that, given its size, population, resources, and strategic importance in the Americas and in the world, Brazil during that period was very much "punching below its weight," both regionally and globally, an attitude wonderfully captured by Vigevani and Cepaluni (2009) as a quest for "autonomy through distance." Such reserve, however, was abandoned once civilians were back in charge.

A major deepening of Brazil's international insertion started as a by-product of the economic liberalization policies launched by the Fernando Collor de Mello administration in 1990, pushing a substantial foreign policy shift onto Itamaraty to get the country to look outward as a "global trader" (Barbosa and César 1994). Privatization processes were married with the launch of the subregional economic space Mercosul, positioning the bloc as an incubator to prepare Brazilian business for global competition. A deeper shift took place as a result of the privatizations when foreign investors brought in new managerial and production techniques or Brazilian managers of domestically held firms took the opportunity to systematically reform their corporate operations and begin a search for new international markets for their products (Amann 1999; Bonelli 1999; Fleury and Fleury 2011).

The impact of Collor's efforts was almost immediate, with exports to bloc partners Argentina, Paraguay, and Uruguay jumping from US$1.38 billion in 1989 to US$4.1 billion in 1992 and just over US$9 billion by 1997. While still a relatively minor component of Brazilian GDP (and one that would drop precipitously with financial crises in Brazil and then Argentina), the exports were predominantly concentrated in manufactured products. This rapid shift created a sudden awareness among the Brazilian industrial elite that they needed to pay attention to the regional and international markets.

This new interest in external economic factors had a crucial impact on the negotiating stands taken toward the Free Trade Area of the Americas. While Brazil arguably never intended to sign on to the deal (Arashiro 2011; Magalhães 1999), a knee-jerk approach against the US-proposed hemispheric trade deal was avoided. As policy-makers involved in the process explained, many countries in Latin America that were becoming small but meaningful economic partners for Brazil found the idea of an agreement with the United States appealing, which meant that direct opposition to the deal could be prejudicial to the emerging regional interests of Brazilian firms. However, there was also a clear sense from the Brazilian agro-industrial sector that they would be a net loser due to US subsidy policies that Washington refused to discuss, and Brazilian industrialists were concerned that the advantages they had gained in Mercosul would be lost if faced with competition from US firms. The strategy devised by Cardoso and his advisors was thus one of never saying no to the Free Trade Area of the Americas (FTAA) but, instead, tying the whole process up in consultative processes and detailed technical discussions. In the end, the negotiations suffocated on their own, largely as a result of a lack of momentum in the United States, epitomized by the thorny political debates around the annual US farm bill and a lack of so-called fast track negotiating authority. Itamaraty implemented this soft veto policy, but the strategic direction and rationale was heavily influenced, if not directed, by the presidency and the country's emerging internationally oriented industrial sector (Magalhães 1999; Barbosa 2011; Lampreia 2010).

Brazil's deliberate turn toward Africa and the global South during the Lula years followed a similar path. While traditionally United States– and Europe-centered sectors in Itamaraty and mainstream business elites saw the attention given to Africa and South America as an ideological extravagance that would fundamentally damage Brazil's core interests (Cabral 2007), the response from Brazil's empreiteiras was one of delight. Trade with Africa is marginal, barely increasing from 4.7 percent of Brazil's total trade in 2002 to 5.7 percent in 2012, or $26.5 billion for the *entire* continent. Yet, this trade was highly concentrated in specific industrial sectors and underpinned by large investments from a small group of major resource and construction companies. Activities that the empreiteiras had been quietly undertaking in Africa and South America from the early 1990s (such as Odebrecht's large infrastructure projects in Angola) mushroomed in the 2000s, benefiting considerably from Lula's developing rock-star status in the global South. Parallel gains were made by companies like mining giant Vale, oil company Petrobras, and electricity utility Eletrobras, all of which engaged in a series of major foreign direct investment operations across the Southern Hemisphere: the empreit-eiras won several billion-dollar contracts for infrastructure projects such as airports, subway systems, ports, and hydroelectric dams (Odebrecht's global revenues in 2013 topped US$ 40 billion), and Petrobras and Vale opened ma-jor new resource extraction operations, a notable example being Vale's $6 billion (and growing) cash investment in the Moatize coal mine projects in Mozambique.

The Mozambique case highlights how the economic logic of the policy shift to Africa was tied to the outlook and interests of a small group rather than to wider societal interests or the views of traditional elites. Just as Vale was ramping up its investment in Moatize and pulling in a string of empre-iteiras to undertake the needed infrastructure construction, the leading Bra-zilian newspaper *O Estado de São Paulo* published an editorial complaining that Brazil's engagement in the country relied on little more than charm and lamenting that China was investing one billion dollars in mineral explora-tion while Brazil's engagement was a paltry US$26 million for an incomplete pharmaceutical factory (*O Estado de São Paulo* 2012b). For the traditional foreign policy elite of Itamaraty the focus of attention had always been the United States and Europe, with attempts to engage areas such as Africa little more than a passing fancy (Dávila 2010). Lost in this geopolitical focus were the economic interests of Brazil's empreiteiras, manufacturers, and resource extraction companies, all of whom, thanks to state support, were rapidly ex-ploiting even larger opportunities in South America and Africa than they could hope to find in the more competitive markets of the United States and European Union. Although these initiatives could be seen as part of a democ-ratizing process because foreign policy was redirected in response to demands from a slightly wider interest segment within Brazil, the regime in the end remained oligarchic.

A Monopoly Challenged

Aside from a limited movement toward democracy, the involvement of new actors and the challenge they represent for Itamaraty's traditional monopoly over the means of diplomacy represents a critical change in Brazil's foreign policy regime. This second mutation can be traced to three main factors. The increased technical requirements of international engagement, particularly on trade and economic issues, strains the capacities of a diplomatic corps that consists mostly of generalists. The weak institutionalization of the country's preferred multilateral channels of diplomacy (from Mercosul on) leaves dip-lomats with few means to manage their own important problems that arise in the country's foreign relations and forces them to appeal to the president. And the growing if still episodic political appeal of foreign policy acts like a honey pot for politicians, particularly presidents. It must be emphasized, however, that without the structural push that deep economic or strategic insertion would provide, these dynamics have had a limited impact. In the end, Itamaraty remains very much in charge.

Generalists Meet the Technical Turn in Global Affairs

The expanding scope and complexity of international negotiations and public policy puts a premium on the kind of technical expertise generally lacking in diplomatic bureaucracies that are staffed by generalists and that value flexibility. This evolution puts pressure on diplomats to involve other branches of government or even outsiders in foreign policy development and implementation (Faria 2012; Faria, Lopes, and Casarões 2013; Pinheiro and Milani 2012). Professional diplomats are pushed toward coordination roles, which remain critical but give them much less control and prestige than if they monopolized the whole policy chain. Professional and institutional cultures, as well as bureaucratic rivalries, predictably play themselves out but with an additional symbolic dimension that is tied to the special prestige of diplomacy and international affairs, long seen—especially by its wordly and polyglot practitioners—as a kind of aristocratic enclave. This change affects several fields, from nuclear energy and health to fisheries, telecoms, and environmental issues. It is, however, around trade that this latent conflict has been playing out most intensely because trade negotiations are highly visible and their outcomes are consequential.

Brazil is no exception, and its deepening insertion has led to significant challenges to the monopoly claimed by the country's diplomats over the country's trade policy. This became particularly apparent in the early 2000s as trade talks within the WTO began to heat up. For critics of Brazil's trade policy, the Itamaraty old boys' network approach to foreign affairs was a major problem. Marcos Jank, an agricultural economist at the University of São Paulo and the Inter-American Development Bank, as well as the founder of the think tank ICONE, the Institute for International Trade Negotiations in São Paulo (Instituto de Estudos do Comércio e Negociações Internacionais), did not mince words: "Brazilian diplomats have a vast know-how when it comes to geopolitical questions, but their experience in conducting trade negotiations is small" (Osse and Cardoso 2002). Jank later went on to extol Itamaraty and the quality of its diplomats, but with a huge caveat: "*The diplomats* do not have the capacity to evaluate the impact on specific [Brazilian] export sectors of offers to reduce or decisions to impose higher import tariffs by another country or trade bloc" (Jank 2003).

Jank's criticism was effectively echoed within Lula's cabinet by two powerful new voices with distinct international interests. Luiz Fernando Furlan had left his position as head of the Brazilian food multinational Sadia to head the Ministry of Development, Industry and Foreign Trade. The Ministry of Agriculture was taken over by Roberto Rodrigues, a highly respected agronomist and engineer in Brazil. Both put major pressure on Itamaraty to open up the trade-policy-making process, using technical studies from Jank's ICONE to demonstrate why shifts in Brazilian positions were necessary and how the international insertion of key sectors of the Brazilian economy had changed. By May 2003 the work of ICONE had proved its value in the run-up to the Cancun WTO ministerial meeting, and Jank and members of his team were included as technical advisors in the Brazilian negotiating teams for the FTAA and WTO (*Gazeta Mercantil* 2003a).

On a working level, Brazil's diplomats praised ICONE, with the head of Itamaraty Economics Department, Ambassador Valdemar Carneiro Leão, telling *Gazeta Mercantil* (2003b), that "Icone is very serious and we have the highest possible regard for it." In practice, however, the diplomats' hold over the file was saved by its politicization, as a broad and popular political agreement to block hemispheric and global attempts at fuller trade liberalization emerged. To stop the FTAA in its tracks and to paralyze the Doha Round by building veto coalitions, negotiating skills were called for, not expertise in trade law or agricultural economics. As global trade discussions heat up again, however, such status-saving situations may become scarce. Encroachments by technical experts on Itamaraty's monopoly have taken place in other areas such as health, human rights, and culture (Pinheiro and Milani 2012). Compared to trade and economic issues, however, their relative marginality in international policy discussions and Brazil's limited global profile in these areas have limited these specialists' overall impact on Itamaraty control over the country's diplomacy.

Weak Multilateral Institutions and Presidential Diplomacy

Since the beginning of its democratization process in the second half of the 1980s, Brazil has been remarkably active as a multilateral entrepreneur. Aside from its fundamental place as the axis of the Mercosul common market, it played a key role in the establishment of the Rio Group, which started as a diplomatic device for South America to help disentangle the disasters of Central America's civil wars and of US involvement in them but gained a second life as a forum through which the countries of the region could resolve their differences and coordinate action without Washington being present. With strong Brazilian impetus, the Rio Group became the Union of South American Nations (Unasul), which gained various councils with more specific mandates, in particular on defence and more recently on public safety.

Finally, South America, Mexico, and the Caribbean were brought together into the Community of Latin America and Caribbean Nations (CELAC), which, for the first time, convened all the countries of the hemisphere except Canada and the United States into a single organization.

Behind these acronyms, however, there has been little substance (Daudelin 2012). Indeed, a shared characteristic of all these endeavours was the limited autonomous capabilities of their secretariats and administrative structures. In practice, they serve as little more than organizing committees for scheduled or emergency meetings of ministers and especially heads of state. The Organization of American States (OAS) and its secretaries-general, perennially shrugged off as weak and ineffective, look by comparison like paragons of institutional capacity and political autonomy. This is one of the main reasons that presidential diplomacy, whereby regional and bilateral issues are settled through the direct intervention of the president, has become such an important theme in debates about international relations in the region (Danese 1999; Cason and Power 2009; Malamud 2005).

In this regard the case of Mercosul is most striking. Even in as dense and complex an economic endeavor as this economic bloc, the tensions and crises that often arise have almost always been resolved by direct presidential intervention. Despite nearly two decades of existence and even with the creation of a regional parliament, the bloc lacks a functioning dispute resolution mechanism or a secretariat with real power and sway (Malamud and Dri 2013). Disputes thus quickly escalate to at least the ministerial level, and when serious, they invariably require a presidential meeting for full resolution.

Efforts by Brazil to expand Mercosul and to build around it mechanisms of cooperation that would span South America did not even include the limited institutional frameworks found in the bloc. The Cardoso presidency's 2000 approach to pan-continental integration—the Initiative for the Integration of the Regional Infrastructure of South America (IIRSA)—explicitly sidestepped political questions by focusing on physical infrastructure. Lula reintroduced a political element to this framework through the Union of South American Nations (UNASUR), which then morphed into Unasul. While clearly meant to put Brazil in a leading political position, Unasul was formed without a centralized, permanent administrative structure that might develop an identity independent of its constituent member states. Unsurprisingly, when regional issues requiring collective management arose, such as the Colombian incursion into Ecuador to bomb a Revolutionary Armed Forces of Colombia (FARC) rebel base on March 1, 2008, the Unasul response relied upon the direct intervention and coordination of presidents, not diplomats or non-existent regional public servants.

The Unasul example shows that, while Itamaraty plays an important role in Brazil's approach to regional governance, the mechanisms that are constructed, de facto and sometimes explicitly, require the direct participation and guidance of presidents and leave very little leeway to the diplomats involved. Such resistance to institutionalization has been most recently embodied by the creation of CELAC, which not only challenges the relevance and legitimacy of the most solidly institutionalized and politically independent grouping in the region — the OAS — but replaces it with an organization that lacks a clear institutional structure with bricks and mortar permanence and some independent political leadership at the top. This ensures that substantive decision-making will take place only at the level of presidential summits.

Brazil's institutional entrepreneurship beyond the region follows exactly the same pattern. The India-Brazil-South Africa (IBSA) initiative (Lima and Hirst 2009) and the Brazil, Russia, India, China (BRICs) grouping (Stuenkel 2015), both of which Brazil embraced enthusiastically, are also devoid of autonomous institutional capabilities and represent little more than vehicles for periodic meetings of heads of states. The extent to which the recently created BRICS development bank will have a degree of autonomy remains unsettled, but there are few indications that its formal leaders will benefit from even as short a leash as those given to the presidents of the World Bank and the International Monetary Fund (IMF). Finally, Brazil's keen support for the summit diplomacy that has typified the last decade takes that anti-institutional trait to its extreme. Summits — Ibero-American, Arab–Latin American, Brazil-Africa, Africa–South America — are indeed best seen as portable tents meant strictly for dialogues between chief executives.

The institutional deficit in Brazil's favored form of multilateralism only makes sense for a country that has little need or will for sustained collective engagement and effective long-term supranational governance. It creates a capacity gap at the international level, however, that makes presidential engagement necessary for concerted action (Burges and Daudelin 2011). To this extent, it opens the door to episodic challenges to Itamaraty's monopoly, especially when the president, as in the case of Lula, finds significant political benefits in global engagements.

A Honey Pot Effect?

Foreign policy rarely matters in domestic politics, especially for countries like Brazil whose borders are secure and whose economies remain largely self-centered. As a rule, electoral competition does not revolve around international affairs, nor can much liquid political capital be generated abroad and used domestically. Consequently, politicians typically have little to gain from active international engagement.

While this interpretation would hold for much of Brazil's recent history,

Lula's two mandates stand as an exception, because so much of Brazil's supposed rise on the global scene had a symbolic quality, especially for Brazilians (Burges 2005; Rohter 2012). De Gaulle's famous—and possibly apocryphal—pun about Brazil's lack of "seriousness" was deeply resented by its elites, all the more so for being difficult to challenge in the face of the country's poor economic performance and disproportionately marginal role in the world and even in the Americas. From this standpoint, Lula's hyperactive international agenda within the context of economic stability and significant progress on education, poverty, and inequality radically redefined Brazil's international image, giving the country, at last, the status that most Brazilians felt it deserved. There is no doubt that seeing Lula being feted everywhere, by the rich and the poor alike, greatly helped cement his domestic stature. The transparent embarrassment of the country's elites, perhaps best embodied by the "serious" media's early insistence on correcting his often tortured Portuguese, was replaced by a generic pride at the image of Brazil—modern, democratic, and open—that he successfully projected in the world. For the poor, his international success neatly complemented the self-esteem effect that his election had created (Burges 2005).

These peculiar reasons no doubt reinforced Lula's successful claim over the country's diplomacy. They were, however, probably unique to his mandates and to the normalization of Brazil's international status, following the stabilization of its economy. It is indeed difficult to imagine his successors drawing much political capital from an active international agenda, which may explain Dilma's retreat into the domestic realm at the start of her first presidency, above and beyond her lack of charisma and the somewhat bland nature, compared to Lula, of her political trajectory. The Golden Age of presidential diplomacy, in other words, may well have passed. With little prospect of changes in the country's strategic and economic environment, Brazilian foreign policy's substantive relevance for domestic politics is unlikely to increase much in the future. The kind of transformation of Brazil's symbolic status that happened at the turn of the century is also probably a unique event. The challenge to Itamaraty's monopoly represented by presidential diplomacy, in other words, probably lies mostly in the technical turn of global affairs and in the thin institutionalization of Brazil's multilateral engagement in the world.

Conclusion

Recent discussions of Brazilian foreign policy have been dominated by four themes: the country's "emergence," particularly as a major *Southern* power (Lima and Hirst 2006; Burges 2009); the political character of its engagement in the world and the rupture represented by the PT's accession to power (Cervo 2000; Vizentini 2005); the quest for autonomy as an underlying and

stable trait of its foreign policy (Hurrell 1986; Fonseca 2004; Vigevani and Cepaluni 2009); and presidential diplomacy as a new way of doing foreign policy
(Cason and Power 2009; Malamud 2005). The analysis proposed here does
not directly challenge those contributions. Our aim instead is to cut across
them to build an interpretation of the country's recent foreign policy based
on a political economy of its insertion in the world and of the impact of that
insertion on some of the key characteristics of Brazil's foreign policy "regime."
We argue that mainly as a result of the slightly deeper strategic and economic
insertion of Brazil in the world, two dominant processes are changing the
country's policy regime: a certain widening of the breadth of social interests
that engage foreign policy, representing less an effective democratization of
that policy regime than the multiplication of democratic moments that see
foreign policy more broadly debated; and a limited challenge to the monopoly of Itamaraty over the means of diplomacy, with the growing involvement
of new actors, particularly outside specialists and the country's presidents.

11

Leslie Elliott Armijo

The Public Bank
Trilemma

Brazil's New
Developmentalism
and the BNDES

WHAT IS BRAZIL'S development model for the twenty-first century? The ubiquitous term "new developmentalism" may best be used to identify the large degree of consensus on economic policies that has characterized all of Brazil's governments since President Fernando Collor. To understand Brazil's development model, I examine the recent trajectory of the country's industrial development bank, the National Bank for Economic and Social Development (Banco Nacional de Desenvolvimento Econômico e Social; BNDES) through the lens of the "public bank trilemma." The trilemma encapsulates the larger conflict inherent in state-led capitalist development: that of balancing autonomous, technocratic decision-making ("Expertise"), and the immediate demands of ordinary citizens for a better life, as expressed through their political representatives ("Democracy"), with the delicate challenge of using state monies and regulatory authority to stimulate voluntary, decentralized, competitive, and efficient private investment ("Markets"). The fights over BNDES operations conveniently illustrate many of Brazil's ongoing debates over the pace, biases, and goals of mixed-capitalist economic growth in a middle-income but still highly unequal country.

Brazil's "New Developmentalism" and the BNDES

The old developmentalism in Brazil and Latin America was the import-substituting industrialization (ISI) of the 1950s through 1970s, which promised, but did not deliver, rapid catch-up with wealthy countries, through protected industrial production for the domestic market. In contrast to ISI, the new developmentalism (ND) of the 1990s through the present has emphasized macroeconomic stability (low inflation), greater participation in global markets, and reducing domestic inequality.[1] Some proponents of ND have championed, in addition, the need to rely on domestic savings rather than foreign loans or investment and, especially, to maintain a competitive (non-overvalued) exchange rate (Bresser-Pereira 2009). The ND is not a sharp break with the past, sharing with the ISI-era a belief in the essential economic role of the state in identifying strategic goals and providing supportive public goods (as in Souza and Miranda 2015). In Brazil, the state has played the central role in financing infrastructure since the early 1950s. Astonishingly, Brazil's federal government, through the BNDES, also has been virtually the only domestic source of medium-to-long-term bank credit for private industry during the entire period from the late 1960s to the present. The BNDES has been central to each phase of Brazilian developmentalism.

Why adopt the BNDES as the symbol of the ND? First, the BNDES, founded in 1952, spans both the old and new developmentalism.[2] Second, it is a dominant institution that has recently become even larger. Its recent growth in annual loan disbursements (shown in nominal *reais* in Figure 11.1), has been truly extraordinary. In 2010 the annual flow of gross new BNDES loans briefly reached 4.3 percent of GDP, before falling back to "only" 3.2 percent in 2011 and averaging about 3.5 percent thereafter.[3] As of late 2015, outstanding BNDES loans stood at 11.2 percent of GDP and accounted for 21 percent of the stock of all credit to firms and households from the entire national financial system. The BNDES also supports Brazilian businesses through consulting and equity participation. By the end of 2014, the bank held total assets worth 16 percent of Brazil's BR$5.52 trillion (about US$2.3 trillion) GDP, of which 75 percent was loans to Brazilian firms, 7 percent investments in corporate equity, and the remaining held in other investments, including 12 percent in government securities.

Brazil's BNDES also looms large in comparative international perspective. Although legally limited to support only Brazilian companies and their customers, the BNDES is significantly larger than the Inter-American Development Bank (IADB), and roughly equivalent in size to the World Bank (Table 11.1). In terms of total assets, the BNDES is the second largest national development bank among emerging economies. As former BNDES presi-

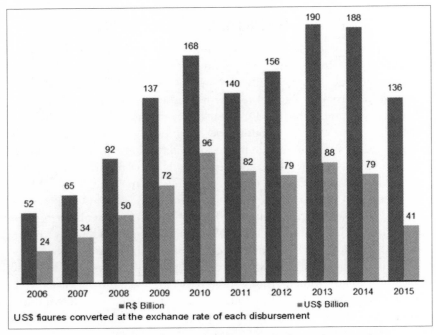

Figure 11.1. BNDES: Evolution of Annual Loan Disbursements, 2006–2015 (BR$billions and US$ billions). *Source*: BNDES 2015d, 43.

dent (2007–2016), Luciano Coutinho, confidently noted, "The Chinese and South Korean development banks lend more than us, but they only do monolines. . . . We do credit, we support capital markets, and we operate through the private banking sector itself" (Wheatley 2009).

Finally, there are clear sub-periods within Brazil's new developmentalism. The governments of presidents Fernando Collor, Itamar Franco, and Fernando Henrique Cardoso in the 1990s through 2002 leaned "neoliberal," because of their emphasis on fiscal responsibility, privatization, and freer trade and capital movements (Armijo and Faucher 2002), while the 2003–2016 period of PT presidents Luiz Inácio Lula da Silva and Dilma Rousseff was more assertively "new developmentalist." Yet Brazil's policy shifts in both directions have been less ideological and extreme than contemporaneous reforms elsewhere in Latin America. There has been substantial continuity in Brazil's ND economic policymaking, as practiced if not always as articulated. Partisan differences within the post-1990 consensus, although they exist, look more significant from within the country than from outside. This said, topical controversies over the future trajectory of the BNDES go to the heart of important nuances currently being debated within Brazil, and within the larger ND consensus.

Table 11.1. Comparison of BNDES with Other Large Development Banks (2014)				
	BNDES	*IADB*	*World Bank*	*China DB*
Total Assets (US$ billions)	330.3	106.3	343.2	1,662.5
Loan Disbursements (US$ billions)	79.3	9.4	44.6	N/A
Income + (–) (US$ billions)	3.2	0.5	(0.8)	15.8
Source: BNDES 2015b, 67.				

The Public Bank Trilemma

The BNDES illustrates what one might term the "public bank trilemma," which is similar to the better known "central bank [regulatory] dilemma." On the one hand, it is accepted wisdom that central banks should be independent of political authorities in carrying out their day-to-day implementation of monetary policy (Goodhart 1990; Bernhard, Broz, and Clark 2003). In this way they can resist pressures to sacrifice price stability for electoral expediency, as by easing liquidity in the months prior to elections, generating the infamous "political-business cycle." Yet on the other hand, monetary policy is not purely a technical matter. Only the legitimate political authorities can decide whether central bank governors should target inflation exclusively, a preference typically favored by the transnational epistemic community of bankers to which they belong (Epstein 1992; Henning 1994), or whether central bankers also should consider how money and credit aggregates influence other outcomes, such as unemployment or the nation's exchange rate. The central bank regulatory dilemma is thus that of balancing the imperatives of the independence of the technical experts ("Expertise") with oversight and goal-setting by the legitimate, democratically chosen authorities ("Democracy").

The challenge of regulating a public commercial or development bank in any modern mixed-capitalist economy is more complex still (Caprio et al. 2005; Bonney 1995; Allen and Gale 2000; Aghion 1999; Bacha 2002; Shleifer 1998). Regulators and managers must simultaneously prioritize three intrinsically contradictory goals: Expertise, Democracy, and Markets. The core rationale for creating a public bank (or having a national industrial policy, more generally) is to empower competent technocrats, operating above the political fray, to aggregate financial resources, typically subsidized by citizens, to make investments (usually long-term) resulting in public goods that otherwise would not be provided ("Expertise") (cf. Shapiro 2007). Like central banks, effective public banks should be independent of partisan and short-term political pressures. Nonetheless, decisions about the outcomes of public bank activities necessarily involve choices about values and thus belong with the country's legitimately elected political authorities, charged to execute the will of the citizenry ("Democracy").[4] In addition, public sector banks in a mixed-capitalist economy must support, rather than undercut or substitute for, private credit and capital markets ("Markets"). A fair evaluation of the performance of any public bank must consider each dimension of this complicated regulatory trilemma.

The public bank trilemma frames this analysis of the BNDES. The initial rationale for public banks, and thus the apex of the triangle, is Expertise. A public bank that cannot plausibly claim to be providing public goods in a competent fashion has no reason to exist. Nonetheless, Expertise alone is insufficient. Following a short historical overview, we will then analyze contemporary tensions in the BNDES between Expertise and Democracy and between Expertise and Markets.

The Shifting Roles of the BNDES over Time

Founded in 1952 to furnish project finance for big infrastructure projects, the BNDES later in the decade also began financing the production of capital goods through its wholly owned subsidiary, FINAME.[5] Following the 1964 military coup, which the new government justified by reference to economic disarray under its civilian predecessors, a barrage of liberalizing reforms attempted to build a solid regulatory framework for capitalist economic growth (Fishlow 1973; Skidmore 1973). However, Brazil's chronic high inflation was not controlled, and long-term, voluntary, private bank credit did not emerge. Consequently, in the late 1960s large business owners, especially from São Paulo, successfully pressed the government to reorient BNDES activity away from financing public infrastructure and instead toward long-term lending to firms, which has remained its core mission ever since. In the 1970s the bank sought to ease fiscal pressures on Brazil's central government, hitherto its primary source of funds, by borrowing cheaply in international markets and on-lending these resources within Brazil. When Brazil's accumulated foreign loans and volatile international conditions led to the debt crisis in the early 1980s, closely followed by the upheaval of the democratic transition, the BNDES was a key component in the federal government's response. The bank helped large Brazilian corporations cope by inaugurating a wholly owned subsidiary, BNDES Participações (BNDESPar), which rescued illiquid firms from bankruptcy through debt-to-equity conversions. When markets recovered, BNDESPar managers sold these shares, in most years turning a profit on the transactions.

In the post–debt crisis 1990s, Brazil's government (and thus the BNDES) embraced pro-market economic reforms. The BNDES ran Brazil's privatization program, ultimately overseeing sales of US$105 billion (BNDES 2002b, 2). As part of the process, economic policymakers usefully cleared out US$18 billion in public debt securities of questionable value (*moedas podres*, or rotten monies) that had been issued by various state firms and entities over the previous twenty years, allowing holders of these securities to spend them in the privatization auctions. From the late 1990s through the present, the BNDES has promoted exports and Brazil's regional and global economic insertion, while also inaugurating new programs for small businesses. The bank has seldom been free of controversy, and earlier arguments over its proper role were as fierce as those that now rage. Nonetheless, and over decades, the BNDES has maintained an enviable reputation for both competence and flexibility. Brazil in 2016 is currently in the throes of both economic and political crises. Present challenges place pressure on each leg of Brazil's public bank management trilemma.

Balancing Expertise and Democracy in the BNDES and the Internationalization of Brazilian Business

The conflict between autonomous, technocratic policymaking (Expertise) and political oversight by the elected authorities, responding to public preferences (Democracy), is illustrated by the way the BNDES has promoted greater engagement with the world economy. There are many different ways to implement an outward economic orientation, ranging from the least to most state interventionist. One may unilaterally remove tariff and non-tariff trade barriers, on the theory that all trade (even when it involves a surge of imports) is good trade, because the country's post-liberalization consumers and firms enjoy better or cheaper goods. A somewhat more activist state will seek the reciprocal removal of trade barriers. More statist still is the belief that "good" trade means the export of manufactures, not commodities, and that it is the government's job to promote this "higher value-added" trade. Both the right-leaning (Collor through Cardoso) and left-leaning (Lula and Dilma) strands of Brazil's new developmentalists have been in agreement that it is better to export airplanes than coffee or soya. Even a recent World Bank report (penned by Brazilians) worries that Brazil's high technology exports grew by only 35 percent (by value) in the decade following 2000—as compared to over 800 percent for China and almost 400 percent for India (Canuto, Cavallari, and Reis 2013).

The BNDES has sought to promote exports, particularly manufactured ones. Brazil's private banks, funding themselves from abroad, provide short-term trade credits to Brazilian firms (Rossi and Prates 2009). However, since foreign customers will not pay the extraordinarily high nominal and real interest rates that have reigned for decades in the free segments of Brazilian markets (see below), longer-term funds to provide suppliers' credit to foreign purchasers of Brazilian exports must also be borrowed abroad or the Brazilian government (and ultimately taxpayers) must subsidize the additional interest cost. In support of this policy goal, BNDES Exim loans (earlier called FI-NAMEX), increased dramatically (prior to the current crisis), rising from 4 percent of total BNDES loan disbursements in 1996 to 11.5 percent in 2009.[6]

More intriguing—and controversial—are the further steps taken by the BNDES since the mid-2000s to promote the "internationalization" of Brazilian business, particularly its policy of promoting "national champions," that is, specific firms judged able to compete with the largest transnationals in global markets. De facto, this means that the taxpayer-supported BNDES acts as a full-service merchant bank to Brazil's largest transnational firms, financing almost any activity that forms part of one of these firms' strategic corporate visions. Most innovative—or merely startling—have been BNDES loans to giant companies such as the meatpacker JBS Friboi, now one of the largest firms in its industry worldwide, to gobble up foreign rivals through mergers and acquisitions (*Latin Finance* 2009). The BNDES also assisted the wood products company Aracruz to recoup foreign exchange bets gone wrong. In 2009 the bank arranged a merger with Brazilian rival Votorantim Papel e Cellulose, forming the new company Fibria (Valle 2012). The BNDES also has opened large credit lines for foreign governments—prominently including those in Andean South America, Lusophone Africa, and Cuba—to acquire Brazilian goods and services, often from one or a handful of companies.

A few firms have received a lot of money. For example, from 2006 to 2012, the BNDES extended US$3.2 billion in loans to the government of Angola, of which almost half purchased consulting and construction services from Brazil's mega-engineering firm Odebrecht (Fellet 2012). From 2008 to 2012 the BNDES lent a cumulative R$40.8 billion (approximately US$22.7 billion) to only six firms, all privately owned: JBS Friboi, Marfrig (both frozen foods), Oi (telecommunications), BRF Brasil Foods (food and beverages), Fibria (pulp and paper), and Ambev (food and beverages) (*O Globo* 2011). Of the BNDES's total loan portfolio of outstanding loans as of mid-2012, 39 percent had gone to the top five borrowers, and a further 28 percent to the fifty next largest borrowers, revealing a high degree of concentration of funding (BNDES 2011, 53). Of BNDES's equity holdings, 80 percent by value are shares of state-owned or de facto controlled firms (such as Petrobras and Vale, in petroleum and mining, respectively), each of which would fit any list of plausible national champions (BNDES 2012, 4). The BNDS also owns large blocs of equity in private firms, including 30.4 percent of Fibria, 20.25 percent of Klabin (pulp and paper), 17.3 percent of JBS Friboi, 13.9 percent of Marfrig,

Table 11.2. Brazilian Export Structure, 2015*				
Partner	% of Total Exports	Of which:		Total to Partner
		Commodities	Semi-manufactured	Manufactured	
Asia	33	73	16	11	100
EU	19	46	15	39	100
Latin America	19	17	3	80	100
United States	17	17	16	67	100
Africa	4	37	23	40	100
World	100	46	14	38	100
China	19				

Note: * Data column 1 adds down; columns 2–4 add across.
Source: MDIC *2015.

12.2 percent of América Latina Logística (transportation infrastructure), and 3.5 percent of Gerdau (construction) (Bugiato 2013, 31).

A related goal of Brazil's ND policies from the mid-1990s onward has been South American economic integration, through both the reduction of intra-continental trade barriers and the promotion of the construction of new transportation and power infrastructure. The BNDES has provided whatever funds it can, within its legal mandate to support only Brazilian firms. (Thus, the BNDES will finance, for example, up to 80 percent of a loan to Ecuador's government to hire a Brazilian construction company to build a dam.) For Brazilian ND governments, the focus on South American integration makes strategic economic as well as political sense. While Brazil's exports to Asia are overwhelmingly commodities, Brazilian exports to Latin America tilt heavily toward manufactures ("good" trade in the ND vision), as shown in Table 11.2.[7] The outward foreign direct investment (also described as "internationalization") of Brazilian firms has also been focused on South America, with Argentina and Venezuela being particularly lucrative host markets, a circumstance that explains the otherwise puzzling support of Brazil's conservative business community for the entry of left-leaning Venezuela into the Mercado Comun do Sul (MERCOSUR) (Lissardy 2011; *Estado de São Paulo* 2012c).

Is there a problem? The Expertise displayed remains high. For example, BNDES officials take great care to demonstrate that the bank is profitable and a good steward of the funds entrusted to it (BNDES 2015c, 2015d) — although this judgment takes as a given its low cost of funds. Some critics maintain that the bank's heavy support for oligopoly players undercuts Democracy. Voices from the left, both within and outside Brazil, conceptualize Brazil's continental policies as expansionist and neoimperialist (Luce 2007; Costas 2012; Zibechi 2012). Others question the goal of BNDES financing for Brazilian firms to move their production—and thus potential Brazilian jobs—abroad. Building on an index developed by the United Nations Conference on Trade and Development (UNCTAD), researchers at the Fundação Dom Cabral calculated a firm's "transnationalization" as the mean of three qualities: assets abroad as a share of total assets, revenues abroad as a share of total revenues, and employment abroad as a share of total employment. By this metric the list of the most transnationalized Brazilian firms—which includes such names as JBS Friboi (54 percent transnationalized, with 62 percent of employees abroad), Gerdau (52 percent), Stefanini IT Solutions (46 percent), Metalfrio (45 percent), Marfrig (45 percent), and Odebrecht (42 percent)—overlaps quite closely with the list of the largest borrowers from the BNDES (Cretoiu et al. 2012, 17). The question is not whether these firms ought to be expanding abroad but whether their corporate strategies ought to receive public subsidies.

In 2011 one incident sparked particular public ire. Brazil's large supermarket chain, Pão de Açucar, proposed a merger with a major competitor, the Brazilian subsidiary of the French supermarket chain Carrefour—in a €2 billion-plus deal arranged by the BNDES. The bank's press statement highlighted the prospect of promoting sales of Brazilian products through the French parent firm's worldwide retail network (Rosas 2011). Nonetheless, five-term federal deputy Darcísio Perondi (PMDB, Rio Grande do Sul), despite being nominally a member of the Dilma government's allied legislative coalition, was among those who quickly attacked the project, calling it crazy to spend monies derived from payroll and social security taxes on a supermarket, particularly given unmet health and education needs, and noting that the merged company easily could employ its resulting oligopoly share of 32 percent of Brazil's retail grocery market to squeeze both small farmer suppliers and customers (Perondi 2011). Public opposition was sufficiently intense that the BNDES backed off, offering the bland excuse that not all of the anticipated private co-funding had materialized (Leahy 2011).

More recently, the revelations of the Lava Jato corruption scandal in 2015–2016 (see Taylor this volume) have subdued BNDES (and Brazilian society's) support for Brazil's large transnational corporations and has put pressure on the BNDES to increase transparency with respect to the precise terms and amounts of its loans to large borrowers. Revelations of corruption within Petrobras, which initially exploded in the context of the company's outward Foreign Direct Investment (FDI) in the United States, generated a sharp plunge in its stock market quotation, and a subsequent BR$15 billion balance sheet "impairment" charge for the BNDES in 2014 and 2015, a major Petrobras shareholder (BNDES 2015b, 6).[8] In 2015 and early 2016 Brazilian courts found the top officers of several of Brazil's largest construction firms, including major BNDES client Odebrecht, guilty of price-fixing and bribery. In mid-2015 Brazil's Congress opened a Parliamentary Inquiry Commission on the BNDES. Asked to provide "more than 10 million pages" of documents, the bank was not in the end accused of wrongdoing yet prudently has instituted several new initiatives to promote greater transparency in its relations with both investors and Brazilian voters. For example, unlike the national development banks of Mexico, Canada, Germany, Spain, and Japan, the BNDES now releases the names of individual client firms (Suchodolski 2016, 7, 10).

Despite understandable differences of opinion over BNDES support for the internationalization of national champions, there is not, strictly speaking, a problem from the viewpoint of the public bank regulatory trilemma — because the bank's policies have been those of the legitimately elected executive branch political authorities. BNDES policies have supported Brazil's ND economic strategy of increasing manufactured exports and also the country's de facto foreign policy strategy of being perceived as a regional leader, thus enhancing its global political status. In the words of Brasília business consultant Thiago de Aragão, "Brazil's number one interest is to make itself influential within the region, and to have its neighbors recognize it as an instrument of regional development" (Lissardy 2011; my translation). Overall, BNDES activity in support of the internationalization of firms, although controversial, has been largely consistent with the need to balance the competing claims of Expertise and Democracy.

Equilibrating Expertise and Markets in the BNDES, Private Banks, and Brazil's Public Finances

The balance within the Expertise versus Markets vector of the public bank regulatory trilemma also has become contentious, revealing clear differences between the center-right and center-left within the larger ND model. There were problems of financial markets in the late 1960s that the BNDES was asked to solve, and a pre–Lava Jato contemporary intra-Expert debate on how the BNDES should complement Brazil's private banks. Disagreements over BNDES finances by mid-2015 had become embroiled in the struggle to impeach President Dilma Rousseff.

For decades, from at least the 1930s through the mid-1990s, Brazil was in the peculiar position of having an economy that suffered from chronic high to very high inflation, yet the country always managed to avoid the disastrous breakdown associated with true hyperinflation (Armijo 1997). One of the consequences of persistent high inflation, however, was the disappearance, or failure to develop, of long-term credit in the economy, as bankers would not loan long-term in a currency that they expected to be devalued on repayment. In the mid-1960s, orthodox economists appointed by the military attempted to end inflation and stimulate private long-term finance (Syvrud 1975; Trubeck 1971; Armijo 1993). After that effort at price stabilization failed, the BNDES reoriented its lending toward long-term support of Brazilian business. This background sets up today's policy conundrum. Ever since the Plano Real (the successful stabilization program of the mid-1990s), Brazil's annual inflation has averaged in the high single digits—the era of chronic, crazy inflation is over. Arguably, continuing the wholesale substitution of Expertise-based, in place of Market-organized, provision of long-term corporate financing in one of the world's largest economies unbalances the public bank triad of goals. However, like other organizations, particularly ones whose leaders understandably perceive their institutions to be at the top of their game, the BNDES resists shrinking.

Probably the most burning contemporary debate about the BNDES within the Expert community centers on the BNDES's sources and costs of financing, and the implications of this for Markets, in the form of private banks. Former senior economic policymakers associated with President Cardoso—including former BNDES and Brazilian Central Bank (BCB) president Pérsio Arida, former BNDES president Luiz Carlos Mendonça de Barros, and former BCB president Gustavo Loyola—have been prominent critics of the BNDES's role in Brazilian financial markets (Arida 2005; Leonel 2010). These center-right critics make four main points. First, the majority of BNDES funding derives from Brazilian taxpayers. Until about 2007, approximately 10 percent of BNDES resources (liabilities) derived from shareholders' (the central government's) equity, and another 75 percent from forced savings, primarily obligatory "investments" by the FAT (Workers' Support Fund, whose resources come from payroll taxes), allocated to the BNDES by the 1988 Constitution. The BNDES has a statutory (but vague) obligation to employ FAT funds for projects that benefit workers by increasing Brazilian employment and production. Although these FAT investments (loans to the BNDES) are safe, they are remunerated at a special "long-term interest rate," the TJLP, which is well below the free market cost of funds in Brazil. There is therefore a question of the opportunity cost to the worker owners of the FAT of directing these monies to the BNDES. Under the PT governments since 2003, the BNDES has greatly expanded lending, especially following the appointment of Luciano Coutinho as its head in 2007, at the start of President Lula's second term. As FAT resources were no longer sufficient, in recent years the BNDES has increasingly been funded by direct transfers from the National Treasury, through special programs including the PAC (Accelerated Growth Program) and PSI (Sustainable Investment Program). Treasury transfers increased from 11 percent of BNDES funding in 2005 to 57 percent by mid-2015 (BNDES 2015b, 43).

Second, these critics contend that it is the BNDES that is pushing up real interest rates in the free segment of the economy (Arida 2005; Romero 2011; Mello and Garcia 2011). There is only a set quantum of savings in Brazil, Therefore, the larger the share accessed by the BNDES at below-market rates, the smaller the share available for all other borrowers—and therefore the higher the price at which credit in the free market will be offered. A rough approximation of the extent of the subsidy enjoyed by the BNDES may be seen by the difference between the SELIC, Brazil's policy interest rate, which is the rate at which the BCB makes short-term loans to commercial banks needing liquidity, and the TJLP, the rate at which the BNDES borrows. Normally, a central bank's policy rate (in the United States, the federal funds rate) is *below* the best rate available to the most creditworthy non-financial business borrowers (in the United States, the prime rate), as banks need to borrow more cheaply than they lend. In Brazil, by contrast, the SELIC is *higher* than the TJLP. Meanwhile, the free market interest rate for thirty-day working capital for excellent corporate borrowers is very high: it fell from 42 percent in January 2009, at the height of the global financial crisis, to "only" 32 percent in mid-2012 (EIU 2012, 41).[9] Naturally, those firms able to do so would prefer to borrow either from the BNDES or abroad. Real annual interest rates to consumers are 70 percent or more.

Third, over the past twenty odd years the BNDES has demonstrated that it can capture resources through bond issues in private capital markets, both within Brazil and internationally. The critics of current funding patterns therefore propose that the BNDES be obliged to move gradually to market sources of funds. If the consequence is a shrinking of the total size of the institution's assets and liabilities, then so be it. Critics' analysis stresses that Expertise, which almost no one questions that the bank displays, should supplement private financial Markets, not replace them.

Fourth and finally, the liberal camp worries that the recent expansion of BNDES lending imperils Brazilian public finances. While monies booked as investments by various social insurance funds paid into by workers (FGTS, PIS/PASEP, and FAT, all of which have provided resources to the BNDES over the years) have no direct fiscal implications, the recent large transfers from the National Treasury have as a counterpart Brazil's public debt: money borrowed from the public (prominently including private banks) at significantly higher rates than the TJLP.[10] Mello and Garcia (2011, 10–11) conclude,

"If BNDES keeps expanding as it did since the 2008 crisis, it will surely constitute a major threat to the solvency of the Brazilian government."

The response from defenders of the BNDES's profile in the PT years, including former BNDES president and long-serving Finance Minister Guido Mantega (March 2006–December 2014), former BNDES president Luciano Coutinho, former BNDES president Carlos Lessa, and many others, coheres around four main points (Lessa 2005; Torres Filho 2005, 2009; Torres Filho and Costa 2012). As Coutinho patiently explains, the reason for large grants of public money to the BNDES is that Brazil has urgent needs for centrally prioritized investments, which provide an invaluable public good (Wheatley 2009). Brazil's recent senior elected officials have been fully supportive of this policy. Thus former President Lula da Silva frequently reiterated his support for the BNDES as essential to the country's commitment to public investment in exports, in industry, in basic research, asserting that, "the world will continue to need more food, and Brazil has all the proper conditions to produce part of that food. . . . [W]e have just discovered a lot of oil, and we do not want to use oil as traditionally the oil countries have used oil. . . . We want to be exporters of oil derivatives, not exporters of oil, because we want to develop a strong oil industry and a strong shipbuilding industry together. We want to build our own drilling rigs, our own offshore platforms, and our own ships. And we want to develop a strong petrochemicals industry" (Barber and Wheatley 2009). The argument for BNDES leadership is that these projects are simply too big, too risky, and too long-term for the private sector to handle: hence the need for public financing.

Second, BNDES officials insist that the bank has nothing to do with Brazil's problem of high interest rates or the related problem of high bank spreads between their deposit and lending interest rates. The origins of Brazil's high interest rates are historically generated expectations being extrapolated forward, combined with oligopoly in the commercial banking sector, the latter compounded by significant barriers to entry into banking. In Coutinho's words, "The [only] distortion is that short-term borrowing rates in Brazil are much higher than in other countries. Our long-term rates are [just] a bit higher than in the US, the UK or South Korea. There's no distortion there" (Wheatley 2009). That is, since the BNDES loans only long-term, and at low rates linked to its low cost of funds (the TJLP), it can hardly be taxed with responsibility for Brazil's abusive short-term rates, which instead derive from high deposit-loan spreads and other inefficiencies in Brazil's commercial and private investment banks.

Third, the activities of the BNDES do not conflict with the private financial sector. On the contrary, the BNDES "crowds in" private financing and investment by working closely with a wide range of private financial actors.

For example, around 50 percent of BNDES lending is "indirect," consisting of on-lending through a nationwide network of private banks. The BNDES helps keep these smaller banks, who are close to their small business customers throughout Brazil, in business. For big projects, including major new infrastructure undertakings such as hydroelectric dams, the BNDES does the project design and provides partial financing but also offers lucrative co-financing opportunities for Brazil's largest financial institutions, whether the big universal banks or smaller investment/merchant banks. Moreover, the BNDES has been a great help in the expansion and technical improvement of Brazil's capital markets—which are finally beginning to provide an alternative domestic source of long-term financing. BNDESPar is one of Brazil's major institutional investors, and its trading activity assists in keeping the market liquid. In other words, the BNDES's current overwhelming dominance of long-term financing in Brazil indeed should change as Brazil modernizes: such a shift is already in progress, and the BNDES is promoting it (Torres and Costa 2012).

Fourth, Brazil's government needs a strong, competent, flexible instrument with which to respond to changing national and international circumstances, and the BNDES has proved its worth on this score time and again (Lessa 2005). To take a recent but stunning example, Brazil performed well in the global financial crisis of 2007–2009, which Finance Minister Mantega countered in two ways. Mantega instituted a series of new temporary capital controls, while also expanding liquidity both directly and by transferring a large sum of money from the National Treasury to the BNDES, which contributed to rapid expansion (see Figure 11.1). Because the BNDES was competent and honest and, together with its nationwide network of private bank partners, had a long list of plausible investment projects essentially ready to go, the stimulus quickly got out to the real economy. Even the International Monetary Fund praised Brazil's crisis management, observing, "Due to deft policy responses and built-in financial system buffers, the financial system weathered the global crisis remarkably well," highlighting the "quasi-fiscal stimulus through the national development bank" and "measures to channel liquidity to small and medium-sized banks facing stress" (Madrid 2012, 6). In December 2012, President Dilma Rousseff again used the BNDES to implement emergency economic stimulus measures (Biller 2012). In early 2016 the BNDES announced an emergency fund to support research on combating the Zika virus.

In sum, the critics on the center-right allege that cheap BNDES funds crowd out the development of private long-term credit and capital markets and are a burden on the taxpayer, primarily going to subsidize large firms. They advocate a smaller BNDES refocused on its core competencies in infrastructure, heavy industry, innovation, and special purpose funds. Defenders of the current center-left trajectory counter that Brazil needs a bank to implement (and in practice often to formulate; see Almeida, Lima-de-Oliveira, and Schneider 2014) a strategic vision of where the country should be heading, that the BNDES in fact complements private banks, and that the bank's essential role in both crisis management and economic development legitimates its government-subsidized funding profile.

The preceding discussion summarizes the largely intra-Expert debate as it stood as of about mid-2013. The political and macroeconomic crisis that has exploded since 2014 has provided some almost surreal twists to recent iterations of the polemics over the proper relationship of the BNDES with private financial Markets—and public finances. As noted, the advocates of a smaller, leaner BNDES have long been critical of transfers from the Treasury, which they argue provide the BNDES with an unfair competitive advantage vis-à-vis private banks. Thus, when President Dilma responded to the deepening recession by appointing a more orthodox economist, Joaquim Levy, as Finance Minister in January 2015, one of his first moves was to end direct Treasury transfers to the BNDES. The problem at that point was perceived, among both economists and other intellectuals loosely arrayed on the center-right of Brazil's domestic political spectrum, as one of the federal government squandering scarce taxpayer resources: the BNDES, and its favored clients, were implicitly imposing on Brazilian society.

However, over the course of 2015, Dilma's detractors, including Social Democracy Party (PSDB) politician and losing 2014 presidential candidate Aécio Neves, tried unsuccessfully to find evidence of personal corruption linked to the president. They eventually seized upon, and subsequently sought to define as not merely slovenly but also explicitly illegal, what was widely acknowledged to be a longtime tactic of financially strapped Brazilian governments: intentionally delaying payments to creditors and suppliers, a practice known as "pedaling." Thus by late 2015 the BNDES—along with two other large public banks, the Banco do Brasil (BB), long one of the country's two largest commercial banks, and Caixa Econômica Federal (CEF), or Federal Savings Bank—rather than being perceived as taking advantage of the National Treasury were, in a sharp cognitive reversal, themselves increasingly portrayed as victims of dodgy public sector accounting (Costa 2015; Pato 2016). The president's accusers noted that all of these public banks had been tasked with disbursing assorted social benefits and other payments to the public—the CEF, for example, was responsible for distributing Bolsa Família payments to poor families (Hunter and Sugiyama this volume). However, intentional delays in transfers from the central government (pedaling) meant that the BNDES and other public banks instead were forced to dip into their own resources to fulfill these obligations, which compromised their own financial integrity.

Although it was true that such delayed payments (technically overdrafts) had been used by previous governments, their magnitude had increased enormously under the PT administrations, rising steadily from only about 0.1 percent of GDP under President Cardoso and during Lula's first term to almost 1.0 percent of GDP following Dilma's reelection in mid-2014 (Pato 2016). The government, worried about this legal tactic, suddenly repaid all its arrears to BNDES on December 30, 2015, issuing Treasury bonds the following week to prevent the surge in liquidity from generating inflation, and sparking further intra-Expert debate on needed reforms of public financial institutions (for example, Duran 2016). Despite what the BNDES carefully referred to as "prepayment" (BNDES 2015c, 1) by the Treasury, the formal impeachment petition filed by the president's opponents in early 2016 accused her of the "crime of responsibility" for intentional and unlawful (not merely incompetent) management of public finances, including those of the BNDES, for partisan political gains.[11] The articles of impeachment ultimately led to Dilma's conviction and removal from office in August 2016.

This has been a sometimes acrimonious policy debate, whose major proponents are past and present government economic officials and other policy elites. Recently (and curiously), certain strands of these quintessentially subtle and technical arguments were hijacked to serve as fodder in the recent presidential impeachment crisis. The larger picture is that BNDES officials throughout all of the PT governments have claimed the mandate of Expertise to increase the size and reach of the bank, while also ostensibly promoting private financial Markets. Their critics, often associated with Cardoso-era officials and the PSDB, claim that the bank's access to large quantities of subsidized funds undermines both healthy national financial development and Brazilian public finances. The intellectual debate remains unsettled, but any change by newly inaugurated President Michel Temer in the operations or mandate of the BNDES, an institution still widely and justly revered, will almost certainly be gradual.

Conclusions

The principal differences between Brazil's old ISI developmentalism of the 1950s through 1970s and the new developmentalism of the 1990s onward lay, first, in the ND's greater enthusiasm toward participation in global markets and, second, in its basis in a radically different underlying Brazilian macroeconomy, one with credibly stable prices and a renewed attention to the evils of intense inequality. There exist two recognizable policy camps within the larger centrist Brazilian economic policy consensus on capitalist developmentalism. The public bank trilemma is a useful framework for thinking about not only the BNDES but also the internal strains within Brazil's ND more generally.

The rationale for a national development bank turns on the autonomous exercise of Expertise to identify public goods that the private financial sector will not provide voluntarily—from promoting a unified South American market and transnational Brazilian "champions" to enabling implementation of a rapid counter-cyclical macroeconomic policy response to a global financial crisis. There is a potential conflict with the imperative of Democracy, most especially when that bank draws heavily on taxpayer funds, which it lends out at subsidized rates to Brazil's largest firms, operating in oligopoly markets. There are also legitimate political conflicts over policy goals, at which point the proper stance of a public bank is to remain, ultimately if not operationally, subordinate to the legitimately constituted political authorities, which the BNDES consistently has done. Overall, Brazil has managed the Expertise-Democracy vector of the public bank regulatory trilemma reasonably well.

The Expertise-Markets vector is more problematic. Brazil's private financial sector, which benefits from on-lending, co-financing, and securities markets support coming from the national development bank, is comfortable with its relationship with the BNDES. But whether the BNDES's dominance is good for financial market functioning (as opposed to the profits of financial institutions) is less clear. Even before the current politicization of public bank finances to be used as a weapon in the impeachment wars, the BNDES's role in public finances has on occasion been ambiguous. For example, journalists in 2013 decried a large loan to the state electricity firm, Eletrobras, whose timing suggested that it would be used to pay stock dividends (including to both the BNDES and central government), thus serving as "creative accounting" to improve the look of public finances (Campos 2013). There is a clear bifurcation between those, mostly on the center-right, who would oblige the BNDES to rely on increasing shares of market financing, consequently shrinking its activities, and those of the center-left, including President Dilma Rousseff, who remained extremely proud of the BNDES's accomplishments—and of its size per se.

While there are extensive areas of new developmentalist agreement across most partisan divides in contemporary Brazil, weak economic and industrial growth rates in Brazil under the Dilma government sharpened the debate (see also Kingstone and Power this volume). Still, the differences that loom large from within the country appear modest from outside. Views on the desirable role of the BNDES, for example, fall out along a partisan (but in fact not terribly wide) divide. No politician with a realistic opportunity to capture national policy influence wants to attack basic private property rights—all agree that capitalism promotes growth. Neither are there influential voices raised that would radically dismantle Brazil's extensive apparatus of state credit and investment. Overall, the underlying national consensus on an activist state as the best option for achieving rapid growth is unlikely to falter. Brazil's basic model of state-led capitalism should continue to guide public policy for the foreseeable future.

NOTES

Chapter 1. The PT in Power, 2003–2016

1. The result of the second round in the presidential election of 2014 was Dilma Rousseff (PT), 51.64 percent, and Aécio Neves (PSDB), 48.36 percent.

2. In September 2010, the newspaper *Folha de São Paulo* and the weekly magazine *Veja* published reports accusing Dilma Rousseff's replacement as Lula's chief of staff, Erenice Guerra, of peddling her influence to help secure contracts and state loans for businesses in negotiations with the government. A legal case was opened as a result of these accusations, but was closed in July 2012 for lack of evidence.

3. Survey conducted by the Brazilian Institute of Public Opinion and Statistics (IBOPE) during the protests of June 20, 2013. The IBOPE interviewed 2002 demonstrators in eight state capitals (São Paulo, Rio de Janeiro, Belo Horizonte, Porto Alegre, Recife, Fortaleza, Salvador, and Brasília).

4. National survey conducted in November 2015 by the Datafolha Institute (study number PO813824).

5. These are the Liberal Party (Partido Liberal; PL), the Communist Party of Brazil (Partido Comunista do Brasil; PCdoB), the National Mobilization Party (Partido da Mobilização Nacional; PMN), and the Brazilian Communist Party (Partido Comunista Brasileiro; PCB).

6. These are the Brazilian Socialist Party (Partido Socialista Brasileiro; PSB), the Democratic Labor Party (Partido Democrático Trabalhista; PDT), the Popular Socialist Party (Partido Popular Socialista; PPS); the Green Party (Partido Verde; PV), and the Brazilian Labor Party (Partido Trabalhista Brasileiro; PTB).

7. These are the Liberal Front Party (Partido da Frente Liberal; PFL), which changed its name to Democrats (Democratas; DEM) in 2007; and the Party of Brazilian Social Democracy (Partido da Social Democracia Brasileira; PSDB), respectively.

8. It is important to remember that the party's National Directorate can overrule these decisions in specific cases.

9. In this chapter we utilize the classification of Brazilian parties along a left–right spectrum established by Zucco (2011) with data from the Brazilian Legislative Survey, conducted by Timothy Power between 1990 and 2009 (Power and Zucco 2011).

10. The PT allied itself with the PFL/DEM on only two occasions. First in 2002, in its support of the gubernatorial candidate Flamarion Portela (Social Liberal Party [Partido Social Liberal]; PSL) in the state of Roraima; and second, in 2010, in the state of Maranhão, when both parties supported the candidacy of Roseana Sarney (PMDB). In both cases, state-specific circumstances led the National Directorate to overrule the decisions of national party meetings and congresses.

Chapter 2. Good Government and Politics as Usual?

This chapter builds on our previous work on state-society relations under the PT (Goldfrank and Wampler 2008). Thanks to Diana Kraiser Miranda for research assistance in updating and revising our work.

1. The aide also had 209,000 *reais* (about US $100,000 at the time) in his suitcase (*Estado de São Paulo* 2005). As the main purpose of this article is to explain the reasons behind the PT's descent into corruption rather than provide an exhaustive accounting, we only use the names of the key politicians.

2. These are the Liberal Party (Partido Liberal; PL), the Popular Party (Partido Popular; PP), the Brazilian Labor Party (Partido Trabalhista Brasileiro; PTB); the Party of the Brazilian Democratic Movement (Partido do Movimento Democrático Brasileiro; PMDB), the Party of Brazilian Social Democracy (Partido da Social Democracia Brasileira; PSDB), and the Liberal Front Party (Partido da Frente Liberal; PFL). The PFL changed its name to Democrats (Democratas; DEM) in 2007.

Chapter 3. Corruption and Accountability in Brazil

Epigraph: Congressman José Dirceu, speaking on September 29, 1992, at the impeachment of President Collor: "O que necessitamos no momento é de uma profunda reforma institucional que elimine da legislação eleitoral partidária as raízes e as causas da corrupção eleitoral, que elimine da legislação penal e tributária brasileira a base para os crimes eleitorais, para a corrupção e, principalmente, para a impunidade" (Leali and Sassine, 2012; author's translation).

1. For example, Cardoso's government faced allegations of buying votes to ensure the passage of a constitutional amendment permitting presidential reelection. More recently, opposition parties of the right and center-right have faced challenges of their own. Supporters of the PT are quick to point to the fact that the Supreme Federal Tribunal has yet to hear the case of the so-called *mensalão tucano*, a scheme by which the former governor of Minas Gerais, Eduardo Azevedo (Partido da Social Democracia Brasileira; PSDB), is alleged to have laundered campaign funds through many of the same unsavory characters at the center of the PT's scandal. In 2010 there was also a *DEM mensalão*, whereby the right-wing Democrats (Democratas; DEM) governor of the Distrito Federal was toppled for leading a similar scheme in the Distrito Federal government. Meanwhile, in a Shakespearean twist, one of the most prominent opposition leaders in the attack against corruption in the Lula administration, Senator Demóstenes Torres (DEM-GO), was rather ignominiously felled in 2012 by his ties to a prominent gambling kingpin, Carlinhos Cachoeira. Allegations that Torres had many hundreds of contacts with Cachoeira and may have benefited financially from sharing government information with him led to his expulsion from the Senate.

2. On the complex dynamics of state and municipal corruption and the effectiveness of local legal accountability regimes see Da Ros (2014) and Macaulay (2011).

3. Because the decision against some of the defendants was very close (six votes to four), their sentencing was subject to a so-called *embargo infringente* appeal, which was decided only in early 2014.

4. The STF issued a potentially pathbreaking ruling in an unrelated case in early 2016, which argued that defendants convicted on first appeal could be sent directly to jail rather than only after all other possible avenues of appeal were exhausted. But this decision was not binding, and there is no guarantee that other judges, or even the STF justices, will rule in the same way in other cases.

5. The STF made two important changes, allowing for the admission of indirect proof collected from witnesses, as well as proof of intent, rather than concrete evidence of consummated corruption. This contrasts sharply with Collor's case, where

in a five-to-three vote, the STF decided that although P. C. Farias had led an illegal campaign finance operation, presumably on behalf of Collor, there was no evidence of Collor's direct involvement. Furthermore, the court adopted a logic of *domínio do fato* to argue that, although Dirceu did not participate directly in corrupt acts, he should have known of the wrongdoing by virtue of his position. Use of this argument has little precedent in Brazilian law.

6. These three potential ameliorating conditions—the statute of limitations, progressive imprisonment, and parole— are worth consideration. The statute of limitations (*prescrição de penas*) is governed by Article 109 of the Criminal Code, with fairly complex rules governing how time to trial will be counted. The statute of limitations can be fairly short relative to average trial times, and is cut in half for those over seventy years old. Progressive imprisonment refers to the existence of three types of incarceration: closed, semi-open, and open. "Closed" refers to prisoners who spend all their time in jail; "semi-open" allows prisoners to work outside prison during the day and return for the evening; and "open" refers to prisoners who sleep in a halfway house. Depending on the sentence received and time served, a prisoner can move from closed to semi-open, or semi-open to open, after completing one-sixth of their prison term. For the mensalão convictions, Congressmen José Genoíno and Roberto Jefferson will serve semi-open jail time because their final, revised sentences were below eight years. Sentenced to ten years for the mensalão, José Dirceu had already moved to a semi-open regime when he was arrested again in November 2013, this time on separate charges related to the Lava Jato scandal. He subsequently was sentenced to another twenty-three years in prison for Lava Jato, the longest penalty issued to date. Parole, known as *liberdade condicional* in the Brazilian legal system, is also a possibility, and available to convicts who have completed one-third of their sentences (or half of their sentences if they are recidivists).

7. "Special" jail cells are not all that "special," of course, in Brazil's overburdened penitentiaries. There is a concerted effort to place college graduates together in jail, but the overcrowding and poor hygiene are not very different from what regular prisoners face. Further, special cells are only available at the trial stage of the criminal process. Upon conviction, prisoners serve together in the general population.

8. Only 9 percent of Brazilians trust others, against a Latin American average of 22 percent, despite the fact that Brazil is near the regional average in terms of trust in government (39 percent versus 40 percent average; Latinobarómetro 2011).

9. These are known as the Lei de Responsabilidade Fiscal (Lei Complementar 101/2000); Ficha Limpa (Lei Complementar 135/2010); Lei de Acesso à Informação (Lei 12.527/2011); Lei sobre Lavagem de Dinheiro (12.683 of 2012); and Lei Anti-Corrupção (Lei 12.846 of 2013).

10. The protections in Brazil's law place it in the top quintile of ninety-two nations with freedom of information laws, at least in de jure terms (Center for Law and Democracy 2012).

11. Amarribo initially was an acronym for the Association of Friends of Ribeirão Bonito, a city in São Paulo state. Amarribo was successful in the early 2000s in fighting corruption within Ribeirão Bonito and sought to share its anti-corruption knowledge beyond that city. By 2008 the organization had established a network of anti-corruption campaigners in various cities and became one of the leading partners behind the popular initiative for the Ficha Limpa law, barring corrupt politicians from running for office. By 2011 it had become a nationally recognized NGO, known as Amarribo Brasil.

Chapter 4. Environmental Politics in Brazil

I would like to thank Laurence Whitehead and the editors for helpful comments on an earlier draft of this chapter. The discussion of Brazilian climate change politics draws on work published with my collaborator, Eduardo Viola (Hochstetler and Viola 2012; Viola and Hochstetler 2015). Research for this chapter was carried out with support of a grant from the Social Sciences and Humanities Research Council of Canada.

1. In 1999, 5.2 percent of the Brazilian population, excluding rural Amazonian areas, was without electricity, and by 2011 this had fallen to well below 1 percent of the total population. See IBGE 1999; IBGE 2012, table 2.6, page 109. Water and sanitation coverage is considerably lower.

2. The Belo Monte plant, currently under construction, is intended as one of the first of a series of large hydropower plants in the Amazon. The first turbines went online in 2016, with the plant set to be fully operational by 2019. It will be the third largest hydroelectric facility in the world in potential volume of electricity produced. While its reservoir is smaller than that of many large hydro projects, the government estimates that twenty thousand people, many of them indigenous, will be displaced; independent estimates are much higher.

3. The website is http://www.ibama.gov.br/licenciamento/index.php.

4. Petrobras, Brazil's state-controlled oil company, found potentially very large oil and gas fields in Brazil's Atlantic coastal waters in 2006. The deposits are known as "pre-salt" because the fuels are in a rock layer deposited below (and chronologically before) a layer of salt that is up to two thousand meters thick. The Tupi field was the first to be more intensively explored in 2009. Its reserves are five thousand meters deep and estimated to hold 5–8 billion barrels of oil equivalent; this is just one of many potential fields in the pre-salt area.

5. Silva's second presidential campaign in 2014 had less direct effects on environmental policies and outcomes.

6. Signatories to the UNFCCC and the Kyoto Protocol hold annual meetings of the parties to the agreements, where they discuss treaty compliance and negotiate additional possible treaties. The discussion here refers to four of these: the 2009 meeting in Copenhagen; the 2011 meeting in Durban; the 2012 meeting in Doha; and the 2015 meeting in Paris.

7. Author observation of the Durban COP 17 meeting, December 2011.

8. See www.globescan.com/radar_overview.htm.

Chapter 5. Checking the Power of Mayors

1. FUNDEF refers to the Fund for the Improvement of Basic Education (Fundo de Manutenção e Desenvolvimento do Ensino Fundamental e Valorização do Magistério) and FUNDEB refers to the Fund for the Improvement of Basic Education and Valorization of Education Professionals (Fundo de Manutenção e Desenvolvimento da Educação Básica e de Valorização dos Profissionais da Educação).

2. For insightful discussions of the politics of education prior to the introduction of FUNDEF, see Brown (2002) and Kosack (2012).

3. Capitation payment systems are based on payment per person rather than on payment per service provided or any other criteria. In the case of FUNDEF, payments

are based on the number of pupils rather than on a flat rate transfer to municipalities.

4. Since it was the federal executive that set the national per capita spending level, it ultimately had discretion over the amount of resources it channelled to FUNDEF. With the 1997 per capita rate set at R$300, the federal government had to provide equalization funds to eight states out of twenty-five—all of them in the North and Northeast—whose per capita spending fell below that value. During the period 1998–2002, the federal government never set the minimum national standard of quality of education that was required by law. More importantly, the per capita spending was not calculated on the basis of the fund's estimated revenue, also required by law. The initial level of R$300 remained the only parameter. In 2012 the federal government transferred funds to ten states, totaling R$10 billion (roughly US$5 billion at the time of writing) (Controladoria Geral da União 2013).

5. The acronym SAEB refers to the Sistema de Avaliação de Ensino Básico (the System for the Evaluation of Basic Education), and consists of two tests: the first—known as the SAEB test—is administered to a sample of fourth-to-eighth-grade students, as well as to senior students in secondary school, in all private and public schools. The second—called Prova Brasil—is the yearly evaluation of fourth-to-eighth-grade students in public schools. The acronym INEP refers to the National Institute for Educational Research, a unit of the Ministry of Education.

6. Using this index for state-level institutions and estimating its impact on municipal corruption (not state-level corruption) greatly reduces the potential endogeneity problems that plague analyses of the quality of institutions.

Chapter 6. Assessing the Bolsa Família

1. In 2001 Brazil's Gini score was 60.1, Haiti's was 59.2 and Bolivia's was 58.5 (World Bank, *World Development Indicators*). We report figures for 2001, as this was the year where World Bank data are available for most countries in the region.

2. The "Eloy Chaves law" provided for the creation of the Caixa de Aposentadoria e Pensão (CAP), a retirement and survivor's pension for Railway Company employees (Malloy 1979, 40).

3. See Rizzotti, Almeida, and Albuquerque (2010) for more on the establishment and regulatory framework of the Unified System of Social Assistance (Sistema Único de Assistência Social; SUAS).

4. Between 2005 and 2006, the federal government "scaled-up" the Bolsa Família program. The Bolsa represented 1.1 percent of total government expenditures and rose to 2.5 percent by the following year, an increase from 0.2 to 0.5 percent of Brazil's GDP in 2006 (Lindert 2006, 67).

5. The interview subjects in our study reported that the threat of suspension was real and that a number of the participants in our study had experienced a suspension (Sugiyama and Hunter 2013). The Ministry of Social Development's goal is to provide struggling families with greater support, and the MDS views such families as needing follow-up with a local social worker.

6. See DAB Portal, "Tipos de benefícios do Programa Bolsa Família," available at http://189.28.128.100/dab/docs/portaldab/documentos/tipos_beneficios_programa_bolsa _familia.pdf/.

7. Lindert (2006) provides an excellent overview on the nuts and bolts of Bolsa Família's administration.

8. Some municipal governments ask that beneficiaries provide more than the minimum required by the MDS and also require a license-to-work card (Carteira de Trabalho).

9. See also Silveira, Campolina, and Van Horn (2013) for a comparison of allotments of time to education and work among children and adolescents who receive vs. do not receive the Bolsa Família.

10. Even healthcare-related conditionalities for mothers—such as prenatal health checkups and breastfeeding—tend to focus on their reproductive roles.

Chapter 7. Progress or Perdition?

1. The law creating the Amnesty Commission dates from 2002, but the commission began its work in 2001 after publication of a presidential decree (*medida provisória*). I thank Marcelo Torelly for this information.

2. This could change. At the time of writing, the alleged murderers of the former congressman Marcelo Rubens Paiva are on trial in a federal court in Rio de Janeiro. See Alfonsín 2015.

3. An official history of the army published in 1998 reflects this lack of a reevaluation of the dictatorship inside the Brazilian armed forces. The chapter on the 1964 coup is an unreconstructed defense of the "revolution" and the "morality" of the armed forces in saving the nation. See Carvalho 1998, 176–99.

4. I owe this insight to Ken Roberts. Pinto (2011, 16) discusses the importance of political parties in transitional justice.

5. I take the word *"jeitão"* from Francisco de Oliveira, who argues that if the *jeitinho* is the hallmark of the marginalized and oppressed, the *jeitão* (the illegal and/or unethical, rapacious, mendacious, or duplicitous subterfuge engaged in to advance special interests) defines Brazil's pattern of national development. See De Oliveira 2012.

6. I use the word "transnational" here to include not just state-to-state international connections, but cross-border connections among NGOs and other relevant actors in the human rights realm.

7. I also heard Steve Stern make this point in a presentation at Tulane University in 2005.

8. For a further discussion of these issues, see Weichert 2012.

9. The committee hearing, organized to demand the formation of the Truth Commission, was chaired by federal deputy Luiza Erundina, then of the Brazilian Socialist Party (Partido Socialista Brasileiro; PSB). She subsequently made criticisms of the way the Truth Commission was put together. Those who testified represented the Family Members of the Politically Killed and Disappeared; the Unified Workers' Central (Central Única dos Trabalhadores; CUT); the National Bar Association (Ordem dos Advogados do Brasil; OAB); the Popular Youth Uprising; Judges for Democracy; the National Confederation of Brazilian [Catholic] Bishops; and Federal Prosecutors for Citizens' Rights (Fazzio 2011).

10. Another problematic issue not dealt with here is who does the coding for these scales, and how qualified and consistent they are in their coding. The PTS score is coded mostly by graduate students under the supervision of Professor Mark Gibney of the Political Science Department at the University of North Carolina (UNC) at Asheville; see www.politicalterrorscale.org. There is less information available about who does the coding for the CIRI scale, under the supervision of the principal investi-

gators Professor David Cingranelli, of the Political Science Department of Binghampton University, Professor David Richards of the Political Science Department of the University of Connecticut, and Assistant Professor Chad Clay, of the Department of International Affairs at the University of Georgia. See http://www.humanrightsdata.com/p/faq.html/. My comments here should not be interpreted as a questioning of the integrity of any of the researchers involved in either of these two projects. Rather, my point is that the large discrepancies in the respective scores for Brazil produced by these two research teams, as well as the inherent difficulties in converting qualitative human rights reports into numerical scores on a limited scale, suggest that relying on this data for fine-grained evaluations of causal mechanisms is problematic and can be misleading.

11. This is an important point that has not received sufficient attention in the literature. Some might defend the use of this data—as imprecise, variable, and arbitrary as it might be—because quantitative analysis can answer fundamental questions about causality. In this view political science, to be rigorous, must use whatever data is available. On the contrary, the use of this kind of data to make inferences about causality creates a spurious rigor, because it claims a degree of accuracy that is unjustified if the creation of the numbers is examined carefully. The claimed degree of variation between the cases is so minute, and the creation of the numbers in the two different rankings so disparate and arbitrary, that causal claims of this nature have to be viewed skeptically.

12. I am grateful to James Green for making this point.

Chapter 8. Toward a (Poor) Middle-Class Democracy?

This article presents partial results of the project on "Middle Income Groups and Politics in Brazil," supported by the National Council for Scientific and Technological Development of Brazil (Conselho Nacional de Desenvolvimento Científico e Tecnológico; CNPq), grant number 454220/2014-6.

1. There are slight differences in the definition of this stratum, which has been labeled middle classes, new middle classes, C class, C stratum, as much as in the criteria used to define it. Neri (2008, 2011b), a pioneer in the study of the issue, defines it as an income category of those whose "mean income equals the mean income of the Brazilian society." The Brazilian Office of Strategic Affairs (Secretaria de Assuntos Estratégicos; SAE) also uses income to define the middle class (SAE 2012a), but its criteria differ from Neri's. Souza and Lamounier (2010), although proposing to combine objective criteria—income, education and occupation—with subjective indicators such as class identity, self-classification and perception of social mobility, chose to use income as the basis for their empirical analysis. Oliveira (2010) defines the middle classes by patterns of consumption and lifestyles. For practical purposes, we will adopt the SAE's criteria and data whenever we have disaggregated data. The SAE defines the middle class as the group whose per capita income varies from R\$291 to R\$1,019, US\$154 to US\$540 (dollar Purchasing Power Parities [PPP] for 2012, using Heston, Summers, and Aten 2012). For all purposes, we will use "middle classes" and "middle income stratum" as interchangeable terms, although we acknowledge that "class" responds to more than a purely income-based definition.

2. There are three very large cash transfer programs: Rural Social Security (Previdência Rural), Continued Cash Benefit (Benefício de Prestação Continuada) and

Family Allowance (Bolsa Família). The first two were created by the 1988 Constitution, and Bolsa Família was established under Lula's government as a result of the restructuring and expansion of previous cash transfer programs created by Cardoso's administration.

3. Nevertheless, levels of education of the younger generation have improved significantly, especially among lower and middle income earners. From 2001 to 2011, the percentage of people with more than eleven years of schooling grew from 9.0 to 26.9 percent among the poorest 20 percent of the Brazilian population; from 13.0 to 37.8 percent among the next 20 percent in the income distribution continuum; from 25.0 to 51.9 percent among the next 20 percent; from 42.7 to 66.7 percent among the next 20 percent; and from 71.1 to 84.4 percent among the richest 20 percent of Brazilians. In other words, those placed around the middle of the income distribution ladder experienced huge increases in education levels. These middle-class students mostly attend private universities, which cater for around 75 percent of all students in higher education.

4. "Between 2000 and 2010, micro and small businesses (MSBs) have created 6.1 million formal jobs, bringing up total employment in these sectors from 8.6 million jobs, in 2000, to 14.7 million, in 2010. In the 2000s, the average growth of jobs in MSBs was 5.5 percent per year. In the first half of the decade, 2.4 million jobs were created in MSBs, an average annual growth of 5.1 percent per year. Between 2005 and 2010, this movement intensified, resulting in 3.7 million jobs, an average annual growth of 6.1 percent per year. Of the 12.6 million formal jobs created in private non-agricultural establishments in the last ten years, 6.1 million were generated by micro and small enterprises. The good performance of MSBs throughout the decade confirmed the economic importance of this sector. In 2010 micro and small enterprises accounted for 99 percent of establishments and 51.6 percent of the formal employment in the private non-agricultural sector, and almost 40 percent of total wages and salaries. On average, during the 2000s, for each R$100 paid to workers in the private non-agricultural sector, approximately R$41 was generated by micro and small enterprises" (SEBRAE 2011).

5. Since we are working with secondary data to assess the impact of class on voting preferences, we are limited to the definition of social strata used by the polling organization. When using data from SAE and Datafolha, we are working with a definition of "middle class" as based on income. In the case of SAE (as we noted earlier), the middle-class family income ranges from 1.8 minimum wages to 6.6 minimum wages, with the lower-middle class ranging from 1.8 to 2.8 minimum wages (SAE 2012a), the mid-middle ranging from 2.8 to 4.1 and the upper-middle from 4.1 to 6.6 minimum wages. In terms of US dollar PPPs these ranges are from $616 to $933; from $933 to $1,356, and from $1,356 to $2,155, respectively. In the case of Datafolha, the range for the group considered middle income is from two to ten minimum wages. Data from Datafolha allows us to disaggregate the middle income group in three segments: the "lower class," or people whose earnings total less than two minimum wages; the "lower middle class," encompassing people with an income of between two and five minimum wages; and the "upper middle class" of people with earnings of between five and ten minimum wages. These divisions correspond to incomes of from $658 to $1,645 and from $1,645 to $3,290 in USD (PPP).

6. "Today, the most heated issues tend to be noneconomic, and support for change on these issues comes from postmaterialists, largely of middle class origin" (Inglehart 1997, 278).

7. Nevertheless, violent homophobic groups exist in several large cities in Brazil and have been responsible for frequent street strikes against real or supposed male homosexuals. Some of these gangs seem to attract middle-class and lower-middle-class youngsters.

8. The question is: "Thinking about left and right in politics, where would you position yourself?"

9. Arranged from the left to the right on the ideological continuum, these are (see Power and Zucco 2011): the Workers' Party (Partido dos Trabalhadores; PT), the Green Party (Partido Verde; PV), the Brazilian Democratic Movement Party (Partido do Movimento Democrático Brasileiro; PMDB) and the Brazilian Social Democratic Party (Partido da Social Democracia Brasileira; PSDB).

10. This narrative is central in the extraordinary documentary film by Dorrit Harrazim and Arthur Fontes, *A Família Braz*, which focuses on members of a Brazilian poor family as they experience upward mobility. The job market and better education, not the government, are seen by the younger members of the family as the tools for social improvement, made possible thanks to their own personal efforts to get better professional and social skills and to take advantage of new learning opportunities.

11. "It is time . . . to reinforce, not to despise, the basic 'middle class' values—study, work, honesty . . . I believe . . . that the traditional middle class, which already played its part in building our nation, remains highly relevant, as it is able to transit its values to emerging groups who are already predisposed to share them, since their improved economic standing also comes from their own effort and hard work" (Cardoso 2012).

12. During the 2010 presidential campaign the PSDB candidate, José Serra, supported by some evangelical denominations, used these issues as part of a negative campaign against Dilma Rousseff, suggesting she favored abortion and same-sex marriage.

13. According to the newspaper *Folha de São Paulo*, at the peak of the movement, on June 20, around a million people took to the streets in several Brazilian cities (*Folha de São Paulo* 2013, C4).

14. The role of social media may have been exaggerated. If it is true that social media was instrumental in rapidly informing thousands of people of events as they unfolded, the traditional media—particularly live television broadcasts showing the street rallies—proved crucial in fomenting a sympathetic reaction among the general public, especially after police reacted with extreme violence to repress demonstrators in São Paulo. There was, in fact, a strong and mutually reinforcing interaction between social and traditional media.

15. FIFA is the International Federation of Football (Fédération Internationale de Football) Association.

16. According to Datafolha surveys, on June 17, 39 percent of participants in the demonstrations in São Paulo were wage earners working in the formal labor market, and 22 percent were students. On June 20, these two groups represented 51 percent and 11 percent respectively of demonstrators interviewed. On these two days, 77 percent and 78 percent respectively of protestors were people with higher education. Singer (2013) summarizes this final full diversity: "Headed by young left-wing activists, the movement ended up attracting diverse and opposing groups. First came a wave of participants typical of Marina Silva voters. Their lifestyle would be characterized as modern, their behavior liberal, their politics centrist, and most of their anger was directed against corruption. Then the conservatives arrived, infuriated by corruption and the PT, upon whom they placed the blame for all of Brazil's problems. Finally, to

complete the political kaleidoscope, the extreme right also took to the streets, transforming the conservatives' rage into violence directed at the socialist parties. Thus, although divided over every issue, the middle class nonetheless paraded as a united force, bound together by its yearning for protest."

17. Brazilian analysts seem to agree with Fukuyama's assessment, although, as the movement is still ongoing, these diagnoses are expressed mostly in newspaper opinion pieces. Among the most interesting are Singer (2013), Coelho (2013), Rodrigues (2013), and Sola (2013).

18. The June 20 survey was conducted around Avenida Paulista, in a middle-class neighborhood. There, only 7 percent of the respondents earned two minimum wages or less, and 32 percent earned more than ten minimum wages. Nevertheless, as the demonstrators moved downtown, it is possible that the crowd assimilated more people from lower-income groups.

Chapter 9. The Economic Context of Social Protests in 2013

1. This chapter covers the cycle of protests in 2013. A separate wave of protests and counter-protests in 2015–2016 centered on Dilma Rousseff's impeachment and subsequent removal from office (see the editors' Introduction to this volume).

2. For a description of the Brazilian class structure, see Boito (2012).

3. A notable exception was the Landless Peasants' Movement (Movimento dos Trabalhadores Rurais Sem Terra; MST), which systematically rejected these employment offers.

4. For a detailed analysis of the class structure in Brazil and its current political implications, see Boito 2012 and Saad-Filho 2014.

5. See Pomar 2013, 42; also www.ibge.gov.br/.

6. These are people in households with per capita income below the poverty line, which is defined as twice the line of extreme poverty. The latter is determined by the cost of a food basket including the minimum calories recommended by FAO and WHO (Ipeadata 2013).

7. This information comes from http://www.denatran.gov.br/frota.htm

8. Former president Lula famously insisted that, during the last decade, much had changed in the homes of the poor in terms of access to consumer goods, but once they stepped outside, they found that nothing had changed in terms of public goods and services (see Saad-Filho 2013, 668).

9. For a detailed review of the events and the social composition of the demonstrations, see Saad-Filho 2013.

10. It has been estimated that up to 91 percent of demonstrators heard about their marches on the Internet (Silva 2013).

11. "There were several demonstrations in the evening of Friday, June 21 and Saturday, June 22. At Paulista Avenue, on Friday evening, three demonstrations took place with different demands and, in the absence of any points of contact, they did not engage with one another: the doctors, the 'gay cure' (a bill in Congress, supported by the evangelical churches, allowing psychologists to treat homosexuals seeking a cure for their supposed 'illness'; the bill was strongly opposed by the left and most social movements, and it was withdrawn on July 1), and another from We Are The Eastern Zone [of São Paulo]" (Fon Filho 2013). The author of this chapter witnessed three small unconnected demonstrations taking place simultaneously, at Paulista Avenue, on Monday, July 1: one led by a street theater group, another by Bolivian workers, and

the third by a loose crowd without any clear demands but obviously very intent on taking photographs of one another. The following evening, Paulista Avenue was paralysed by a large demonstration of bus drivers and, the next evening, twenty thousand health sector workers demonstrated there.

12. An opinion poll carried out in eight state capitals on June 20 (a day of large demonstrations) suggested that 63 percent of the demonstrators were aged fourteen to twenty-nine, 92 percent had completed at least secondary school, 52 percent were students, 76 percent were in paid employment, and only 45 percent earned less than five minimum wages. In other words, they had attended school for much longer and had much higher incomes than the population average (*O Globo* 2013b; Bueno 2013).

13. Data from www.ipeadata.gov.br/ and UOL Economia 2016.

14. See Saad-Filho 2014. The relationship between neoliberalism and democracy is examined in Ayers and Saad-Filho 2014.

15. The classic analysis of the political role of the lumpenproletariat is outlined in Marx (1851).

16. For a detailed analysis of the social composition of the protests (insofar as this is possible), see Chauí (2013) and Saad-Filho (2013).

17. For an open admission of successive mistakes in the coverage of the preparations for the World Cup in Brazil's largest weekly news magazine, see *Brasil 247* 2014.

18. For an extraordinary admission that the media took up the mantle of political opposition to the PT administrations, see the interview of the president of the National Association of Newspapers, Maria Judith Brito, at Farah 2010. Broader studies of media bias, invariably against the government, can be found at Manchetômetro (http://www.manchetometro.com.br) and Observatório da Imprensa (http://www.observatoriodaimprensa.com.br).

19. For a detailed analysis, see Saad-Filho 2014 and Saad-Filho and Morais 2014.

Chapter 11. The Public Bank Trilemma

Thanks, without responsibility, are due to this volume's editors, our anonymous reviewers, Laura Randall, and Fernando Barrera Sotelino.

1. For further discussion of contemporary Brazilian and Latin American political economy, see Bresser-Pereira 2009; Kingstone 2011; Castelo 2012; Zanetta 2012; Ban 2013; Souza and Miranda 2015. Matthew Taylor's (2015) analysis identifies significant continuity in Brazilian public policies, even across ideologically distinct presidential administrations.

2. For other analyses of the contemporary political economy of the BNDES, see Stallings with Studart 2006, 222–60; Von Mettenheim 2010; Hochstetler and Montero 2013; Doctor 2013; Almeida, Lima-de-Oliveira, and Schneider 2014.

3. Data in this paragraph have been drawn from BNDES 2015a, 2015b, and BCB 2016.

4. The Expertise-Democracy leg of the public bank trilemma is close to Peter Evans's (1995) concept of the need for "embedded autonomy" within a developmental state. Almeida, Lima-de-Oliveira, and Schneider (2014) reference Evans's frame in their analysis of the BNDES.

5. For the history of the BNDES, see Willis 2013; Armijo 1993, 1997; BNDES 2002a; Stallings with Studart 2006; von Mettenheim 2010; Doctor 2013.

6. Rossi and Prates (2009, 24) concluded that the share of total financing from the

BNDES system that was export-related was fully 33 percent in 2003 but had fallen to only 13 percent of disbursements in 2008. Other sources show smaller shares.

7. Besides South America, the other major export destination where manufactured goods dominate is the United States, where Brazil's largest export by value continues to be commuter aircraft. In 2009 the United States was displaced as Brazil's largest trading partner by China, where Brazilian exports are heavily skewed toward commodities (see Table 11.2).

8. By early 2016 Petrobras's finances had become dire. In February Brazil's government announced it had accepted a $10 billion loan from the China Development Bank to Petrobras, sufficient to make its foreign debt payments for 2016, which would be repaid in future oil sales. Brazil (or at least Petrobras) thus joined the ranks of resource-rich pariah states shut out of global capital markets, including Venezuela and Kirchner-era Argentina.

9. Another reason that Brazilian interest rates remain stubbornly high is that commercial banks get so little of their funding from the free market (since they also access on-loaned BNDES funds, which are at the below-market TJLP rate). BCB must therefore raise rates in order to get an impact on the volume of credit.

10. The social insurance funds are Fundo de Garantia do Tempo de Serviço (FGTS),

Programa de Integração Social/Programa de Formação do *Patrimônio* do Servidor Público (PIS/PASEP), and Fundo de Amparo ao Trabalhador (FAT).

11. Brazil is hardly alone in employing various accounting tricks to improve the look of public finances. See Irwin 2016.

REFERENCES

Aarão Reis Filho, Daniel. 2013. "O governo Lula e a construção da memória do regime civil-militar." In *O Passado que não passa*, edited by António Costa Pinto and Francisco Carlos Palomanes Martinho, 215–34. Rio de Janeiro: Civilização Brasileira.

Abers, Rebecca N. 2000. *Inventing Local Democracy: Grassroots Politics in Brazil*. Boulder: Lynne Rienner.

Abers, Rebecca N. 2016. "Conflitos, mobilizações e a participação institucionalizada: a relação com a sociedade civil no construção de grandes obras de infraestrutura." Brasília: Instituto de Pesquisa Econômica Aplicada, Relatório de Pesquisa. February.

Abers, Rebecca N., and Marília Silva de Oliveira. 2015. "Nomeações políticas no Ministério do Meio Ambiente (2003–2013): interconexões entre ONGs, partidos e governos." *Opinião Pública* 21 (2): 1–29.

Abers, Rebecca N., and Marisa von Bülow. 2011. "Movimentos sociais na teoria e na prática: como estudar o ativismo através da fronteira entre Estado e sociedade?" *Sociologias* 13, no. 28 (September–December): 52–84.

Abrão, Paulo, and Marcelo Torelly. 2011. "The Reparations Program as the Linchpin of Transitional Justice in Brazil." In *Transitional Justice: Handbook for Latin America*, edited by Félix Reátegui, 443–85. Brasília: Brazilian Amnesty Commission, Ministry of Justice/International Center for Transitional Justice.

Acselrad, Henri, Selene Herculano, and José Augusto Pádua. 2003. *Justiça ambiental e cidadania*. Rio de Janeiro: Relume Dumará.

Aghion, B. 1999. "Development Banking." *Journal of Development Economics*, no. 58: 83–100.

Alfonsin, Jaques Távora. 2015. "O caso Rubens Paiva: processo volta a tramitar." *Carta Maior*, September 30. http://cartamaior.com.br/?/Editoria/Principios-Fundamentais/O-caso-Rubens-Paiva-processo-volta-a-tramitar/40/34633.

Allen, F., and D. Gale. 2000. *Comparing Financial Systems*. Cambridge, MA: MIT Press.

Almeida, Mansueto, Renato Lima-de-Oliveira, and Ben Ross Schneider. 2014. "Política industrial e empresas estatais no Brasil: BNDES e Petrobras." In *Capacidades estatais e democracia: arranjos institucionais e políticas públicas*, edited by A. de Gomide and R. R. C. Pires. Brasília: IPEA.

Almeida, Maria Hermínia Tavares de, and Emmanoel Nunes de Oliveira. 2010. "Nuevas capas medias y política en Brasil." In *Clases medias y gobernabilidad en América Latina*, edited by Ludolfo Paramio, 103–18. Madrid: Editorial Pablo Iglesias.

Almeida, Maria Hermínia Tavares de, Alexandre Barbosa Pereira, and Umberto Mignozzetti. 2011. "Brasil: las capas medias en las elecciones presidenciales de 2010." In *Clases medias y procesos electorales en América Latina*, edited by Ludolfo Paramio, 208–25. Madrid: Ed. Catarata.

Almeida, Paulo Roberto de, and Rubens Antônio Barbosa, eds. 2006. *Relações Brasil-Estados Unidos: assimetrias e convergências*. São Paulo: Editora Saraiva.

Almond, Gabriel, and Sidney Verba. 1963. *The Civic Culture: Political Attitudes and Democracy in Five Nations*. Boston: Little, Brown.

Alston, Lee, Marcus André Melo, Bernardo Mueller, and Carlos Pereira. 2009. "The Choices Governors Make: Checks and Balances, and the Provision of Public Goods in the Brazilian States." Paper presented at the National Bureau for Economic Research. NBER summer conference, Boston.

Amann, Edmund. 1999. "Technological Self-Reliance in Brazil: Achievements and Prospects: Some Evidence from the Non-serial Capital Goods Sector." *Oxford Development Studies* 27 (3): 329–57.

Amann, Edmund. 2009. "Technology, Public Policy, and the Emergence of Brazilian Multinationals." In *Brazil as an Economic Superpower? Understanding Brazil's Changing Role in the the Global Economy*, edited by Lael Brainard and Leonardo Martinez-Diaz, 187–220. Washington, DC: Brookings Institution Press.

Amaral, Oswaldo E. do. 2011. "Ainda conectado: O PT e seus vínculos com a sociedade." *Opinião Pública* 17, no. 1 (June): 1–44.

Amaral, Oswaldo E. do, and Pedro Floriano Ribeiro. 2015. "Por que Dilma de novo? Uma análise exploratória do Estudo Eleitoral Brasileiro de 2014." *Revista de Sociologia e Política* 23 (56): 107–23.

Ames, Barry. 1987. *Political Survival: Politicians and Public Policy in Latin America*. Berkeley: University of California Press.

Ames, Barry. 2001. *The Deadlock of Democracy in Brazil*. Ann Arbor: University of Michigan Press.

Amorim Neto, Octavio. 2007. "Algumas consequências políticas de Lula: novos padrões de formação e recrutamento ministerial, controle de agenda e produção legislativa." In *Instituições representativas no Brasil: balanço e reforma*, edited by Jairo Nicolau and Timothy Power, 55–73. Belo Horizonte: UFMG.

Angelsen, Arild. 2012. *Analysing REDD+: Challenges and Choices*. Bogor: Center for International Forestry Research.

Arantes, Rogério B. 2011. "The Federal Police and the Ministério Público." In *Corruption and Democracy in Brazil: The Struggle for Accountability*, edited by Timothy J. Power and Matthew M. Taylor, 184–217. Notre Dame, IN: University of Notre Dame Press.

Arashiro, Zuleika. 2011. *Negotiating the Free Trade Area of the Americas*. New York: Palgrave Macmillan.

Arends-Kuenning, M. 2009. "A Report Card for Lula: Progress in Education." In *Brazil under Lula*, edited by J. Love and W. Baer. London: Palgrave.

Arida, Pérsio. 2005. *Mecanismos compulsórios e mercados de capitais: propostas de política econômica*. Texto para Discussão 8, Instituto de Estudos de Política Econômica, Casa das Garças. May.

Armijo, Leslie Elliott. 1993. "Brazilian Politics and Patterns of Financial Regulation, 1950–1991." In *The Politics of Finance in Developing Countries*, edited by S. Haggard, C. Lee, and S. Maxfield. Ithaca, NY: Cornell University Press.

Armijo, Leslie Elliott. 1997. "Brazil: Business-Government Financial Relations in the Land of 'Super-Inflation.'" In *Government and Business Finance: Global Perspectives on Economic Development*, edited by R. Bingham and E. W. Hill. Newark: CUPR Press of Rutgers University.

Armijo, Leslie Elliott, and Philippe Faucher. 2002. "'We Have a Consensus': Explaining Political Support for Market Reforms in Latin America." *Latin American Politics and Society* 44 (2): 1–40.

Arns, Paulo Evaristo. 1996. *Brasil: Nunca Mais.* São Paulo: Editora Vozes.

Arretche, Marta. 2004. "Federalismo e políticas sociais no Brasil: problemas de coordenação e autonomia." *São Paulo em Perspectiva* 18 (2): 17–26.

Arruda, Roldão. 2012. "Caserna longe da crise com governo." In *O Estado de São Paulo*, March 17.

Atencio, Rebecca. 2014. *Memory's Turn: Culture and Transitional Justice in Brazil.* Madison: University of Wisconsin Press.

Attuch, Leonardo. 2006. *A CPI que abalou o Brasil: os bastidores da imprensa e os segredos do PT.* Futura: São Paulo.

Avritzer, Leonardo. 2011. "Governabilidade, sistema político e corrupção no Brasil." In *Corrupção e sistema político no Brasil*, edited by Leonardo Avritzer and Fernando Filgueiras. Rio de Janeiro: Ed. Civilização Brasileira.

Avritzer, Leonardo, and Clóvis Henrique Leite de Souza. 2013. "Conferências Nacionais: atores, dinâmicas participativas e efetividade." Brasília: IPEA.

Ayers, A., and A. Saad-Filho. 2014. "Democracy against Neoliberalism: Paradoxes, Limitations, Transcendence." *Critical Sociology* 41 (4–5): 597–618.

Bacha, Edmar. 2002. "Do Consenso de Washington ao Dissenso de Cambridge." In *Desenvolvimento em debate: novos rumos do desenvolvimento no mundo*, edited by A. C. Castro. Rio de Janeiro: BNDES.

Baierle, Sergio. 1998. "The Explosion of Experience: The Emergence of a New Ethical-Political Principle in Popular Movements in Porto Alegre, Brazil." In *Cultures of Politics/Politics of Cultures: Re-visioning Latin American Social Movements*, edited by Sonia E. Alvarez, Evelina Dagnino, and Arturo Escobar. Boulder, CO: Westview Press.

Baiocchi, Gianpaolo. 2005. *Militants and Citizens: The Politics of Participation in Porto Alegre.* Stanford, CA: Stanford University Press.

Balán, Manuel. 2014. "Surviving Corruption in Brazil: Lula's and Dilma's Success despite Corruption Allegations and Its Consequences." *Journal of Politics in Latin America* 6 (3): 67–93.

Balbachevsky, Elisabeth, and Denilde Holzhacker. 2004. "Identidade, oposição e pragmatismo: o conteúdo estratégico da decisão eleitoral em 13 anos de eleições." *Opinião Pública* 10, no. 2 (November): 242–53.

Ban, Cornel. 2013. "Brazil's Liberal Neo-developmentalism: New Paradigm or Edited Orthodoxy?" *Review of International Political Economy.* Available at Online First.

Banco Central do Brasil (BCB). 2016. "Financial System Credit Operations." Economy and Finances Data. http://www.bcb.gov.br.

Banco Nacional de Desenvolvimento Econômico e Social (BNDES). 2002a. *BNDES: Cinquenta anos de desenvolvimento*, June. http://www.bndes.gov.br.

Banco Nacional de Desenvolvimento Econômico e Social (BNDES). 2002b. "Privatization in Brazil." Powerpoint presentation, September 2002. http://www.bndes.gov.br.

Banco Nacional de Desenvolvimento Econômico e Social (BNDES). 2011. "Financial and Institutional Aspects." Powerpoint presentation, June 2011. http://www.bndes.gov.br.

Banco Nacional de Desenvolvimento Econômico e Social (BNDES). 2012. *Annual Report 2011.* Rio de Janeiro: BNDES. http://www.bndes.gov.br.

Banco Nacional de Desenvolvimento Econômico e Social (BNDES). 2015a. *Annual Report 2014*. Rio de Janeiro: BNDES.

Banco Nacional de Desenvolvimento Econômico e Social (BNDES). 2015b. "Corporate Presentation: Financial Area." June 2015. Powerpoint presentation at Investor Relations. http://www.bndes.gov.br.

Banco Nacional de Desenvolvimento Econômico e Social (BNDES). 2015c. "Economic and Financial Release, Highlights 4Q15." December 2015. Powerpoint presentation at Investor Relations. http://www.bndes.gov.br.

Banco Nacional de Desenvolvimento Econômico e Social (BNDES). 2015d. "Investor Presentation." December 2015. Powerpoint presentation at Investor Relations. http://www.bndes.gov.br.

Bandeira, Luiz Alberto Moniz. 2003. *Brasil, Argentina e Estados Unidos: Conflito e integração na América do Sul da Tríplice Aliança ao Mercosul, 1870–2003*. Rio de Janeiro: Editora Revan.

Bandeira, Luiz Alberto Moniz. 2004. *As relações perigosas: Brasil–Estados Unidos (de Collor a Lula, 1990–2004)*. Rio de Janeiro: Civilização Brasileira.

Barahona de Brito, Alexandra. 2011. "Transitional Justice and Memory: Exploring Perspectives." In *Dealing with the Legacy of Authoritarianism*, edited by Antônio Costa Pinto and Leonardo Morlino, 21–38. London: Routledge.

Barahona de Brito, Alexandra, and Mario Sznajder. 2011. "The Politics of the Past: The Southern Cone and Southern Europe in Comparative Perspective." In *Dealing with the Legacy of Authoritarianism*, edited by Antônio Costa Pinto and Leonardo Morlino, 145–63. London: Routledge.

Barber, Lionel, and Jonathan Wheatley. 2009. "The Real Reward." Interview with President Luiz Inácio (Lula) da Silva. *Financial Times*, November 8.

Barbosa, Rubem. 2011. *O Dissenso de Washington*. São Paulo: Editora Agir.

Barbosa, Rubens Antônio, and Luís Panelli César. 1994. "O Brasil como 'global trader.'" In *Temas de Política Externa Brasileira II, vol. 1*, edited by Gélson Fonseca Júnior and Sérgio Henrique Nabuco de Castro. São Paulo: Paz e Terra.

Barreto, Fernando de Mello. 2001. *Os sucessores do Barão, 1912–1964*. São Paulo: Editora Paz e Terra.

Barreto, Fernando de Mello. 2006. *Os sucessores do Barão: relações exteriores do Brasil, vol. 2: 1964–1985*. São Paulo: Paz e Terra.

Barros, Ricardo Paes de, Mirela de Carvalho, Samuel Franco, and Rosane Mendonça. 2010. "A importância das cotas para a focalização do Programa Bolsa Família." In *Bolsa Família 2003–2010: avanços e desafios*, vol. 2, edited by Jorge Abrahão de Castro and Lúcia Modesto. Brasília, IPEA.

Barros, Ricardo Paes de, D. Grosner, and A. Mascarenhas. 2012. *Vozes da classe média: caderno 2—desigualdade, heterogeneidade e diversidade*. Brasília: Presidência da República.

BASIC Experts. 2011. *Equitable Access to Sustainable Development: Contribution to the Body of Scientific Knowledge*. Beijing: BASIC Expert Group.

Bastagli, Francesca. 2011. "Conditional Cash Transfers as a Tool of Social Policy." *Economic and Political Weekly* 46, no. 21 (May 21): 61–66.

Bastos, E. K. X. 2012. *Distribuição funcional da renda no Brasil: Estimativas anuais e construção de uma série trimestral*. Texto para Discussão IPEA, no. 1702. Brasília: IPEA.

BCB. *See* Banco Central do Brasil (BCB)

Bernhard, William, J. Lawrence Broz, and William Roberts Clark, eds. 2003. *The Political Economy of Monetary Institutions*. Cambridge, MA: MIT Press.

Bersch, Katherine, Sergio Praça, and Matthew M. Taylor. 2017. "State Capacity, Bureaucratic Politicization, and Corruption in the Brazilian State." *Governance: An International Journal of Policy, Administration, and Institutions* 30, no. 1 (January): 105–24.

Bethell, Leslie, and Celso Castro. 2008. "Politics in Brazil under Military Rule, 1964–1985." In *The Cambridge History of Latin America, Volume 9, Brazil since 1930*, edited by Leslie Bethell, 165–230. Cambridge: Cambridge University Press.

Biller, David. 2012. "Rousseff's Stimulus Measures to Spur Brazil Economy: Timeline." *Bloomberg*, December 6.

Birdsall, Nancy, and Richard H. Sabot, eds. 1996. *Opportunity Foregone: Education in Brazil*, Washington, DC: Inter-American Development Bank.

BNDES. *See* Banco Nacional de Desenvolvimento Econômico e Social (BNDES)

BNDES News. 2010. "BNDES and the Stock Exchange Launch Efficient Carbon Index at COP 16." Press release. December 8. http://www.bndes.gov.br.

Boas, Taylor, F. Daniel Hidalgo, and Neal Richardson. 2014. "The Spoils of Victory: Campaign Donations and Government Contracts in Brazil." *Journal of Politics* 76 (2): 415–29.

Boito, Armando. 2003. "A hegemonia neoliberal no Governo Lula." *Crítica Marxista*, no. 17: 1–16.

Boito, Armando. 2012. "Governos Lula: a nova burguesia nacional no poder." In *Política e classes sociais no Brasil dos anos 2000*, edited by A. Boito and A. Galvão, 67–104. São Paulo: Alameda.

Bonelli, Regis. 1999. "A Note on Foreign Direct Investment and Industrial Competitiveness in Brazil." *Oxford Development Studies* 27 (3): 305–27.

Bonney, Richard, ed. 1995. *Economic Systems and State Finance*. Oxford: Oxford University Press.

Braga, Maria do Socorro, Pedro Ribeiro, and Oswaldo Amaral. 2016. "El sistema de partidos en Brasil: estabilidad e institucionalización, 1982–2014." In *Los sistemas de partidos de América Latina [1978–2015]*, edited by Flavia Freidenberg, 69–133. México: Instituto Nacional Electoral e Instituto de Investigaciones Jurídicas, Universidad Nacional Autónoma de México.

Brainard, Lael, and Leonardo Martinez-Diaz, eds. 2009. *Brazil as an Economic Superpower? Understanding Brazil's Changing Role in the Global Economy*. Washington, DC: Brookings Institution Press.

Brandão, André, Salete Da Dalt, and Victor Hugo Gouvêa. 2008. "Food and Nutrition Security among Beneficiaries of the Bolsa Família Program." In *Evaluation of MDS Policies and Programs-Results (Vol. 2): Bolsa Família Program and Social Assistance*, edited by Jeni Vaitsman and Rômulo Paes-Souza, 97–116. Brasília: Ministry of Social Development and the Fight Against Hunger.

Brasil 247. 2014. "Chefão da Abril: 'Imprensa pecou feio. É a vida.'" June 29. http://www.brasil247.com/pt/247/midiatech/145063/Chef%20percentC3%20percentA3o-da-Abril-Imprensa-pecou-feio-%20percentC3%20percent89-a-vida.htm.

Bratman, Eve. 2015. "Passive Revolution in the Green Economy: Activism and the Belo Monte Dam." *International Environmental Agreements*, no. 15: 61–77.

Brazilian Delegation. 1993. *Conferência das Nações Unidas sobre Meio Ambiente e Desenvolvimento: relatório da delegação brasileira.* Brasilia: Fundação Alexandre de Gusmão, Instituto de Pesquisa de Relações Internacionais.

Bresser-Pereira, Luiz Carlos. 2009. "From Old to New Developmentalism in Latin America." In *Handbook of Latin America Economics,* edited by José Antonio Ocampo and Jaime Ros. New York: Oxford University Press.

Brown, David S. 2002. "Democracy, Authoritarianism and Education Finance in Brazil." *Journal of Latin American Studies* 34 (115): 141.

Bruns, Barbara, David Evans, and Javier Luque. 2012. *Achieving World-Class Education in Brazil: The Next Agenda.* Washington, DC: World Bank.

Bruns, Barbara, D. P. Filmer, and H. A. Patrinos. 2011. *Making Schools Work: New Evidence on Accountability Reforms.* Washington, DC: World Bank.

Buarque de Holanda, Sérgio. 1971. *Raízes do Brasil.* Vol. 6. Rio de Janeiro: José Olympio.

Buarque de Holanda, Sérgio. 1972. *Do Império à República.* São Paulo: DIFEL.

Bueno, Natalia S. 2013. "Who Is Protesting in Brazil?" *The Smoke-Filled Room,* June 27. https://thesmokefilledroomblog.wordpress.com/2013/06/27/who-is-protesting-in-brazil.

Bugiato, Caio Martins. 2013. "The Role of BNDES in the Expansion of Business of the Brazilian Inner Bourgeoisie." Unpublished paper. University of Campinas.

Burges, Sean W. 2005. "*Auto-Estima* in Brazil: The Rhetorical Logic of Lula's South-South Foreign Policy." *International Journal* 60, no. 3 (autumn): 1133–51.

Burges, Sean W. 2009. *Brazilian Foreign Policy after the Cold War.* Gainesville: University of Florida Press.

Burges, Sean W., and Jean Daudelin. 2011. "Moving In, Carving Out, Proliferating: The Many Faces of Brazil's Multilateralism since 1989." *Pensamiento Próprio* 16, no. 33 (January–June): 35–64.

Cabral, Otávio. 2007. "Nem na ditadura: Entrevista com Embaixador Roberto Abdenur." *Veja,* February 7.

Campello, Daniela, and Cesar Zucco Jr. 2015. "Understanding the Rising Popularity of Brazilian Presidents." In *Emergent Brazil: Key Perspectives on a New Global Power,* edited by Jeffrey Needell, 51–67. Gainesville: University of Florida Press.

Campello, Tereza, and Marcelo Côrtes Neri, eds. 2013. *Programa Bolsa Família: uma década de inclusão e cidadania.* Brasília: IPEA.

Campos, Eduardo. 2013. "BNDES empresta e Eletrobras paga dividendos." *Valor Econômico.* July 10.

Campos, Mauro Macedo. 2009. "Democracia, partidos e eleições: Os custos do sistema partidário-eleitoral no Brasil." Unpublished Ph.D. dissertation, Universidade Federal de Minas Gerais.

Canuto, Octaviano, Matheus Cavallari, and José Guilherme Reis. 2013. "The Brazilian Competitiveness Cliff." *Economic Premise,* no. 105. Washington, DC: World Bank.

Caprio, Gerard, Jonathan L. Riechter, Robert E. Litan, and Michael Pomerleano, eds. 2005. *The Future of State-Owned Financial Institutions.* Washington, DC: Brookings Institution Press.

Cardoso, Fernando Henrique. 2012. "A classe média na berlinda." *O Estado de São Paulo,* 2. June 1.

Carvalho, José Murilo de. 2008. "Passado, presente e futuro da corrupção brasileira." In *Corrupção: Ensaios e críticas,* edited by Leonardo Avritzer, Newton Bignotto,

Juarez Guimarães, and Heloisa Maria Murgel Starling. Belo Horizonte: Editora UFMG.

Carvalho, Luiz Paulo Macedo. 1998. *The Army in Brazilian History. Volume 3: Republic.* Rio de Janeiro: Biblioteca do Exército, Odebrecht.

Cason, Jeffrey W., and Timothy J. Power. 2009. "Presidentialization, Pluralization, and the Rollback of Itamaraty: Explaining Change in Brazilian Foreign Policy-Making in the Cardoso Lula Era." *International Political Science Review* 30 (2): 117–40.

Castelo, Rodrigo. 2012. "O novo desenvolvimentismo e a decadência ideológica do pensamento econômico brasileiro." *Serviço Social & Sociedade* 112 (December): 613–36.

Castro, Jorge Abrahão. 1998. "O Fundo de Manutenção e Desenvolvimento do Ensino e Valorização do Magistério (Fundef) e seu impacto no financiamento do ensino fundamental." Discussion Paper no. 604. Brazil: IPEA.

Castro, Jorge Abrahão, José Aparecido Carlos Ribeiro, José Valente Chaves, Bruno Carvalho Duarte. 2012. "Gasto Social Federal: prioridade macroeconômica no período 1995–2010." *IPEA Nota Técnica,* no. 9 (September). Brasília, IPEA.

Cecchini, Simone, and Aldo Madariaga. 2011. "Conditional Cash Transfer Programmes: The Recent Experience in Latin America and the Caribbean." *Cuadernos de la CEPAL,* no. 95.

Ceneviva, Ricardo. 2011. "O nível de governo importa para a qualidade da política pública? O caso da educação fundamental no Brasil." Doctoral thesis in political science, University of São Paulo.

Center for Law and Democracy. 2012. "Global RTI Rating." http://www.law-democracy.org/live/global-rti-rating.

Centro de Referência de Assistência Social (CRAS). 2011. Author focus group with CRAS research team members. Camaragibe, Pernambuco, July 2.

Cervo, Amado Luiz. 2000. "Sob o signo neoliberal: as relações internacionais da América Latina." *Revista Brasileira de Política Internacional* 43 (2): 5–27.

Chauí, Marilena. 2013. *As manifestações de junho de 2013 na cidade de São Paulo.* http://www.teoriaedebate.org.br/materias/nacional/manifestacoes-de-junho-de-2013-na-cidade-de-sao-paulo.

Chaves, J. V., and J. A. C Ribeiro. 2012. "Gasto social federal: uma análise da execução orçamentária de 2011." *IPEA Nota Técnica,* no.13.

Coelho, Marcelo. 2013. "Manifestações expõem o fato de que o poder não muda?" *Folha de São Paulo,* June 6, C4.

Collier, David, and Ruth Berins Collier. 1991. *Shaping the Political Arena: Critical Junctures, the Labor Movement, and Regime Dynamics in Latin America.* Princeton, NJ: Princeton University Press.

Collins, Cath. 2010. *Post-transitional Justice: Human Rights Trials in Chile and El Salvador.* Pittsburgh: University of Pittsburgh Press.

Comisión Nacional de Verdad y Reconciliación. 1993. *Report of the Chilean National Commission on Truth and Reconciliation.* South Bend: University of Notre Dame Press.

Comisión Nacional sobre la Desaparación de Personas (CONADEP). 1986. *Nunca Más.* New York: Farrar, Straus Giroux.

Comissão Nacional da Verdade. 2014. *Relatório.* 3 vols. Brasília: Comissão Nacional da Verdade.

CONADEP. *See* Comisión Nacional sobre la Desaparación de Personas (CONADEP)

Conrad, Björn. 2012. "China in Copenhagen: Reconciling the 'Beijing Climate Revolution' and the 'Copenhagen Climate Obstinacy.'" *China Quarterly*, no. 210: 435–55.

Constanzi, R. N., and F. Fagundes. 2010. "Perfil dos beneficiários do Programa Bolsa Família." In *Bolsa Família 2003–2010: avanços e desafios*, edited by J. A. Castro and L. Modesto, 249–70. Brasília: IPEA.

Controladoria Geral da União. 2013. "Relatorio de Acompanhamento de Programas de Governo n. 22. Complementação da União ao Fundo de Manutenção e Desenvolvimento da Educação Básica e de Valorização Dos Profissionais da Educação." Fundeb, Brasilia: CGU.

Cordeiro, Gabriela. 2011. Author interview with coordinator of citizenship services (Programa Balcão da Cidadania). Jaboatão dos Guararapes, Pernambuco, July 5.

Costa, Ana Clara. 2015. "'O governo fez bancos do Estado pagarem as suas despesas — e isso não é pedalada': Interview with José Roberto Afonso." *Veja*, April 22. http://abr.ai/1HtxrB8.

Costa, Breno, and Bernardo Mello Franco. 2011. "Maiores casos de corrupção no país ainda se arrastam na Justiça." *Folha de São Paulo*, September 3.

Costas, Ruth. 2012. "Aos 60 anos, 'BNDES do século 21' atrai polêmicas e atenção internacional." *BBC Brasil*, August 20.

Crandall, Britta H. 2011. *Hemispheric Giants: The Misunderstood History of US-Brazilian Relations*. Lanham, MD: Rowman and Littlefield.

Cretoiu, S. L., L. L. Barakat, V. S. Nogueira, and L. M. Diniz. 2012. "Ranking FDC das transnacionais brasileiras 2012." *Caderno de Ideias*, no. 1215. Nova Lima, Minas Gerais: Fundação Dom Cabral.

Cullenward, Danny, and David G. Victor. 2006. "Special Issue on the Dam Debate and Its Discontents: An Editorial Comment." *Climatic Change*, no. 75: 81–86.

Cunha, Alexandre dos Santos, Bernardo Abreu de Medeiros, and Luseni Maria C. de Aquino. 2010. "Corrupção e controle democráticos no Brasil." In *Estado, instituições e democracia: República*. Brasília: IPEA.

Cunha, Luiz Claudio. 2013. "A verdade sobre a Comissao da Verdade." *O Globo*, July 5.

D'Araujo, Maria Celina. 2011. "PSDB e PT e o Poder Executivo." *Desigualdade e Diversidade*, edição especial (December): 65–100.

Da Matta, Roberto. 1979. *Carnavais, malandros e heróis: Para uma sociologia do dilema brasileiro*. Rio de Janeiro: Zahar Editores.

Da Ros, Luciano. 2014. "Mayors in the Dock: Judicial Responses to Local Corruption in Brazil." Unpublished Ph.D. dissertation, University of Illinois at Chicago.

Dahl, Robert A. 1985. *Controlling Nuclear Weapons: Democracy versus Guardianship*. Syracuse: Syracuse University Press.

Danese, Sérgio. 1999. *Diplomacia presidencial: história e critica*. Rio de Janeiro: Topbooks.

Daudelin, Jean. 1995. "The Politics of Oligarchy: 'Democracy' and Canada's Recent Conversion to Latin America." In *Democracy and Foreign Policy, Canada among Nations 1995*, edited by Maxwell A. Cameron and Maureen Appel Molot, 145–65. Ottawa: Carleton University Press.

Daudelin, Jean. 2012. "Brasil y la 'desintegración' de América Latina." *Política Exterior* 149 (September/October): 50–57.

Dávila, Jerry. 2010. *Hotel Trópico: Brazil and the Challenge of African Decolonization, 1950–1980*. Durham, NC: Duke University Press.

Duverger, Maurice. 1954. *Political Parties: Their Organization and Activity in the Modern State.* New York: John Wiley and Sons.

De Brauw, Alan, Daniel Gilligan, John Hoddinott, and Shalini Roy. 2014 "The Impact of Bolsa Família on Women's Decision-Making Power." *World Development* 59 (July): 487–504.

De Brauw, Alan, Daniel Gilligan, John Hoddinott, and Shalini Roy. 2015. "The Impact of Bolsa Família on Schooling." *World Development* 70 (June): 303–16.

De Oliveira, Francisco. 2012. "Jeitinho e jeitão." *Piauí*, no 73 (October): 32–34.

Dimitrov, Radoslav S. 2010. "Inside UN Climate Change Negotiations: The Copenhagen Conference." *Review of Policy Research* 27 (6): 795–821.

Doctor, Mahrukh. 2013. "Assessing the Changing Roles of the Brazilian Development Bank." Revision of paper presented at Annual Meeting of the Latin American Studies Association. Washington, DC, May 29–June 1.

Draibe, Sonia. 2004. "Federal Leverage in a Decentralized System: Education Reform in Brazil." In *Crucial Needs, Weak Incentives: Social Sector Reform, Democratization, and Globalization in Latin America*, edited by Robert R. Kaufman and Joan M. Nelson, 375–406. Baltimore: Johns Hopkins University Press.

Duran, Camila Villard. 2016. "The Task Ahead for Brazil." Blogpost at Project Syndicate, April 15. http://www.project-syndicate.org.

Economia-IG. 2012. "Com Bolsa Família, País reduziu trabalho infantil." September 21. http://economia.ig.com.br.

The Economist. 2010. "Brazil's Bolsa Família: How to Get Children out of Jobs and into School." July 29.

The Economist. 2013. "The Road to Hell." September 28.

Epstein, Gerald. 1992. "Political Economy and Comparative Central Banking." *Review of Radical Political Economics* 24 (1): 1–30.

ESEB. *See* Estudo Eleitoral Brasileiro (ESEB)

Estado de São Paulo. 2005. "Assessor do PT é preso com US$ 100 mil sob a roupa." July 9.

Estado de São Paulo. 2012a. "A amplitude da corrupção." December 30.

Estado de São Paulo. 2012b. "Haja charme . . ." Editorial. *O Estado de São Paulo*, August 26.

Estado de São Paulo. 2012c. "Empresários brasileiros esperam ampliar negócios com a reeleição de Chávez." October 8.

Estudo Eleitoral Brasileiro (ESEB). 2006. *Centro de Estudos de Opinão Pública-Cesop/ Unicamp.*

Estudo Eleitoral Brasileiro (ESEB). 2010. *Centro de Estudos de Opinão Pública-Cesop/ Unicamp.*

Evans, Peter. 1995. *Embedded Autonomy: States and Industrial Transformation.* Princeton, NJ: Princeton University Press.

Falcão, Tiago, and Patricia Viera da Costa. 2014. "A linha de extrema pobreza e o público-alvo do plano Brasil sem Miséria." In *O Brasil sem Miséria*, edited by Tereza Campello, Tiago Falcão, and Patricia Viera da Costa, 67–96. Brasília, Ministério de Desenvolvimento Social.

Faoro, Raymundo. 1958. *Os donos do poder: Formação do patronato político brasileiro.* Porto Alegre: Editora Globo.

Farah, Tatiana. 2010. "Entidadades de imprensa e Fecomercio estudam ir ao STF contra plano de direitos humanos." *O Globo Política.* http://oglobo.globo.com/politica

References

/entidades-de-imprensa-fecomercio-estudam-ir-ao-stf-contra-plano-de-direitos
-humanos-3037045.

Faria, Carlos Aurélio Pimenta de. 2012. "O Itamaraty e a política externa brasileira: do insulamento à busca de coordenação dos atores governamentais e de cooperação com os agentes societários." *Revista Contexto Internacional* 34 (1): 311–55.

Faria, Carlos Aurélio Pimenta de, Dawisson Belém Lopes, and Guilherme Casarões. 2013. "Itamaraty on the Move: Institutional and Political Change in Brazilian Foreign Service under Lula da Silva's Presidency (2003–2010)." *Bulletin of Latin American Research* 32, no. 4 (October): 468–82.

Faria, Cláudia F. 2005. *O Estado em movimento: complexidade social e participação política no Rio Grande do Sul.* Doctoral dissertation, Department of Political Science, Federal University of Rio Grande do Sul.

Fausto, Ruy. 2005. "Para além da gangrene." *Lua Nova*, no. 65: 203–28.

Fazzio, Gabriel Landi. 2011. "A Comissão da Verdade e a luta social." *PT*. http://www .pt.org.br.

Fellet, João. 2012. "Com BNDES e negócios com politicos, Odebrecht ergue 'império' en Angola." *BBC Brasil*, September 18.

Fenwick, Tracy Beck. 2009. "Avoiding Governors." *Latin American Research Review* 44 (1): 102–31.

Ferraz, C., and F. Finan. 2011. "Electoral Accountability and Corruption: Evidence from Audits of Local Governments." *American Economic Review* 101, no. 2 (June): 1274–311.

Ferraz, Lucas. 2012. "O lado 'dark' da resistência: a luta armada e o justiçamento de militantes na ditadura." *Folha de São Paulo*, June 17, 6.

Figueiredo, Argelina Cheibub, and Fernando Limongi. 1999. *Executivo e legislativo na nova ordem constitucional.* Rio de Janeiro: Editora FGV.

Filgueiras, Fernando. 2011. "Transparência e controle da corrupção no Brasil." In *Corrupção e sistema político no Brasil*, edited by Leonardo Avritzer and Fernando Filgueiras, 133–62. Rio de Janeiro: Civilização Brasileira.

Filgueiras, Fernando, and Ana Luiza Melo Aranha. 2011. "Controle de corrupção e burocracia de linha de frente: regras, discricionaridade e reformas no Brasil." *Dados: Revista de Ciencias Sociais* 54 (2): 349–87.

Fishlow, Albert. 1973. "Some Reflections on Post-1964 Brazilian Economic Policy." In *Authoritarian Brazil: Origins, Policies, and Future*, edited by Alfred Stepan. New Haven: Yale University Press.

Fiszbein, Ariel, and Norbert Schady. 2009. *Conditional Cash Transfers: A World Bank Policy Research Report.* Washington, DC: World Bank.

Fleischer, David. 1997. "Political Corruption in Brazil: The Delicate Connection with Campaign Finance." *Crime, Law, and Social Change*, no. 25: 297–321.

Fleischer, David. 2012. *Brazil Focus Weekly Report.* February 18–March 2. Brasília.

Fleischer, David, and Leonardo Barreto. 2009. "El impacto de la justicia electoral sobre el sistema político brasileño." *América Latina Hoy*, no. 51: 117–38.

Fleitas, Diego M., German Lodola Ortiz de Rozas, and Hernan Flom. 2014. "Delito y violencia en América Latina y el Caribe: perfil de la región." Buenos Aires: Asociación para el Análisis de Políticas Publicas. https://aa.ou.org.uk/2014/homicides -in-central-america-up-99-per-cent.

Fleury, Afonso, and Maria Tereza Leme Fleury, 2011. *Brazilian Multinationals: Competences for Internationalization.* Cambridge: Cambridge University Press.

Flynn, Peter. 2005. "Brazil and Lula, 2005: Crisis, Corruption, and Change in Political Perspective." *Third World Quarterly* 26 (8): 1221–67.

Folha de São Paulo. 2005. "PF investiga furto de dinheiro apreendido em operação no Rio." September 20.

Folha de São Paulo. 2013. "Que país sai dos protestos?" June 6, C4.

Fon Filho, Aton. 2013. "A direita sai de casa pela porta da esquerda." *Viomundo*, June 26. http://www.viomundo.com.br/politica/aton-fon-filho-a-direita-sai-de-casa-pela-porta-da-esquerda.html.

Fonseca, Gelson. 2004. *A legitimidade e outras questões internacionais: poder e ética entre as nações*. São Paulo: Paz e Terra.

Foreque, Flávia, and Márcio Falcão. 2013. "Com alfinetadas ao regime militar, Congresso devolve mandato de João Goulart." *Folha de São Paulo*, December 18.

Forum Brasileiro de Segurança Pública. 2014. *8º Anuário Brasileiro de Segurança Pública*. São Paulo: Forum Brasileiro de Segurança Pública.

Franchini, Roger. 2011. *Toupeira: A história do assalto ao Banco Central*. São Paulo: Editora Planeta.

Franco, Bernardo Mello. 2012. "Maioria quer punição dos réus do mensalão, mas acha que ninguém vai preso." *Folha de São Paulo*, August 8.

Freire de Lacerda, A. D. 2002. "O PT e a unidade partidária como problema." *Dados* 45 (1): 39–76.

Fried, Brian J. 2012. "Distributive Politics and Conditional Cash Transfers." *World Development* 40, no. 5 (May): 1042–53.

Fuggle, Richard. 2005. "Have Impact Assessments Passed Their 'Sell-By' Date?" *Newsletter International Association for Impact Assessment* 16 (3): 1, 6.

Fukuyama, Francis. 2013. "The Middle Class Revolution." *Wall Street Journal*, 28 June.

Fundação Perseu Abramo. 2006. "Governo Lula, imagem dos partidos e cultura política." http://www2.fpa.org.br/portal/modules/wfdownloads/viewcat.php?cid=65.

García-Escribano, Mercedes, Carlos Góes, and Izabela Karpowicz. 2015. "Filling the Gap: Infrastucture Investment in Brazil." IMF Working Paper 15/180. Washington, DC: International Monetary Fund. July.

Garrido, Beatriz. 2011. Author interview with coordinator of the Promotion of Civil Registry of Births. Brasília, 28 June.

Gazeta Mercantil. 2003a. "Negociadores brasileiros terão apoio privado." May 5.

Gazeta Mercantil. 2003b. "Itamaraty elogia criação de instituto." May 7.

Gazola Hellman, Aline. 2015. "How Does Bolsa Família Work?" Technical Note 856. Washington, DC: Inter-American Development Bank.

Gilligan, Daniel, and Anna Fruttero. 2011. "The Impact of Bolsa Família on Education and Health Outcomes in Brazil." Report on select findings of IFPRI evaluation done by Alan de Brauw, Daniel Gilligan, John Hoddinott, and Shalini Roy. Presentation at Second Generation of CCTs Evaluation Conference, World Bank. October 24.

Gois, Ancelmo. 2005. "Apresentação: O samba do mensalão." In *Memorial do escândalo: os bastidores da crise e da corrupção no governo Lula*, edited by Gerson Camarotti and Bernardo de la Peña, 13–14. Geração Editorial: São Paulo.

Goldfrank, Benjamin. 2004. "Conclusion: The End of Politics or a New Beginning for the Left." In *The Left in the City: Participatory Local Governments in Latin America*, edited by Daniel Chavez and Benjamin Goldfrank, 193–211. LAB/TNI: London.

Goldfrank, Benjamin. 2007. "The Politics of Deepening Local Democracy: Decentralization, Party Institutionalization, and Participation." *Comparative Politics* 39 (2): 147–68.

Goldfrank, Benjamin. 2011. "The Left and Participatory Democracy: Brazil, Uruguay, and Venezuela." In *The Resurgence of the Latin American Left*, edited by Steven Levitsky and Kenneth Roberts, 162–83. Baltimore: Johns Hopkins University Press.

Goldfrank, Benjamin, and Brian Wampler. 2008. "From the Petista Way of Governing to the Brazilian Way: How the PT Changed." *Revista Debates* 2 (2): 245–71.

Gómez, Hernán B. 2015. "Participation under Lula: Between Electoral Politics and Governability." *Latin American Politics and Society* 57 (2): 1–20.

Gonçalves, Sonia. 2014. "The Effects of Participatory Budgeting on Municipal Expenditures and Infant Mortality in Brazil." *World Development* 53 (1): 94–110.

González, Eduardo. 2012. *Observações sobre o mandato legal da Comissão Nacional da Verdade do Brasil.* New York: International Center for Transitional Justice. May.

Goodhart, Charles. 1990. *The Evolution of Central Banks.* Cambridge, MA: MIT Press.

Hall, Anthony. 2006. "From Fome Zero to Bolsa Família: Social Policies and Poverty Alleviation under Lula." *Journal of Latin American Studies* 38 (4): 689–709.

Hall, Anthony. 2008. "Brazil's Bolsa Família: A Double-Edged Sword?" *Development and Change* 39 (5): 799–822.

Hall, Anthony. 2012. "The Last Shall Be First: Political Dimensions of Conditional Cash Transfers in Brazil." *Journal of Policy Practice* 11 (1–2): 25–41.

Hallding, Karl, Marie Olsson, Aaron Atteridge, Antto Vihma, Marcus Carson, and Mikael Román. 2011. *Together Alone: BASIC Countries and the Climate Change Conundrum.* Stockholm: Stockholm Environment Institute.

Hanushek, Eric A., Paul E. Peterson, and Ludger Woessmann. 2012. "Achievement Growth: International and U.S. State Trends in Student Performance." Harvard's Program on Education Policy and Governance (PEPG) and Education Next Taubman Center for State and Local Government. Harvard Kennedy School PEPG Report 12-03. July.

Harbison, Ralph W., and Eric A. Hanushek. 1992. *Educational Performance of the Poor: Lessons from Rural Northeast Brazil.* New York: Oxford University Press.

Harbitz, Mia, and Maria del Carmen Tamargo. 2009. "The Significance of Legal Identity in Situations of Poverty and Social Exclusion." Washington, DC: Inter-American Development Bank.

Harrazim, Dorrit, and Arthur Fontes. 2010. *A família Braz: dois tempos.* Documentary film.

Hayner, Patricia. 2011. *Unspeakable Truths: Transitional Justice and the Challenge of Truth Commissions.* New York: Routledge.

Henning, Randall. 1994. *Currencies and Politics in the United States, Germany, and Japan.* Washington: Institute for International Economics.

Heston, Alan, Robert Summers, and Bettina Aten. 2012. "Penn World Table Version 7.1." Center for International Comparisons of Production, Income, and Prices at the University of Pennsylvania. July.

Hirst, Mônica. 2005. *The United States and Brazil: A Long Road of Unmet Expectations.* New York: Routledge.

Hochstetler, Kathryn. 2011. "The Politics of Environmental Licensing: Energy Projects of the Past and Future in Brazil." *Studies in Comparative International Development* 46 (4): 349–71.

Hochstetler, Kathryn, and Margaret E. Keck. 2007. *Greening Brazil: Environmental Activism in State and Society*. Durham, NC: Duke University Press.

Hochstetler, Kathryn, and Alfred P. Montero. 2013. "The Renewed Developmentalist State: The National Development Bank and the Brazil Model." *Journal of Development Studies* 49 (11): 1484–99.

Hochstetler, Kathryn, and J. Ricardo Tranjan. 2016. Environment and Consultation in the Brazilian Democratic Developmental State. *Comparative Politics* 48 (4).

Hochstetler, Kathryn, and Eduardo Viola. 2012. "Brazil and the Politics of Climate Change: Beyond the Global Commons." *Environmental Politics* 21 (5): 753–71.

Hoffmann, Rodolfo. 2003. "Inequality in Brazil: The Contribution of Pensions." *Revista Brasileira de Economia* 57, no. 4 (October–December): 755–73.

Hollanda, Francisco Mauro Brasil de. 2001. *O gás no Mercosul: uma perspectiva brasileira*. Brasília: FUNAG.

Hopkin, Jonathan. 2010. "The Comparative Method." In *Theory and Methods in Political Science*, edited by David Marsh and Gerry Stoker, 285–307. Houndmills: Palgrave Macmillan.

Huber, Evelyn. 1996. "Options for Social Policy in Latin America." In *Welfare States in Transition*, edited by G. Esping-Anderson, 141–91. London: Sage.

Hunter, Wendy. 2010. *The Transformation of the Workers' Party in Brazil, 1989–2009*. New York: CUP.

Hunter, Wendy, and Timothy J. Power. 2007. "Rewarding Lula: Executive Power, Social Policy, and the Brazilian Elections of 2006." *Latin American Politics and Society* 49 (1): 1–30.

Hunter, Wendy, and Natasha Borges Sugiyama. 2009. "Democracy and Social Policy in Brazil: Advancing Basic Needs, Preserving Privileged Interests." *Latin American Politics and Society* 51 (2): 29–57.

Hunter, Wendy, and Natasha Borges Sugiyama. 2011. "Documenting Citizenship: Contemporary Efforts toward Social Inclusion in Brazil." Paper prepared for presentation at the annual meeting of the American Political Science Association, Seattle, September 1–4.

Hunter, Wendy, and Natasha Borges Sugiyama. 2014. "Transforming Subjects into Citizens: Insights from Brazil's Bolsa Família." *Perspectives on Politics* 12, no. 4 (December): 829–45.

Hunter, Wendy, and Natasha Borges Sugiyama. Forthcoming. "Making the Newest Citizens: The Quest for Universal Birth Registration in Contemporary Brazil." Unpublished manuscript.

Huntington, Samuel P. 1991. *The Third Wave*. Norman: University of Oklahoma Press.

Hurrell, Andrew. 1986. "The Quest for Autonomy: The Evolution of Brazil's Role in the International System, 1964–1985." D.Phil dissertation, University of Oxford.

Hurrell, Andrew, and Sandeep Sengupta. 2012. "Emerging Powers, North-South Relations, and Global Climate Politics." *International Affairs* 88 (3): 463–84.

IBAMA. 2009. Author interview with anonymous environmental impact assessment (EIA) analyst at the Brazilian Institute of the Environment and Renewable Natural Resources (IBAMA), Brasília. June.

IBASE. 2008. *Repercussões do Programa Bolsa Família na segurança alimentar e nutricional das famílias beneficiadas*. Rio de Janeiro: IBASE.

IBGE. *See* Instituto Brasileiro de Geografia e Estatística (IBGE)

ILO. 2011. "Understanding the Brazilian Success in Reducing Child Labor: Empirical Evidence and Policy Lessons." Understanding Children's Work WP 2011, ILO Office, Rome.

Infraero (Empresa Brasileira de Infraestrutura Aeroportuária). 2016. "Estatísticas." http://www.infraero.gov.br/index.php/estatistica-dos-aeroportos.html.

Inglehart, Ronald. 1977. *The Silent Revolution: Changing Values and Political Styles among Western Publics*. Princeton, NJ: Princeton University Press.

Inglehart, Ronald. 1997. *Modernization and Post-Modernization*. Princeton, NJ: Princeton University Press.

Instituto Brasileiro de Geografia e Estatística (IBGE). 1999. "Education and Life Conditions 1999." http://www.ibge.gov.br/english/estatistica/populacao/condicaodevida /indicadoresminimos/tabela3.shtm#a36.

Instituto Brasileiro de Geografia e Estatística (IBGE). 2012. "Síntese de Indicadores Sociais 2012." http://www.ibge.gov.br.

Ipeadata. 2013. "Pobreza—taxa de extrema pobreza." http://www.ipeadata.gov.br.

Irwin, Timothy C. 2016. "How Much Progress Have Governments Made in Getting Assets and Liabilities on Balance Sheet?" IMF Working Paper 16/95. Washington, DC: International Monetary Fund. April.

Istoé. 2007. "Batida Suspeita: Como o acidente com um advogado de bingos e caça-níqueis revelou o esquema de propina na polícia de São Paulo." June 6.

Jank, Marcos Sawaya. 2003. "Suporte para negociações externas." *Gazeta Mercantil*, May 6.

Jenkins, Rhys. 2015. "Is Chinese Competition Causing Deindustrialization in Brazil?" *Latin American Perspectives* 42 (6): 42–63.

Johnson, Ken. 2001. "Brazil and the Politics of the Climate Change Negotiations." *Journal of Environment and Development* 10 (2): 178–206.

Jornal do Brasil. 2006. March 28, 1.

Keck, Margaret E. 1991. *PT, a lógica da diferença; o Partido dos Trabalhadores na construção da democracia brasileira*. São Paulo: Editora Ática.

Keck, Margaret E. 1992. *The Workers' Party and Democratization in Brazil*. New Haven: Yale University Press.

Keck, Margaret E., and Kathryn Sikkink. 1998. *Activists beyond Borders: Advocacy Networks in International Politics*. Ithaca: Cornell University Press.

King, Ed. 2015. "Foie Gras, Oysters, and a Climate Deal: How the Paris Pact Was Won." *Climate Change News*. December 14.

Kingstone, Peter. 2011. *The Political Economy of Latin America: Reflections on Neoliberalism and Development*. New York: Routledge.

Kolk, Ans. 1998. "From Conflict to Cooperation International Policies to Protect the Brazilian Amazon." *World Development* 26 (8): 1481–93.

Kosack, Stephen. 2012. *The Education of Nations: How the Political Organization of the Poor, Not Democracy, Led Governments to Invest in Mass Education*. New York: Oxford University Press.

Lamounier, Bolivar. 1996. "Brazil: The Hyperactive Paralysis Syndrome." In *Constructing Democratic Governance: Latin America and the Caribbean in the 1990s*, edited by Jorge I. Domínguez and Abraham Lowenthal, 166–87. Baltimore: Johns Hopkins University Press.

Lampreia, Luiz Felipe. 2010. *O Brasil e os ventos do mundo*. Rio de Janeiro: Editora Objetiva.

Latin Finance. 2009. "Best Multilateral: Cranking Out Champions." November 1.

Latinobarómetro. 2011. "Informe 2011." Santiago: Corporación Latinobarómetro.

Leahy, Joe. 2011. "Questions Surround Brazil Bank in Carrefour Deal." *Financial Times*, July 13.

Leal, Victor Nunes. 1977. *Coronelismo: Municipality and Representative Government in Brazil*. Cambridge: Cambridge University Press.

Leal, Victor Nunes. 1997. *Coronelismo, enxada e voto*. 3rd ed. Rio de Janeiro: Nova Fronteira.

Leali, Francisco, and Vinicius Sassine. 2012. "Vinte anos depois, Collor ainda responde no STF por crimes." *O Globo*, September 28.

Leão, Danuza. 2012. "Ser especial." *Folha de São Paulo*, November 25, C-2.

Leite, Adailton Amaral Barbosa. 2010. "Descentralização, responsabilização e (des) controle: determinantes e impactos da corrupção e má gestão dos recursos federais nos municipios brasileiros." PhD dissertation in Political Science, Universidade Federal de Pernambuco.

Leonel, Josué. 2010. "BNDES limita desenvolvimento do crédito privado, diz Loyola." *Brasil Econômico*, July 16.

Lessa, Carlos. 2005. "Atrofiar, privatizar ou, se possível, fechar o BNDES." *Valor Econômico*, August 3.

Licio, Elaine Cristina, Lucio R. Rennó, and Henrique Carlos de O. de Castro. 2009. "Bolsa Família e voto na eleição presidencial de 2006." *Opinião Pública* 15 (1): 31–54.

Lima, Maria Regina Soares de, and Monica Hirst. 2006. "Brazil as an Intermediate State and Regional Power: Action, Choice, and Responsibilities." *International Affairs* 82 (1): 21–40.

Lima, Maria Regina Soares de, and Monica Hirst, eds. 2009. *Brasil, Índia e África do Sul: Desafios e oportunidades para novas parceiras*. São Paulo: Paz e Terra.

Lima, Maria Regina Soares de, and Gerson Moura. 1982. "A trajetória do pragmatismo: uma análise da política externa brasileira." *Dados* 25 (3): 349–64.

Lima, Nísia T., Gerschman, Silvia Gerschman, Edler, Flavio C. Edler, and Suárez, Julio M. Suárez. 2005. *Saúde e democracia: história e perspectivas do SUS*. Rio de Janeiro: FIOCRUZ.

Limongi, Fernando, and Rafael Cortez. 2010. "As eleições de 2010 e o quadro partidário." *Novos Estudos* 88 (November): 21–37.

Lindert, Kathy. 2007. "Brazil: Bolsa Família: Scaling Up Cash Transfers to the Poor." In *MfDR: Principles in Action: Sourcebook on Emerging Good Practice*, 67–74. Washington, DC: OECD/World Bank. http://www.mfdr.org/sourcebook.html.

Lindert, Kathy, Anja Linder, Jason Hobbs, and Bénédicte de la Brière. 2007. *The Nuts and Bolts of Brazil's Bolsa Família Program*. Social Protection Discussion Paper 0709. Washington, DC: World Bank.

Lipset, Seymour Martin. 1959. "Some Social Requisites of Democracy: Economic Development and Political Legitimacy." *American Political Science Review* 53, no. 1 (March): 69–105.

Lissardy, Gerardo. 2011. "BNDES impulse maior presença brasileira en América Latina." *BBC Brasil*, November 9.

Lopes, Dawisson Belém. 2013. *Política externa e democracia no Brasil*. São Paulo: Editora UNESP.

Lopez, Felix Garcia, and Fabio de Sá e Silva. 2014. "Valores e estrutura social no Brasil." *Textos para Discussão* 1946. Brasília: IPEA.

Luce, Mathias Seibel. 2007. "O subimperialismo brasileiro revisitado: a política de integração regional do governo Lula (2003–2007)." Unpublished paper. Graduate Program in International Relations, Federal University of Rio Grande do Sul.

Lucon, Oswaldo, and José Goldemberg. 2010. "São Paulo—The 'Other' Brazil: Different Pathways on Climate Change for State and Federal Governments." *Journal of Environment and Development* 19 (3): 335–57.

Lula da Silva, Luiz Inácio. 2009. Speech at the UN Climate Change Conference, Copenhagen, Denmark, December 18. http://www.itamaraty.gov.br/sala-de-imprensa /discursos-artigos-entrevistas-e-outras-comunicacoes/presidente-da-republica -federativa-do-brasil/318494324985-discurso-do-presidente-da-republica-luiz-inacio.

Lupu, Noam. 2016. *Party Brands in Crisis: Partisanship, Brand Dilution, and the Breakdown of Political Parties in Latin America*. New York: Cambridge University Press.

Macaulay, Fiona. 2011. "Federalism and State Criminal Justice Systems." In *Corruption and Democracy in Brazil: The Struggle for Accountability*, edited by Timothy J. Power and Matthew M. Taylor, 218–49. Notre Dame, IN: University of Notre Dame Press.

Madrid, Pamela. 2012. *Brazil: Financial System Stability Assessment*. Washington, DC: International Monetary Fund.

Magalhães, Fernando Simas. 1999. *Cúpula das Américas de 1994: Papel negociador do Brasil, em busca de uma agenda hemisférica*. Brasília: Fundação Alexandre de Gusmão.

Mainwaring, Scott, Timothy J. Power, and Fernando Bizzarro. Forthcoming. "The Uneven Institutionalization of a Party System: Brazil." In *Party Systems in Latin America: Institutionalization, Decay, and Collapse*, edited by Scott Mainwaring. New York: Cambridge University Press.

Mainwaring, Scott, and Christoper Welna, eds. 2003. *Democratic Accountability in Latin America*. New York: Oxford University Press.

Malamud, Andrés. 2005. "Presidential Diplomacy and the Institutional Underpinnings of MERCOSUR: An Empirical Examination." *Latin American Research Review* 40 (1): 138–64.

Malamud, Andrés, and Clarissa Dri. 2013. "Spillover Effects and Supranational Parliaments: The Case of Mercosur." *Journal of Iberian and Latin American Research* 19 (2): 224–38.

Malloy, James M. 1979. *The Politics of Social Security in Brazil*. Pittsburgh: University of Pittsburgh Press.

Manchetômetro. http://www.manchetometro.com.br.

March, James, and Johan Olsen. 2009. "Elaborating the 'New Institutionalism.'" In *The Oxford Handbook of Political Science*, edited by Robert Goodin, 159–75. Oxford: Oxford University Press.

Marchini Neto, Dirceu. 2012. "A constituição brasileira de 1988 e os direitos humanos: garantias fundamentais e políticas de memória." *Revista Científica FacMais* 2 (1): 81–96.

Markun, Paulo. 2004. *O sapo e o príncipe: Personagens, fatos e fábulas do Brasil contemporâneo*. Rio de Janeiro: Objetiva.

Marques, R. M., M. G. Leite, A. Mendes, and M. R. J. Ferreira. 2009. "Discutindo o papel do Programa Bolsa Família na decisão das eleições presidenciais brasileiras de 2006." *Revista de Economia Política* 29 (1): 114–32.

Martins, Ricardo Chaves de Rezende. 2012. *O Poder Legislativo e as políticas públicas educacionais no período 1995–2010*. Brasilia: Câmara dos Deputados.

Marx, Karl. 1851. *The Eighteenth Brumaire of Louis Bonaparte*. Various editions.

Mattei, Lauro. 2012. "Políticas públicas de combate à pobreza no Brasil: o caso do Programa Bolsa Família." *Revista da Sociedade Brasileira de Economia Política*, no. 33: 147–76.

McAdam, Doug, and Hillary Shaffer Boudet. 2012. *Putting Social Movements in Their Place: Explaining Opposition to Energy Projects in the United States, 2000–2005.* Cambridge: Cambridge University Press.

McAllister, Lesley. 2008. *Making Law Matter: Environmental Protection and Legal Institutions in Brazil.* Stanford: Stanford University Press.

MDIC. *See* Ministério de Desenvolvimento, Indústria e Comércio Exterior (MDIC)

MDS. *See* Ministério de Desenvolvimento Social (MDS)

Medeiros, Marcelo de Almeida, and Maria Isabel Meunier Ferraz. 2010. "Le Brésil de Lula et l'intégration regionale." In *Relations internationales du Brésil: les chemins de la puissance*, edited by Denis Rolland and Antônio Carlos Lessa, 37–50. Paris: L'Harmattan.

Medeiros, Marcelo, Tatiana Britto, and Fábio Soares. 2007. "Transferência de renda no Brasil." *Novos Estudos CEBRAP* 79 (November): 5–21.

Medeiros, Marcelo, and Pedro H. G. F. Souza. 2015. "State Transfers, Taxes, and Income Inequality in Brazil." *Brazilian Political Science Review* 9 (2): 3–29.

Mello, João Manoel P. de, and Márcio G. P. Garcia. 2011. "Bye, Bye Financial Repression, Hello Financial Deepening: The Anatomy of a Financial Boom." Texto para Discussão #594, PUC-Rio: Departamento de Economia.

Mello, Luis de, and M. Hoppe. 2006. "Educational Attainment in Brazil: The Experience of Fundef." *Economics Department Working Paper*, no. 424. Paris: Organization for Economic Cooperation and Development.

Melo, Marcus André. 2008. "Unexpected Successes, Unanticipated Failures: Social Policy from Cardoso to Lula." In *Democratic Brazil Revisited*, edited by Peter Kingstone and Timothy Power, 161–84. Pittsburgh: University of Pittsburgh Press.

Melo, Marcus André, A. Leite, and E. Rocha. 2012. "Competitive Corruption: Evidence from Randomized Municipal Audits in Brazil." Paper prepared for presentation at the American Political Science Association, New Orleans, September.

Melo, Marcus André, and Carlos Pereira. 2013. *Making Brazil Work: Checking the President in a Multiparty System.* New York: Palgrave.

Melo, Marcus André, Carlos Pereira, and Carlos Mauricio Figueiredo. 2009. "Political and Institutional Checks on Corruption: Explaining the Performance of Brazilian Audit Institutions." *Comparative Political Studies* 42 (9): 1217–44.

Mendes, Marcos. 2004. "Análise das irregularidades na administração municipal do FUNDEF: Constatações do programa de fiscalização a partir de sorteios públicos da Controladoria-Geral da União." São Paulo: Transparência Brasil.

Meneguello, Rachel. 1989. *PT: A formação de um partido, 1979–1982.* São Paulo: Paz e Terra.

Meneguello, Rachel. 1995. "Electoral Behavior in Brazil: The 1994 Presidential Elections." *International Social Science Journal*, no. 146: 145–62.

Meneguello, Rachel. 2005. "Government Popularity and Public Attitudes to Social Security Reform in Brazil." *International Journal of Public Opinion Research*, no. 17: 173–89.

Meneguello, Rachel. 2010. "Cidadãos e política: diagnóstico da adesão democrática, comportamento e valores." In *Estado, Instituições e Democracia*, edited by José Carlos Cardoso and José Carlos dos Santos, 189–95. Brasilia: IPEA.

Meneguello, Rachel. 2011. "Las elecciones de 2010 y los rumbos del sistema de partidos brasileño: política nacional, fragmentación y lógica de coaliciones." In *América Latina: política y elecciones del bicentenario (2009–2010)*, edited by Manuel Alcántara de Sáez and María Laura Tagina, 449–88. Madrid: Centro de Estudios Políticos y Constitucionales.

Meneguello, Rachel. 2012a. "As bases do apoio ao regime democrático no Brasil e o papel dos programas sociais como intermediários do sistema." Paper presented at the International Congress of the Latin American Studies Association, San Francisco.

Meneguello, Rachel. 2012b. "O impacto do PT no sistema partidário brasileiro: coalizões e capacidade organizativa." Paper presented at the workshop on "The PT from Lula to Dilma: Explaining Change in the Brazilian Workers' Party." Brazilian Studies Programme, University of Oxford.

Meneguello, Rachel, and Oswaldo E. do Amaral. 2008. "Ainda novidade: uma revisão das transformações do Partido dos Trabalhadores no Brasil." University of Oxford, *BSP Occasional Papers*, no. 2: 1–25.

Menezes Filho, Naercio. 2012. "Educação estagnada." *Valor Econômico*, September 28. http://www.valor.com.br/opiniao/2847940/educacao-estagnada.

Meyer, Emilio Peluso Neder. 2012. *Ditadura e responsabilização: elementos para uma justiça de transição no Brasil*. Belo Horizonte: Arraes Editores.

Mezarobba, Glenda. 2010. "Between Reparations, Half-Truths, and Impunity: The Difficult Break with the Legacy of the Dictatorship in Brazil." *Sur* 7, no. 13 (December): 7–25.

Mezarobba, Glenda. 2015. "Justiça de Transição e a Comissão da Verdade." In *1964: do Golpe à Democracia*, edited by Angela Alonso and Miriam Dolhnikoff, 343–58. São Paulo: Hedra.

Michener, Greg. 2011. "FOI Laws around the World." *Journal of Democracy* 22 (2): 145–59.

Michener, Gregory. 2015. "How Cabinet Size and Legislative Control Shape the Strength of Transparency Laws." *Governance*, no. 28: 77–94.

Ministério de Ciência e Tecnologia. 2010. *Brazil's Second National Communication to the United Nations Framework Convention on Climate Change*. http://www.mct .gov.br/index.php/content/view/326751.html.

Ministério de Desenvolvimento, Indústria e Comércio Exterior (MDIC). 2015. *Balança Comércial Brasileira, Mensal*, Brasília: MDIC. December. http://www .desenvolvimento.gov.br.

Ministério de Minas e Energia. 2010. *Plano decenal de expansão de energia 2019*. Brasília: Ministêrio de Minas e Energia, Empresa de Pesquisa Energética.

Ministério de Planejamento. 2011. "Orçamento federal ao alcance de todos: projeto de lei orçamentária annual PLOA." http://www.planejamento.gov.br/secretarias /upload/Arquivos/sof/ploa2012/110831_orc_fed_alc_todos.pdf.

Minow, Martha. 1998. *Between Vengeance and Forgiveness*. Boston: Beacon Press.

Moisés, José Álvaro. 2013. "Corrupção política e democracia no Brasil contemporâneo." In *A desconfiança política e os seus impactos na qualidade da democracia — o caso do Brasil*, edited by José Álvaro Moisés, and Rachel Meneguello, 201–36. São Paulo: EDUSP.

Moisés, José Álvaro, and Rachel Meneguello, eds. 2013. *A desconfiança política e os seus impactos na qualidade da democracia—o caso do Brasil*. São Paulo: EDUSP.

Molyneux, Maxine. 2006. "Mothers at the Service of the New Poverty Agenda: Progresa/ Oportunidades, Mexico's Conditional Transfer Programme." *Social Policy and Administration* 40 (4): 425–49.

Montero, Alfred P. 2010. "No Country for Leftists?" *Journal of Politics in Latin America* 2, no. 2 (January): 102–31.

Moraes, Reginaldo. 2005. "Notas sobre o imbróglio do Governo Lula, 2005." *Lua Nova*, no. 65: 179–202.

Morais, L., and A. Saad-Filho. 2003. "Snatching Defeat from the Jaws of Victory? Lula, the Workers' Party, and the Prospects for Change in Brazil." *Capital & Class*, no. 81: 17–23.

Morais, L., and A. Saad-Filho. 2005. "Lula and the Continuity of Neoliberalism in Brazil: Strategic Choice, Economic Imperative or Political Schizophrenia?" *Historical Materialism* 13 (1): 3–31.

Morais, L., and A. Saad-Filho. 2011. "Brazil beyond Lula: Forging Ahead or Pausing for Breath?" *Latin American Perspectives* 38 (2): 31–44.

Morais, L., and A. Saad-Filho. 2012. "Neo-developmentalism and the Challenges of Economic Policy-Making under Dilma Rousseff." *Critical Sociology* 38 (6): 789–98.

Nassar, André Meloni. 2009. "Brazil as an Agricultural and Agroenergy Superpower." In *Brazil as an Economic Superpower? Understanding Brazil's Changing Role in the Global Economy*, edited by Lael Brainard and Leonardo Martinez-Diaz, 187–220. Washington, DC: Brookings Institution Press.

Nepstad, Daniel, Britaldo S. Soares-Filho, Frank Merry, André Lima, Paulo Moutinho, John Carter, Maria Bowman, Andrea Cattaneo, Hermann Rodrigues, Stephan Schwartzman, David G. McGrath, Claudia M. Stickler, Ruben Lubowski, Pedro Piris-Cabezas, Sergio Rivero, Ane Alencar, Oriana Almeida, and Osvaldo Stella. 2009. "The End of Deforestation in the Brazilian Amazon." *Science*, no. 326: 1350–51.

Neri, Marcelo. 2007. *Miséria, desigualdade e políticas de renda: O real do Lula*. Rio de Janeiro: FGV/CPS.

Neri, Marcelo. 2008. *Miséria e nova classe média na década da igualdade*. Rio de Janeiro: FGV/CPS.

Neri, Marcelo. 2010. *A nova classe média: o lado brilhante dos pobres*. Rio de Janeiro: FGV/CPS.

Neri, Marcelo. 2011a. *Desigualdade de renda na década inclusiva*. Rio de Janeiro: FGV/CPS.

Neri, Marcelo. 2011b. *A nova classe média: o lado brilhante da base da pirâmide*. Rio de Janeiro: Editora Saraiva.

Nêumanne Pinto, José. 1992. *A República na lama: Uma tragédia brasileira*. Vol. 2. São Paulo: Geração Editorial.

New York Times. 2004. "Corruption Accusations Rise from Brazil Mayor's Death." February 1.

Nino, Carlos Santiago. 1996. *Radical Evil on Trial*. New Haven: Yale University Press.

Nunes, Edson. 1997. *A gramática política no Brasil: Clientelismo e insulamento burocrático*. Rio de Janeiro: Editora Zahar.

Nylen, William. 2000. "The Making of a Loyal Opposition: The Workers' Party (PT) and the Consolidation of Democracy in Brazil." In *Democratic Brazil: Actors, In-*

References

stitutions, and Processes, edited by Peter Kingstone and Timothy Power, 126–43. Pittsburgh: University of Pittsburgh Press.

Observatório da Imprensa. http://www.observatoriodaimprensa.com.br.

O'Donnell, Guillermo. 1998. "Horizontal Accountability in New Polyarchies." *Journal of Democracy* 9 (3): 112–26.

O'Donnell, Guillermo. 1996. "Illusions about Consolidation." *Journal of Democracy* 7 (2): 34–51.

O Globo. 2011. "Apesar do financiamento do BNDES, multinacionais não se livram das dívidas." *O Globo Gazeta Online*. December 17.

O Globo. 2012. "Quadrilha nas estradas—Polícia Rodoviária tem 80 denunciados no Rio." November 1.

O Globo. 2013a. "Oficiais da PM fizeram guarda ilegal para Liesa." February 9.

O Globo. 2013b. "Veja pesquisa completa do Ibope sobre os manifestantes." June 24.

O Globo. 2015. "Dilma anuncia reforma com redução de 39 para 31 ministérios." October 2.

Oliveira, Fabiana Luci. 2010. "Movilidad social e económica en Brasil—¿una nueva clase media?" In *Las clases medias en Iberoamérica—Retrospectivas y nuevas tendencias*, edited by Rolando Franco, Martin Openhayn, and Artur León, 168–229. Mexico City: Siglo XXI Editores.

Oreiro, José Luis, and Carmen A. Feijó. 2010. "Desindustrialização: conceituação, causas, efeitos e o caso brasileiro." *Revista de Economia Política* 30 (2): 219–32.

Osse, José Sergio, and Cíntia Cardoso. 2002. "Agropecuária perde US$7.8 bi por ano." *Folha de São Paulo*, August 19.

Paes-Sousa, Rômulo, Leonor Maria Pacheco Santos, and Édina Shisue Miazaki. 2011. "Effects of a Conditional Cash Transfer Programme on Child Nutrition in Brazil." *Bulletin of the World Health Organization*, no. 89: 496–503.

Pagliarini, Andre. 2015. "Brazil's Truth Commission: An Interview with Paulo Sergio Pinheiro." Providence, RI: Watson Institute, Brown University.

Panebianco, Angelo. 1988. *Political Parties: Organization and Power*. New York: Cambridge University Press.

Partido dos Trabalhadores (PT). 2001. *Resoluções do 12° Encontro Nacional do Partido dos Trabalhadores*. São Paulo: PT/FPA.

Partido dos Trabalhadores (PT). 2006. *Resoluções do 13° Encontro Nacional do Partido dos Trabalhadores*. São Paulo: PT.

Partido dos Trabalhadores (PT). 2007. *Resoluções do 3° Congresso do Partido dos Trabalhadores*. Porto Alegre: PT.

Partido dos Trabalhadores (PT). 2010. *Resoluções do 4° Congresso do Partido dos Trabalhadores*. Brasília: PT.

Partido dos Trabalhadores (PT). 2011. *Resolução Política do 4° Congresso Extraordinário do Partido dos Trabalhadores*. Brasília: PT.

Passos, Najila. 2012. "Entidade pedem comissão da verdade e revisão da Lei da Anistia." *Agência Carta Maior*, April 10.

Pato, Gustavo. 2016. "Pedaladas fiscais dispararam sob Dilma, diz relatório do Banco Central." *Folha de São Paulo*, April 6.

Pêgo, Bolívar, Júlio César Roma, José Gustavo Feres, and Larissa Schmidt. 2016. "Condicionantes institucionais a execução dos investimentos em infraestrutura econômica no Brasil: licenciamento ambiental." Brasília: Instituto de Pesquisa Econômica Aplicada.

Pereira, Anthony. 2000. "An Ugly Democracy? State Violence and the Rule of Law in Postauthoritarian Brazil." In *Democratic Brazil: Actors, Institutions, and Processes*, edited by Peter Kingstone and Timothy Power, 217–35. Pittsburgh: University of Pittsburgh Press.

Pereira, Anthony. 2005. *Political (In)justice: Authoritarianism and the Rule of Law in Brazil, Chile, and Argentina*. Pittsburgh: University of Pittsburgh Press.

Pereira, Carlos, Timothy J. Power, and Eric D. Raile. 2011. "Presidentialism, Coalitions, and Accountability." In *Corruption and Democracy in Brazil: The Struggle for Accountability*, edited by Timothy J. Power and Matthew M. Taylor, 31–55. Notre Dame, IN: University of Notre Dame Press.

Peres, Paulo, Paolo Ricci, and Lucio Rennó. 2011. "A variação da volatilidade eleitoral no Brasil: um teste das explicações políticas, econômicas e sociais." *Latin American Research Review* 46 (3): 46–68.

Perondi, Darsício. 2011. "Perondi critica BNDES." June 30. http://darcisioperondi .com.br/perondi-critica-bndes.

Peters, B. Guy. 2005. *Institutional Theory in Political Science: The "New Institutionalism."* London: Continuum.

Pinheiro, Leticia, and Carlos R. S. Milani, eds. 2012. *Política externa brasileira: As prácticas da política a a política das prácticas*. Rio de Janeiro: Editora FGV.

Pinto, Antônio Costa. 2011. "Introduction." In *Dealing with the Legacy of Authoritarianism*, edited by Antônio Costa Pinto and Leonardo Morlino, 1–20. London: Routledge.

Pitkin, Hanna. 1967. *The Concept of Representation*. Berkeley: University of California Press.

PNUD Brasil. 2012. "Pesquisa avalia impactos do programa." July 20.

Pochmann, M. 2010. "Estrutura social no Brasil: mudanças recentes." *Serviço Social & Sociedade*, no. 104: 637–49.

Pochmann, M. 2011. "Políticas sociais e padrão de mudanças no Brasil durante o Governo Lula." *SER Social* 13 (28): 12–40.

Pochmann, M. 2012. *Nova classe média?* São Paulo: Boitempo.

Pogrebinschi, Thamy. 2012. "Participation as Representation: Democratic Policymaking in Brazil." In *New Institutions for Participatory Democracy in Latin America: Voice and Consequence*, edited by Maxwell A. Cameron, Eric Hershberg, and Kenneth E. Sharpe, 53–74. New York: Palgrave Macmillan.

Pogrebinschi, Thamy, and David Samuels. 2014. "The Impact of Participatory Democracy: Evidence from Brazil's National Public Policy Conferences." *Comparative Politics* 46 (3): 313–32.

Pomar, W. 2013. "Debatendo classes e luta de classes no Brasil." http://novo.fpabramo .org.br.

Portal Brasil. 2011. "Água e Luz Para Todos." September 29. http://www.brasil.gov.br /cidadania-e-justica/2011/10/agua-e-luz-para-todos.

Porto, Mauro P. 2011. "The Media and Political Accountability." In *Corruption and Democracy in Brazil: The Struggle for Accountability*, edited by Timothy J. Power and Matthew M. Taylor, 103–26. Notre Dame, IN: University of Notre Dame Press.

Porzecanski, Arturo. 2009. "Latin America: The Missing Financial Crisis." Economic Commission for Latin America and the Caribbean Studies and Perspective Series, no. 6. Washington DC. October.

Possas, Mariana Thorstensen, and Lucia Elena Bastos. 2015. "Truth and Memory in

Brazil: Challenges to 'New' Categories of Human Rights." In "Human Rights in Brazil: When Democracy Is Not Enough," edited by Nancy Cardia. São Paulo: manuscript.

Power, Timothy. 2010. "Optimism, Pessimism, and Coalitional Presidentialism: Debating the Institutional Design of Brazilian Democracy." *Bulletin of Latin American Research* 29 (1): 18–33.

Power, Timothy. 2014. "Continuity in a Changing Brazil: The Transition from Lula to Dilma." In *Brazil under Lula: A Country in Transformation*, edited by Fábio de Castro, Kees Koonings, and Marianne Wiesebron, 10–35. London: Palgrave.

Power, Timothy J., and Matthew M. Taylor. 2011. *Corruption and Democracy in Brazil: The Struggle for Accountability*. Notre Dame, IN: University of Notre Dame Press.

Power, Timothy, and Cesar Zucco. eds. 2011. *O Congresso por ele mesmo: auto percepções da classe política brasileira*. Belo Horizonte: Editora UFMG.

Power, Timothy. 2008. "Centering Democracy? Ideological Cleavages and Convergence in the Brazilian Political Class." In *Democratic Brazil Revisited*, edited by Peter Kingstone and Timothy Power, 81–106. Pittsburgh: University of Pittsburgh Press.

Praça, Sérgio. 2011. "Corrupcão e reforma institucional no Brasil 1988–2008." *Opinião Pública* 17 (1): 137–62.

Praça, Sérgio, and Matthew M. Taylor. 2014. "Inching toward Accountability: The Evolution of Brazil's Anticorruption Institutions, 1985–2010." *Latin American Politics and Society* 56, no. 2: 27–48.

Przeworski, Adam. 1991. *Democracy and the Market: Political and Economic Reforms in Eastern Europe and Latin America*. Cambridge: Cambridge University Press.

Przeworski, Adam, Susan Stokes, and Bernard Manin, eds. 1999. *Democracy, Accountability, Representation*. New York: Cambridge University Press.

PT. *See* Partido dos Trabalhadores (PT)

Rasella, Davide, Rosana Aquino, Carlos A. T. Santos, Rômulo Paes-Souz, and Mauricio L. Barreto. 2013. "Effect of a Conditional Cash Transfer Programme on Childhood Mortality." *The Lancet* 382: 57–64.

Rego, Walquiria Leão, and Alessandro Pinzani. 2014. *Vozes do Bolsa Família: autonomia, dinheiro e cidadania*. São Paulo: Editora UNESP.

Reid, Walter V., Oswaldo Lucon, Suani Teixeira Coelho, and Patricia Guardabassi. 2005. *No Reason to Wait: The Benefits of Greenhouse Gas Reduction in São Paulo and California*. Menlo Park: The William and Flora Hewlett Foundation.

Reinikka, R., and J. Svensson. 2005. "Fighting Corruption to Improve Schooling: Evidence from a Newspaper Campaign in Uganda." *Journal of the European Economic Association* 3 (2–3): 259–67.

Ribeiro, Pedro. 2010. *Dos sindicatos ao governo: a organização nacional do PT de 1980 a 2005*. São Carlos: Editora UFSCar.

Ribeiro, A. Jr. 2012. *A privataria tucana*. São Paulo: Geração Editorial.

Rizzotti, Maria Luiza, Aidê Cançado Almeida, and Simone Aparecida Albuquerque. 2010. "Sistema unico de assistência social: sua contribuição na protecção social brasileira." In *Bolsa Família 2003–2010: avanços e desafios*, vol. 1, edited by Jorge Abrahão de Castro and Lúcia Modesto, 137–50. Brasília: IPEA.

Roberts, J. Timmons, and Bradley C. Parks. 2007. *A Climate of Injustice: Global Inequality, North-South Politics, and Climate Policy*. Cambridge, MA: MIT Press.

Rodrigues, Fernando. 2013. "Atos reforçam imaginário do Estado com fundos infinitos." *Folha de São Paulo*, June 6, C4.

Rodrigues, Leôncio Martins. 1997. "PT: A New Actor in Brazilian Politics." In *Political Culture, Social Movements, and Democratic Transitions in South America in the Twentieth Century*, edited by Fernando Devoto and Torcuato Di Tella. Milan: Feltrinelli.

Rohter, Larry. 2012. *Brazil on the Rise: The Story of a Country Transformed*. New York: Palgrave Macmillan.

Romero, Critina. 2011. "Crédito subsidiado impede queda de juros." *Valor Econômico*, December 13.

Rosas, Rafael. 2011. "BNDES estuda crédito de 2 bi de euros para Pão de Açúcar." *Valor Econômico*, June 28.

Rosenn, Keith S., and Richard Downes. 1999. *Corruption and Political Reform in Brazil: The Impact of Collor's Impeachment*. Boulder: Lynne Rienner.

Rossi, P., and D. M. Prates. 2009. "Projeto de estudos sobre a indústria financeira brasileira e o papel dos bancos públicos." Campinas, MG: Fundação Economia de Campinas (FECAMP).

Rossinholi, Marisa. 2008. "Política de financiamento da educação básica no Brasil: do Fundef ao Fundeb." Doctoral thesis, Universidade Metodista de Piracicaba.

Saad-Filho, A. 2013. "Mass Protests under 'Left Neoliberalism': Brazil, June–July 2013." *Critical Sociology* 39 (5): 657–69.

Saad-Filho, A. 2014. "Brazil: Development Strategies and Social Change from Import-Substitution to the 'Events of June.'" *Studies in Political Economy* 94 (June).

Saad-Filho, A., and M. L. R. Mollo. 2002. "Inflation and Stabilisation in Brazil: A Political Economy Analysis." *Review of Radical Political Economics* 34 (2): 109–35.

Saad-Filho, A., and M. L. R. Mollo. 2006. "Neoliberal Economic Policies in Brazil (1994–2005): Cardoso, Lula, and the Need for a Democratic Alternative." *New Political Economy* 11 (1): 99–123.

Saad-Filho, A., and L. Morais. 2014. "Mass Protests: Brazilian Spring or Brazilian Malaise?" In *Socialist Register*, edited by L. Panitch, G. Albo, and V. Chibber, 227–46, London: Merlin Press.

Sadek, Maria Tereza. 1995. *A justiça eleitoral e a consolidação da democracia no Brasil*. São Paulo: Konrad Adenauer Stiftung.

SAE. *See* Secretaria de Assuntos Estratégicos (SAE).

Samuels, David. 2001. "Money, Elections, and Democracy in Brazil." *Latin American Politics and Society* 43 (2): 27–48.

Samuels, David. 2004. "From Socialism to Social Democracy: Party Organization and the Transformation of the Workers' Party in Brazil." *Comparative Political Studies* 37 (9): 999–1024.

Samuels, David. 2006. "Financiamento de campanhas no Brasil e propostas de reforma no Brasil." In *Reforma política: lições da história recente*, edited by Gláucio Ary Dillon Soares and Lucio Rennó, 133–53. Rio de Janeiro: Editora FGV.

Samuels, David. 2013. "Brazilian Democracy in the PT Era." In *Constructing Democratic Governance in Latin America*, edited by Jorge Dominguez and Michael Shifter, 177–203. Baltimore: Johns Hopkins University Press.

Sánchez, Luis E. 2010. "Environmental Impact Assessment Teaching at the University of São Paulo: Evolving Approaches to Different Needs." *Journal of Environmental Assessment Policy and Management* 12 (3): 245–62.

References

Sánchez, Luis E. 2012. Author interview with former president of the International Association of Impact Analysis. São Paulo. June.

Sanders, Elizabeth. 2006. "Historical Institutionalism." In *The Oxford Handbook of Political Institutions*, edited by R. A. W. Rhodes, Sarah Binder, and Bert Rockman, 39–55. Oxford: Oxford University Press.

Santos, Fabiano, and Márcio G. Vilarouca. 2008. "Political Institutions and Governability from FHC to Lula." In *Democratic Brazil Revisited*, edited by Peter Kingstone and Timothy Power. Pittsburgh: University of Pittsburgh Press.

Sardinha, Edson, and Fábio Góis. 2013. "Maioria da mesa do Senado está sob investigação." *Congresso em Foco*, February 5.

Scharlemann, Jörn P. W., and William F. Laurance. 2008. "How Green Are Biofuels?" *Science* 319 (5859): 43–44.

Schmitter, Philippe C. 1992. "The Consolidation of Democracy and Representation of Social Groups." *American Behavioral Scientist* 35, nos. 4–5 (March–June): 442–49.

Schneider, Ben Ross. 1995. "Democratic Consolidations: Some Broad Comparisons and Sweeping Arguments." *Latin American Research Review*, no. 30: 215–34.

Schneider, Ben Ross. 2009. "Big Business in Brazil: Leveraging Natural Endowments and State Support for International Expansion." In *Brazil as an Economic Superpower? Understanding Brazil's Changing Role in the the Global Economy*, edited by Lael Brainard and Leonardo Martinez-Diaz, 159–86. Washington, DC: Brookings Institution Press.

Schneider, Ben Ross, ed. 2016. *New Order and Progress: Development and Democracy in Brazil*. New York: Oxford University Press.

Schwarzer, Helmut, and Ana Carolina Querino. 2002. *Benefícios sociais e pobreza: programas não-contributivos da seguridade social brasileira*. Discussion Paper no. 929. Brasília: IPEA.

SEBRAE. *See* Serviço Brasileiro de Apoio às Micro e Pequenas Empresas (SEBRAE)

Secretaria de Assuntos Estratégicos (SAE). 2012a. *Comissão para definição da classe média no Brasil*. Brasilia: Presidência da República.

Secretaria de Assuntos Estratégicos (SAE). 2012b. *Vozes da classe média*. Brasilia: Presidência da República.

Serviço Brasileiro de Apoio às Micro e Pequenas Empresas (SEBRAE). 2011. *Anuário do trabalho na micro e pequena empresa: 2010–2011*. São Paulo: Dieese.

Shapiro, Helen. 2007. "Industrial Policy and Growth." UN Department of Economic and Social Affairs (UN/DESA), Working Paper #53. August.

Shleifer, A. 1998. "State versus Private Ownership." *Journal of Economic Perspectives* 12 (4): 133–50.

Sikkink, Katherine. 2011. *The Justice Cascade*. New York: W. W. Norton.

Sikkink, Katherine, and Bridget Marchesi. 2015. "Nothing but the Truth: Brazil's Truth Commission Looks Back." *Foreign Affairs*, February 26.

Silva, Alessandro. 2013. "O que vemos nas ruas?" *Jornal da Unicamp* 567 (July).

Silveira, Fernando Gaigar, Bernardo Campolina, and Ross Van Horn. 2013. "Impactos do Programa Bolsa Família na alocação do tempo entre escola e trabalho de crianças e adolescentes de 10 a 18 Anos." In *Programa Bolsa Família: uma década de inclusão e cidadania*, edited by Tereza Campello and Marcelo Côrtes Neri, 305–26. Brasília: IPEA.

Singer, A. 2009. "Raízes sociais e ideológicas do lulismo." *Novos Estudos Cebrap*, no. 85: 83–102.

Singer, A. 2010. "A segunda alma do Partido dos Trabalhadores." *Novos Estudos Ce-brap*, no. 88: 89–111.

Singer, A. 2013. "Enigma popular." *Folha de São Paulo*, June 6, A2.

Skidmore, Thomas E. 1973. "Politics and Economic Policy Making in Authoritarian Brazil, 1937–1971." In *Authoritarian Brazil: Origins, Policies, and Future*, edited by Alfred Stepan, 3–46. New Haven: Yale University Press.

Smith, Joseph. 2010. *Brazil and the United States: Convergence and Divergence*. Athens: University of Georgia Press.

Smith, Roger. 2008. "Historical Institutionalism and the Study of Law." In *The Oxford Handbook of Law and Politics*, edited by Keith Whittington, Daniel Kelemen, and Gregory Caldeira, 46–59. Oxford: Oxford University Press.

Soares, Fábio Veras. 2011. "Brazil's Bolsa Família: A Review." *Economic and Political Weekly*, no. 46: 21.

Soares, Fábio Veras, Rafael Perez Ribas, and Rafael Guerreiro Osório. 2010. "Evaluating the Impact of Brazil's Bolsa Família: Cash Transfer Programs in Comparative Perspective." *Latin American Research Review* 45 (2): 174–90.

Soares, Fábio Veras, and Elydia Silva. 2010. "Conditional Cash Transfer Programmes and Gender Vulnerabilities in Latin America: Case Studies from Brazil, Chile, and Colombia." London: Overseas Development Institute.

Soares, Gláucio, and Sonia Terron. 2010. "As bases eleitorais de Lula e do PT: do distanciamento ao divórcio." *Opinião Pública* 16, no. 2 (November): 310–37.

Soares, Sergei. 2006. "Distribuição de renda no Brasil de 1976 a 2004 com ênfase no período entre 2001 e 2004." *Textos para Discussão* 1166. Brasília: IPEA.

Soares, Sergei. 2012. "Bolsa Família, Its Design, Its Impacts, and Possibilities for the Future." Working Paper, no. 89. Brasília: International Policy Centre for Inclusive Growth. February.

Soares, Sergei, and Natalia Sátyro. 2010. "O Programa Bolsa Familia: desenho institucional e possibilidades futuras." In *Bolsa Familia: 2003–2010: avanços e Desafios*, Vol. 1, edited by Jorge Abrahão Castro and Lúcia Modesto, 25–56. Brasilia: IPEA.

Soares, Sergei, Pedro Herculano G. Ferreira de Souza, Rafael Guerreiro Osório, and Fernando Gaiger Silveira. 2010. "Os impactos do benefício do Programa Bolsa Família sobre a desigualdade e a pobreza." In *Bolsa Família, 2003–2010: avanços e desafios*, Vol. 2, edited by Jorge Abrahão Castro and Lucia Modesto, 25–52. Brasília, IPEA.

Sola, Lourdes. 2013. "Uma primavera no outono?" *O Estado de São Paulo*, June 8, A2.

Souza, Amaury, and Bolivar Lamounier. 2010. "A classe média brasileira—ambições, valores e projetos de sociedade." Rio de Janeiro: Elsevier.

Souza, André de Melo e, and Pedro Miranda, eds. 2015. *Brasil em Desenvolvimento 2015*. Brasília: IPEA.

Souza, Jessé. 2010. *Batalhadores brasileiros. Os nova classe média ou nova classe trabalhadora*. Belo Horizonte: Editora UFMG.

Souza, Pedro Herculano Guimarães Ferreira de, and Rafael Guerreiro Osorio. 2013. "O perfil da pobreza no Brasil e suas mudanças entre 2003 e 2011." In *Programa Bolsa Família: uma década de inclusão e cidadania*, edited by Tereza Campello and Marcelo Côrtes Neri, 139–56. Brasília: IPEA.

Speck, Bruno Wilhelm. 2011. "Auditing Institutions." In *Corruption and Democracy in Brazil: The Struggle for Accountability*, edited by Timothy J. Power and Matthew M. Taylor, 127–61. Notre Dame, IN: University of Notre Dame Press.

Speck, Bruno Wilhelm. 2012a. "O financiamento político e a corrupção no Brasil." In *Temas de corrupção política*, edited by Rita de Cássia Biason, 49–98. São Paulo: Balão Editorial.

Speck, Bruno Wilhelm. 2012b. "Os limites da transparência." *Revista MPD Dialógico* 8 (38): 22–23.

Spektor, Matias. 2002. "O Brasil e Argentina entre a cordialidade oficial e o projeto de integração: a política externa do Governo de Ernesto Geisel (1974–1979)." *Revista Brasileira de Política Internacional* 45 (1): 117–45.

Spektor, Matias. 2004. "Origens e direção do pragmatismo ecumênico e responsável (1974–1979)." *Revista Brasileira de Política Internacional* 47, no. 2 (July–December): 191–222.

Spektor, Matias. 2009. *Kissinger e o Brasil*. Rio de Janeiro: Editora Zahar.

Stallings, Barbara, with Rogélio Studart. 2006. *Finance for Development: Latin America in Comparative Perspective*. Washington, DC: Brookings Institution Press.

Stern, Steve. 2004. *Remembering Pinochet's Chile: On the Eve of London 1998: The Memory Box of Pinochet's Chile*. Durham: Duke University Press.

Stuenkel, Oliver. 2015. *The BRICS and the Future of the Global Order*. Lanham, MD: Lexington Books.

Suárez, Mireya, and Marlene Libardoni. 2008. "The Impact of the Bolsa Família Program: Changes and Continuities in the Social Status of Women." In *Evaluation of MDS Policies and Programs-Results (Vol II): Bolsa Família Program and Social Assistance*, edited by Jeni Vaitsman and Rômulo Paes-Souza, 117–60. Brasília: Ministério de Desenvolvimento Social.

Suchodolski, Sergio. 2016. "BNDES and Transparency: Past, Present, and Future." Powerpoint presentation, Columbia University, April 20.

Sugiyama, Natasha Borges. 2011. "The Diffusion of Conditional Cash Transfer Programs in the Americas." *Global Social Policy* 11 (2–3): 250–78.

Sugiyama, Natasha Borges. 2012. *Diffusion of Good Government: Social Sector Reforms in Brazil*. South Bend, IN: University of Notre Dame Press.

Sugiyama, Natasha Borges, and Wendy Hunter. 2013. "Whither Clientelism: Good Government and Brazil's Bolsa Família Program." *Comparative Politics* 46, no. 1 (October): 43–62.

Syvrud, Donald. 1975. *Foundations of Brazilian Economic Growth*. Stanford, CA: Hoover Institution Press.

Tapajós, Luziele, Júnia Quiroga, Rovane B. Schwengber Ritzi, and Marcel Frederico de Lima Taga. 2010. "A importância da avaliação no contexto da Bolsa Família." In *Bolsa Família 2003–2010: avanços e desafios, Vol II*, edited by Jorge Abrahão Castro and Lucia Modesto, 73–88. Brasília: IPEA.

Tarrow, Sidney. 2011. *Power in Movement: Social Movements and Contentious Politics*. 3rd ed. Cambridge: Cambridge University Press.

Taylor, Matthew M. 2008. *Judging Policy: Courts and Policy Reform in Democratic Brazil*. Stanford: Stanford University Press.

Taylor, Matthew M. 2009. "Corruption, Accountability Reforms, and Democracy in Brazil." In *Corruption and Democracy in Latin America*, edited by Charles Blake and Stephen Morris, 150–68. Pittsburgh: University of Pittsburgh Press.

Taylor, Matthew M. 2015. "The Unchanging Core of Brazilian State Capitalism, 1985–2015." Working Paper 2015-8. School of International Service, American University, Washington, DC. October 14.

Taylor, Matthew M., and Vinicius Buranelli. 2007. "Ending Up in Pizza: Accountability as a Problem of Institutional Arrangement in Brazil." *Latin American Politics and Society* 49 (1): 59–87.

Teitel, Ruti. 2002. *Transitional Justice*. New York: Oxford University Press.

Teixeira, Izabella Mônica Vieira. 2008. "O uso da avaliação ambiental estratégica no planejamento da oferta de blocos para exploração e produção de petróleo e gás natural no Brasil: uma proposta." PhD dissertation in Energy Planning, Federal University of Rio de Janeiro.

Teixeira, Marco Antonio Carvalho, Gabriela de Brelàz, Gustavo Andrey de Almeida, Eduardo José Grin, Fernanda Cristina da Silva, Miriam Pires Vale, Robson Zuccolotto, and Thomaz Anderson Barbosa da Silva. 2013. "Global Initiative for Fiscal Transparency. Country Reports: Brazil." Report Commissioned by the Global Initiative for Fiscal Transparency.

Ter-Minassian, Tereza. 2013. "Improving Social Spending for a Better Life for All in Brazil." Vox LACEA. http://www.vox.lacea.org/?q=brazil_social_spending.

Tible, Jean. 2013. "O fenômeno político do lulismo e a construção de uma nova classe social." In *Classes sociais no Brasil de hoje*, edited by Rui Falcão, 68–77. São Paulo: Fundação Perseu Abramo.

Torelly, Marcelo. 2015a. "Challenging Impunity in Brazil: Assessing the Role of the National Truth Commission in the Transitional Justice Process." Brasilia: unpublished manuscript.

Torelly, Marcelo. 2015b. "Somos todos constituintes." *Revista de História da Biblioteca Nacional* 114 (March): 37–41.

Torres Filho, E.T. 2005. "A reforma do sistema FAT-BNDES: críticas à proposta arida." *Revista do BNDES* 12, no. 24 (December): 31–42.

Torres Filho, E. T. 2009. "Papel dos bancos públicos: o caso do BNDES." Powerpoint presentation, 5th Jornada de Estudos de Regulação, November. Rio de Janeiro: IPEA.

Torres Filho, E. T., and F. N. Costa. 2012. "BNDES e o financiamento do desenvolvimento." *Economia e Sociedade* 21 (December): 975–1009.

Touchton, Michael, and Brian Wampler. 2014. "Improving Social Well-Being through New Democratic Institutions." *Comparative Political Studies* 47 (10): 1442–69.

Touchton, Michael, Natasha Borges Sugiyama, and Brian Wampler. 2017. "Democracy at Work: Moving Beyond Elections to Improve Well-Being." *American Political Science Review* 111, no. 1 (February): 68–82.

Transparency International. 2010/2011. "Global Corruption Barometer 2010/11." Available at gcb.transparency.org/gcb201011/results.

Trubeck, David M. 1971. "Law, Planning, and the Development of the Brazilian Capital Market." *The Bulletin*, nos. 72–73. Institute of Finance, School of Business Administration, New York University. April.

Tribunal Supremo Eleitoral. Electoral Supreme Court website. http://www.tse.jus.br/eleicoes.

UOL Economia. 2016. "Cotações: Câmbio, Conversor de Moedas, Bolsas e Índices—Dólar Comercial." http://economia.uol.com.br/cotacoes/cambio/dolar-comercial-estados-unidos.

Valle, Sabrina. 2012. "Aracruz: quem vai levar a culpa?" *Estado de São Paulo*, January 9.

Van Biezen, Ingrid, Peter Mair, and Thomas Poguntke. 2012. "Going, Going . . . Gone? The Decline of Party Membership in Contemporary Europe." *European Journal of Political Research*, no. 51: 24–56.

Van Eeuwen, Daniel. 2010. "Les relations Washington-Brasília entre bipolarité conflictuelle e 'rivalité cordiale.'" In *Relations internationales du Brésil: les chemins de la puissance*, edited by Denis Rolland and Antônio Carlos Lessa. Paris: L'Harmattan.

Van Zyl, Paul. 2011. "Promoting Transitional Justice in Post-conflict Societies." In *Transitional Justice: Handbook for Latin America*, edited by Félix Reátegui, 45–67. Brasília: Brazilian Amnesty Commission, Ministry of Justice/International Center for Transitional Justice.

Vaz Ferreira, Luciano, and Fabio Costa Morosini. 2013. "The Implementation of International Anti-corruption Law in Business: Legal Control of Corruption Directed to Transnational Corporations." *Austral: Brazilian Journal of Strategy & International Relations* 2 (3): 241–60.

Veiga, Pedro da Motta. 2007. "Política commercial no Brasil: Características, condicionantes domésticos e policy-making." In *Polítics Comerciais Comparadas: Desempenho e modelos organizacionais*, edited by Marcos Sawaya Jank and Simão Davi Silber. São Paulo: Editora Singular.

Venturi, Gustavo. 2010. "PT 30 anos: crescimento e mudanças na preferência partidária." *Perseu*, no 5: 197–214

Verba, Sidney, Kay L. Schlozman, and Henry E. Brady. 1995. *Voice and Equality: Civic Voluntarism in American Politics*. Cambridge, MA: Harvard University Press.

Vidigal, Carlos Eduardo. 2010. "The Brazil-Argentine Axis during the Lula da Silva Government (2003–2010)." In *Relations internationales du Brésil: les chemins de la puissance*, edited by Denis Rolland and Antônio Carlos Lessa. Paris: L'Harmattan.

Vigevani, Tullo, and Gabriel Cepaluni. 2009. *Brazilian Foreign Policy in Changing Times: The Quest for Autonomy from Sarney to Lula*, translated by Leandro Moura. Lanham, MD: Lexington Books.

Vihma, Antto. 2011. "India and the Global Climate Governance: Between Principles and Pragmatism." *Journal of Environment and Development* 20 (1): 69–94.

Viola, Eduardo. 2010. *Impasses e perspectivas da negociação climática global e mudanças na posição brasileira.* http://www.cindesbrasil.org.

Viola, Eduardo, and Kathryn Hochstetler. 2015. "Brazil in Global Climate Governance." In *Handbook on Global Climate Governance*, edited by K. Bäckstrand and E. Lövbrand, 237–48. Edward Elgar Publishers.

Vizentini, Paulo Fagundes. 2005. *Relações internacionais do Brasil: de Vargas a Lula.* São Paulo: Editora Fundação Perseu Abramo.

Von Mettenheim, K. E. 2010. *Federal Banking in Brazil: Policies and Competitive Advantages.* London: Pickering and Chatto.

Wainwright, Hilary, and Sue Branford, eds. 2006. *In the Eye of the Storm: Left-Wing Activists Discuss the Political Crisis in Brazil*. Transnational Institute. http://www.tni.org/reports/newpol/brasildossier.htm.

Wampler, Brian. 2015. *Activating Democracy in Brazil: Popular Participation, Social Justice, and Interlocking Institutions*. Notre Dame, IN: University of Notre Dame Press.

Wampler, Brian, and Leonardo Avritzer. 2004. "Participatory Publics: Civil Society and New Institutions in Democratic Brazil." *Comparative Politics* 36 (3): 291–312.

Weichert, Marlon Alberto. 2012. "Visão critica dos óbices à promoção da justiça no Brasil." Paper prepared for the conference "Transitional Justice: Comparative Analyses of Brazil and Germany," held at Goethe University, Frankfurt, July 17.

Weyland, Kurt. 1996. *Democracy without Equity: Failures of Reform in Brazil*. Pittsburgh: University of Pittsburgh Press.

Weymouth, Lally. 2013. "An Interview with Dilma Rousseff, Brazil's President-Elect." *Washington Post*, December 3.

Wheatley, Jonathan. 2009. "Interview with Luciano Coutinho, President of the Development Bank, the BNDES." Special report on Brazil. *Financial Times*, November 4.

Whitehead, Laurence. 2002. *Democratization: Theory and Experience*. Oxford: Oxford University Press.

Wilcken, Patrick. 2012. "Brazil's Reckoning." *New Left Review* (November–December): 63–80.

Willis, Eliza Jane. 2013. "A Historical Case Study of a Pocket of Effectiveness: Brazil's National Economic Development Bank (BNDE)." In *State Performance and Reform in Developing Countries: Pockets of Effectiveness*, edited by Michael Roll. New York: Routledge.

Wilson, Richard. 2001. *The Politics of Truth and Reconciliation in South Africa*. Cambridge. Cambridge University Press.

Wong, Laura R., and Cassio M. Turra. 2007. "O Sub-Registro de Nascimentos no Brasil." InterAmerican Development Bank, project ATN/NS-8915-RS.

Wood, Reed, and Mark Gibney. 2010. "The Political Terror Scale (PTS): A Re-introduction and a Comparison to CIRI." *Human Rights Quarterly* 32, no. 2 (May): 367–400.

World Bank. 2002. "Brazil Municipal Education Resources, Incentives, and Results." Report No. 24413-BR. 2 vols. Washington, DC: World Bank.

World Bank. 2008. *Environmental Licensing for Hydroelectric Projects in Brazil: A Contribution to the Debate, Volume 1 (of 3 Volumes): Summary Report*. Brazil Country Management Unit, Report No. 40995-BR. Washington, DC: World Bank.

World Bank. 2002–2012. *World Development Indicators Online*. Database. http://www.data.worldbank.org/indicator/SI.POV.GINI/countries?display=default. By year.

Wu, V. 2010. "Por que a grande mídia e a oposição resolveram jogar sujo." *Carta Maior*, September 21. http://www.cartamaior.com.br/templates/materiaMostrar.cfm?materia_id=16980&boletim_id=764&componente_id=12686.

Zamboni, Yves. 2012. "Avaliando o avaliador: evidências sobre um experimento de campo sobre auditorias da CGU." PhD dissertation in Public Administration, Getúlio Vargas Foundation, Brazil.

Zamboni, Yves, and Stephan Litschig. 2006. "Law Enforcement and Local Governance in Brazil: Evidence from Random Audit Reports." Columbia University. Unpublished manuscript.

Zanetta, Rafael A. F. 2012. "The Risk of the New Developmentalism: 'Brasil Maior' Plan and Bureaucratic Rings." Working paper. http://papers.ssrn.com/sol3/papers.cfm?abstract_id=2120002.

Zibechi, Raúl. 2012. *Brasil potencia. Entre la integración regional y un nuevo imperialismo*. Bogotá: Ediciones desde abajo.

Zucco, Cesar Zucco. 2008. "The President's 'New' Constituency." *Journal of Latin American Studies*, no. 40: 29–49.

Zucco, Cesar. 2011. "Esquerda, Direita e Governo: a ideologia dos partidos políticos brasileiros." In *O Congresso por ele mesmo: auto percepções da classe política brasileira*, edited by Timothy Power and Cesar Zucco, 37–60. Belo Horizonte: Editora UFMG.

CONTRIBUTORS

Maria Hermínia Tavares de Almeida is emeritus professor of political science at the University of São Paulo and senior researcher at the Centro Brasileiro de Análise e Planejamento (CEBRAP). She is past president of both the Latin American Studies Association (LASA) and the Brazilian Political Science Association (ABCP). She has published the books *Crise econômica e interesses organizados* (Edusp, 1993) and, with Gian Luca Gardini, *Foreign Policy Responses to the Rise of Brazil—Balancing Power in Emerging States* (Palgrave, 2016).

Oswaldo E. do Amaral is an assistant professor at the Department of Political Science and a researcher at the Public Opinion Studies Centre (CESOP) at the State University of Campinas (Unicamp), in Brazil. Between 2013 and 2017, he was co-coordinator of the Research Group on Political Parties and Party Systems of the Latin American Political Science Association (ALACIP). He has published several books and articles about the Workers' Party (PT), the Brazilian party system, party organization, and electoral behavior.

Leslie Elliott Armijo teaches Development at the School for International Studies, Simon Fraser University, Canada. She studies the public policies of emerging powers, especially in financial regulation, the infrastructure/environment nexus, migration, and South-South cooperation. Recent publications include *Unexpected Outcomes: How Emerging Economies Survived the Global Financial Crisis* (co-edited with Carol Wise and Saori N. Katada, Brookings 2015); *The Financial Statecraft of Emerging Powers: Shield and Sword in Asia and Latin America* (co-edited with Saori N. Katada, Palgrave 2014). Her most recent article, with Sybil Rhodes, is "Can International Relations and Comparative Politics Be Policy Relevant? Theory and Methods for Incorporating Political Context" (*Politics & Policy*, 2015).

Sean W. Burges is a senior lecturer in international relations at the Australian National University and a senior research fellow with the Council on Hemispheric Affairs in Washington, DC. He is author of *Brazilian Foreign Policy after the Cold War* (Florida, 2009) and *Brazil in the World: The International Relations of a South American Giant* (Manchester, 2017), as well as over thirty scholarly journal articles and book chapters on Brazilian foreign policy, inter-American affairs, and South-South relations.

Jean Daudelin is associate professor of international affairs at Carleton University, in Ottawa, and research fellow at the *Núcleo de Estudos e Pesquisas em Criminalidade, Violência e Políticas* Públicas *de Segurança* at the Federal University of Pernambuco. He currently studies illegal markets and violence in Brazil's Northeast. His recent publications include "Not Killer Methods: A Few Things We Do Wrong When Studying Violence in Latin America," in Tina Hilgers and Laura Macdonald, eds., *Violence in Latin America and the Caribbean* (Cambridge, 2017) and "Coming of Age: Recent Scholarship on Brazilian Foreign Policy," in *Latin American Research Review* (2013).

Benjamin Goldfrank is associate professor and department chair at Seton Hall University's School of Diplomacy and International Relations. His research interests focus on the comparative analysis of Latin American politics and, especially, experiments in participatory democracy. He teaches classes on Latin American politics, society, and economic development as well as US foreign policy toward the region. He is the author of *Deepening Local Democracy in Latin America: Participation, Decentralization, and the Left* and co-editor of *The Left in the City: Participatory Local Governments in Latin America*.

Fernando Guarnieri is a Brazilian political scientist. He earned his PhD from University of São Paulo (USP). He is an adjunct professor of political science at the Instituto de Estudos Sociais e Políticos (IESP) of the State University of Rio de Janeiro (UERJ) and a researcher at the Comparative and International Studies Research Center (NECI/USP) and at the Brazilian Centre of Analysis and Planning (CEBRAP). His current research focuses on the dynamics of political competition in Brazil, the origins and evolution of the Brazilian party system, and the formation of political cleavages.

Kathryn Hochstetler is professor of international development at the London School of Economics and Political Science. She has published widely on environmental politics in Brazil, including the prize-winning *Greening Brazil: Environmental Activism in State and Society* (Duke University Press, with Margaret Keck). Her current projects include a book on the adoption of wind and solar power in Brazil and South Africa and research on the environmental and developmental impacts of BNDES's support for infrastructure projects in Brazil and worldwide.

Wendy Hunter, professor of government at the University of Texas, studies comparative politics with an emphasis on Latin America. She has conducted research on the military in Brazil and the Southern Cone and on various social policy topics in Latin America and elsewhere. She is currently researching identity documentation among low-income populations in the developing world. She is the author of *The Transformation of the Workers' Party in Brazil, 1989–2009* (Cambridge University Press, 2010) and *Eroding Military Influence in Brazil: Politicians against Soldiers* (University of North Carolina Press, 1997).

Peter Kingstone is professor of politics and development and co-founder of the Department of International Development at King's College London. He is author of several books on Latin America, including *Crafting Coalitions for Reform: Business Preferences, Political Institutions and Neoliberal Reform in Brazil, The Political Economy of Latin America: Reflections on Neoliberalism and Development* as well as co-editor of *Democratic Brazil: Actors, Institutions and Processes, Democratic Brazil Revisited,* and the *Handbook of Latin American Politics.* He has published various articles and book chapters on the subject of democratization and the politics of neoliberal economic reforms.

Marcus André Melo is a professor of political science at the Federal University of Pernambuco and a former Fulbright scholar at MIT and visiting professor at Yale University. He is the co-author of *Against the Odds: Institutions, Politicians, and the Struggle against Poverty* (Columbia University Press, 2012), *Making Brazil Work: Checking the President in a Multiparty System* (Palgrave, 2013), and *Brazil in Transition: Beliefs, Leadership, and Institutional Change* (Princeton University Press, 2016). His work has also appeared in *Journal of Democracy, Legislative Studies Quarterly, Political Research Quarterly,* and the *Journal of Comparative Economics.*

Rachel Meneguello is professor of political science, past director of the Center for Studies on Public Opinion (CESOP) at the University of Campinas (UNICAMP), Brazil, and editor of the journal *Opinião Pública.* Between 2004–2008 and 2012–2016 she served on the board of directors of the Brazilian Political Science Association and was a member of the executive committee of the Asociación Latinoamericana de Ciencia Política (ALACIP). Her publications deal mainly with political parties, political behavior, and mass support for democracy. She is the author of *PT: A formação de um partido (1979–1982)* and *Partidos e governos no Brasil contemporâneo.* She was twice awarded the Elizabeth Nelson Prize from the World Association of Public Opinion Research (WAPOR) and is a member of the steering committee of the Comparative Study of Electoral Systems Project (CSES).

Anthony W. Pereira is a professor and the founding director of the Brazil Institute at King's College London. He obtained his BA from Sussex University in 1982 and his MA and PhD degrees from Harvard University in 1986 and 1991 respectively. Before coming to King's in 2010, he held positions at the New School, the Fletcher School, the University of East Anglia, and Tulane University. His research interests include the issues of authoritarian rule, democracy, human rights, and transitional justice. Among his publications are *Ditadura e Repressão* (Paz e Terra, 2010) and *The Brazilian Economy Today* (Palgrave, 2015).

Timothy J. Power is university lecturer in Brazilian studies and a fellow of St. Antony's College at the University of Oxford. His research addresses issues of democracy and political institutions in Brazil, especially parties, elections, executive-legislative relations, and presidential governance. He is a former president of the Brazilian Studies Association (BRASA) and former treasurer of the Latin American Studies Association (LASA). His most recent book, with Paul Chaisty and Nic Cheeseman, is *Coalitional Presidentialism in Comparative Perspective: Minority Presidents in Multiparty Systems* (Oxford University Press, forthcoming).

Alfredo Saad-Filho is professor of political economy at SOAS, University of London, and was a senior economic affairs officer at the UN Conference on Trade and Development. He has degrees in economics from the Universities of Brasília (Brazil) and London (SOAS) and has taught in universities and research institutions in Brazil, Canada, Italy, Japan, Mozambique, Switzerland, and the United Kingdom. His research interests include the political economy of development, industrial policy, neoliberalism, democracy, alternative economic policies, Latin American political and economic development, inflation and stabilization, and the labor theory of value.

Natasha Borges Sugiyama is associate professor of political science at the University of Wisconsin–Milwaukee. Her research examines the politics of poverty alleviation, social policy reform, citizenship development, and human development. She is author of *Diffusion of Good Governance: Social Sector Reforms in Brazil* (University of Notre Dame Press, 2013). Her research has appeared in numerous journals, including *American Political Science Review*, *Comparative Politics*, *Comparative Political Studies*, *Journal of Development Studies*, *Latin American Research Review*, *Latin American Politics and Society*, and *Perspectives on Politics*. Her current research examines democratic pathways to improvements in well-being.

Matthew M. Taylor is an associate professor at the School of International Service at American University, and adjunct senior fellow for Latin America at the Council on Foreign Relations. Taylor is the author of *Judging Policy: Courts and Policy Reform in Democratic Brazil*, co-editor with Timothy J. Power of *Corruption and Democracy in Brazil: The Struggle for Accountability*, and co-editor with Oliver Stuenkel of *Brazil on the Global Stage: Power, Ideas, and the Liberal International Order*.

Brian Wampler is a professor of political science at Boise State University. He is the author of *Activating Democracy in Brazil: Popular Participation, Social Justice and Interlocking Institutions* (University of Notre Dame Press, 2015) and *Participatory Budgeting in Brazil: Cooperation, Contestation, and Accountability* (Pennsylvania State University Press, 2007). Wampler's research focuses on citizen participation, civil society, and institution building. He has published articles in journals such as *American Political Science Review, Comparative Politics, Comparative Political Studies, World Development,* and *Latin American Politics and Society*.

INDEX